Emily Jane Brontë

and

Her Music

Emily Jane Brontë

and

Her Music

JOHN HENNESSY

Published by WK Publishing

A CIP catalogue record for this book is available from the British Library.

ISBN 978-1-9996836-0-3 (Paperback)
ISBN 978-1-9996836-1-0 (Hardback)

Book layout and cover design by Clare Brayshaw

Cover image is an original watercolour by Daisy Hennessy

Prepared and printed by:

York Publishing Services Ltd
64 Hallfield Road
Layerthorpe
York YO31 7ZQ

Tel: 01904 431213

Website: www.yps-publishing.co.uk

Contents

Emily Jane Brontë (1818-1848)
By Branwell Brontë
(Original in the National Portrait Gallery)

Acknowledgements

It would not have been possible to write this work without the assistance of the staff at the Brontë Parsonage Museum. Ann Dinsdale, Principal Curator, sanctioned my research. I am particularly indebted to Sarah Laycock, Curator, whose expertise, and patient and friendly support throughout, both in the Parsonage library and in correspondence, was invaluable. I was permitted access to Emily's own music scores and allowed to reproduce images of some of the Parsonage treasures in my work.

I am very grateful to Ken Forrest who gave me an insight into his remarkable restoration of the Parsonage piano and who has contributed his 'Notes on Playing the John Green Cabinet Upright Piano', included with his permission in Appendix Four. Isabelle Oehmichen's intriguing assessment of the challenge of playing the Parsonage piano in recital is reproduced with her permission in Appendix Six. I was able to draw upon the literary scholarship of Edward Chitham for advice in regard to aspects of Chapter Three, and the encyclopaedic knowledge of the Haworth historian, Steven Wood. Olivia Wahnon de Oliveira, librarian of the Conservatoire Royale de Bruxelles, gave me details of musical life in Brussels during the years 1842-1843 , and provided important information concerning their ownership of Anton Schindler's first edition biography of Beethoven. Julie

Akhurst provided me with a copy of the 1899 sale catalogue of the library of the Heaton family of Ponden Hall. Finally, my thanks are due to the Brontë scholar, the late Virginia Rushton, for her friendship and encouragement.

Recourse has, of course, been made to a considerable number of literary sources, as evidenced by the Select Bibliography in Appendix Two. Specific mention must be made of two classic works of scholarship – Juliet Barker's *The Brontës*, and Margaret Smith's *The Letters of Charlotte Brontë*. All references to the text of the sisters' novels, and Elizabeth Gaskell's *The Life of Charlotte Brontë*, pertain to the Haworth Edition of 1899–1900; those to Emily's poems to C.W. Hatfield's 1941 edition.

John Hennessy
2018

Introduction

When, in 1857, just two years after her subject's death, Elizabeth Gaskell published her *Life of Charlotte Brontë*, she would probably not have envisaged that she was to be the first in a very long line of people who were to feel a need to express themselves about the Brontë family, their lives, their environment and their writings. During the last century and a half, the accumulated bibliography has been immense as to quantity and, frequently, rich in scholarship.

It seems that there have been few areas of the Brontë's lives which have not been subjected to microscopic analysis. Perhaps, though, there is one facet of those lives, particularly Emily's, which has not received quite the attention which it ought to have had. The word 'music' is regularly used in literary analyses of the sisters' writings, particularly as regards its rhythmic structure or metre. It is known that music played an important and enjoyable role in the siblings' lives while growing up into adulthood, but did this enjoyment of music have any effect on their creative output? Emily was, beyond dispute, the most musically accomplished of the four surviving Brontë children. Her knowledge and love of music, the part it played in her life and the influence it had upon her writing, is the subject of this study.

This is a simple enough concept in principle, but unfortunately one which, in reality, is nowhere near as straightforward a proposition as might be assumed or wished. Everybody who has ever sought to evaluate or comment upon the elusive genius that is Emily Brontë has faced the same intractable problem; the author John Hewish referred to her as being 'biographer-proof'. Other than those of her literary writings that survive, which might be said to constitute her autobiography, and which include the nine *devoirs* which she wrote during her time as a student at the Pensionnat Heger in Brussels in 1842, there is little additional tangible, as opposed to anecdotal, material upon which to work. Furthermore, the extent to which, if at all, Charlotte Brontë destroyed various of Emily's manuscripts after her sister's death, including perhaps the beginnings of a second novel, in what she perceived as a justifiable exercise to protect Emily's reputation from the welter of vitriolic criticism that the publication of *Wuthering Heights* had precipitated, will always be a matter for debate – scholars have differed in their opinions. Four diary papers, three brief letters to Ellen Nussey and a fragment of an account book remain to provide a glimpse into Emily's daily life. It is also a matter of particular frustration that there is an almost complete lack of positive information about Emily's musical experiences, potentially of considerable significance, during the important nine months which she spent with Charlotte in Brussels in 1842. As a consequence, in an assessment of this nature, a certain amount of speculation becomes inevitable. When in the pages which follow factual evidence is unavailable, this will be acknowledged and all available data will be discussed. The reader will be free to form her or his opinions.

Such is the conundrum of this complex and extraordinary woman. She always has, and forever will, move lesser individuals to attempt to understand her, to try to discern her *modus operandi*, perhaps to obtain an insight into her approach to the unfathomable mysteries of the Universe, the Creation, and Infinity. Was she a mystic? It is certainly not the claim of the present writer that this study will provide conclusive answers to the myriad questions which her literary genius poses. It is rather that a look into her musicality, as one of a number of influences on her writing, might be of value.

Writing a century or so after Beethoven had completed his *Große Fuge,* Igor Stravinsky referred to that ground-breaking masterwork as 'this contemporary work which shall forever remain contemporary'. Is there any more appropriate way to describe *Wuthering Heights* or Emily's poetry? Beethoven, whose influence upon Emily's literary creativity might well have been considerable, will feature prominently throughout the following pages.

Prologue

Riches I hold in light esteem
And Love I laugh to scorn
And lust of Fame was but a dream
That vanished in the morn –
And if I pray, the only prayer
That moves my lips for me
Is – 'Leave the heart that now I bear
And give me liberty'.
Yes, as my swift days near their goal
'Tis all that I implore –
Through life and death, a chainless soul
With courage to endure!
Emily Jane Brontë – 1 March 1841

CHAPTER ONE

A Century of Change 1750–1850

A Social Context
The Changing Face of Western Music
Music in England

A Social Context

To say that the years of the second half of the eighteenth century and the first half of the nineteenth were a period of massive change and upheaval is a considerable understatement. The Industrial Revolution, conveniently said to have begun with the accession to the throne of George III in 1760, brought about enormous changes in the lifestyle of the people which, with hindsight, can be seen to have been both inevitable and beneficial, but which at the time, in many cases, caused considerable distress. An obvious example was the invention of various types of machinery, such as Samuel Crompton's spinning mule in 1779 and Edmund Cartwright's power loom for spinning cotton in 1785, which many skilled craftsmen believed was depriving them of their livelihoods. A movement, begun in Nottingham in 1811, supposedly under the leadership of one Ned Ludd, took to wrecking this factory machinery. The violence spread rapidly and by 1812 had reached the heartlands of the woollen and cotton industries, Yorkshire and Lancashire. In one celebrated incident, on 11 April 1812, the cloth-weaving mill at Rawfolds near Cleckheaton, owned by William Cartwright, was attacked by Luddites. This incident was used by Charlotte Brontë in *Shirley* as the basis for the attack on Robert Gerard Moore's Hollow's Mill. (1) Interestingly, although the action is set at the time of Luddite unrest, the novel was actually written during another period of tension (as well as personal distress) in 1848–1849, as a tidal wave of revolutionary fervour was sweeping Europe, and when Chartist agitation in this country had reached its height (see below). The Revd Patrick Brontë was incumbent of nearby Hartshead and, although sympathetic to the feelings of the rioters, nonetheless did not condone their use of violence.

William Cartwright's Mill at Rawfolds

However, the era was one of progress, albeit slow at times, its benefits often being unequally distributed. The long drawn-out and costly – both economically and in terms of loss of life – Napoleonic wars ended with Wellington's victory at the Battle of Waterloo in 1815. Apart from the Crimean War of 1854-1856, and the Boer War of 1899–1902, Britain was to be spared major conflict for all but a few months short of a century. The Duke of Wellington, soldier, and prime minister between 1828 and 1830 – he briefly formed an administration again, in 1834 – was a particular hero

The Duke of Wellington
A copy of this 1844 Daguerro type hangs in the Parsonage Dining Room, a present from George Smith (of Smith, Elder and Company)

of the Brontë family. Patrick visited the site of the Battle of Waterloo in 1842 after having escorted Charlotte and Emily to the Pensionnat Heger in Brussels for their time of study there, and Branwell and Charlotte used the Duke as a key character in their early stories.

An important piece of legislation was the Reform Act of 1832 which enfranchised the upper-middle classes, albeit that it was dependent upon a property qualification and women were excluded, the number of voters doubling to about one million. Although a Whig measure, Patrick Brontë supported it. The Chartist movement, during the decade from 1838, was active in pressing for male suffrage, equal electoral districts, payment of members of parliament, abolition of property qualifications for members, voting by ballot, and annual parliaments. Chartism was always most popular in the north of England, with mass meetings of Chartists being commonplace. In August 1842, it was estimated that ten thousand Chartists gathered on Lees Moor, while in April 1848 the Haworth Chartist, Archibald Leighton addressed some eight thousand people on Farnhill Moor near Kildwick, six miles north of Haworth; between four and five thousand gathered the next day in Keighley market place. (2) It was not a movement that was immediately successful and, for a variety of reasons, it gradually petered out, but most of its aims were eventually achieved.

Patrick Brontë, although a Tory, was very much a progressive in regard to local social matters, and he encouraged his children accordingly. He was prominent in petitioning the General Board of Health in London to obtain a long-overdue system for the supply of fresh water in Haworth where, hitherto, sanitary conditions had been appalling. This had lead to an average life expectancy of twenty-five years, with over forty-one per cent of children dying before the age of six. The result was the publication of the Babbage Report of 1850, which recommended improvements in regard to the water supply, sewage disposal and toilets, but which unfortunately, for reasons pertaining to the self-interest of various local landowners, took eight years to be fully implemented.

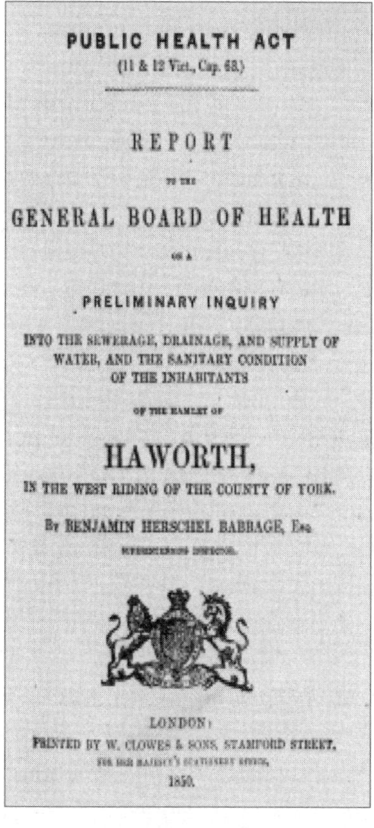

PUBLIC HEALTH ACT
(11 & 12 Vict., Cap. 63.)

REPORT
TO THE
GENERAL BOARD OF HEALTH
ON A
PRELIMINARY INQUIRY
INTO THE SEWERAGE, DRAINAGE, AND SUPPLY OF WATER, AND THE SANITARY CONDITION OF THE INHABITANTS
OF THE HAMLET OF
HAWORTH,
IN THE WEST RIDING OF THE COUNTY OF YORK.

By BENJAMIN HERSCHEL BABBAGE, Esq.

LONDON:
PRINTED BY W. CLOWES & SONS, STAMFORD STREET,
1850.

Report of the General Board of Health, 1850
Benjamin Herschel Babbage

Patrick was also a trustee of the Keighley Savings Bank, founded in 1819, a year after similar banks had opened in Bradford, Leeds and Huddersfield. It is generally accepted that the first such institution had been established in a small cottage by the Revd. Henry Duncan at Ruthwell in Dumfriesshire in 1810, the underlying principle being that of self-help for the poor. The use of capital punishment was widespread in the early years of the nineteenth century, as many as two hundred and twenty offences being punished with the death penalty. Vehemently opposed to this state of affairs, Patrick addressed the issue in his short story *The Maid of Killarney*, published in 1818, as well as in letters to local newspapers such as the *Leeds Mercury*. By 1861, the year of Patrick's death, the number of capital offences stood at just four – murder, treason, piracy, and arson in a royal dockyard. There were improvements in road construction and, in 1830, the world's first passenger railway, running from Liverpool to Manchester, was opened. 'Railway mania' reached a peak in the 1840s, with the three Brontë sisters investing their aunt's legacy in railway shares. The railway reached Leeds in 1834, Bradford in 1846 and Keighley a year later, but Haworth was not connected by rail to Keighley until 1867. Branwell took employment with the Manchester and Leeds Railway. He was dismissed in 1842 following the discovery of a shortfall of £11.1s.7d in the company's accounts.

As far back as 1772, Lord Mansfield's judgement in the *Somerset Case*, had had the *de facto* effect that slavery in England and Wales (Scotland subsequently) did not exist under English law, thereby establishing the rights of those black people employed as domestic servants in England. In 1807, the *Slave Trade Act* outlawed the trading of slaves and, finally, in 1833, slavery in the British Empire was abolished, William Wilberforce, a Yorkshireman, being one of the main champions of the abolitionist cause. Patrick Brontë, along with other evangelical clergymen, had organised petitions to Parliament proposing abolition some three years earlier. (Wilberforce was one of a small number of sponsors whose financial support had enabled Patrick to complete his university degree at St. John's College, Cambridge, where he had studied from 1802 to 1806). Another cause which gained Patrick's support was that of Catholic emancipation which was achieved, subject to certain limits, in 1829. In 1833, the *Factory Act* made it illegal to employ children under the age of nine in factories, and limited the work of those under thirteen to forty-eight hours a week and those between thirteen and eighteen to sixty-nine hours a week. The following year, the *Poor Law Amendment Act* made the receipt of public assistance conditional upon residence in workhouses, with gender segregation meaning that families were split up. Patrick Brontë was one of many who opposed this legislation. In 1840, Rowland Hill's penny post was introduced and, in 1846, the *Corn Laws* of 1815 were repealed, thereby reducing the price of bread. There were regular scientific and medical discoveries, further areas in which Patrick took a keen interest, as evidenced by his ownership, considerably annotated, of Graham's *Modern Domestic Medicine* (1826).

The Changing Face of Western Music

It is often thought convenient to regard the history of western music in terms of 'periods', for example Baroque, Classical and Romantic. It is, however, dangerous to regard one period as starting the instant the previous one has ended – there is a degree of overlapping. It may be said that, as regards music, the Baroque era came to a close about the end of the 1750s with the deaths of J.S. Bach (1750) and Handel (1759). Each was a master of counterpoint, but it is wrong to suggest that neither wrote homophonic music, and it is certainly incorrect to assume that geniuses such as Mozart, Beethoven and others eschewed counterpoint in their writing. It is more accurate to say that about this time there was a change of compositional emphasis from the horizontal, involving the skilful interweaving of melodic lines, to the vertical, which meant harmony based on chords.

There had been anticipations of this change in direction in the writings of Domenico Scarlatti (born in the same year, 1685, as Bach and Handel), François Couperin born 1668, and Jean-Phillipe Rameau born 1683. Now it was Carl Philipp Emanuel Bach, Johann Sebastian's third son, who was one of the first to embrace the changing style. He began to develop the concept of 'sonata form', a movement consisting of three sections. The first of these, the 'exposition', contained a first subject group comprising a number of short themes or figures initially in the tonic. It was followed, usually after a short transition, by the second subject group which introduced other ideas, usually in the dominant or relative major, in which key the exposition closed. The second section was described as the 'development', which involved the working out of the material of the exposition, though sometimes a new idea in the form of an episode was introduced as well, before the third section, the 'recapitulation', returned to the music of the exposition, sometimes varied, but now with both subject groups in the tonic. A coda, or tailpiece, might be added to conclude the movement. This sonata form was very often, though not exclusively, used as the first movement of a complete work – symphony, chamber music, such as string trio or string quartet, or pianoforte sonata. Such a work might consist of three or four movements – if the latter, the first movement would very likely be followed by a slow movement, then by a minuet (alternatively a scherzo) and lastly a finale. This final movement was usually, though again not always, in rondo form, consisting of a main theme played three or four times, with contrasting episodes interspersed. It could be illustrated as ABACABA, where A is the main theme, B the first episode and C the second episode. There might be a coda to conclude.

The main musical centre in the late eighteenth and early nineteenth centuries was Vienna, for there at various times lived the four greatest composers of the era – Haydn, Mozart, Beethoven and Schubert, although Schubert was the only one to have been born there. Between them they wrote symphonies, piano sonatas, concertos, chamber music, songs and sacred music. Mozart wrote twenty operas and Beethoven just one, *Fidelio*. During this time the modern orchestra was formed. This was the Classical era. But when did it end and when did the next one – the Romantic – begin? Berlioz, Mendelssohn, Chopin, Schumann and Liszt were all born between the years 1803–1811, and all can be described as belonging to the Romantic era. It is often said that the two eras – Classical and Romantic – were spanned by Beethoven and Schubert and, in so far as the forms which Beethoven brought to their classical apotheoses also provided a starting point for the Romantics, who were already active by the time of his death in 1827, the suggestion is valid. But, Beethoven's music cannot be definitively classified, and he could not be described as a composer of 'romantic' music. Rossini is probably as good an example as any of a composer who linked the two periods.

Put in very simple terms, Romanticism tends to involve visionary and imaginative aspects of art, rather than just its formal, classical nature. In addition to symphonies, the Romantic composers began to write symphonic poems on a programmatic basis, concert overtures and incidental music. The German *lied* (song), particularly as developed by Schubert and Schumann, became immensely popular. Then there were the operas. In Germany, Carl Maria von Weber was the first major composer in the genre, and in Italy, Gioacchino Rossini, Gaetano Donizetti and Vincenzo Bellini, all born within a decade of each other at the turn of the century, were prolific. Short piano pieces in free forms, with names rather than just opus numbers, proliferated; they often exploited the increasing tonal possibilities of the piano as it was being developed. These developments in piano manufacture included the transition from wooden frames to stronger iron ones, the use of thicker strings and larger hammers, the increase of the keyboard range, and Sébastien Érard's double-escapement device.

Music in England

Music which was accessible to the people existed in a variety of forms in the England of the early nineteenth century. Inevitably, London was well catered for, public concerts having long been established as part of the musical life of the capital. Music festivals were held regularly in Westminster Abbey, and programmes were given at venues such as the King's Concert Rooms in Hanover Square. In 1765, Johann Christian Bach and Karl Friederich Abel inaugurated a series of concerts, initially in Carlisle House, Soho Square, then from 1775 at Hanover Square; all told they continued for eighteen years. Later, in 1837, the composer and pianist Ignaz Moscheles gave a series of 'classical soirées' here. The programme consisted of two Beethoven sonatas, opp. 31 no. 2 and 81a, three preludes and fugues from the '48' of Bach, keyboard works by Scarlatti and Handel, as well as songs by Purcell and Mendelssohn, a duet by Mozart and a glee by William Jackson of Exeter. Subsequently, the German-born violinist and impresario, Johann Peter Salomon (1745–1815), who settled in London in 1781, brought Haydn to the city twice during the 1790s for a famous series of concerts, for which the composer's last twelve symphonies were written – hence they are known as Haydn's 'London' symphonies.

Salomon was a co-founder, in January 1813, of the Philharmonic Society now, from 1912, the Royal Philharmonic Society, formed for the encouragement of orchestral and instrumental concerts. Other founder members included Muzio Clementi, Johann Baptist Cramer, Thomas Attwood, and William Ayrton, who acted as honorary treasurer. The Society commissioned Beethoven's ninth symphony, plus a tenth which never materialised, and gave its first English performance, under Sir George Smart, in March 1825. It also presented Beethoven with a Broadwood pianoforte. From 1833 until 1868, the Society's concerts were held in the Hanover Rooms. Music by practically all the major composers was presented, with many of the leading musicians of the time performing. The Royal Academy of Music, founded by Lord Burghersh, the 11th Earl of Westmorland, was opened in London in March 1822. William Crotch was the first principal, and the composer and pianist Cipriani Potter, who had met Beethoven on a number of occasions and had impressed him, was appointed pianoforte teacher, taking over as principal in 1832. Clementi and Attwood were also involved. There were various musical events, such as elaborate balls, in the great houses of the aristocracy and the upper classes, and in a number of social clubs known as Almack's, as well as concerts in the pleasure gardens in the capital, such as Vauxhall and Marylebone. Sadler's Wells was originally another of the pleasure gardens, complete with medicinal spring, before a theatre was built on the site. Like Covent Garden, rebuilt in 1809 after a fire the previous year, it catered for the expanding middle-class population's desire for musical entertainment. London seemed to act as a magnet for all the best of the European pianists; Clementi, Cramer, Dussek, Field, Hummel, Kalkbrenner, Moscheles, Steibelt and Woelfl were all active in the capital during the first part of the nineteenth century.

In the provinces, societies and festivals sprang up, particularly in the cities. The Three Choirs Festival, held alternatively in the cathedrals of Gloucester, Hereford and Worcester, dates from the very early eighteenth century. The first Birmingham music festival took place as early as 1768, and in 1846 Mendelssohn's oratorio *Elijah* received its first performance there. The Liverpool Philharmonic Society was founded in 1840, although concerts of various kinds had been held in the city for many years prior to that date. As early as 1796, it was reported that 'the Public Concert Room is large and finished with great elegance. The present form was adopted to gain room for the accommodation of the musical festival which takes place once every three years. It will admit thirteen hundred persons commodiously. The orchestra is well-formed and arranged. The organ is more powerful than fine toned, and has a great effect in choruses and full pieces'. (1) The magnificent St. George's Hall, completed in 1854, has a concert room which is still in use. The first York Musical Festival was held in 1791. At the 1823 event, which included a performance of Beethoven's Fifth Symphony, the orchestra comprised one hundred and eighty members and the chorus two hundred and eighty-five, with the numbers being further increased for the Festival two years later. Beethoven's Sixth Symphony was played in 1828. In 1848 in Manchester, Charles Hallé began putting on chamber concerts which led to the formation of the Hallé Orchestra a decade later. The orchestras were all-male preserves; the country's main ones were professional, but there were many amateur orchestras as well.

Concerts were, of course, given to provide enjoyment to audiences consisting of an increasingly wide social range, but sometimes there was a specific reason for staging one. A benefit concert could be put on to raise money for a specific charity or purpose, the performances of *Messiah* given by Handel at the Foundling Hospital in London, each year from 1750 until his death in 1759, being particularly notable examples. Occasionally there would be an opportunity to hear one of the great virtuosi of the day. The composer and violinist Niccolo Paganini played at Halifax on 9 February 1832, (2) and Franz Liszt performed there in 1841, on which occasion he improvised a set of variations upon the National Anthem, prompting the *Halifax Guardian* to proclaim: 'We never remember a concert which was marked by so much enthusiasm, or so many rapturous encores as that night'. (3) This concert was organised by Joseph Henry Frobisher, organist of Halifax Parish Church, who was known to Branwell Brontë.

Choral societies also became popular. In West Yorkshire, the Halifax Choral Society, formed in 1817 and claiming to be the oldest in the country with an unbroken history, gave its first concert, a performance of Haydn's *Creation*, within its first year. In fact, a Halifax Musical Club had been formed as early as 1767 for the practice of choral music, and in 1784, a group of singers from Halifax and Luddenden participated in the Handel Festival in London. A contemporary report states that 'in this manufacturing town the poorer classes are, so to speak, born musicians. They meet constantly at their own habitations for practice, and after a hard day's toil their solace is a glee party or a trial of choral music'. (4)

William Priestley (Halifax Choral Society)

The man most responsible for the Society's formation was William Priestley, a lover of music who built up a considerable library of music scores, particularly of the German masters, with a special emphasis on choral works, and who thereby greatly assisted the Society in the expansion of its repertoire. He was also active in the establishment of the public library in Halifax. The Society's programme for 1826 stated that 'the Vocal and Instrumental Band will consist entirely of native talent', (5) while by 1830, the orchestra numbered sixty players. The renowned soprano Mrs Susan Sunderland, *nee* Susannah Sykes (1819–1905), first appeared on the Society's programme in 1830 as a soloist in Handel's oratorio *Alexander's Feast,* and she performed with them for the next thirty years. The 'Sunderland Vocal Prize' for natives of West Yorkshire was founded in her name. Oratorios were staple fare at Society concerts, one such event in 1830 drawing eulogies from the *Halifax Chronicle*'s reviewer, who referred to 'the very great perfection evinced by the chorus and band'. (6) Handel wrote a considerable number of oratorios including *Esther*, the first English oratorio, *Israel in Egypt*, *Messiah*, *Jephtha*, *Samson*, said to be a favourite of Branwell Brontë, (7) and *Saul*, three numbers of which Anne Brontë copied into her *Song Book*. (8)

In addition to Haydn's *Creation*, Mendelssohn's *St Paul* and *Elijah* were also performed regularly. A particularly close relationship was established with Mendelssohn, the score of whose *Psalm 114* was donated to the Society. According to Benjamin Binns, a member of the family of Haworth tailors, Patrick Brontë was 'passionately fond of oratorio'. In 1820, a choral society was formed at Bradford, followed by one in Keighley in 1834 and in Huddersfield in 1836.

Nor was it solely in the cities that societies were to be found, albeit they were on a smaller scale – Haworth Philharmonic Society was formed round about the year 1780. The *Bradford Observer* reported on 10 April 1834 that 'The Philharmonic Society in this place held a concert in the large room of the Black Bull Inn, on Tuesday, April 1st. The songs, catches and glees were well selected. Miss Parker sang with much sweetness and was well applauded. Mr. Parker was in fine voice and sang with his usual effect. Mr. Clark sang several comic songs with much taste, and was encored, particularly in the song of Miss Levi which kept the audience in continual laughter. The concert was numerously and respectfully attended, and the company went away highly gratified'. Then, in December 1842, shortly after Emily and Charlotte had returned from Brussels, another concert was reported, this time by the *Keighley, Halifax and Bradford and Huddersfield Saturday Observer.* 'On Wednesday evening a vocal and instrumental concert took place in the Sunday School, Haworth. The leader of the orchestra was the celebrated Mr. G.F. Hoffman, the German violinist, who astonished a numerous audience by his extraordinary abilities as a musician, especially by his performance on the 'cello entitled 'Farmyard'. The principal vocalists were Mr. Parker of Haworth, Mrs. Boocock of the Haworth concert ... all was performed with first rate ability amidst unbounded applause'. (9) There was a similar society at Keighley, where a music festival was held in 1834. Abraham Sunderland, at this time the young Brontës' music teacher, conducted the choir and orchestra, so there must have been every chance that his students attended.

Particularly popular, too, especially in Lancashire and Yorkshire, were brass bands; Charlotte was known to have been an admirer. After the Napoleonic wars, returning soldiers who had learnt to play musical instruments while in the army began to form bands for recreational enjoyment, with competitions beginning round about 1818. The forerunner of the internationally-renowned Black Dyke Mills Band was formed in 1816, at Queensbury between Halifax and Haworth; the present day band has existed uninterrupted since 1855. On 4 February, 1833, on the occasion of the opening of the new premises of the Three Graces Lodge, the Keighley Band led the procession from there to Haworth Church, the fee of thirty shillings being charged. Haworth has had a brass band from at least 1854, and in 1895 it played at the opening of the Brontë Museum, then housed on the first floor of the Yorkshire Penny Bank at the top of Main Street. (10) In *Wuthering Heights*, the Gimmerton band was 'fifteen strong, consisting of a trumpet, a trombone, clarinets, bassoons, French horns, and a bass viol, besides singers', (11) while the Whitsun-procession band in *Shirley* included flutes, clarion, and drums. (12)

Of course, music formed an important part of the life of the churches. Patrick Brontë had been appointed perpetual curate at Thornton Chapel near Bradford in 1815. In its archives is to be found –

'An account of the musical instruments and books belonging to this chapel and which it is the business of the minister and churchwardens always to take care of and preserve for the use of the said chapel:

1 Violincello [*sic*] and Bow,
1 Tenor Violin and Bow,
2 Treble Violins and Bows,
1 Holroyd's Psalmody,
1 Stansfield's Psalmody
[Yorkshire psalmody published in 1731],
1 Knapp's Church Melody [1753],
1 Folio Orators of Joshua,
2 Volumes of Anthems by [William] Croft,
A Copy of Purcell's *Te Deum* [1694]
Some Volumes of Manuscript Music,
1 Steel Fork for Pitching Tunes,
1 Book of Hymns.' (13)

Upon being installed as incumbent at Haworth, Patrick wasted no time in purchasing 'a set of music books … which may be had at about six pounds owing to their being second-handed'. The Vestry records for 28 April 1821 show that

Thomas Parker was authorised to effect the purchase 'out of the church rate'. Furthermore, 'three singing books were delivered by David Feather in the Vestry on 17 October 1823, viz: Boy's Anthems 2nd Volume, one book Ratcliff's Anthems, one ditto Ebdon's Services'. A 1773 volume entitled *Select Hymns with Tunes annexed, selected chiefly for the People called Methodists,* beautifully inscribed 'Jane Branwell, formerly, but now Jane Fennell', is housed in the Parsonage. It is not certain which hymn books were in use in Haworth Parish Church during the Brontës' time, but in the catalogue of the sale of the property of the Revd. Arthur Bell Nicholls at Sotheby's on 26 and 27 July, 1907, Lot Fifteen is described as 'Hymn Books (3) by I[saac] Watts, with autograph signature in each volume: C. Brontë, April 6th, 1845, E.J. Brontë, A. Brontë, 1843–4'. Furthermore, in another Sotheby's auction, this one of the property of J.H. Dixon of Harrogate, held on 15 December 1916, the catalogue lists two copies of *Psalms of David, with Hymns and Songs by I[saac] Watts*, one owned by Tabitha Brown of Haworth, daughter of the sexton, and the other by Patrick Brontë, with the inscription 'Minister, Haworth Church' stamped in gold on the upper cover. There are two further inscriptions, one dated 1842, referring to a sermon preached by Patrick.

The Parsonage also has an interesting little volume containing one hundred and twenty-three hymns, the purchase price having being eight (old) pence. Part of the title of this book has been heavily scored out in ink, but the words that remain are *Hymns for the Use of Sunday Schools.* Published by R. Aked, Low Street, Keighley on 1 May 1821, the address (preface) contains the phrase 'hymns for infant minds'. It bears an inscription by Patrick Brontë – 'To be kept for the purpose of selecting hymns for the Annual

Sunday School Sermon at Haworth. Those selected must be marked in order to prevent any being used a second time – as repetition is to be avoided'. Also in the Parsonage library are a number of service sheets which seem to pertain to the aforementioned Sunday School services. As regards those which took place during the years 1827 to 1855, a total of sixty-five hymns are printed. Fourteen are taken from *Hymns for the Use of Sunday Schools,* the last occasion being for the 1838 service. Ten of these are Watts' compositions (five of them being included in the *Methodist Hymn Book*) the remaining four being by other writers. Aked was initially the publisher of these service sheets, but John Greenwood took over in 1850.

Not all churches possessed an organ at this time – Haworth's was not installed until 1834 – a collection of stringed and wind instruments, usually situated in the west gallery or 'singers' loft, providing an accompaniment for the singers and congregation instead. Interestingly, when, in 1785, the Archbishop of York required parishioners in Bradford to show cause why an organ should not be installed in that town's parish church, the inhabitants of Haworth (in the Bradford deanery) objected to their having to pay a share of their rates for this purpose.

As regards the standards of musical performance in Haworth Church, a Brontë enthusiast, E.P. Evans recounts a visit to Haworth in the summer of 1871. Attending a service in the church conducted by the rector, the Revd. John Wade, Patrick Brontë's successor, in the company of the Haworth carpenter William Wood, he professed himself 'surprised at the excellence of the singing; the organ was well played and the children's voices had evidently received careful training. The psalms for the day were chanted in full, and even in the Lord's Prayer and the Creed the organ and the choir followed the rector, sentence by sentence, with soft, sweet melody, and low but distinct articulation'. This event, of course, occurred well after the Brontë's time, but Evans goes on to relate that, 'having expressed surprise afterwards at the proficiency in school children', Wood informed him that 'the improvement dated from Mr. (the Revd. Arthur Bell) Nicholl's arrival in the parish as Mr. Brontë's curate'. He had been licensed to the Curacy of Haworth on 9 June 1845. 'Before that time the music had been simple, as one would expect to find it in so remote and small a parish; but he had at once taken the matter in hand, and introduced a portion of the choral service of the cathedrals, to the satisfaction of all concerned'. (14)

CHAPTER TWO

Musical and Cultural Influences

Haworth
Brussels
Beethoven
Romanticism

Haworth

Haworth Old Church
Apart from the Tower it was rebuilt in 1879
(Brontë Society)

In her *Life of Charlotte Brontë*, Elizabeth Gaskell, having written of the rough living conditions existing in Haworth in the time of the Brontës and the coarseness of its inhabitants, went on to say – 'There are some things, however, which rather tend to soften the idea of the rudeness of Haworth. No rural district has been more markedly the abode of musical taste and acquirement, and this at a period when it was difficult to find them to the same extent apart from towns in advance of their times. I have gone to Haworth and found an orchestra to meet me, filled with local performers, vocal and instrumental, to whom the best works of Handel, Haydn, Mozart and Marcello, etc. etc., were familiar as household words. By knowledge, taste and voice they were markedly separate from ordinary village choirs, and have been put in extensive requisition for the solo and chorus of many an imposing festival. One man still survives, who for fifty years has had one of the finest tenor voices I ever heard, and with it a refined and cultivated taste'. (1) The tenor so described was Thomas Parker (1787–1866) who once sang before Queen Victoria. He performed on many occasions at events in Haworth and other local venues, for example in St. Michael's Church on 24 July 1843 with Mrs. Sunderland in a programme of music by Handel, Haydn, Mozart and Beethoven, the performance giving 'great satisfaction to a rather thin but highly respectable audience', (2) and on 20 July 1846, when he was the beneficiary at a 'Programme of Oratorio Selection, performed in Haworth Church, under Distinguished Patronage'. Branwell Brontë painted his portrait in oils in 1838.

Thomas Parker

There were a number of poets of varying degrees of accomplishment in and around the Haworth area, as attested by Charles F. Forshaw in his *The Poets of Keighley, Bingley, Haworth and District*, published in 1891. Included in their number was the Revd. Patrick Brontë, who had published his *Rural Minstrel* in 1813 and *Cottage Poems* two years earlier.

That the four young Brontës heard a good deal of music in Haworth is not in doubt; their father is known to have taken them to concerts within the village. After the installation of the organ, the church became a regular venue for concerts. It would be pleasing to speculate that the sisters were escorted to performances further afield, in Keighley, Halifax, Bradford, or even Leeds. Branwell might well have attended concerts in these places when he was working away from home; he was known to have frequented the Talbot Inn at Halifax, behind which were the Assembly Rooms, a regular venue for public concerts. There was plenty of musical activity within the Parsonage. For the middle, as well as the upper, classes in the first half of the nineteenth century, music in the home was an important element of family life, and not just for the purposes of enjoyment. Girls were expected to learn to sing and play a musical instrument, most often the pianoforte, as an 'accomplishment', particularly if they were to pursue employment as governesses. Otherwise, music was unlikely to have been a profession for a woman in nineteenth-century England, except perhaps as a singer or, occasionally, a teacher.

One of the outcomes of the technological advances brought about by the Industrial Revolution had been a great increase in the publishing of music scores. Vincent Novello founded his publishing house in 1811, with Chappell and Co following a year later. There was a considerable quantity of sheet music in the Parsonage, including *The Musical Library,* published during the years 1834 to 1837 by William Clowes and Son; the Parsonage edition is dated 1844. Likewise, the mass production of musical instruments, and increasing affluence for a greater proportion of the population than hitherto, contributed to a considerable growth of music-making within the home, a piano being regarded as essential in many middle-class households. The music performed obviously depended upon the degree of accomplishment attained by each player, but a competent amateur pianist would have expected her or his repertoire to include pieces ranging from simple waltzes, fantasias and marches to more advanced works, such as sonatas by Haydn, Mozart, Dussek, Clementi and Beethoven, and miniatures by composers such as Schumann and Mendelssohn, for example the latter's eight books of *Lieder ohne Worter* (Songs Without Words). There would also have been pianoforte arrangements of popular songs of the day, such as Henry Bishop's 'Home Sweet Home', and folk songs such as 'Ye Banks and Braes o' Bonnie Doon', as well as transcriptions of operatic overtures and arias, perhaps even symphonies. Hymns and sacred songs were popular on a Sunday evening.

According to Ellen Nussey, there was no piano at the Parsonage at the time of her first visit on 19 July 1833, but a little later 'there was the addition of a piano'. (3) On 17 November 1831, the *Leeds Intelligencer* carried an advertisement for a 'superior rosewood cabinet piano' costing 90 guineas new, but selling at less than half price. (4) Such an outlay would have been considerable, perhaps prohibitive, for a clergyman whose income was never in excess of £200 per annum. But it might have been that the purchase was made possible by Aunt Branwell, who had some financial independence, or perhaps it was a gift from friends of the family, such as godparents, wishing to see the precocious young children develop their cultural potential further. (Emily's godparents were John and Jane Fennell and their daughter, also named Jane).

The Cabinet Piano in Patrick Brontë's Study (Brontë Society)

The Parsonage piano has a gold-painted panel above the keyboard upon which is inscribed the name John Green, a music agent (and business associate of Clementi) of 33 Soho Square, London, and the date of its construction lies probably between 1820 and 1825.

The compass of the instrument is FF-c4 (where c1 = middle C), comprising forty ivory and twenty-eight ebony keys. It is cased in Honduras mahogany, with two fluted tapering legs resting on castors supporting the keyboard, under which are two hinged doors. The strings are covered by a maroon silk screen tightly pleated from the centre, repaired during the 1980s, with a brass strip around the edge.

Two candle boards may be swivelled out by using a tiny ivory knob – in the Brontë's lifetime, candles provided the only source of light by which to read the music when daylight had faded. The hammers are leather-covered. There is a sustaining pedal and an *una corda* shift pedal; the bi-chords (two strings) extend over the whole of the compass, there being no monochords or tri-chords. The instrument is 106 centimetres wide, 61 centimetres deep and 199 centimetres tall; thus the strings are the length of those of a grand piano, with consequent benefits in tone, albeit that they are in an upright frame. The height of the instrument dictates that it is a cabinet, not cottage, piano as some writers have stated. Emily and Anne played on it regularly, sometimes together. Branwell probably played it as well, but it is known that Charlotte, though keenly interested in music, was discouraged from taking piano lessons at Roe Head because of her short-sightedness. Consequently, on occasion, she lost the opportunity of employment. As she explained to Ellen Nussey, in a letter dated 12 November 1840, in regard to an offer from Mrs. Brooke of Huddersfield, 'I can't give her music and singing so of course the negotiation is null and void'. Charlotte also related that, upon returning from an extended visit to London in 1851, she found that her father had had the piano removed from his study to a location upstairs.

It was lent to the curate of Oxenhope (and Master of Haworth Grammar School) the Revd. Joseph Brett Grant, probably after the deaths of all the children, before being returned to the Parsonage for the sale of family items after Patrick's death in 1861, which sale took place on 1 and 2 October. It was purchased on the first day by John Booth of Oxenhope for the sum of five guineas. (5) (Another item in the sale, described as 'Music books, etc.,' went to a Mr. Thompson for the sum of eight shillings). Subsequently, the piano passed to Joseph Henry Dixon, an amateur musician and owner of a private museum in Harrogate. It is listed as number 318 in his catalogue, with the following annotations – 'Charlotte Brontë's Piano. Played upon by her for many years in the vicarage [*sic*] at Haworth,' [as has already been noted this is probably an inaccurate statement] and 'I hereby beg to state that the piano in the possession of Mr. John Booth of Shaw, Oxenhope, was formerly in my possession, lent me by the Revd. P. Brontë and consequently that it was originally the property of the Brontë family. (Signed) J.B. Grant, A.B., Vicar of Oxenhope. (Dated) Mar. 27/66'. After Dixon's death, it was put up for auction at Sotheby's on 15 December 1916 as lot 656. The next day an account of the sale appeared in *The Yorkshire Observer*, as follows – 'A piano said to be that in the vicarage [*sic*] at Haworth when Charlotte died, sold for £10. This piano, an upright 'cottage' [*sic*] shape, in mahogany case with satin wood inlay, and front panel covered with pleated silk, was stated to be that originally sold at Haworth Rectory [*sic*] on the death of Charlotte's father in 1861'. (6) The purchaser was a person named 'Brand'. However, in 1917 it was donated to the Brontë Society by Mrs. Harriet Dixon in memory of her late husband. (7) It was then housed in the Society's Museum on the first floor of the Yorkshire Penny Bank at the top of Main Street until 1928, when the Parsonage was bought for the Brontë Society by Sir James Roberts, and it was returned there. It is shown in a photograph of the Parsonage dining room taken in 1929, when that room was used to house the recently acquired bequest of the collection of Henry Houston Bonnell. (8) For how long it remained there is uncertain. The Bonnell Collection was re-housed in the extension to the Parsonage completed in 1960, about which time the first serious attempts were made to show the building as the Brontë home, and postcards from that decade indicate that the piano had been returned to Patrick's study by then. A music stool used by the family was returned to the Parsonage by way of gift in 1929.

In early 2008, a Brontë Society member, Virginia Esson, generously offered to finance the piano's restoration. It was one of the Society's trustees, Virginia Rushton, who arranged for this enormous task to be entrusted to Ken Forrest, who subsequently spent two-and-a-half years engaged in research, involving much travelling, including to New York, prior to dismantling the instrument and restoring it to its original condition. He makes an interesting observation. Given that the instrument was made for the playing of music from the Classical era – Haydn, Mozart and others – its falling into dereliction could perhaps have been through its being used to play music of the later Romantic era, for example Liszt, necessitating advanced technique and, frequently, loud dynamics. This could have resulted in the breaking of the hammer shanks and the springing of the leather and vellum hinge joints. Emily and Anne owned no Liszt scores, but subsequent owners might well have done, and caused irreparable damage to an instrument which was not built for the performance of such music.

The vast accumulation of soot, dust and general detritus had to be removed before the work could begin in earnest, and it was only then that the apparent hopelessness of the task was revealed. The original soundboard could be preserved, although many of the guide pins and hitch pins needed to be carefully removed and replaced. The instrument had to be completely re-strung, not of itself too great a problem. But the action was in a very damaged state and there were no surviving dampers or their levers and linkages. What really was a concern was the fact that there were no instruments of a sticker under-damper action available anywhere from which replacement parts could be copied. Furthermore, even the most comprehensive reference works on the history of the piano contained no examples of such an action to act as a guide. In addition, leather strips had been glued onto some of the original leather hammer heads, particularly the middle ones, in an amateurish way, with the result that they were unlikely to strike the newly-installed strings properly; hence they had to be replaced. Eventually, a new damper system was devised and the mechanism was fully restored. The instrument's strain-resisting structure and the soundboard were found to withstand the tension of the re-stringing and, in June 2010, the Brontë's cabinet piano was returned to the Parsonage in pristine order. On 4 June 2010, a second plaque was added, close to Green's original, acknowledging this remarkable restoration work. It bears the inscription

'In loving memory of Emily Jane Brontë'.

Brontë enthusiasts everywhere owe an incalculable debt of gratitude to Ken Forrest and Virginia Esson. In 2010, the Belarusian pianist, Maya Irgalina, gave a recital of pieces known to have been played by Emily more than one hundred and sixty years previously. There have since been a number of broadcasts and recitals, most notably by the French pianist, Isabelle Oehmichen.

Robert K. Wallace has suggested that Emily returned from Brussels in 1842 to 'a new upright piano placed in Patrick Brontë's study'. (9) In correspondence with the present writer, he has acknowledged that he is unsure of the provenance for this assertion. Furthermore, Ken Forrest, as well as the staff at the Brontë Parsonage Museum, present and past, have said that they have no evidence to support this statement. (10) Consequently, it is considered that there was never a second piano in the Parsonage, a view with which Professor Wallace now concurs.

Abraham Stansfield Sunderland (1800–1855) gave musical tuition to the Brontë children, though from what date it is not clear. Branwell had started to play the flute, perhaps as early as 1828, one of his stories from that year, *The History of the Rebellion in My Fellows*, having been written on music manuscript paper, and he made a collection of flute pieces, begun in November 1831 and completed some three months later. (11) It is probable that he started organ lessons with Sunderland after the installation of the organ in Haworth Church in March 1834. As to when the girls began their piano lessons, again it is not possible to say with certainty. In Emily's and Anne's diary paper dated 24 November 1834, Emily writes 'Anne and I have not done our music exercise which consists of b major' … 'Mr. Sunderland expected'. But, some of their scores were acquired before 1834, so it is possible that lessons were taken at Sunderland's house, or perhaps in the church or the newly built schoolroom, before the Parsonage piano arrived.

In January 1834, Abraham Sunderland was involved in a Haworth Philharmonic Society music festival when he conducted the orchestra and choir for the section devoted to sacred music, the principal soloist being Thomas Parker. Sunderland also arranged the concert in Haworth Church to celebrate the installation of the organ, with a performance of Handel's 'Messiah'. Whether the whole of the oratorio was given or just parts of it, is not certain; Charlotte relates that '[the aria] "I know that my Redeemer liveth" rang through the church'. The celebrated organist John Greenwood also performed, the event being satirised by Charlotte. (12) In a letter dated 15 August 1896, Abraham Sunderland's daughter-in-law, Susan, recounted that it was after this concert that her father-in-law was entertained by the Brontë family, 'with whom he was intimate', and that it was then that Charlotte presented to him one of her pencil drawings completed early in the previous year, a copy of a drawing, 'Cockermouth', by Thomas Allom (from an engraving by R. Sands). Patrick had had a struggle to have the organ installed, there having been for some reason opposition from the singers. However, in a letter to George Taylor of the Manor House, Stanbury, he wrote, 'I have consulted the proper law authorities and have found that when the licensed minister gives leave, no other can hinder any performance of the kind in the Church, and it will not do for me to be dictated to by the singers'. (13)

The organ, installed in 1834, was built by Nicholson of Rochdale. It comprised two manuals – Great, with eight stops (principal, twelfth, fifteenth, cornet, sesquialta, open diapason, stop diapason and viola da gamba) and Swell, with six stops (principal, diapason, cornopean, clarion, fifteenth, and tenor(h)orn) along with couplers, and pedal organ with a range of one-and-a-half octaves. Upon the church being rebuilt from 1879, the organ was dismantled and removed to the schoolroom, where services were being held temporarily, before finding its way to the private museum of J.H. Dixon at Oatlands in Harrogate. (14) (The present organ was built by James Jepson Binns of Bramley).

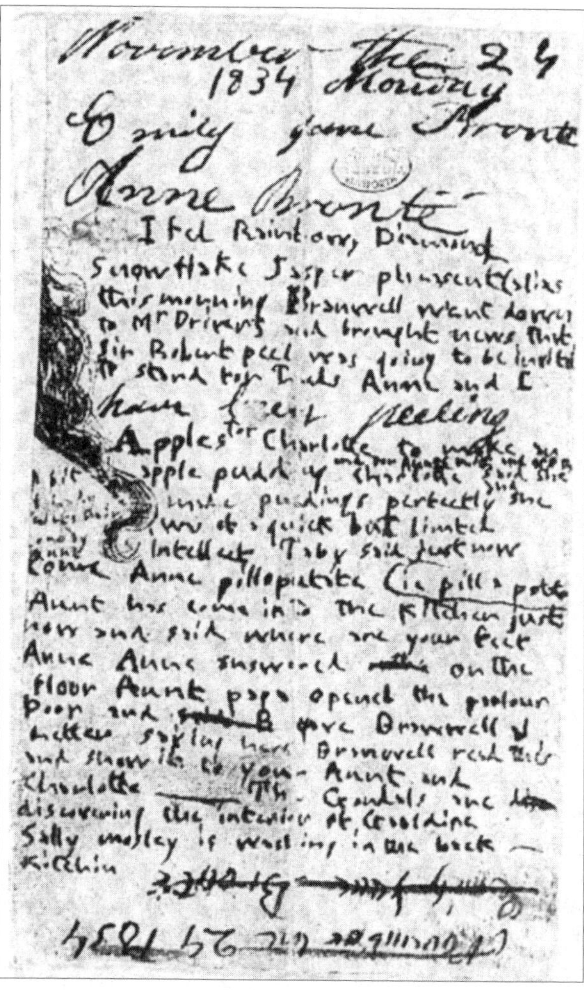

November the 24
1834 Monday
Emily Jane Brontë
Anne Brontë
I fed Rainbow, Diamond
Snowflake Jasper pheasent (alias
this morning Branwell went down
to Mr Drivers and brought news that
Sir Robert peel was going to be invited
to stand for Leeds Anne and I
have been peeling
Apples for Charlotte to make an
apple pudding [illegible] Charlotte said she
made puddings perfectly she
was of a quick but limited
intellect Taby said just now
Come Anne pillopatate (ie pill a potate
Aunt has come into the Kitchen just
now and said where are your feet
Anne Anne answered On the
floor Aunt papa opened the parlour
Door and gave Branwell a
Letter saying here Branwell read this
and show it to your Aunt and
Charlotte The Gondals are
discovering the interior of Gaaldine
Sally mosley is washing in the back
Kitchin

November the 24 1834

Emily's and Anne's Diary Paper, 24 November 1834,
First Page, actual size
(Brontë Society)
The reference to music practice is on lines 8 and 9;
that to Mr. Sunderland is on line 15.

It is past Twelve o'clock Anne and I have not tided ourselvs, done our bed work or done our lessons and we want to go out to play we are going to have for Dinner Boiled Beef Turnips, potato's and applepudding the Kitchin is in a very untidy state Anne and I have not Done our music exercise which consists of b major Taby said on my putting a pen in her face Ya pitter pottering there instead of pilling a potate I answered O Dear, O Dear, O Dear I will derectly with that I get up, take a knife and begin pilling (finished pilling the potatos papa going to walk Mr Sunderland expected

Anne and I say I wonder what we shall be like and what we shall be and where we shall be if all goes on well in the year 1874 - in which year I shall be in my 54th year Anne will be going in her 55th year Branwell will be going in his 58th year And Charlotte in her 59th year hoping we shall all be well at that time We close our paper

Emily and Anne
November the 24 1834

Emily's and Anne's Diary paper, 24 November, 1834,
Second Page, actual size
(Brontë Society)

Returning to the subject of Emily's possible attendance at public concerts, a speculative thought concerns her time as a teacher at Miss Elizabeth Patchett's school at Law Hill near Halifax, from September 1838 to late March or early April 1839. Located nearby was High Sunderland Hall, a building which had some external characteristics, particularly shields and carvings on the gateway and entrance, which might have been in Emily's mind when she was creating the farmhouse Wuthering Heights (although Ponden Hall, three miles from Haworth, is generally regarded as being in most respects the model for the Heights, and Top Withins a likely location.) Emily was well-acquainted with High Sunderland, at which time it was owned by William Priestley. It is certain that Priestley knew Elizabeth Patchett. Accordingly, it might well be surmised that the schoolmistress took her pupils to musical events recommended by Mr. Priestley, and just perhaps that Miss Patchett's young teacher went along too. One such concert given while Emily was at Law Hill, which attracted a glowing review in the *Halifax Guardian*, featured Johann Strauss and his waltz band. (15)

The Brontë children had a considerable library available to them at the Parsonage. As will be seen later in this chapter, the works of Byron and Scott were to have a major influence on them. Shakespeare, too, was well known to them; an 1843 copy of his works survives in the Parsonage, but they were well-versed in him before that year. *Blackwood's Edinburgh Magazine*, founded in 1817, was read regularly. (An extensive set, now housed in the Parsonage dining room, is not the one owned by the family). A Tory publication, it nonetheless published the writings of the radicals of British Romanticism such as Percy Bysshe Shelley and Samuel Taylor Coleridge. The most important writer for the magazine was the often severely critical John Wilson. The contributions of James Hogg, the 'Ettrick Shepherd', concerning Scottish folklore and customs were particularly attractive; so too were the many horror fiction stories which appeared on a regular basis. Many translations and critiques of German literature appeared in the magazine over the years. Charlotte referred to *Blackwood's Edinburgh Magazine* as 'the most able periodical there is', (16) and Coleridge gave it as his opinion that '"Blackwood's" reigned as the unprecedented phenomenon in the world of letters'. As will subsequently be seen, 'Blackwood's' occasionally featured articles of musical criticism, sometimes referring to Beethoven, potentially a matter of significance.

Fraser's Magazine for Town and Country, founded in London in 1830, was another Tory literary journal and a rival to 'Blackwood's' which the young Brontës began reading early in its existence. Hogg, whose *Private Memoirs and Confessions of a Justified Sinner* was known to the children, Robert Southey, William Makepeace Thackeray, whom Charlotte was to meet on a number of occasions in the future, Thomas Carlyle, John Stuart Mill and George Henry Lewes all contributed to its pages, the latter having reviewed *Jane Eyre* in the December 1847 edition. Lewes also wrote a biography of Goethe. Anne Brontë's *The Three Guides* was published in the August 1848 edition. There was also *The Quarterly Review*, to which Southey and Scott were regular contributors.

Aesop's Fables, an inspiration for the juvenile play *Our Fellows*, and *Arabian Nights Entertainment*, which Charlotte mentions in Chapter Twelve of *Shirley*, were read, as was the poetry of Robert Burns. William Wordsworth's poetry and John Milton's works, including *Paradise Lost,* were favourites of Patrick Brontë and were well known to all the family – Charlotte owned a 1797 copy of *Paradise Lost* which contains many marked passages. In her letter of 4 July 1834 to Ellen Nussey, she advised, 'If you like poetry, let it be first rate', then went on to recommend Milton, Shakespeare, [James] Thomson, a copy of whose works had been owned by Mrs. Brontë, Goldsmith, Pope ('if you will though I don't like him'), Scott, Byron, [Thomas] Campbell, Wordsworth and Southey. (17) Another favourite of hers was John Bunyan's *Pilgrim's Progress*. Newspapers, including the *Leeds Intelligencer*, a Tory publication, and the *Leeds Mercury*, a Whig journal, were subscribed to, while the high Tory *John Bull*, was apparently borrowed from a Mr. Driver who lived locally.

There was a *Deutsches Lesebuch* (Lessons in German Literature) and Rabenhorst's *Pocket Dictionary of the German and English Languages,* Volume 1, each inscribed by Anne, the latter dated September 14 1843, and Charlotte's *New Testament* in German, inscribed by her: *Herr Heger hat mir dieses Buch gegeben. Brussels, Mai 1843.* (M. Heger has given me this book. Brussels, May 1843). Emily's *Book of Common Prayer* is inscribed 'Emily Jane Brontë, from her sister C. Brontë, Febr. 1st 1842' (four days before the sisters' departure for Brussels), while Anne's contains the words 'Given to Anne Brontë by her Godmother'. Elizabeth Gaskell refers to Emily's 'studying German out of an open book propped up before her' as she made the bread. (18) At about the age of twenty, Emily started to translate *Ars Poetica* of Horace. She, and Branwell, would probably have read their father's copy of Homer's *The Iliad*, inscribed with the words 'Patrick Brontë: My prize for having always kept in the first class at St. John's College, Cambridge. P. Brontë, A.B. To be retained *semper*'. *The Works of Virgil*, translated by John Dryden, contains annotations by Charlotte and Branwell. There was a French Dictionary and *A New and Easy Guide to the Pronunciation and Spelling of the French Language*, each containing inscriptions or annotations by Charlotte. The Revd. J. Goldsmith's *A Grammar of General Geography for the use of Schools and Young Persons*, 1823 edition, is interesting in that it includes sketches by both Branwell and Charlotte, and under the heading 'A Vocabulary of Proper Names', additions by Anne of the names of places in the Gondal stories. And there was Thomas Bewick's *A History of British Birds*, initially published in two volumes in 1797 and 1804 respectively, the Brontë's edition being a later one of 1816. (19) All the children made copies of Bewick's wood engravings, being encouraged to do so by their drawing teacher, John Bradley of Keighley.

It is believed that books were borrowed from the extensive library of the Heaton family at Ponden Hall. By any stretch of the imagination, this was an extraordinary library of immense erudition, the breaking up of which, at a sale at Keighley on 4 November 1899, was a tragedy. No less than 1385 items were disposed of, including a quite priceless first folio Shakespeare. The categories listed in the sale catalogue were – agriculture, arithmetic, biography, brewing, drama, essays, farriery, gardening, geography, grammar, health and medicine, history, law (including Peter

Thomas Bewick's Merlin Hawk

Lovelass's *The Laws Disposing of a Person's Estate*, potentially of significance to Emily in the writing of her novel), magazines, medicines, miscellaneous, music (see below), natural history, poetry, political economy, travels, religion and science. (20) In a painstaking work of scholarship, the library historian Bob Duckett has listed the twenty-four titles in the thirty-two music volumes:

Ritson's *Collection of English Songs* (1783);
Banquet of Thalia, the fashionable songsters pocket memorial (1790);
Bickerstaff – *The Maid of the Mill*, a comic opera (1765);
The Charmer – a choice collection of songs, Scots and English (1782);
Cockle – *Simple Minstrelsy* (1812);
Collection of Celebrated Songs (nd);
Collection of Songs (1762) and (1782);
Dibdin – *A Collection of Songs* (1814);
Edinburgh Musical Miscellany – Scotch, English, Irish Songs (1808);
Evans – *Old Ballads, with some of modern date* (1784);
Humorous and Other Songs (1776);
Ritson – *Ancient Songs* (1792);
Selection of English Songs (1783);
The Skylark – a well-chosen selection of English songs (1772);
Songs, English and Scotch (1736);
Songs with Airs (nd);
Songster's Favourite Companion (nd);
Tosi – *Observations on the florid song, sentiments ancient and modern* (1742);
Town and Country Songster or, *Vocal Companion* (1790);

Union Song Book – Collection of Scottish and English Songs (1781);
Vocal Magazine, Volume 1 (1778);
Vocal Miscellany, Volume 1 (1738);
Wakefield – *The Warbling Muses*, 731 songs in all subjects (1749);
Watts – *Hymns and Spiritual Songs* (1856). (21)

There were circulating libraries in Halifax, one of which was run by the Leyland family, known to Branwell, and Benjamin Binns recalls seeing the sisters 'trudging' four miles to Keighley to borrow books from a Mr. Hudson, a bookseller and druggist in the High Street. There was also a library at the Keighley Mechanics Institute. Founded in 1825, with an initial membership of seventy-one, the object of the Institute was to bring the Arts and Sciences 'within the reach of the most humble'. Patrick Brontë was a member, his number being 213; so too the Revd. William Weightman, curate at Haworth from 1839 until his death from cholera in 1842. Each gave lectures to the Institute. Many Brontë biographers have asserted that the family borrowed books from this source. However, in a persuasive article in *Brontë Studies*, Bob Duckett insists that this is an incorrect assumption. (22) Furthermore, Juliet Barker states that only sons, not daughters, could accompany their father to the library, (23) so perhaps this long-held assumption is ill-founded.

Patrick Brontë had a number of paintings in his Parsonage, including a mezzotint of John Martin's 'Belshazzar's Feast', the dramatically austere nature of which quite possibly influenced the young Brontës' earliest writings. At the Parsonage sale on 1 and 2 October referred to above, an item listed as 'Belshazzar's Feast' was sold for the sum of fifteen shillings – no purchaser's name is quoted. It has subsequently been returned to the Parsonage.

Brussels

Emily and Charlotte attended Madame Zoë Claire Heger's Pensionnat for nine months in 1842, having left Haworth with their father and their friends Joseph and Mary Taylor on 8 February of that year, arriving at the Pensionnat a week later.

Rue d'Isabelle, Brussels
The Pensionnat Heger was situated at Number 32 on the left-hand side of the road.
(From La Rue Isabelle et le Jardin des Arbaletriers – Victor Tahon)

The reason for Emily's accompanying her elder sister was probably her desire to improve her fluency in foreign languages – French and German – in order that the idea which she and her sisters had mooted, to open a school of their own, might be brought to fruition. In the event their plans came to nothing; no students were forthcoming – they were only seeking some half-dozen – and the idea was dropped.

It was scarcely a surprise that Emily and Madame Heger's husband, Constantin, the languages master at the Pensionnat, did not exactly get on with each other. In a letter to Ellen Nussey written in May 1842, Charlotte described him as 'very choleric and irritable in temperament', and added: 'Emily and he don't draw well together at all'. (1) Emily disliked his method of reading and analysing extracts of French authors, such as Victor Hugo, François-René Chateaubriand, Alphonse de Lamartine, and Charles-Hubert Millevoye, and then requiring that she respond in similar style, rather than in her own fashion. This, she concluded, would stifle her originality of thought. Yet, despite everything, she made progress, as her nine surviving *devoirs* indicate – she was less accomplished in French than Charlotte was when they first arrived in Brussels – and they are important, foreshadowing themes subsequently used in *Wuthering Heights* and the late poetry. (A *devoir* is a student exercise or composition.)

In *Lettre,* dated 16 July, a student writes to her music teacher, inviting her to a small musical party at her house. In reply, the teacher, in declining, comments that 'at least I will not undergo the mortification of witnessing the poor results of my work with you; because I have heard that you are to play a piece on this occasion, and forgive me if I advise you (out of pure friendship) to choose a time when everyone is occupied with something other than music, for I fear that your performance will be a little too remarkable. Still, I would not wish to discourage you …' (2) This is interesting, given that Emily was probably receiving piano lessons at the time, music (at the parents' expense) being included in the Pensionnat prospectus.

The Misses Bronte's Establishment

FOR

THE BOARD AND EDUCATION

OF A LIMITED NUMBER OF

YOUNG LADIES,

THE PARSONAGE, HAWORTH,

NEAR BRADFORD.

Terms.

	£.	s.	d.
BOARD AND EDUCATION, including Writing, Arithmetic, History, Grammar, Geography, and Needle Work, per Annum, ...	35	0	0
French, .. German, .. Latin .. } .. .. each per Quarter, ...	1	1	0
Music, .. Drawing, .. } .. .. each per Quarter, ...	1	1	0
Use of Piano Forte, per Quarter, ...	0	5	0
Washing, per Quarter, ...	0	15	0

Each Young Lady to be provided with One Pair of Sheets, Pillow Cases, Four Towels, a Dessert and Tea-spoon.

A Quarter's Notice, or a Quarter's Board, is required previous to the Removal of a Pupil.

Prospectus for the Sisters' Proposed School
'Music and Drawing, each per Quarter £1.1.0'
Use of Piano Forte, per Quarter £0.5.0
(Brontë Society)

Also of significance is *Le Roi Harold avant la Bataille de Hastings* (King Harold before the Battle of Hastings), written in June 1842, wherein Emily equates Harold's readiness to die – to submit to Death's touch – to the blow which strikes off a slave's shackles. But, it is *Le Papillon* (The Butterfly) dated 11 August, which has attracted the greatest critical comment. Charlotte submitted a *devoir* on the same day entitled *La Chenille* (The Caterpillar).

During a walk through a forest, the writer, in a dark mood, reflects – 'Nature is an inexplicable puzzle, life exists on a principle of destruction; every creature must be the relentless instrument of death to the others, or himself cease to live. Nevertheless, we celebrate the day of our birth, and we praise God that we entered such a world. In the course of my soliloquy I picked a flower by my side. It was pretty and newly opened, but an ugly caterpillar had hidden himself among the petals and already they were drawing up and withering. "Sad image of the earth and its inhabitants!" I exclaimed. "This worm lives only by destroying the plant which protects him; why was he created and why was man created? He torments, he kills, he devours; he suffers, dies, is devoured – that's his whole story. It is true that there is a heaven for the saint, but the saint leaves enough misery here below to sadden him even before the throne of God." I threw the flower to the ground; at that moment the universe appeared to me to be a vast machine constructed only to bring forth evil; I almost doubted the goodness of God for not annihilating man on the day of his first sin. "The world should have been destroyed," I said, "crushed, just like I crushed this reptile which has done nothing during his life but make everything he touches as disgusting as himself." I had scarcely taken my foot off the poor insect when, like a censuring angel sent from heaven there fluttered through the trees a butterfly with large wings of gleaming gold and purple; it shone only a moment before my eyes, then, rising among the leaves, it vanished into the blue skies above. I was silent, but an inner voice said to me, "Let not the creature judge his creator, here is a symbol of the world to come; just as the ugly caterpillar is the beginning of the splendid butterfly, this globe is the embryo of a new heaven and of a new earth whose merest beauty infinitely surpasses mortal imagination. When you see the glorious outcome of what now seems to you so mean, how you will despise your blind presumption in blaming Omnipotence for not having destroyed nature in its infancy". God is the God of justice and mercy; then assuredly, each pain that he inflicts upon His creatures, be they human or animal, rational or irrational, each suffering of our unhappy nature is only a seed for that divine harvest which will be gathered when sin having spent its last drop of poison, death having thrown its last dart, both will expire on the funeral pyre of a universe in flame, and will leave their former victims to an eternal realm of happiness and glory'. The translation from the French is Lorine White Nagel's. (3)

Interestingly, there is a passage in the Introduction to the second volume of Bewick's *The History of British Birds* which Emily might have brought to mind while writing this *devoir* – '[I]t is a melancholy reflection that, from man downwards to the smallest living creature, all are found to prey upon and devour each other.' (4) Elizabeth Gaskell, who met Monsieur Heger a year after Charlotte's death, wrote that Emily's teacher admired her 'head for logic, and a capacity for argument, unusual in a man and rare in a woman', but also noted her 'stubborn tenacity of will, which rendered her obtuse to all reasoning where her own wishes, or her own sense of right, was concerned'. And in a further statement which might nowadays raise a few eyebrows, also said: 'She should have been a man – a great navigator'. (5)

Apart from her friendships with Mary Taylor and, until she died of cholera in Belgium in October 1842, Mary's sister Martha, Emily found nothing to enjoy from a social standpoint; nor did she make any concession to the prevailing fashions of Brussels' society, obstinately sticking to her existing outmoded clothes, and asserting that 'I wish to be as God made me'. It was the fourteen-year-old student Laetitia Wheelwright, a contemporary of Emily and Charlotte at the Pensionnat, who related this statement. She went on to say, 'I simply disliked her [Emily] from the start', and told how Emily taught music to the three youngest Wheelwright sisters (Frances, Sarah Ann and Julia) for four months, but only in play hours so as not to curtail her own school hours, 'naturally causing tears to small children, the eldest ten and the youngest seven'. As regards her competence in music, she described Emily as 'something of a proficient.' (6) With one of her students, however, the sixteen-year-old Belgian girl Louise de Bassompierre, she did strike up a relationship, sufficient for her to present Louise with a pencil drawing of a fir tree, signed and dated, before she returned home. Writing to the Brontë Society many years later, in March 1913, Mademoiselle Bassompierre had this to say – 'Miss Emily was much less brilliant than her sister, but much more friendly. She was advanced in her studies, and she had acquired a genuine talent. She gave me a pretty, autographed, picture, which I have looked after carefully'. (7) Another Louise, the daughter of M. and Mme. Heger , born in 1839, made a particular impression on Charlotte; she appears in *Villette* as Georgette Beck, and she subsequently taught music at the Pensionnat. (8)

Other than the above remarks, there appear to be no surviving records as to the details of Emily's teaching, such as the pieces she taught and the standards of her pupils, nor specific details as to the tuition which she herself received – the repertoire she studied, and the names of her teacher(s). Mary Robinson, Emily's first biographer, refers to Emily as 'the assistant music-mistress' (9), but does not name the teacher(s) to whom, apparently, she was assistant. In a letter to Ellen Nussey dated 6 March 1843, Charlotte writes that Monsieur and Madame Heger's sitting room was, in the daytime, 'a public room, where the music masters and mistresses are constantly passing in and out', (10) which at least shows that there actually were music teachers at the Pensionnat. In a further letter to Ellen, probably written in July 1842, Charlotte states, 'Emily is making rapid progress in French, German, Music and Drawing'. She also relates that 'I consider it doubtful whether I shall come home in September or not – Madame Heger has made a proposal for both me and Emily to stay another half-year – offering to dismiss her English master and take me as English teacher – also to employ Emily some part of each day in teaching music to a certain number of the pupils'. (11) But, Brontë scholars have differed in their opinions as to the identity of Emily's music teacher(s) while she was in Brussels.

Winifred Gérin, quoting Clement K. Shorter, states that 'Emily studied music with M. Chapelle, M. Heger's brother-in-law, a professor of the Conservatoire Royale de Bruxelles, the visiting master at the Pensionnat'. In her novel *Villette*, Charlotte based her character M. Paul Emanuel upon Constantin Heger, and she probably used M.

Chapelle, to whom she taught English, as the model for M. Josef Emanuel, half-brother to M. Paul, who visited Madame Beck's Pensionnat twice a week to give piano lessons. (12) Gérin goes on to relate that 'the progress she [Emily] made ... was exceptional enough for the Hegers to decide on giving her lessons next half with the finest teacher in Belgium'. (13) Robert K. Wallace does not believe that Monsieur Chapelle was ever connected with the Conservatoire, citing Monsieur P. Raspe, librarian of the Conservatoire in 1986, as his authority. (14) The present writer has also contacted the Conservatoire, and was informed by the current librarian, Ms. Olivia Wahnon de Oliveira, that Monsieur Chapelle was not a piano teacher there, the two piano teachers in 1842 being Monsieur Michelot (the elder) and Madame Lambert. (15) Akiko Higuchi agrees with this, further suggesting that 'there seems to be a good case for Christian Friedrich Johann Girschner (1794–1860) being her teacher'. He was a minor German composer and professor of organ at the Conservatoire Royal de Bruxelles from 1842 to 1848, whose *Jagd Chor* (Hunters' Chorus) was included in a concert which he conducted in the Waux-Hall, now the Theatre du Parc, in the Parc de Bruxelles in August, 1843. Professor Higuchi sees links with this piece of music on this occasion and *Villette.* (16).

On 5 November 1842, Monsieur Heger wrote to Patrick Brontë, expressing sympathy at the death of Aunt Elizabeth Branwell, and reporting that *Miss Emily allait apprendre le piano: reçevoir les leçons du meilleur professeur que nous ayons en Belgique, et déjà elle avait elles-mêmes de petites élèves.* A number of writers over the years have read this as 'Miss Emily *was learning* the piano, receiving lessons from the best professor in Belgium, and she already had little pupils'. But this is not correct. The proper translation of M. Heger's words is – 'Miss Emily *was about to learn the piano,* to receive lessons from the best teacher we have in Belgium, and she herself already had little pupils'. This is the interpretation of both Margaret Smith, in her remarkably comprehensive work on Charlotte's correspondence, (17) and Juliet Barker (18); it is also the present writer's. Tantalisingly, though, Monsieur Heger does not name the teacher. Margaret Smith, in a note appended to her translation of the letter, the original manuscript of which has been lost, opts for Monsieur Chapelle as the teacher – 'EJB was about to receive lessons from M. Chapelle, brother-in-law of M. Heger's first wife, and teacher of music at the Brussels' Conservatoire', (19) but, as has been shown above, Chapelle was not a teacher there, although he may well have been, in the not-altogether impartial opinion of M. Heger, the aforementioned 'best teacher' in Belgium who *would have* given Emily piano tuition had she returned to Belgium and, in view of Charlotte's characterisations in *Villette,* detailed above, might in any case have been a teacher at the Pensionnat during the time that she *was* there. In *The Oxford Companion to the Brontës,* it is stated that 'Emily was prevented from taking lessons from one of the foremost teachers in Brussels only by her abrupt departure for home …after the news of the sudden death of Aunt Branwell.'(20) The date of the sisters' arrival home was 8 November.

Collating the above data, the following conclusions may be drawn. It is fairly certain that Emily was receiving music tuition during her time at the Pensionnat, and that that tuition would have included piano lessons, but the names of her teacher(s) cannot be identified with absolute certainty. It does, though, seem probable that she missed out on piano lessons from a more eminent piano teacher than the one with whom she had previously studied by not returning. What she might have learnt from a period of study with a teacher of such enhanced standing, as regards her piano technique, the repertoire, including perhaps Beethoven's sonatas, and music in general, can only be a matter for conjecture.

A further area for consideration concerns the cultural life of the city. It is known that Charlotte went to the Théâtre de la Monnaie on a date between 22 July and 20 August 1842 to see the celebrated actress Rachel perform; Rachel became Vashti in chapter 23 of *Villette*. Then, in the autumn of that year, she went to the Salon where some of the paintings that she saw, most notably 'Cleopatra', were later described in the novel. (21) It is probable that Emily accompanied her sister on these visits. As regards musical concerts, it is not certain that they attended any during their time in the Belgian capital, but it might well be imagined that they did, perhaps escorted by Monsieur and Madame Heger; indeed it may well have been an intrinsic part of Emily's study, as required by her music teacher. They would at least have been able to read reports in the daily newspapers.

Concerts were presented regularly by the Société Philharmonique and the Société Royale de la Grand Harmonie, and music by Beethoven was definitely performed. It is known that at least three concerts held in Brussels during the months in 1842 that Emily lived there included his works. According to *La Belgique Musicale,* the concert on 12 March included one of the three *Leonore* Overtures and the *Eroica* Symphony, while the one held on 24 April included the Seventh Symphony. Each of these concerts was held at the Salle de la Loyauté. (22) As will shortly be seen, Beethoven's influence on Emily Brontë was likely to have been considerable. The third concert was an important event which took place on 24 July at the Temple des Augustins, to celebrate an anniversary of Belgian independence from the Dutch which had occurred in 1830 (confirmed by the Treaty of London in 1839) and the accession to the throne of Leopold I, an uncle of Queen Victoria, in 1831. The orchestra was under the direction of François-Joseph Fétis, and featured the virtuoso pianism of Liszt who played his *Reminiscences de Norma* and *Fantaisie sur les motifs favoris de l'opéra La Sonnambula* (Bellini transcriptions). The thought that Franz Liszt and Emily Jane Brontë might just perhaps have been in the same room together is a distinctly intriguing one.

François-Joseph Fétis (1784–1871), musicologist, composer, critic and teacher, was a leading figure in Brussels' musical life at this time. From 1821, he had been a professor at the newly opened Paris Conservatoire where the founder of that institution, François-Antoine Habeneck (1781–1849) had, in that same year, begun staging regular concerts of the Beethoven symphonies, thereby greatly influencing Fétis (as well as the twenty-five year old Hector Berlioz, albeit that that composer and Habeneck never got on well with each other). In 1833, Fétis was appointed director of the Brussels Conservatoire and *maitre de chapelle* to Leopold I. He was also court conductor and he performed as conductor of the Conservatoire orchestra at the concert given in July 1842, described above.

Speculation as to whether or not the sisters attended concerts in the capital may be taken a step further. In the autumn of 1842, Berlioz, now aged thirty-eight, visited Brussels to conduct two concerts. The first of them, given on 26 September at the Hall of the Société Royale de la Grande Harmonie, included, *inter alia*, the following of his works:

Stanzas from the Prologue of 'Romeo and Juliet' (Shakespeare);
Le jeune Pâtre breton (sung by Marie Recio, with solo horn and orchestra);
Second Movement, *Marche des Pèlerins* ('Pilgrim's March') from 'Harold in Italy', opus 16, M. Ernst (viola), (Byron);
Symphonie funèbre et triomphale, opus 15 (a work for two orchestras and chorus, with trombone solo played by M. Schmidt).

The second of Berlioz's concerts, held on 9th October 1842 in the Temple des Augustins featured these of his works –

Overture *Les francs-juges;*
Orchestral arrangement of Weber's *Invitation to the Dance*;
Second Movement, *Marche des Pèlerins* (Pilgrim's March), from *Harold in Italy*, opus 16, J.B. Singalee (viola), (Byron);
Symphonie Fantastique – épisode *de la vie d'un artiste.*

The orchestration of Weber's *Invitation to the Dance* is significant in that the original piano score was twice in Emily's collection – one copy in what is now known as the 'Parrish Collection', and one in *The Musical Library*, each to be discussed in Part Two. Again, the possibility of Emily's having seen Berlioz conducting his own works is exciting. The Brontë scholar, the late Virginia Rushton, was of the opinion that Berlioz was a distinct influence on Emily Brontë.

It will be seen that works inspired by Shakespeare and Byron feature in the programmes; Emily had a passion for Byron, was acquainted with his works, and had also read Thomas Moore's *Life of Byron.* Berlioz was another to have been influenced by Byron. In addition to *Harold in Italy*, which was based upon Byron's *Childe Harold's Pilgrimage*, a copy of which was owned, and inscribed, by Branwell Brontë, Berlioz wrote the overture *Le Corsaire*, opus 21, also based on a Byron poem. Furthermore, his *opera de concert, La damnation de Faust*, opus 24, was inspired by Goethe's drama, and his overtures *Waverley*, opus 2, and *Rob Roy* were settings of Sir Walter Scott's works. As will be seen, Byron, Scott and the German Romantics were a considerable influence upon Emily Brontë.

Berlioz's *Symphonie Fantastique* is one of the most definitive of all works of music of the Romantic period. Inspired by the composer's infatuation for the actress Harriet Smithson, its five movements are all titled. Translated from the French they are (first movement) 'Dreams, Passions', (second movement) 'A Ball', (third movement) 'Scene in the Fields', (fourth movement) 'March to the Scaffold', and (fifth movement) 'Witches' Sabbath'. It is known that Fétis was not a fan of either Berlioz or the symphony. But, Berlioz was certainly an enthusiast of Beethoven; he championed Beethoven's music, writing extensively on the subject. One of his most valuable efforts was a treatise entitled *A Critical Study of the Symphonies of Beethoven,* a work couched very much in 'romantic' terms. Sir George Grove, in his *Beethoven and His Nine Symphonies* quotes Berlioz extensively. (23)

It seems that, for many years, biographers were disinclined to place overmuch emphasis upon Emily's musical abilities and the inspiration it might well have given her as an influence on her writing. As early as 1883, Mary Robinson, while acknowledging the importance of Emily's study of the German language and her reading of the works of the German Romantic authors, nonetheless regarded her French and music studies as being 'the mere necessary acquirement of a governess', (24) an opinion which is surely inaccurate. Much later, in 1971, The Bodley Head in London published *Emily Brontë: A Peculiar Music,* a title which refers to the description given by Charlotte when she first encountered her sister's poetry. This was an edition of twenty-nine poems and copies of the diary papers for 'young readers', chosen, introduced and annotated by Naomi Lewis. It included an informative introductory essay and a thoughtfully written chapter which briefly discussed each of the selected poems, while placing them into context. A review of this book in *Brontë Society Transactions* contained the following statement: 'We are reminded also of Emily's deep attachment to her home and its immediate surroundings and of the *complete lack of impact which a long absence in Brussels made upon her*' [present writer's italics]. (25) If this statement is to be interpreted as underestimating the significance of Emily's time in the Belgian capital, the present writer disagrees. While it is undeniable that Emily would have been homesick, and that subsequently she made no reference to Brussels in *Wuthering Heights*, unlike Charlotte, whose novels *The Professor* and *Villette* were set there, it is surely the case that Emily's nine months spent at the Pensionnat were of considerable importance to her creative development; her vision, already exceptional, had been yet further enhanced. The very fact that she had advanced her study of the French and German languages, in a foreign environment, had enabled her to expand her fertile intellect further into the fields of European literature, art, architecture and music, it being remembered that she and her brother and sisters were already well-versed in German Romantic literature as a result of their voracious reading at home. The further fact that not long after returning to Haworth she purchased *The Musical Library*, which volumes contained music of a more erudite nature than many of those works which she had studied at home previously, suggests that she had started to become better acquainted with the works of the great composers, one way or another, while she was in Brussels, and it is nowadays much more readily accepted that Emily's musicality was a key component in her literary creativity.

Emily never returned to Brussels; she had worked hard to achieve what she wanted. She was so busy that, while there, she had time to write only one complete poem, entitled *H. A. and A. S.*, and begin two others, one entitled *Written in Aspin Castle* (a Gothic tale) and the second opening with the line 'The evening passes fast away'; the Hatfield numbers are 153–155. These latter two were completed on 6 February of the following year. This was in contrast to her time at Law Hill when she wrote some of her best-known poetry. (Hatfield dates twenty-four of her poems to the eight month period from 30 August 1838 during most of which time Emily was at Law Hill: H76–H99). Furthermore, her aunt's legacy of approximately £300 removed the need for her to seek a career as a governess.

Charlotte, however, did go back. There is a programme of one Brussels concert which is preserved in the Parsonage archives. It is of a *Grand Concert,* held at La Salle de la Société Royale de la Grande Harmonie on 24 October 1843, some eleven months after Emily had returned from Brussels, and the inference is that Charlotte attended that particular event, maybe with Monsieur or Madame Heger, perhaps both. Interestingly though, it was discovered in Emily's writing desk after her death. Although it is difficult to imagine what attraction the majority of the items performed could have held for Emily, the fact that she retained it in her writing desk means that it had some significance for her; accordingly, the programme is listed here.

1. Duo de *Norma* — Bellini
2. *Adagio,* theme and variations for Violin, composed and played by — M. Emiliani
3. Duo from *Picaro et Diego* — Dalayrac
4. Air from *Rinaldo* — Handel
5. English Air (1667)
6. Elegy for Violin — Stradella
7. Quatuor from *l'irato* — Erast
   (althought the composer was actually Étienne Méhul)
8. Fantasy for Violin composed and played by — M Emiliani
9. Scene and Romance from *Rosamunde,* — Alary

Furthermore, on 10 December of that year, another concert was held, this one given by the Société Royale de la Grande Harmonie and attended by Leopold I and Queen Louise. The music performed was by Bellini, Mozart, Spohr, and the contemporary Belgian composers Joseph François Snel, and Armand Limnander. In *Villette*, Lucy Snowe attends just such a concert, patronised by royalty, and including a *'lottery au benefice des pauvres'*, at which piano students from the conservatoire perform, as had been the case at the actual concert. (26) It seems reasonable to assume that Charlotte attended on this occasion too, and that concert-going in the Belgian capital was something which she, and possibly her sister too when she was there, regarded as a valued feature of the environment in which they lived.

The Pensionnat Heger at the time that Charlotte and Emily were pupils Le Soir, Brussels (Brontë Society)

Beethoven

The inclination to link Emily Brontë and Beethoven is irresistible. Each, according to the standards of the time, was unconventional as to behaviour and dress, and could appear to be off-hand or downright rude. Each had an innate empathy with Nature which considerably inspired and influenced their work. Emily's love of the moors surrounding her home, the flora and fauna, the weather, night and day and the seasons, is well known.

'High waving heather, 'neath stormy blasts bending,
Midnight and moonlight and bright shining stars;
Darkness and glory rejoicingly blending,
Earth rising to heaven and heaven descending,
Man's spirit away from its drear dungeon sending,
Bursting the fetters and breaking the bars.' (1)

The writer Herbert Dingle has recorded that only twenty-six of the one hundred and ninety-three of the poems in C.W. Hatfield's authoritative 1941 edition of *The Complete Poems of Emily Jane Brontë* fail to refer to the state of Nature at the time and, of these, several are the merest fragments, that one hundred and three open with references to the air and sky, and nineteen to the earth. Interestingly, he goes on to compare the meteorological records in the Haworth area on the various dates that Emily wrote her poetry with the material contained therein. (2) As her sister Charlotte put it; 'her native hills were far more to her than a spectacle; they were what she lived in, and by, as much as the wild birds, their tenants, or as the heather, their produce'. (3)

Likewise, a number of his contemporaries have related that Beethoven, too, would take himself off into the countryside on long solitary walks, pencil and notebook in the pocket of his overcoat, ready to jot down any ideas which occurred to him for working on when he returned home. Beethoven's pupil and friend, Ferdinand Ries, relates an incident that occurred on one of his walks in the country with the composer. 'Beethoven muttered and howled the whole time without emitting any definite notes. When I asked him what he was doing he answered, "A theme for the last *allegro* of the sonata [*Appassionata*] has occurred to me". When we reached the house he ran, without stopping to take off his hat, to the piano. I sat in a corner, and he soon forgot all about me. At last he got up; he was astonished to find me still there, and said, "I cannot give you a lesson today: I must go on working" '. (4)

It is not suggested that Emily Brontë was prone to work herself up into such paroxysms as Beethoven apparently was wont to do. However, the intrinsic need for communion with Nature, out in the countryside, preferably alone, was a common feature of the personalities of each of them. In her *Biographical Notice of Ellis and Acton Bell* (the pseudonyms which Emily and Anne used when publishing their books) which preceded the 1850 edition of Emily's *Wuthering Heights* and Anne's *Agnes Grey,* Charlotte Brontë (whose own pseudonym was Currer Bell) referred to her sisters in this way: 'They always wrote from the impulse of nature'. (5)

The fact that Emily Jane Brontë and Ludwig van Beethoven could justifiably be described as being unique in their own fields suggests a correlative proposition – that the very uniqueness of these two creative artists of genius might prompt a discussion of their similarities. The eminent critic Harold C. Schonberg had this to say about the composer: 'The difference between Beethoven and all other musicians before him – aside from things like genius and unparalleled force – was that Beethoven looked upon himself as an artist, and he stood up for his rights as an artist … he was a force of nature'. (6) The musicologist and Nobel Prize-winning author Romain Rolland describes Beethoven's twin emotions as being 'vast love and vast scorn'. Later on he refers to [Beethoven's] 'direct expression of personal soul and the constructive intelligence'. (7) Thus, although Beethoven's music so frequently invokes the most intense emotions, this is not at the expense of classical principles of structure. Or, as Berlioz said, 'In Beethoven there is a poetic idea constantly at work; yet music is wholly in command'. (8) As to Emily, her biographer Winifred Gérin refers to the 'incompatibility between the mundane facts of her life and her aspirations'. She then continues by relating this situation 'not to the Victorian age of her maturity, but the romantic age of her adolescence; the era of Byron, Beethoven and Blake'. (9) (Beethoven and William Blake died in the same year – 1827). And would anybody ever suggest that Emily was unable to 'stand up for herself', or, Stevie Davies apart, take issue with a description of her as 'a force of nature'? The modus operandi of each of them was similar, in that each could well be engaged on more than one work at the same time. Each, too, would revise and 'fine tune' material until completely satisfied, sometimes leaving incomplete fragments if necessary. It was during the early 1840s, particularly during her nine months in Brussels in 1842 and upon her return to Haworth, that Emily probably came to know something of Beethoven, and (at least some of) his music, and very possibly be influenced by it.

From a very early stage, it has been felt necessary to divide Beethoven's music into stylistic periods, usually three, designated early, middle and late. (Liszt disagreed, proposing two categories – the first in which Beethoven was influenced by other composers, and the second in which he wasn't). Some authorities claim that it was François-Joseph Fétis who initiated this concept; others that it began with two of the composer's earliest biographers, Anton Schindler and Wilhelm Lenz writing, respectively, in 1840 and 1852, and *prima facie*, it is a theory which has much to commend it. Care must be taken, however, in selecting the criteria to be employed in partitioning his *oeuvre*. Dates of composition and opus numbers (which reflect dates of publication, not composition) are obviously of significance. So too, though, might be various important events in the composer's life, for example, his move from Bonn to Vienna in 1792, the effect of his increasing deafness as expressed in the *Heiligenstadt Testament* of 1802, his chaotic financial circumstances and patronage arrangements, various romantic affairs as portrayed in the letter to the 'Immortal Beloved', his enforced withdrawal from public performance on account of his ill health, and domestic matters such as the bitter dispute with his sister-in-law, Johanna, over custody of his nephew Karl. This method of categorisation is appropriate for the string quartets, with the possible exception of opus 95, and also holds up well for the piano sonatas provided a little flexibility is used and a degree of overlapping is acknowledged. Thus, it might be suggested that the sonatas opp. 2–22, with opus 49, comprise the early period; as Charles Rosen said of opus 22, 'this sonata is Beethoven's farewell to the eighteenth century', (10) , though Lenz includes it in the next period. Then, opp. 26–90 could be said to be the middle period, and opp. 101–111, the late. In due course, it will be seen that Emily Brontë possessed the scores of a small number of movements from the early sonatas up to opus 26. The apportioning of the symphonies into the various periods will be considered shortly.

The depths of despair to which Beethoven had sunk by 1802, at which date he was not yet thirty-two years of age, are only too well shown by the *Heiligenstadt Testament*. Anxious to leave the stress of life in Vienna for the more tranquil surroundings of the countryside where he felt more relaxed – and able to commune with Nature – he set down his desperate thoughts in a document dated 6 October 1802 (with a codicil added four days later). His deafness, by now acute, was an appalling handicap for a musician – composer and pianist – and he acknowledged his desperation to hide it from people; indeed, suicide was a consideration. The depth of emotion in Beethoven's testament is evidence of a very stressed soul, but also one belonging to someone who already was a genius with, as it transpired, much more to come.

But what of Emily? Had she experienced any traumas that had had a seriously adverse effect on her life? At the age of just three, she had lost her mother to cancer. Following that, her two elder sisters, Maria and Elizabeth, had succumbed to pulmonary tuberculosis, by which time Emily was seven. Maria was regarded, by her father in particular, as being a particularly mature girl, likely to have had an important influence on her younger siblings. Instead, their upbringing was entrusted to their mother's sister, Aunt Elizabeth Branwell, and the redoubtable Tabitha Aykroyd – 'Tabby' – a local woman and servant in the Parsonage, with whose blunt, homespun, Yorkshire pragmatism, and veritable mine of local folklore, Emily readily empathised. Beethoven, too, had had an unsteady childhood, with the loss of his mother when he was sixteen, a dissolute father, and the necessity to attend to the welfare of his younger brothers.

By the turn of the millennium, Beethoven had been living in Vienna for eight years. By then, he had written a considerable number of works, rich in quality, and, in 1801, he began work on his second symphony in D, opus 36, completing it in the following year. A four-movement work, it is not a derivative of the symphonies of Haydn and Mozart; even compared with the first symphony, there is an advancement of musical ideas. Berlioz referred to it as being 'noble, energetic and proud'. (11) The second symphony is of greater dimensions than the first, with the *adagio* introduction being thirty-three bars long compared with twelve in the first symphony, a foretaste of the substantial introductions in the fourth and seventh symphonies. The two hundred and seventy-six bar second movement *larghetto* is one of the longest slow movements in Beethoven's entire *oeuvre*, while the third movement is a *scherzo* instead of a minuet. In the finale, *allegro molto*, there is the sense of driven, on-going movement, a typical Beethoven characteristic. Another feature of this movement is the huge coda; Beethoven was to write an even bigger one in his next symphony, *Eroica*. Nicholas Marston states that '[the coda of the Second Symphony's finale's] force is such that it grounds not only the last movement but the whole work. The sense of a psychological 'journey' from beginning to end which is thus created became an essential feature of Beethoven's symphonic style'. (12) The second symphony might well be said to bridge the early and middle periods of Beethoven's work. Intriguingly, it was completed in the year of the *Heiligenstadt Testament*, in which Beethoven poured out his despair at his deafness. There is, though, no semblance of despair in the second symphony. Its second and third movements feature in Emily's edition of *The Musical Library*, to be discussed in Part Two, with the markings on the contents page of that eight-volume work suggesting that she was giving special attention to these inner movements in her practice.

The reaction of one music critic, writing after the second symphony had been heard in Leipzig for the first time, a short while after the work's first performance in Vienna, is interesting. Its finale was described as 'a gross enormity, an immense wounded snake, unwilling to die, but writhing in its last agonies, and bleeding to death'. (13) This sort of criticism was not dissimilar to some of the vehemence of the early reviews of *Wuthering Heights*, for example that of the writer Elizabeth Rigby, who referred to the book's 'repulsive vulgarity', (14) while the reviewer in *Douglas Jerrold's Weekly Newspaper* opined – '*Wuthering Heights* is a strange sort of book, baffling all regular criticism ... the ideas predominant in [the reader's] mind are likely to be brutal cruelty and semi-savage love. There seems to us great power in this book, but it is a purposeless power, which we feel a great desire to see turned to better account. In *Wuthering Heights* the reader is shocked, disgusted, almost sickened by details of cruelty, inhumanity and the most diabolical hate and vengeance, and anon come passages of powerful testimony to the supreme power of love – even over demons in human form. The women in the book are of a strange, fiendish-angelic nature, tantalising and terrible, and the men are indescribable out of the book itself. We strongly recommend all our readers who love novelty to get this story, for we can promise them that they have never read anything like it before'. (15) Emily knew of this writer's criticism – it was one of five such reviews found in her writingdesk after her death, the other four being those in *The Examiner*, *Britannia,* and *Atlas*, all from January 1848, with one unidentified. (16) And the Scottish writer Peter Bayne, having 'no hesitation in [describing Emily Brontë as] one of the most extraordinary women that ever lived', went on to pronounce it 'unquestionably and irredeemably monstrous', and belonging to 'the horror school of fiction'. (17) There were plenty more reviews of similar ilk. Progressive and innovative art often seems to attract an initial negative response, precisely because it is progressive and innovative. (It is only fair to state, however, that these are only examples of unfavourable criticism extracted from much fuller reviews; not everything that was said about *Wuthering Heights* at the time of its publication was of a condemnatory nature).

Between the composition of the first and second symphonies, Beethoven had composed music for the ballet *Die Geschöpfe des Prometheus* (The Creatures of Prometheus), his opus 43. This work is unusual in that it is one of only two extended ballet scores to have survived from music's Classical period, the other being Gluck's *Don Juan.* Based upon the Greek myth, Prometheus creates two human figures out of clay, bringing them to life with fire which he has stolen from heaven. However, upon finding that they lack any sort of emotion, he leads them to Parnassus to be instructed in the Arts by Apollo, Bacchus and the Muses. The result, according to the original programme's synopsis, is that 'through the power of harmony [the two humans are made] susceptible to all the passions of human life'. The Beethoven scholar Barry Cooper has referred to the 'Prometheus' story as being 'essentially the civilising power of art – a subject close to Beethoven's heart'. (18) It is known that Charlotte was intrigued by it, and Emily had two copies of a transcription of the overture. (19)

In 1803, Beethoven wrote one of the most important works in the history of music – his third symphony in E flat known as *Eroica*, opus 55. Nearly twice as long as any previous symphony, it is a work of the composer's middle period. He had originally intended to dedicate it to Napoleon, whose republican ideals he admired. However, according to Ferdinand Ries, when he informed Beethoven that Napoleon had proclaimed himself emperor, the irate composer flew into a rage, tore up the title page of the symphony, and threw it to the ground, shouting; 'Is he then, too, nothing more than an ordinary human being? Now he, too, will trample on all human rights and indulge only his ambition. He will exalt himself above all others, become a tyrant!' (20) The first edition bears the changed inscription, translated from the Italian as 'Sinfonia *Eroica* ... to celebrate the memory of a great man'; the new dedicatee was to be Prince Lobkowitz. (Beethoven's attitude to Napoleon did mellow with the passing of time, Carl Czerny reporting in 1824 – 'Napoleon [Beethoven] said, earlier I couldn't have tolerated him. Now I think completely otherwise') (21). It is known that even as children the Brontë sisters and Branwell had been fascinated by Napoleon, despite his having been the adversary of the family's hero Wellington. Indeed, Branwell had used him prominently in the early *Glass Town* and *Angria* sagas and, when she was at the Pensionnat Heger , Charlotte had written an essay entitled 'The Death of Napoleon'. Byron, too, admired him, and Sir Walter Scott wrote a biography entitled *Life of Napoleon Buonaparte.* The *adagio assai* second movement, *Marcia funèbre*, was included in *The Musical Library*, but not specifically ink-marked on the contents page of Emily's copy. (22) The celebrated 'Prometheus' theme of the finale had already been used by Beethoven as the final number in *The Creatures of Prometheus* ballet music, referred to above. (It is also the seventh of the twelve *Contradanses*, WoO 12, and the theme for the *Prometheus Variations* for piano, opus 35). Professor Cooper makes an interesting point when he suggests that 'the narrative implied by Beethoven's structure is that the first movement depicts the hero's life, the second his death, the third his resurrection, and the fourth his apotheosis on

Parnassus, like the creatures of Prometheus in the ballet'. (23)

Beethoven wrote only one opera. One of the most pertinent reasons for this was the fact that so few subjects that were offered to him matched up to his high ideals, or as he put it: '[the subject] must be something I can take up with sincerity and love'. Eventually, Joseph Sonnleithner gave him a libretto based upon *Léonore, ou L'amour conjugal*, a work by Jean Nicolas Bouilly, originally written in 1798 for the French composer Pierre Gaveaux, which Beethoven took up enthusiastically. Stemming from France's Reign of Terror, though with the action set instead in Spain, it concerns the rescue, from what would have been an unjust death, of a political prisoner; in short, it encapsulated the principle of liberty and justice triumphing over tyranny, which was an ideal dear to Beethoven's heart. Furthermore, the rescue was to be carried out by a woman, Leonore, disguised as a jailer's assistant, willing to risk her own life to save that of her husband. This too appealed to Beethoven's conception of womanhood – noble, devoted and heroic. At the climax of the action in Act Two, when Leonore reveals her true identity, Beethoven sets the words *Töt' erst sein Weib!* ('First kill his wife!') to a chord of E flat major and Leonore's top B flat – a stunning Neapolitan effect, given that the key is D major. The composition of the opera, originally called *Leonore* but subsequently re-named *Fidelio*, the name that Leonore assumes in her disguise, underwent two revisions after the first performance in 1805, before the version which we know today, with its altered title and new overture, was finally premiered on 23 May 1814. The setting of words to music never came as easily to Beethoven as it did to Mozart and Schubert – compare, for example, Beethoven's effort

(WoO 131) at setting Goethe's *Erlkönig* with Schubert's masterpiece (D 328). Interestingly, Edward Chitham has put forward the hypothesis that *Wuthering Heights* too was revised, and considerably expanded, after its initial rejection by a publisher. (24)

We know that Emily knew the overture to the opera and the first act march – their piano transcriptions are in *The Musical Library*, Instrumental section. (25) Given that three of the vocal numbers are in that publication's Vocal section, (26) it may be assumed that she also knew the plot; we can be fairly optimistic that she approved of it and, perhaps, was inspired by it. She, along with her sisters and brother, had always been intrigued by Gothic novels with their haunted castles and prisoners in dungeons – indeed, it is thought that as children they had played out their games in the vaulted cellar under the Parsonage – and many of their early *Glass Town* and *Angria* tales bear witness to this. Emily carried some of these early ideas forward into her depiction of Catherine Earnshaw and Heathcliff in *Wuthering Heights*. Furthermore, Isabella, Nelly and Cathy are, at various stages, kept prisoner by Heathcliff; ghosts and dreams run right through the novel. Then again, in Sir Walter Scott's *Rob Roy*, which along with other *Waverley Novels* Emily had read, Diana Vernon is a strong, independently minded character, of the sort very likely to have appealed to Emily. Leonore, Diana Vernon, Catherine Earnshaw and Emily Brontë were all strong, principled women – the sort Beethoven admired.

The obvious prima facie connection between the sixth symphony of Beethoven and Emily Brontë is its depiction of the outdoors and nature; the name *Pastoral*, though not bestowed upon it by Beethoven, has always been applied to it. Berlioz, though, sounds a note of caution: 'But let us be clear: we are not dealing here with [a] picture postcard and prettified shepherds ... we are dealing here with real nature'. (27) It is unusual in that it has five movements, rather than the conventional four, and that each one has a descriptive title. Translated from the German, these are (first movement) 'Awakening of happy feelings on arrival in the country', (second movement) 'Scene at the brook', (third movement) 'Joyous gathering of country folk', (fourth movement) 'Tempest, storm', and (fifth movement) 'Shepherd's song of thanksgiving after the storm'. The last three movements follow each other without a break. Beethoven was concerned to explain that the work was 'more an expression of feeling than painting'. A selection from the sixth symphony is included in *The Musical library.*

The seventh symphony, completed four years after the sixth, reverts to the normal four-movement structure. Wagner described it as 'the apotheosis of the dance'. The poignant second movement, the piano transcription of which is ink-marked on the contents page of *The Musical Library,* (28) is directed to be played *allegretto*, that is to say not *andante* or *adagio,* as might have been expected in that era. The contrast with the bright outer movements is obtained by way of its low orchestral colouring. It is written in the tonic minor, with a melody in the tonic major inserted, causing Berlioz to declare: 'But a ray of hope appears; these heartbreaking sounds are followed by a transparent melody, pure, simple, gentle, sad and resigned like patience smiling to suffering'. (29) The rhythm is an important feature – a dactyl (a foot of three syllables, one long followed by two short), followed by a spondee (a foot of two long syllables) played relentlessly. Beethoven's seventh symphony, opus 92, is chronologically the last work of his which we are certain was definitely known to Emily. One wonders if she ever became aware of his late works.

It should occasion no surprise that such singular individuals as Ludwig van Beethoven and Emily Jane Brontë should have held deep, intensely personal, feelings about God, and that such beliefs would inevitably be at a variance with those of the churches and conventional religious feelings of the age. Stevie Davies has gone so far as to entitle her 1994 study *Emily Brontë: Heretic*. Emily did attend church on occasions, but probably without any pretence of deep Christian spirituality, and it is unlikely that she taught a great deal in the Sunday School which her father had founded in 1832, whereas Charlotte was appointed Superintendent. Her frustration with the dogma and rituals of the established church were expressed in her poem *My Comforter*. (30) Close as she was to her younger sister Anne, her communion with God was different; if Anne's faith could be described as conventional, Emily's was anything but. For her, the relationship which she had with her Creator was hers and hers alone. Mary Taylor related an incident to Elizabeth Gaskell which occurred when she and the sisters were talking of religion. Mary had told an inquirer that her religious creed was a matter between God and herself. 'Emily, who was lying on the hearth rug exclaimed "That's right". This was all I ever heard Emily say on religious subjects'. (31)

Nature was paramount. In a memorable piece of writing, Winifred Gérin considered that, whilst to Anne 'Nature was a pathway to God … to Emily, Nature became an end in itself'. (32) She also pointed out that Emily seems never to have undergone any sort of religious crisis in her younger life; Anne's approach to faith had been proscribed by her aunt's strictures, and Charlotte had been unhappily affected by the Calvinistic teachings of the Revd. Carus Wilson at the Clergy Daughters' School˙ at Cowan Bridge. Emily's 1842 *devoir, Le Papillon*, which so pointedly expressed aspects of her religious views, has been discussed earlier in this chapter. (33) Now, in a manuscript dated 2 January 1846, Emily Jane Brontë set down her own personal creed in words which have moved generations who have read them ever since. *No Coward Soul is Mine* is considered by many to be the apotheosis of her work.

No coward soul is mine
No trembler in the world's storm-troubled sphere
I see Heaven's glories shine
And Faith shines equal arming me from Fear

O God within my breast
Almighty ever-present Deity
Life, that in me hast rest
As I, Undying Life, have power in thee

Vain are the thousand creeds
That move men's hearts, unutterably vain
Worthless as withered weeds
Or idlest froth amid the boundless main

To waken doubt in one
Holding so fast by thy infinity
So surely anchored on
The steadfast rock of Immortality

With wide-embracing love
Thy spirit animates eternal years
Pervades and broods above
Changes, sustains, dissolves, creates and rears

Though Earth and moon were gone
And suns and universes ceased to be
And thou wert left alone
Every Existence would exist in thee

There is not room for Death
Nor atom that his might could render void
Since thou art Being and Breath
And what thou art may never be destroyed. (34)

As for Beethoven, his whole personality rebelled against anything which remotely smacked of convention, discipline imposed by other humans, especially those possessed of titles, or vague assumptions blindly to be followed come what may; an approach not dissimilar to Emily Brontë's. Beethoven was born and initially brought up a Catholic, but in adult life he was not a practising one. His biographer, Anton Schindler, wrote in the appendix to his *Biographie von Ludwig van Beethoven* (Life of Ludwig van Beethoven) of 1840: 'his religious views rested less upon the creed of the church, than that they had their origin in deism. Without having a manufactured theory before him, he plainly recognised the existence of God in the world as well as the world in God. This theory he found in the whole of Nature'. (35) The *Oxford English Dictionary* defines 'deism' as 'belief in the existence of a supreme being arising from reason rather than revelation'. This is in contrast to 'theism' – 'belief in the existence of a God supernaturally revealed to [humans], and sustaining a personal relation to his creatures'. Another view that might be an apt description of Beethoven's feelings is the principle that God is identifiable with the forces of nature – a creed known as 'pantheism', and a belief which might well be said to equate with that of Emily Brontë. Certainly, Beethoven's profound love of nature was an intrinsic component of his personality. In any event, he was not religious in a conventional sense, like Emily, having no need for regular church attendance or any sort of human intermediary. This is not to say that he entirely rejected Christianity; on his death bed he did receive the last sacrament. And, of course, he wrote a number of religious works – the oratorio *Christus am Őlberge* (Christ on the Mount of Olives), opus 85, the Mass in C, opus 86, and the *Missa Solemnis,* opus 123.

It was in 1819 that Beethoven began work on his 'Mass in D', the *Missa Solemnis,* intended for the following year's installation of his friend, pupil and patron, the Archduke Rudolph, as Archbishop of Olmütz. The ceremony was to take place in the suitably grand setting of the medieval Cologne Cathedral. In fact, so enormous was the task which Beethoven had set himself that the work took four years to complete, and it did not receive its first performance until a year after that in St. Petersburg. The opening is dramatic; after a short orchestral *tutti,* the two-bar *Kyrie* (Lord have mercy) of the chorus is cut short by a solo tenor's suppliant repeat of the same word. Donald Francis Tovey refers to Beethoven's bringing out 'an overwhelming and overwhelmed sense of the Divine glory, with which he invariably and immediately contrasts the nothingness of man'. Throughout the text, the omnipotence of the Godhead is reflected by Beethoven's extraordinarily vehement writing; he makes considerable demands upon the performers, especially the singers. Tovey also states that [the *Missa Solemnis*] 'could not have been written except by a man to whom the prayer for peace with which every Mass concludes [*Dona nobis pacem*] was, as

Beethoven calls it, a 'prayer for outward as well as inward peace'. (36)

In her poem *To Imagination*, the manuscript being dated 3 September 1844, Emily Brontë wrote –

'So hopeless is the world without,
The world within I doubly prize'. (37)

In 2012, Barry Cooper discovered in a sketch book in Berlin, a harmonisation by Beethoven, apparently suitable for organ, of the Gregorian chant *Pange lingua,* probably written for the Archduke in 1820. According to Professor Cooper, Beethoven's treatment of this ancient melody presages the *Heiliger Dankgesang eines Genesenen an die Gottheit, in der lydischen Tonart* (Sacred Song of Thanksgiving to the Deity from a Convalescent, in the Lydian Mode) of his string quartet in A minor, opus 132. Written in the last few years of the composer's life, this quartet is one of the triptych including opus 130 in B flat, with its original *Große Fuge* finale, and opus 131 in C sharp minor. These works are ethereal, transcendental, timeless, and encapsulate the apotheosis of their composer's creative genius.

As time went on, Beethoven took to reading mystic tracts from different cultures, particularly those from the orient. Schiller had written an essay entitled *Die Sendung Moses* (The Letter of Moses) on oriental religions, and Beethoven kept three ideals from this work under a glass frame on his desk –

'I am that which is'

'I am all what is, what was, what will be;
no mortal man has lifted my veil'

'He is only and solely of himself,
and to this only one all things owe their existence'

One wonders if the words attributed to the Dutch philosopher Baruch Spinoza (1632–1677) 'He [or she] who knows Nature knows God', could be said to describe the philosophy of Emily Jane Brontë and of Ludwig van Beethoven?

Of course, in comparing the personalities and creative output of two such singular souls – each, by any criterion, a genius – so much must, of necessity, be at best subjective and on occasion plainly speculative. Robert K. Wallace has regarded *Wuthering Heights* as being a work in three parts, which he seeks to explain by way of an analysis of three of Beethoven's works – in fact he chooses three piano sonatas – one from each of the periods of the composer's creative life. These are opus 13, in C minor, *Pathetique*, opus 57 in F minor, *Appassionata,* and the last sonata of all, opus 111, also in C minor (although its second, final, movement is in the tonic major). It is an interesting hypothesis, scholarly written, and caringly expounded. (38) Certainly, the passion and fury of *Appassionata* can be seen as reflective of Heathcliff's and Catherine's tormented relationship, though it is pertinent to note the calmness of the middle movement *andante* as being redolent of the occasions when their stubbornly forthright individual personalities attain a mutuality. As to the finale of opus 111, the *Arietta,* it requires no great stretch of the imagination to relate this ethereal wonder, in particular its fourth variation and coda, to the peace which, in death, Emily's immortal lovers hopefully achieve. Charles Rosen refers to the last page of the sonata as being 'almost entirely *pianissimo* with a sonority of diaphanous delicacy and refinement, most of it in the highest register', (39) while

Professor Wallace compares the endings of the novel and the sonata, referring to the latter's 'gradual loosening of earthly ties', leading to 'the unmeasured stillness of eternity'. (40)

In 1840, Anton Schindler's *Biographie von Ludwig van Beethoven,* was published in Műnster. A year later, Ignaz Moscheles' English translation, in two volumes, was produced in London by Henry Colburn. The question immediately arises as to whether or not Emily ever read this work, in either its original or translated version. Once again, we are in the realms of speculation. The Parsonage records are silent on the matter, neither is either version listed in the 1899 sale catalogue of the valuable library of the Heaton family at Ponden Hall or shown in the records of either the Keighley Mechanics Institute or the Halifax Public Library. However, the present writer has contacted the Conservatoire Royale de Bruxelles, and has been informed by the librarian that an 1840 first edition of Schindler's biography is owned by the Conservatoire. It is not known exactly when it was acquired, but, *if* it be surmised that it arrived there shortly after publication, and just before Emily and Charlotte went to Brussels in 1842 with the predominant intention of improving their fluency in the French and German languages, and *if* this volume was perhaps borrowed by Monsieur Heger or his music teacher colleague at the Pensionnat, which institution surely had links with the Conservatoire, it is not unreasonable to assume that Emily might have read at least some of it, despite, or *perhaps because,* it was written in German. If so, she wouldn't have had to have read a great deal of it in order to learn of the tale of Beethoven's smashed violin, which came about, apparently, as a result of an argument with his mother about a spider interfering with his practice, which is described at the very beginning of the first chapter of Schindler's biography. (41) In *Wuthering Heights*, the violin which Mr. Earnshaw brings back from Liverpool as a present for Hindley is presented to him 'crushed to morsels'. (42) Is this merely coincidental? The tale of Beethoven's smashed violin is almost certainly apocryphal – he himself denied it in later life – but this would not have been of concern to Emily, had she read the story. (Likewise, the fact that, by the late twentieth century, it had become clear that Schindler had been much prone to lying and generally dishonest behaviour is not relevant to the present discussion, as, once again, Emily would have been completely unaware of such malpractice.). One is led to wonder if Emily did in fact read Schindler's biography, and whether any aspects of Beethoven's personality found their way into her creation of Heathcliff.

Certainly, it can be said that each bore physical resemblances to the other, stocky of build and unkempt with, in bygone days, the word 'dark' having been used to describe them both. Each was mistrustful of, and rude towards, other people, and obstinacy was certainly a shared characteristic. They were of the same generation, Beethoven having been born in 1770, and Heathcliff probably six years earlier – as a foundling, his exact date of birth is not stated. Each was named after a child whose death had occurred shortly beforehand; in Beethoven's case, this was his elder brother, Ludwig Maria, who died on 8 April 1769, six days after his baptism, and in Heathcliff's, a son of the Earnshaw's who had died in childhood, a short while earlier. Each was attracted to women of a higher social standing, Beethoven on more than one occasion, invariably unsuccessfully. Heathcliff's 'Oh Cathy! Oh, my life!' is redolent of Beethoven's 'My Angel, my all, my other self' addressed to the 'Immortal Beloved'. Finally, each died during a storm in springtime.

Schindler wrote of Beethoven's last years that, often '[his] inward mind alone was active; but the outward sense no longer co-operated with it'. In *The Prisoner*, Emily wrote –

'Mute music soothes my breast – unuttered harmony,
That I could never dream, till Earth was lost to me'.

'Then dawns the Invisible: the Unseen its truth reveals.
My outward sense is gone, my inward essence feels:
Its wings are almost free – its home, its harbour found,
Measuring the gulf, it stoops and dares the final bound'.
(43)

It has already been noted that from the earliest days at Haworth Parsonage *Blackwood's Edinburgh Magazine* was read regularly, the young Brontës becoming acquainted with its contents remarkably early in life. A number of articles were written upon musical themes, and Beethoven was occasionally referred to. In March 1830, an article entitled 'Musical Literature', described Beethoven's *Sinfonia Pastorale* as 'an exquisite specimen of descriptive music', going on to declare that 'the works of Beethoven and Weber contain sounds that would have made every hair of Handel's wig stand upright with horror, and probably would have been the death of the gentle Corelli'. (44) *Wellington's Victory,* opus 91, also known as 'The Battle of Vitoria', was referred to in an article of 1841, 'honouring Wellington's victory, and rejoicing over the French defeat'. (45) (This was a battle in 1813 in the Peninsula War, a conflict in which the Brontë children had taken an interest when they were growing up). Reference is made to Beethoven's 'mighty and terrific discords with subtle concords' (46) and his 'fearfully dramatic harmony'. (47) Then, in October 1847, the issue of Beethoven's deafness was addressed. The author, having referred to [Beethoven's] 'gigantic genius' and having opined that 'the discords of Beethoven are better than the harmonies of all other musicians', went on to list a number of his works – *Fidelio, Christus am Őlberge, Eroica, Adelaide,* and *Missa Solemnis,* and refer to 'the doom of Ludwig Von [*sic*] Beethoven'. The interest in this article lies in the fact that the author refers to Schindler's remark, quoted above, pertaining to the inward and outward senses, continuing – 'the outpourings of his fancy became scarcely intelligible'. (48) At the date of publication of this last article, Emily's literary creativity was to all intents finished, so it cannot be said that she was positively influenced by it. Yet this was the sort of reading material which she had been devouring for nearly three-quarters of her short life.

She was aware of at least some details of Beethoven's life. At the conclusion of the fourth Instrumental volume of *The Musical Library*, of which Emily owned the complete set, there are mini-biographies of the composers whose works have featured therein. That of Beethoven is just ninety-seven words long. Having given his place of birth as Bonn, date of birth as 1774, instead of the correct year of 1770, and the place and date of his death, Vienna, 1827, the editor goes on to say that he 'received more honors [*sic*] at his funeral than were bestowed on him while living! His life was devoid of incident, for during the greater portion of it he suffered under the infliction of deafness, which confined him to one country, and deterred him from entering into society; but he is indisputably the musical glory of the present century'.

So, finally, the question to be asked is whether or not Emily Brontë was influenced in any way by Beethoven, and the answer must necessarily depend upon the extent to which she came to know of him – played or heard his music, or read of his life and the complexities of his philosophy and personality. It would be convenient, and exciting, to think that the creator of Heathcliff and Catherine was fully aware of, perhaps even could play, the *Appassionata* sonata, that it was running through her mind during the writing of a novel which, in the late 1840s was unique, and remains to this day a defining work in the history of English literature. Yet again, though, we are faced with the inconvenient fact that there is no hard evidence to suggest that Emily ever heard Beethoven's opus 57, much less that, notwithstanding Charlotte's and Ellen Nussey's eulogies about her pianistic abilities, she was capable of performing one of the most demanding works in the pianist's repertoire. And what of the late works – the last five piano sonatas, the *Diabelli Variations,* the ninth symphony, the final string quartets and the *Missa Solemnis*? These are deeply spiritual works which ask questions of the listener or performer; music which might be said to go straight to the soul. Of the *adagio sostenuto* of the opus 106 sonata, *Hammerklavier,* Beethoven wrote in one of his sketchbooks – 'Holy peace, how beautiful, how glorious. Here is God: here rest to serve Him.' No doubt, had Emily become acquainted with these works during her time in Brussels, she would have been profoundly moved and greatly influenced by them. Again, frustratingly, there is no way of telling if she ever came to know them, although it is a possibility, given that there was a considerable degree of sophistication in the musical life of the city at that time. As will be seen, she did own a few Beethoven scores, some unfortunately considerably abridged, most of them contained in *The Musical Library*, which she acquired in

1844, a short while after her return from Brussels. This fact could be taken to suggest that she encountered his music in some form or other while she was there, but to what extent it is unlikely that we shall ever, conclusively, find out.

But even so, to whatever (limited) extent Emily Jane Brontë knew of, and was inspired by, the works of Ludwig van Beethoven, it is clear that the two of them were possessed of similarities – their stubborn, downright wilful personalities, determinedly unconventional philosophies, and unique compositional *modus operandi.* All of these characteristics were reflected in the genius of their works, for which posterity shall forever be grateful. The extent to which they can be compared will always be a matter for wholly subjective conjecture. What is not in doubt, though, is that they were two geniuses who never met but who, in the minds of so many whose lives have been enriched by them, will always be inextricably linked.

Romanticism

Encyclopaedia Britannica describes 'Romanticism' as 'an attitude or intellectual orientation that characterized many works of literature, painting, music, architecture, criticism and historiography in Western civilization over a period from the late eighteenth to the mid-nineteenth century. Romanticism can be seen as a rejection of the precepts of order, calm, harmony, balance, idealization, and rationality that typified Classicism in general and late eighteenth-century Neoclassicism in particular. It was also to an extent a reaction against the Enlightenment and against eighteenth-century rationalism and physical materialism in general. Romanticism emphasized the individual, the subjective, the irrational, the imaginative, the personal, the spontaneous, the emotional, the visionary and the transcendental.'

The encyclopaedia article goes on to emphasise the characteristics of Romanticism – an appreciation of nature was an essential feature, so too the creative spirit of the artist, which was regarded as being of greater importance than the strict adherence to formal rules and traditions. Imagination was emphasised as a gateway to transcendent experience and spiritual truth. Folk culture, national and ethnic cultural origins, and the medieval era were all relevant, along with an obsession with the exotic, the remote, the mysterious, the weird, the occult, the monstrous, the diseased and the satanic.

Romanticism in music was briefly considered in Chapter One, *The Changing Face of Western Music*, and earlier in this chapter. In architecture, there was a revival of the medieval Gothic style. In the visual arts, an early English exponent was William Blake (1757–1827), a poet and philosopher as well as an artist, who regarded art, imagination and religion as synonymous. He was followed by Joseph Mallord William Turner (1775–1851) and John Constable (1776–1837), two of the greatest of all landscape painters, who portrayed a dynamic natural world through the medium of the dramatic effects of light, colour and atmosphere. Turner's art, for example *The Fighting Temeraire* and *Rain, Steam and Speed*, foreshadowed the school of Impressionism. Constable, whose most well-loved work is *The Haywain*, exerted a considerable influence on the French artist Eugene Delacroix (1798–1863), noted for his use of rich colour. Another French artist, and friend of Delacroix, was Théodore Géricault (1791–1824), whose best-known painting is *The Raft of the Medusa*. In Germany, the greatest Romantic artist was Caspar David Friedrich (1774–1840). Praised by Goethe, his work, for example *The Wanderer above the Sea of Fog*, featured vast and desolate landscapes, often with a solitary human figure marvelling at Nature's awesome power. In similar fashion, Wordsworth's poem *The Prelude* concludes with the poet standing on Snowdon's summit in moonlight with 'a silent sea of hoary mist' at his feet.

Turning to Romanticism in literature, the movement was particularly strong in Germany. Johann Christoph Friedrich von Schiller (1759–1805) was a dramatist and poet, a copy of whose *Sämtliche Werke* (Complete Works) 1838 edition, was owned by Patrick Brontë. (Disposed of in the sale of 1861, it was returned to the Parsonage in 1971). He wrote ballad poetry and some fragment poetry, as did Emily, for example in her Gothic poem *The Prisoner (A Fragment).* Schiller's work regularly featured in *Blackwood's Magazine*, which was read religiously by the Brontë family. Schiller is popularly known for *An die Freude* (Ode to Joy), part of which was set by Beethoven in the finale of his ninth symphony, *The Choral*, including the line which, if she had known it, must have appealed to Emily – *Űber Sternen müß ein lieber Vater wohnen* (Above the Stars must a loving Father dwell). His drama *Die Räuber* (The Robbers), published in 1781, was performed within a year in Bonn. It was an important work, dealing with such conflicting ideas as personal liberty and law and concepts of good and evil. Beethoven probably knew it well. Charlotte Brontë certainly did – in Chapter 28 of *Jane Eyre*, Diana and Mary Rivers are reading it when Jane first meets them. It is very likely, therefore, that Emily also knew it.

Schiller was a friend of the polymath Johann Wolfgang von Goethe (1749–1832), poet, novelist, playwright, scientist and philosopher amongst other things. While studying law at Strasbourg, Goethe came under the influence of Johann Gottfried Herder, the pioneer of German Romanticism. Goethe's best-known works are *Die Leiden des jungen Werthers* (The Sorrows of Young Werther), *Wilhelm Meister's Theatralische Sendung* (Wilhelm Meister's Theatrical Letter) and his version of Christopher Marlowe's *Faust*, which took him most of his life to complete. *Werther* emanates from the *Sturm und Drang* (Storm and Stress) period of the 1770s, which witnessed a movement advocating passion and individuality as opposed to the doctrines of rationalism and restraint of Neoclassicism, and was an influence on the German Romantic movement soon to follow. The work is a collection of letters written by a young, passionate, and sensitive artist to his friend Wilhelm; it was translated into English by Thomas Carlyle (1795–1881), as was *Wilhelm Meister*, which book contains the poetry of Mignon's songs. Carlyle was one of a number of British literary men – Scott and Coleridge were others – who wrote critical essays and provided translations of the works of their German counterparts. *Faust* is a disillusioned scholar who seeks happiness in the real world. He makes a pact with the Devil, through whose representative, Mephistopheles, he schemes to bring about the seduction and death of Gretchen, a village girl; this in turn eventually brings Faust to the brink of moral degradation, though in Goethe's version of the tale, he is saved by God's grace. Berlioz set the Faust story for voices and orchestra in his *La damnation de Faust*

Goethe's poetry is often Gothic – for example *Erlkönig* (Erl King) which was memorably set to music by Schubert, as his D 328. This tells of the death of a child at the hands of a supernatural being, despite the father's attempts at rescue.

The German translation from the Danish was by Herder.

Wer reitet so spät durch Nacht und Wind?
Es ist den Vater mit seinem Kind,
Er hat den Knaben wohl in dem Arm,
Er faßt ihn sicher, er hält ihn warm.

Who rides so late through night and wind?
It is the father with his child,
He has the child firmly in his arm,
He holds him to keep him warm.

Then, in the final verse –

Dem Vater grauset's, er reitet geschwind,
Er hält in Armen das ächzende Kind,
Erreicht den Hof mit Müh und Not;
In seinem Armen das Kind war tot.

The father is horrified, he rides on fast,
He holds in his arms the moaning child,
Reaches the courtyard, troubled with dread,
In his arms the child was dead.

One wonders how Schubert might have treated Emily's poetry had he known any of it; he died in 1828 when she was ten.

Goethe's poetry was known to, and admired by, Beethoven who set several of his works to music as songs – opp. 52 numbers 4 and 7, 75, numbers 1 *Mignon*, 2 and 3, 83 numbers 1, 2, and 3, and WoO 74, 127, 134 and 151. He also wrote the *Overture and Incidental Music,* consisting of nine numbers, to Goethe's *Egmont,* opus 84, in 1809–1810. It was no surprise that Beethoven was so taken with this subject, embracing as it does the subject of national liberation. Set in sixteenth-century Flanders, at the time under Spanish rule, the title character, a benevolent nobleman seeking a more liberal treatment of his people, is executed by the governor. Claerchen, who is in love with Egmont, foresees this, tries unsuccessfully to rescue him, and proceeds to poison herself. Beethoven's final Goethe setting was of *Meersstille und glückliche Fahrt* (Calm Sea and a Prosperous Voyage), opus 112, which he dedicated to the author. (Mendelssohn also set it.) Composer and poet did in fact meet while holidaying at Teplitz in 1812. In 1823, Beethoven wrote to Goethe, 'The admiration, the love and the esteem which already in my youth I cherished for the one and only immortal Goethe have persisted'. (1) For his part, the poet, while respecting Beethoven's genius, nonetheless found his demeanour somewhat uncouth. 'Never have I met an artist of such spiritual concentration and intensity, such vitality and great-heartedness. I can well understand how hard he must find it to adapt to the world and its ways'. (2) Goethe was a big influence on the composer – each shared a belief in 'fate' as a demonic force which could override man's reason. In fact, the works of few, if any, poets have been set to music as often as Goethe's have been.

It is probable that Emily knew of Goethe's work; four of Beethoven's settings of his were included in her edition of *The Musical Library*, Vocal volumes – opp. 52 numbers 4 and 7, 75 number 1, and 83 number 3 – and the entry in *The Oxford Companion to the Brontës* states: 'It would be unusual if the Brontës were not familiar with Goethe's *Faust* and *The Sorrows of Young Werther*, 'if only in translation'. (3) Charlotte certainly knew of him for, in a letter to her publishers, Smith, Elder and Company, she wrote, 'You are right about Goethe, you are very right, he is clear, deep, but very cold. I acknowledge him great, but cannot feel him genial'. (4) One of his poems, though, *Nacht Denken* (Night Thoughts), which he addresses to the stars, does bear similarities to one of Emily's. The penultimate verse of her poem *Stars,* published in 1846, reads –

Oh, stars and dreams, and gentle night;
Oh, night and stars return!
And hide me from the hostile light,
That does not warm, but burn. (5)

The 'hostile light' to which Emily refers is the sun.

A generation after Goethe came the Schlegel brothers, August Wilhelm (1767–1845) and Karl Wilhelm Friedrich (1772–1829) of the Jena School, Johann Ludwig Tieck (1773–1853), poet and critic, and Georg Friedrich von Hardenberg (1772–1801), who went under the pseudonym 'Novalis', another polymath referred to as the 'Prophet of Romanticism'. In *Hymnen an die Nacht* (Hymns to the Night), another example of 'fragment poetry', which he wrote after the early death of the fifteen-year-old Sophie von Kuehn with whom he had fallen in love, Novalis used the silence of the night to picture the immortal spiritual world of eternity after death –

'The night inspirits him'

'Surely, life advances,
To eternal life';

'The world of the stars is dissolved
Into a golden wine of life,
We will enjoy them
And become bright stars'.

This concept is not dissimilar to Emily Brontë's, as expressed by her in *The Visionary* (Julian M. and A.G. Rochelle), again, using the night and stars –

'Silent is the house: all are laid asleep:
One alone looks out o'er the snow-wreaths deep;

The little lamp burns straight, its rays shoot strong and far:
I trim it well, to be the wanderer's guiding star.' (6)

Beethoven's pupil Karl Czerny relates that 'the E major *adagio* in the second *Razumovsky Quartet,* opus 59, no. 2, occurred to him [Beethoven] when contemplating the starry sky and thinking of the music of the spheres'. (7) *Musica universalis* – Music (or Harmony) of the Spheres – is an ancient philosophical concept that regards proportions in the movements of celestial bodies, such as the sun, planets and moon, as a form of music. Furthermore, in one of his 1820 conversation books, Beethoven wrote the words – 'the moral law within me and the starry sky above me – Kant!!' The inference in this postulate is that God is an infinite being, not available to finite human senses or reason – 'We cannot talk to one we cannot comprehend, and we cannot comprehend God; we can only believe in him' – so on earth humans must reason out their own morality and happiness. These words of Immanuel Kant (1724–1804) come from his *Critique of Practical Reason* of 1788, and pose the question as to what extent Beethoven read Kant's works. Albeit that, shortly after his own arrival in Vienna in 1794, his life-long friend Franz Gerhard Wegeler (1765–1848) had tried to persuade Beethoven to attend a series of lectures on the subject of Kant's philosophy, but without success, (8) Beethoven had probably read at least a certain amount. Kant, Goethe and Beethoven might all be said to have bridged the Age of Enlightenment and the Romantic Age.

E(rnest) T(heodor) A(madeus) Hoffmann (1776–1822) was a German writer, composer and music critic, whose *Das Majorat* (The Primogeniture) has some similarities to the plot of *Wuthering Heights.* Hoffmann's celebrated 'Tales' appeared in translation in *Blackwood's* and *Fraser's.* (His character *Der Kapellmeister* was the inspiration for Schumann's set of piano pieces *Kreisleriana*). Scott was particularly influenced by him, and by Goethe. Other German Romantics included Clemens Brentano and Joseph von Eichendorff. In France, the works of Alexander Dumas, *père et fils*, were a feature of Monsieur Heger's tuition during Emily's and Charlotte's time of study in Brussels at the Pensionnat.

In her Introduction to the Haworth Edition of *Wuthering Heights*, Mrs. Humphrey A. Ward wrote – '*Wuthering Heights* is a book of the late Romantic movement, betraying the influences of German Romantic imagination, as Charlotte's work betrays the influence of Victor Hugo and George Sand. The Romantic tendency to invent and delight in monsters, *l'exaltation du moi,* [roughly translated as 'to be full of oneself'] which has been said to be the secret of the whole Romantic revolt against Classical models and restraints, the love of violent speech and action, the preference for the hideous in character and the abnormal in situation – of all of these there are abundant examples in *Wuthering Heights* … [which] is then the product of romantic imagination, working probably under influences from German literature, and marvellously fused with local knowledge and a realistic power which, within its own range, has seldom been surpassed'. (9)

One of the first publications in England which may be described as Romantic, entitled *Lyrical Ballads with a Few Other Poems,* was a collaboration between William Wordsworth (1770–1850) and Samuel Taylor Coleridge (1772–1834), published in 1798. These two, along with Robert Southey (1774–1843), commonly termed the 'Lake Poets', had a cultural affinity with the German Romantics. They were well known to all the Brontë siblings, Branwell in particular being an enthusiast.

Percy Bysshe Shelley (1792–1822), a radical social reformer whose poetry reflected his belief that liberty of the individual was the basis of happiness, was a conspicuous influence on all, especially Emily. His *Epipsychidion* of 1821 has similarities with *Wuthering Heights* – the love between two humans which transcends earthly limits, especially where the narrator says 'I am not thine: I am a part of thee'. In Chapter Nine of *Wuthering Heights* Catherine declares: 'Nelly, I *am* Heathcliff!' Edward Chitham has speculated that Emily's *It is too late to call thee now,* written in April 1840, refers to Shelley in its third and final stanza –

Yet, ever in my grateful breast,
Thy darling shade shall cherished be;
For God alone doth know how blest
My early years have been in thee! (10)

Shelley was an atheist who, according to Chitham, 'sought Eternity like Emily; he was willing to look for it through death'. His pantheistic views are reflected in his *Ode to the West Wind* and *Mont Blanc.* He was another who was moved by the 'Prometheus' legend; his *Prometheus Unbound,* a lyrical drama in four acts, was published in 1819.

As has already been noted, Sir Walter Scott (1771–1832) and Lord Byron (1788–1824) were influential figures in the lives of the developing Brontës. The childrens' interest in the writings of Scott had been stimulated at an early age by their eager readings of their father's editions of his works. In 1828, Aunt Branwell gave them a copy of *Tales of a Grandfather,* in the customary three volumes, inscribed 'These volumes were written by Sir Walter Scott, and the Hugh Little John mentioned in them is Master Lockhart, grandson to Sir Walter – A New Year's gift by Miss E.B. to her dear little nephew and nieces Patrick, Charlotte, Emily and Anne, 1828'. An 1834 edition of George Allen's *Life of Sir Walter Scott* was also owned. All of this reading proved a fertile ground for gleaning material for the children's early literary efforts – the *Glasstown, Angria* and *Gondal* sagas, particularly as regards the Scottish landscape of mountains, glens, castles, flora and fauna. All four alluded to, or directly quoted from, Scott's novels in their later works. His *Minstrelsy of the Scottish Border* of the years 1802–1803, and *The Lay of the Last Minstrel* (1805), a copy of which was bought by Patrick a year later upon his graduating from St. John's College, Cambridge, were early favourites of the Brontës, as was *The Lady of the Lake.* From this latter work, seven songs were translated into German by Adam Storck, the third of which, *Ellen's dritter Gesang,* beginning with the words *Ave Maria,* was set by Schubert, as his D839. Two more of Scott's poems, *The Vision of Don Roderick* and *Rokeby,* were owned by Charlotte, having been presented to her by Miss Wooler, headmistress of Roe Head School where Charlotte, and briefly Emily, had been pupils, and Charlotte was subsequently a teacher. Barbara and Gareth Lloyd Evans state that the rhythms used by Emily in a good deal of her poetry are conventional ballad metres 'derived probably from Scott'. (11) Charlotte's opinions of Scott were voiced in a letter to Ellen Nussey dated 4 July 1834 – 'Scott's sweet, wild, romantic poetry can do you no harm', and '[for] fiction read Scott alone [;] all novels after his are worthless'. (12) Scott was one of the earliest exponents of the historical and regional novel, his sequence of 'Waverley' novels concerning Scottish history beginning in 1814. Then, starting with *Ivanhoe* in 1820, he turned his attention to English history.

George Gordon, Lord Byron, was the most influential of the English Romantic poets, and his effect on the juvenilia of the four young Brontës was considerable. Many themes and characters which Emily and Anne worked into their Gondal saga are recognisable from Byron's writing. He certainly influenced Emily in her creation of the complex character that is Heathcliff, described by Winifred Gérin as – 'the Byronic hero *par excellence*, in whom is embodied the sin of pride to a Satanic degree'. (13) She goes on to say that 'Emily seemed to have had something of both admiration and sympathy for Satan – it seemed to suit her own wilful and independent nature to create heroes in Satan's image'. Byron's *Childe Harold* and *Manfred* evince the struggle between the will of the individual against Nature's forces, the rule of God, and the rule of Law. *Prometheus* was written in 1816. His characters were often unconventional, antisocial or ill-fated. Some, like Lara (another one of his most important creations), had mysterious origins, as Heathcliff had. Byron himself was famously described by

Lady Caroline Lamb as 'mad, bad, and dangerous to know'. Included in his considerable output were six poems on the subject of Napoleon.

Thomas Moore, in his *Letters and Journals of Lord Byron, with Notices of his Life* (usually abbreviated to the title of *Life of Byron*) published in 1830, relates an incident in regard to the poet's early love for Mary Chaworth. Infatuated with her, and believing that she returned his love, he was devastated and humiliated to overhear her saying to her maid – 'Do you think that I care for that lame boy?' Byron rushed out of Mary's house, Annesley Park, and ran home to Newstead Abbey, some three miles away. (14) In *Wuthering Heights* Heathcliff overhears Catherine telling Nelly that it would degrade her to marry him. Like Byron, Heathcliff is humiliated and runs away, not to be heard of for another three years. (15)

Although Matthew Arnold's *Haworth Churchyard* was written upon the death of Charlotte Brontë in 1855, and published in *Fraser's Magazine* two months later, the following of its lines refer to Emily –

'... and she
(How shall I sing her?) whose soul
Knew no fellow for might,
Passion, vehemence, grief,
Daring, since Byron died,
That world-famed son of fire – she, who sank
Baffled, unknown, self-consumed;
Whose too-bold dying song,
Stirr'd, like a clarion-blast, my soul'.

By way of a postscript to this brief assessment of the Romantic movement as an influence on the literary creativity of Emily Brontë, it may be added that Beethoven had this to say about his own creativity –'You will ask me whence I take my ideas? That I cannot say with any degree of certainty: they come to me uninvited, directly or indirectly. I could almost grasp them in my hands, out in Nature's open, in the woods, during my promenades, in the silence of the night, at the earliest dawn. They are roused by my moods which in the poet's case are transmuted into words, and in mine into tones, that sound, roar and storm until at last they take shape for me as notes'. (16)

CHAPTER THREE

Emily Brontë's Musicality

Musical and Literary Rhythm
Emily the Pianist

Musical and Literary Rhythm

In a talk given to the Ilkley Literary Festival in 2011, Bonnie Greer, then President of the Brontë Society, said 'Emily's state of being was musicality … [she] heard the music of her environment and it is captured in the words of *Wuthering Heights*'. (1) This was, Greer said, the concept of synaesthesia. The *Oxford English Dictionary* defines 'synaesthesia' as 'the production of a mental-sense impression relating to one sense by the stimulation of another sense'. The present writer experienced it in a simple way at a very young age when, upon starting to learn to play the piano, he found it the case that each note of the chromatic scale was emphatically related to a specific colour. In very simplistic terms, in the context being discussed, synaesthesia is a concept which maintains that, in performing or listening to music, something in addition to the actual score is suggested – the visual and literary arts, perhaps, or nature – thereby heightening the emotion of the work and its effect on the performer or listener. By the same reckoning, a poet's musicality might subconsciously influence his or her creative writing.

There has always been a close relationship between poetry and music stemming, at least, from Greek and Roman times. The *Oxford English Dictionary* defines 'ode', a word of Greek origin, as 'a poem meant to be sung'. Emily is known to have studied and translated the Roman poet Horace's *Ars Poetica,* and it is likely that this work was an influence upon her writing. Poetry and music do share certain characteristics – vowel sounds (assonance), repetition, phrase or line lengths, and overall patterning and structure. Derek Roper, in his authoritative 1995 edition of Emily's poems, has made the very interesting observation that – 'Emily was highly sensitive to the sound of words, less so to their appearance', (2) which statement might be considered to be an example of her 'musicality'.

Emily had originally written her poems on various tiny scraps of paper which she stored in a tin box. Subsequently, during the winter of 1839–40, she copied a selection of these poems into a notebook, now designated MS (manuscript) C. Then, in February 1844, she began two more books of transcriptions, this time written in tiny printed characters rather than the cursive hand of MS C. MS A is headed with her initials and date of transcription, while MS B bears the inscription 'Emily Jane Brontë. Transcribed February 1844/ Gondal Poems'. MS A, often referred to as the 'Honresfeld' manuscript after the name of the house of William Law who had purchased the document, has long since been lost, though fortunately there is a clear photograph of it in the Parsonage. Also extant are a further forty-six single-leaved manuscripts written on various slips of paper or card. With the exception of MS A, all other manuscripts are in safe-keeping, either in the Brontë Parsonage Museum, British Museum, Pierpoint Morgan Museum, New York, Berg Collection, New York, Princeton University, New Jersey, or the University of Texas, Austin.

In 1850, after the deaths of her sisters, Charlotte added a selection of their poetry to a reprint of *Wuthering Heights* and *Agnes Grey*. Half of Emily's poems were taken from MS A and half from MS B. It is probable that there was a discernable degree of revision of Emily's work by Charlotte. Also included in this edition was a biographical notice about her sisters, written by Charlotte, which included the following paragraph –

'One day, in the autumn of 1845, I accidentally alighted on a MS volume of verse in my sister Emily's handwriting. Of course, I was not surprised, knowing that she could and did write verse: I looked it over, and something more than surprise seized me – a deep conviction that these were not common effusions, nor at all like the poetry women generally write. I thought them condensed and terse, vigorous and genuine. To my ear they had also a peculiar music – wild, melancholy and elevating.' (3) There have been a number of further editions of Emily's poetry, the most important ones being C.W. Hatfield's of 1941, and Derek Roper's, mentioned above.

As early as 1846, Sydney Dobell, writing anonymously in the *Athenaeum*, referred to the three Brontë authors as 'a family in whom appears to run the instinct of song', and referring specifically to Ellis Bell [Emily Brontë] – 'How musical he can be, and how lightly and easily the music falls from his heart and pen'. (4) Again, E.S. Dallas, writing in *Blackwood's Edinburgh Magazine* in 1857, refers to '[Ellis's] music of expression which Currer, with all her wonderful felicity of diction, never attained.' (5) On the other hand, in 1911, two years before being appointed Poet Laureate, Robert Bridges wrote – 'Her [Emily's] biographers, it is true, assert that she was musical; but proficiency in her day, and at a girls' boarding school, implies little; and it would be difficult to find in her writings any evidence of the true musical faculty. In her poems she is certainly not delicately conscious of the music either of her rhythm or of her rhyme'; (6) that view seems to be very much a minority one. More recently, Stevie Davies has referred to the *cantabile* quality of her writing revealing 'a musical ear attuned to phrasings and cadences of an expressive but restrained reverie'; she also considers *Wuthering Heights* to be 'a musician's novel'. (7) The composer Nick Peros thinks 'that the length of Emily's poems is perfect for musical setting and there is such a musicality to her verses' (8) while Lord David Cecil refers to the general outline of *Wuthering Heights* as being 'as logical as a fugue'. (9)

Some of Emily's poems are actually entitled 'Song', as is the one entitled *Song to A.A.*, whose first line reads 'This shall be thy lullaby', (10) while in *Harp of wild and dream-like strain*, and *For him who struck thy foreign string* the poet addresses, respectively, the harp and her guitar. (11) Emily's poetry is often of a hymn-like metre; for example, *The linnet in the rocky dells* (Hatfield 173), and *The winter wind is loud and wild* (Hatfield 177) are both common metre (CM), while *The night of storms has passed* is short metre (SM) (12). In June 1838, she wrote ten poetical fragments, each of which comprises four-beat lines, such as are often found in songs or hymns, and are common in her poetry. (13) To take one example, the following lines (Hatfield 66) could easily be sung to the tune of Charles Wesley's hymn of 1747 *Love divine all loves excelling* (14) with the metre 8 7 8 7 –

Lonely at her window sitting,
While the evening stole away,
Fitful winds, foreboding, flitting
Through a sky of cloudy grey. (15)

Versification, or prosody, can be described by the use of the metrical foot. A foot consists of two, three or four syllables, each one of which may be stressed or unstressed. The most common feet in English are –

Disyllable	iamb	unstressed + stressed
	trochee	stressed + unstressed
	spondee	stressed + stressed
Trisyllable	dactyl	stressed + two unstressed
	anapaest	two unstressed + stressed.

Thus, 'Lonely at her Window sitting', above, is trochaic.

Emily's versification skills were complex, considerable, and closely linked to her understanding of music. One example may be given. The three fragments, the first of which was written in November 1837, *The night is darkening round me*, *I'll come when thou art saddest*, and *I would have touched the heavenly key*, when read consecutively, comprise thirty-five lines, of varying metrical feet, both disyllable and trisyllable. (16)

(Hatfield 36)
The night is darkening round me,
The wild winds coldly blow;
But a tyrant spell has bound me
And I cannot, cannot go.

The giant trees are bending
Their bare boughs weighed with snow,
And the storm is fast descending
And yet I cannot go.

Clouds beyond clouds above me,
Wastes upon wastes below;
But nothing drear can move me:
I will not, cannot go.

(Hatfield 37)
I'll come when though art saddest,
Laid alone in the darkened room;
When the mad day's mirth has vanished,
And the smile of joy is banished
From evening's chilly gloom.

I'll come when the heart's real feeling
Has entire, unbiased sway,
And my influence o'er thee stealing,
Grief deepening, joy congealing,
Shall bear thy soul away.

Listen,'tis just the hour,
The awful time for thee;
Dost thou not feel upon thy soul
A flood of strange sensations roll,
Forerunners of a sterner power,
Heralds of me?

(Hatfield 38)
I would have touched the heavenly key
That spoke alike of bliss and thee;
I would have woke the entrancing song,
But its words died upon my tongue;
And then I knew that [entrancing*] strain
Could never speak of joy again;
And then I felt … (unfinished)

*Hatfield reads Emily's difficult handwriting as 'entheal' – which word does not exist – and defines its meaning as 'hallowed'. Edward Chitham has explained that the correct interpretation is 'entrancing'.

The first five stanzas contain twenty-two lines, each of three strong beats; so, too, are the first two lines of the sixth stanza. However, the next three lines are each of four strong beats, with the last line comprising just two. The first six lines of the final stanza also consist of four strong beats, before the seventh line, 'And then I felt …' is left unfinished.

One of Emily's best-loved poems, of love and mourning, is *Remembrance*, whose first line reads 'Cold in the earth, and the deep snow piled above thee!' (Hatfield 182). The Poet Laureate, C. Day Lewis, has this to say about its rhythmic structure – 'The line here is basically a pentameter; but it is pulled out of ordinary pentameter rhythm and given a different shape by three devices – by putting a stress on the first syllable of each line, by a marked caesura after the second foot, and by the use of feminine rhymes in lines one and three of each stanza. The effect of this rhythm I find extremely powerful, extremely appropriate. It is a dragging effect, as of feet moving in a funeral march; an *andante maestoso* it is the *slowest* rhythm I know in English poetry, and the most sombre.' (17)

As regards the rhythms in the one hundred and seventy-six pieces in *The Musical Library*, Instrumental volumes, to be analysed in Part Two, ninety per cent are written in simple time – 4–4, 2–2 (cut-**C**, sometimes referred to as *alla breve*) 2–4, 3–4, and a single 6–4. The four compound time signatures used are 3–8, 6–8, 9–8 and 12–8. (A number of the pieces contain more than one of these time signatures.) As has already been noted, in regard to the *allegretto* second movement of Beethoven's symphony number seven, the metre of a piece of music can also be described in terms of its metrical feet. (18)

One wonders, though, if it was only in this particular, rhythmic, respect that Emily was influenced by the music which she encountered. Surely, it was also the case that the music which she knew was a source of inspiration to her. But this does not mean to say that she regularly incorporated into her work events or occasions wherein music played a specific role. In fact, there are only a few direct references to music in *Wuthering Heights.* Unlike in her sisters' novels, nobody in the Grange or the Heights plays the piano; in *Jane Eyre*, there is a cabinet piano in the library of Thornfield Hall, and in *The Tenant of Wildfell Hall*, there is a similar instrument in Helen Graham's studio in the Hall. The Christmas Day visit to Thrushcross Grange of the Gimmerton Band has already been noted. (19) There are also three references to ballads –*Chevy Chase*, mentioned by Cathy (20), *Fairy Annie's Wedding*, sung by Nelly (21) and a particularly interesting one which occurs after the infant Hareton is dropped over the banister, fortuitously to be caught by Heathcliff. Nelly takes the baby into the kitchen and, cradling him in her arms, hums a song that begins –

'It was far in the night, and the bairnies grat,
The mither beneath the mools heard that'. (22)

'The bairnies grat' translates as 'the little children wept'; 'mither' is 'mother', and 'mools' is another word for 'earth'. This is a good example of a stanza from a border ballad of the type that Emily and her sisters were well acquainted with. They knew Scott's *Minstrelsy of the Scottish Border*, and were also used to hearing their long-standing servant and friend, 'Tabby' Aykroyd, singing ballads in the local dialect. In fact, Scott refers to the above lines in his Note XLIX to *The*

Lady of the Lake. Canto Four, number xii, is entitled *Alice Brand*, which according to Scott's note is founded upon a translation from the sixteenth-century Danish fairy tale, *Kaempe Viser*. They form the two-line eleventh verse of 'The Ghaist's Warning' included in that tale.

Emily the Pianist

The development in Emily's love and understanding of music can be seen further by making a comparison of the scores which she, along with Anne, accumulated up to the time of her departure for the Pensionnat Heger and those which she acquired after her return. Every single score which the sisters are known to have owned will be discussed in Part Two of this work. Some assessment of Emily's ability as a pianist may now also be attempted.

Frustratingly, while there are occasional references to Emily's playing of the piano, sometimes of the works of Beethoven, in the writings of various authors over the years, these invariably seem to be unsubstantiated. For example, Winifred Gérin writes that 'the girls possessed … Beethoven's piano sonatas and a keyboard scoring of his overtures'. (1) This is an infuriatingly vague statement which is not supported by any assessment of the scores preserved in the Parsonage archives, except to the limited extent that there are a very small number of single movements from the sonatas, and some transcriptions of parts of other works, mostly contained in Emily's copy of *The Musical Library*. Annoyingly, many of the pieces therein have been severely abridged by the editor; see, for example, the slow movements of Beethoven's second and third symphonies, and the opening movement of his opus 26 piano sonata.

Then again, Charlotte is reported as saying that 'Emily used to practise Beethoven's earlier sonatas with fire and spirit'. More than one writer has used this statement, without being able to provide its source. (2) If Charlotte did make this statement, did she mean *complete* sonatas, or just separate movements? If the former, the inference is that her sister became acquainted with them during her time in Brussels, for no complete scores of Beethoven sonatas belonging to Emily are in the collections at Haworth or Princeton University. Unfortunately, the Conservatoire Royale de Bruxelles has no record of any early editions, so Charlotte's statement remains unsubstantiated. (3) However, her use of the word 'earlier' is interesting in that it presupposes a comparison with 'later' sonatas and this, in turn, hints at the possibility that Emily had access to a complete set, in opus number order, at the Pensionnat. (As has already been noted, from a very early stage, the thirty-two sonatas were referred to as being from Beethoven's 'early', 'middle', or 'late' periods. (4) It is relevant to note that, the two short opus 49 *Sonates faciles* apart, the performance of each one of Beethoven's early piano sonatas requires a considerable level of technical expertise and a perceptive intellectual insight.

Approximately sixty per cent of the music in the three volumes of scores purchased in the 1830s which are still in the Parsonage, and those now housed in the 'Parrish Collection' at Princeton University, consists of music by what may be termed lesser-known composers. Variations on themes, transcriptions of operatic arias, overtures and national airs, fantasias, and dances, especially waltzes and quadrilles, are the works which go to make up most of the items in these two collections. Many, though not all, of these pieces are of less than outstanding quality, sometimes lacking in depth of emotion, and not requiring the pianist to be possessed of any great insight into the musicality and inner meaning of the piece. These scores are the sort of piano music to which Robert Schumann might have applied the word 'Philistine'. Yet it would be quite wrong to write off altogether the contents of these volumes of scores which Emily, along with Anne, acquired and worked upon during her late teens. A careful examination of these original manuscripts reveals a number of interesting facts. Firstly, the many pre-Brussels scores under review were clearly acquired piecemeal and only later bound together in the volumes now housed at Haworth. Secondly, a large number of them bear pencil fingering markings, possibly Emily's and/or Anne's, but equally likely to be those of their teacher, Abraham Sunderland. It may be deduced that Emily, in particular, worked upon a considerable number of pieces in her rapidly accumulating collection, and these were of diverse musical forms. Furthermore, many of them required an advanced technical ability, dexterous figuration being not uncommon. What does have to be said, though, is that complete works written specifically for the piano by the great composers of the Classical era – Haydn, Clementi, Mozart, Dussek, Beethoven and Schubert – and, indeed, the major composers of the new Romantic era growing simultaneously with Emily herself, are conspicuous by their absence.

By way of contrast, *The Musical Library* contains works, many of which are more profound and musically valuable; Emily's is the 1844 – not the first – edition. One hundred and seventy-six pieces are included in the Instrumental section – there is also a Vocal section – many by Handel, Haydn, Mozart and Beethoven, as well as a number by such important composers as Clementi, Dussek, Hummel,

Weber and Gluck, though, unfortunately, not John Field. Twenty pieces are marked on the contents pages of the 'Instrumental' volumes, presumably by Emily, indicating that she would give precedence to these in her practice. In addition, some works not so marked may well also have been worked upon, given that a number of other pages in the volumes show evidence of a certain amount of wear and tear. Not every selection of the editor of *The Musical Library* was one of the highest erudition. It remains a frustration, not only that so many selections were truncated, but also that *complete* piano sonatas were omitted – only two, both by Clementi, were included – at the expense of rather too many orchestral transcriptions, not all of which transferred easily to the new idiom, and a few choices were decidedly trite. Of the twenty pieces which it is presumed that Emily marked, sixteen were transcriptions of orchestral or choral works, and six of the twenty were abridged. Nonetheless, she now had available for study a considerable number of interesting works, and these included twenty by Beethoven – three sonata movements, three sets of piano variations and a rondo, three transcriptions of chamber works, four transcriptions of movements from the symphonies, two operatic transcriptions and three ballet transcriptions, along with one work of dubious authenticity.

As to the standard that Emily reached in her playing, it is not easy to come to a definitive conclusion. Ellen Nussey, herself an amateur pianist of limited accomplishment, spoke highly of her ability, describing her playing as 'amazing in style, touch, and expression, like a professor absorbed heart and soul in his theme'. Her opinion, however, was hardly impartial; nor was it likely to have been particularly informed. Charlotte's close friend, Mary Taylor, an accomplished pianist who taught piano and who, while living in Germany, had taken lessons from Friedrich Hallé, father of Charles, the founder of the Hallé orchestra, would have been an ideal person to comment, but there seems to be no record of any thoughts she had on the subject. In a letter to Ellen Nussey dated 9 June 1838, Charlotte refers to Mary's having played on the Parsonage piano during a visit she made with her sister, Martha. Mary Robinson wrote of Emily's time in Brussels – 'She worked hard at music; and in half a year the stumbling schoolgirl became a brilliant and proficient musician. Her playing is said to have been singularly accurate, vivid, and full of fire'. (5) 'Is said to have been', but by whom? Realistically, there is no way of telling what level of competence Emily attained in regard to each of the pieces she studied.

Yet her collection of scores was extensive, and if an assumption is made that she did, in fact, reach a decent amateur level of performance in such pieces as Clementi's Sonata in E flat, opus 7, no. 1, Beethoven's Variations on Paisiello's Air 'Quanto e' bello, WoO 69, Rondo in C, opus 51, no. 1, and a selection of the various orchestral transcriptions, in addition to the more difficult of the works from her pre-Brussels days, the necessary technical demands of these pieces would indicate a very definite ability. Any attempt to draw comparisons with modern assessment criteria, for example the examinations of the Associated Board of the Royal Schools of Music, would be inappropriate; few of the works of which Emily owned the scores would be considered for inclusion in the Grade Eight or Diploma pianoforte syllabuses. However, it is interesting to recall that, in her diary paper of 24 November, 1834, (6) Emily referred to her and Anne as not having 'done [their] music exercise, which consists of B major'. Emily was sixteen at that date, the piano had been in the Parsonage for about a year, and she and her younger sister had been having piano lessons from Abraham Sunderland, probably for at least that year. In today's Associated Board examinations, the scale of B major is a requirement of the Grade Four pianoforte and theory syllabuses. It may be surmised that, by the time of her return from Brussels eight years later, Emily's standard of playing had increased considerably from that level.

Certainly, over a period of time, Emily developed a competence in, and a joy of, music. She had also, from her earliest days, an all-embracing love of the natural environment into which she was born and grew to maturity. In *Wuthering Heights*, Catherine describes 'her most perfect idea of heaven's happiness' as 'rocking in a rustling green tree, with a west wind blowing, and the bright white clouds flitting rapidly above; and not only larks, but throstles and blackbirds, and linnets and cuckoos pouring out music on every side …'. (7) Surely it is no exaggeration to say that Emily Brontë's deep-rooted appreciation of Music – her *musicality* – combined with her innate empathy with Nature, which itself has its own sounds and rhythms and which was the only environment in which she felt completely at home – her *spirituality* – was fundamental to the creative genius of her last few years.

CHAPTER FOUR

Music Scores Owned by the Brontë Family

Thirty-seven Pieces – The 'Parrish Collection'
Three Volumes purchased in the 1830s
The Musical Library – 'Instrumental'
The Musical Library – 'Vocal'
Anne Brontë's Song Book and Vocal Scores
Branwell Brontë's Flute Book

Volume of Thirty-seven pieces of Sheet Music for the Pianoforte belonging to Emily and Anne Brontë – The 'Parrish Collection'

This volume of the sisters' piano music is bound in black pebble cloth, with a black leather spine and corners, tooled and lettered on the spine with the word 'Music'. Its height is 34 centimetres. Pasted on to the inside cover is a sheet upon which are written the words 'This Music Book was bought at an auction of relics of The Brontë Family in Yorkshire, England'. Pasted on to the foot of the sheet is an undated newspaper clipping concerning 'The Brontë Museum'. The names of Emily and Anne Brontë, together with dates indicating that the music was acquired in the early-to-mid-1830s, appear at the head of the first pages of many of the pieces though, having been written in pencil, many of them are now practically illegible, and parts have been trimmed away. It is not certain in whose handwriting these names and dates are written, nor is it clear whose pencil fingerings appear in the scores – one assumes the most likely person is Emily's and Anne's teacher who, as has already been noted, was Abraham Sunderland, though some of the markings could be the sisters' own. It is interesting to note that a number of the pieces are pianoforte duets, and it may be supposed that the two sisters played them together. This is obviously a set of scores which left the Parsonage, never to return, perhaps in 1861. It would be interesting to know who collated and bound the individual sheets; it is known that the volume was rebound in Canada on its way to new owners in California. It now resides in the 'Parrish Collection' at Princeton University, New Jersey, as item number 112 in the catalogue of Brontë material, listed on the university's website.

Morris Longstreth Parrish, a Wall Street stockbroker, was an avid accumulator of the works of Victorian novelists. He bequeathed over seven thousand volumes to Princeton University, involving first editions from 1806–1958, though the majority date from the 1830s to the 1930s. In addition to these music scores, the 'Parrish Collection' includes a further one hundred and twenty-one items comprising various editions of all the Brontë works, in different languages and in excellent condition, as well as manuscripts and letters.

Contents

1. Plachy, Wenzel. 'Three Characteristic Marches for Two Performers on the Piano Forte', opus 9. Printed by T. Boosey and Co., London. There is some fingering in pencil.

Wenzel Plachy (1785–1858) was a Bohemian who was best known for being one of the composers approached by the publisher Anton Diabelli to contribute a variation on his waltz theme, the proceeds to go to the widows of soldiers killed in the Napoleonic Wars. In fact, a total of fifty composers responded, Plachy's effort of sixty-four bars *con fuoco* being number thirty-two in the published edition. Beethoven also received an invitation, but declined it, and wrote his own set of thirty-three *Diabelli Variations*, opus 120, one of the masterpieces of the genre. The firm of T. Boosey and Co., music publishers and instrument makers, was established by Thomas Boosey at 28 Holles Street, Oxford Street, London, in 1816, Boosey having been a bookseller from about 1792.

2. Latour, T. 'Two Duetts for Two Performers on the Piano Forte, from the Favourite Airs in the Ballet of *La Dansomanie*'. Composed and arranged for the Rt. Honourable the Ladies

Charlotte and Mary Hill … Book 1st… London: printed and sold by R(obert) Birchall. The inscription is 'Misses E. and A. Brontë, 20th September 1834'. There is some fingering in pencil, and some in ink on the verso of page 23.

La Dansomanie is a ballet-pantomime in two acts by Pierre Gardel, with music by Étienne Méhul, premiered in 1800 at the Paris Opera. It is a transposition of Molière's *Le Bourgeois gentilhomme.* Jean Théodore Latour (1766–1837) was a French pianist and composer of, inter alia, sonatinas which were ideal for student use. He held an appointment as official pianist to the Prince Regent (later George IV). From 1789 to 1819, the premises of the publisher Robert Birchall were at 133, New Bond Street, London. He published many of Beethoven's works, including a number of original English editions.

3. Steibelt, Daniel. 'Two Duetts for Two Performers on the Piano Forte, from the Favourite Airs in the Ballet of *La Belle Laitière*'. Composed by D. Steibelt and arranged by T. Latour, Pianiste to His Royal Highness the Prince Regent. Book 2 … London: printed and sold by Rt. Birchall [1814]. The inscription is 'Misses E. and A. Brontë, 22nd August 1834'. There is some fingering in pencil.

La Belle Laitière is a ballet in two acts written in 1805. It consists of an overture with eleven numbers in the first act and fourteen in the second. Daniel Steibelt (1765–1823) was born in Berlin, the son of a harpsichord and pianoforte maker. Coming under the patronage of the crown prince, subsequently Frederick William II, a keen amateur cellist who for a while, bizarrely, was rumoured to be Beethoven's father, Steibelt was sent to study harpsichord and composition with Johann Philipp Kirnberger. After a spell in the army, he moved to Paris to begin his career as composer and virtuoso, before travelling to England in late 1796. During the next two years he played works at the famous Salomon concerts which included his own piano concertos, the third of which contains the popular 'Storm Rondo'. He wrote eight such concertos in all. Further travelling ensued, to Hamburg, Dresden, Prague, Berlin and Vienna. It was in this city, at the palace of Count Moritz von Fries on the Josefsplatz, in the spring of 1800, that Steibelt unwisely took on Beethoven in a pianoforte 'duel', coming off very much the worse. Steibelt wrote a number of ballets, *La Belle Laitière* being produced at the King's Theatre in London on 26 January 1805. In 1808, he went to St Petersburg to take up an appointment by Tsar Alexander, where he continued to compose up to his death on 2 October 1823. He composed prolifically for the pianoforte and wrote chamber music and music for the stage. He also compiled a pianoforte method.

4. Haigh, Thomas. 'Corelli's Fourth Solo, arranged as a Duet for Two Performers on the Piano Forte'. Published by Clementi and Co., London. The inscription is 'Misses E. and A. Brontë, 1833'. There is some fingering in pencil.

Thomas Haigh (1769–1808) was born in London. A violinist, pianist and composer, he studied composition under Haydn during the latter's visit to the capital in 1791–2. Although many of his works were written for the two instruments at which he was accomplished, his most prolific output was in the genre of making arrangements, as this piece shows. He died in London. Arcangelo Corelli (1653–1713) was an

Italian composer renowned for his *sonates da camera* and *concerti grossi,* which had a considerable influence upon Handel and Bach. Muzio Clementi (1752–1832), who was born in Rome, was a composer, particularly of pianoforte sonatas, and pianist of high renown who, after the bankruptcy of the publishing house of Longman and Broderip in 1778, entered into a new partnership with Longman until 1801 when Longman left. Clementi then became head of a new firm at 131 Cheapside, with Messrs. Banger, Hyde, Collard and Davis. Clementi left the firm, which also had a fine reputation for the manufacture of pianofortes, in 1831 , one year before his death at Evesham.

5. Rossini, Gioacchino **Antonio.** 'The Overture to *Tancredi,* arranged as a Duett for two Performers'. Published by George Walker, London. Inscribed 'Misses E. and A. Brontë, 1st July 1834'. There is some pencil fingering.

The two-act opera (*melodramma eroico) Tancredi* was written in 1813, and produced on 6 February of that year at the Teatro La Fenice in Venice. The libretto was by Gaetano Rossi, based on Tasso's *Gerusalemme liberata* and Voltaire's tragedy *Tancrede.* The overture, marked *andante marcato,* is in common time, and contains extremes of dynamics. Gioacchino Antonio Rossini (1792–1868) was born in Pesaro, the son of a town trumpeter and singer. Although apprenticed to a blacksmith as a child, he entered the Liceo Comunale of Bologna in 1806 where he started writing comic operas. In 1814, he was appointed to the musical directorship of the two Neapolitan opera houses where his operatic output continued with, inter alia, *Il Barbiere di Siviglia* (The Barber of Seville) *La Cenerentola* (Cinderella) and, in 1823, *Semiramide.* (In July 1848, Charlotte and Anne Brontë, though not Emily who had remained in Haworth, were escorted to a performance of *Il Barbiere di Siviglia* at the Royal Opera House, Covent Garden, by Charlotte's publisher George Smith and his family). The previous year Rossini had visited Vienna on his honeymoon and met Beethoven who, in writing to Louis Spohr, said that Rossini had supplanted him in popularity. Beethoven admired the Italian style of vocal writing. A trip to London followed before, in 1824, he moved to Paris to take up the position of director of the Théâtre des Italiens and, a year later, as composer to Charles X. While in Paris, he composed three operas, including *Guillaume Tell*, before leaving for Italy in 1836. However, he and his second wife returned to the French capital in 1855 where they lived for the remainder of his days. He wrote little music during the last thirty years of his life, though the *Petite Messe Solennelle*, begun in 1863, is notable. George Walker established his publishing house at 106, Great Portland Street, London, about the year 1795. He remained there until 1821, moving to 17 Soho Square until about 1848.

6. Handel, George Frideric. 'The "Hallelujah" Chorus from the Oratorio of "Messiah". Composed by Handel and arranged as a Duett for Two Performers on the Piano Forte by T. Haigh ... York: Printed and sold by Knapton, White and Knapton, and may be had in London at W. Bainbridge's Patent Flageolet Manufactory'. The inscription is 'Misses E. and A. Brontë, 1834'. There is some pencil fingering.

The oratorio *Messiah* is Handel's most well-known work. He wrote it in an incredibly short period of time – Grove states twenty-four days, between 22 August and 14 September 1741 – and it received its first performance, in the Great Music Hall, Fishamble Street, Dublin, in the following year. The first English performance was at the Covent Garden Theatre on 23 March 1743. In its finished form – Handel revised and rewrote much of the work after the first performance – it consists of fifty-three numbers in three parts, beginning with an overture in the French style, and is scored for soprano, alto (male or female), tenor and bass soloists, chorus and orchestra. The earliest published score is that of Randall and Abell, dated 1767, and the earliest public performance in a church was probably that given in Westminster Abbey during the Handel Commemoration in 1784. Often, however, particularly when a performance is given in a church by an amateur society, the accompaniment is provided by an organ. In such cases, a vocal score is used, a particularly well known one being the Novello edition of 1902, edited by Ebenezer Prout. *Messiah* is known to have been performed in Haworth Parish Church. The popular 'Hallelujah' Chorus is the final number of Part Two, the text being taken from the 'Book of Revelation', as follows – chapter 9, verse 6 ('Hallelujah' and text line one), chapter 11, verse 15 (text lines two and three) and chapter 19, verse 16 (text line four)..

Hallelujah!
(i) For the Lord God omnipotent reigneth;
(ii) The kingdom of this world is become
the Kingdom of our Lord and of His Christ;
(iii) And He shall reign for ever and ever;
(iv) King of Kings and Lord of Lords.

In fact, the text of *Messiah* was assembled by Charles Jennens (*c*1700–1773) patron of the arts, who had already done likewise with Handel's oratorios *Saul* and *Israel in Egypt*. George Frideric Handel (1685–1759) was born in Halle, Germany, the son of a barber-surgeon who did not wish his son to pursue a career in music. Accordingly, Handel studied law at Halle University, only turning to music when his father died. There followed spells in Hamburg, Italy and, in 1710 , Hanover, where he was appointed to the post of court conductor. Shortly, he moved to London where he was to spend the rest of his life, becoming a naturalised Englishman in 1726. Handel's output was prodigious, comprising more than three dozen Italian operas, over two dozen oratorios, church music, including the 'Chandos' Anthems and the four 'Coronation' Anthems written for George II, and a considerable quantity of chamber music, harpsichord and organ works, on each of which instruments Handel was a virtuoso.

7. Handel, George Frideric. ' "And the Glory of the Lord", Chorus from "Messiah" '. Arranged as a Duet for Two Performers on the Piano Forte by T. Haigh, London. Published by Clementi and Co., London. The inscription is 'Misses E. and A. Brontë', with the date being illegible. Pages 3–7 have been damaged and crudely repaired. There is some pencil fingering.

The text is taken from 'Isaiah', chapter 40, verse 5.

And the Glory of the Lord shall be revealed,
And all flesh shall see it together,
For the mouth of the Lord hath spoken it.

8. Handel, George Frideric. 'Coronation Anthem'. Arranged from the Original Score as a Grand Duett for Two Performers on One Piano Forte by H[enry] G[eorge] Nixon, organist to the Royal Bavarian Embassy in London. Published by Walker and Son, London. The inscription is 'Misses E. and A. Brontë', with the date being illegible. There is some fingering in pencil.

Handel wrote four 'Coronation Anthems' for the Coronation of King George II on 11 October 1727 – 'Zadok the Priest' (the shortest and most popular), 'The King Shall Rejoice', 'Let Thy Hand be Strengthened' and 'My Heart is Inditing'. The *Norwich Mercury*, on 16 September announced that 'Mr. Hendel [*sic*], the famous composer to the Opera, is appointed by the King to compose the anthem at the Coronation which is to be sung in Westminster Abbey at the Grand Ceremony'. 'Zadok the Priest' has been sung at every Coronation since. On 14 October, the same journal printed an account of the rehearsal which had taken place eight days earlier, at which there were – 'forty voices and about one hundred violins, trumpets, hautboys, kettledrums and bass proportionable; besides an organ which was erected behind the Altar; and both the Musick and the Performers were the Admiration of all the Audience'. The Leipzig publishing house of Breitkopf und Härtel was founded in 1719 by Bernhard Christoph Breitkopf. One of the music world's most eminent publishing firms, its catalogue over nearly three centuries is immense, with complete editions of the works of numerous composers.

9. Moscheles, Ignaz. 'Three Waltzes for Two Performers on the Piano Forte … Book 1 … Published for the Proprietors by Metzler and Son, Music Sellers, London … New and Superior Edition'. Inscribed 'Misses E. and A. Brontë, 22nd October 1833'. There is fingering in pencil.

Ignaz Moscheles (1794–1870) was a pianist, conductor and composer born in Prague. In his teens, he moved to Vienna to study with Albrechtsberger and Salieri (with both of whom Beethoven had studied) and, in 1814, the publishing house of Artaria and Co. commissioned him to make a pianoforte arrangement of *Fidelio* under Beethoven's supervision. He travelled extensively in his capacity as a virtuoso, settling for a time in London in 1826, where, six years later, he conducted the London premiere of the *Missa Solemnis*. He was one of the first pianists to perform Beethoven's piano sonatas in public. From 1846 to his death, he was professor of pianoforte at the Leipzig Conservatory, founded by Mendelssohn, to whom he had given lessons more than twenty years earlier. His prolific output of compositions included eight piano concertos, twenty-four études, opus 70, and *Charakteristiche Studien*, opus 95. Importantly, in 1841, he translated Anton Schindler's biography of Beethoven into English. (1) The German Valentin Metzler opened a shop in Wardour Street , London, for the sale of flutes and other musical instruments about the year 1788.

10. Griffin, George Eugene. 'Concerto No. 1 for the Piano Forte, with Accompaniments for a Full Orchestra', opus 1. Dedicated to Mr. J.B. Cramer … London. Published by Cramer, Addison and Beale and by Clementi and Co., London. The inscription is 'Miss A. Brontë', the date being illegible.

George Eugene Griffin (1781–1863) was born in London. He gave the first performance of his first Piano Concerto in A, opus 1, no. 1 – there were three concertos altogether – at the age of sixteen. It includes a set of variations on the tune 'The Blue Bell of Scotland'. With the exception of three string quartets, opus 8, all his compositional output was for pianoforte, with or without other instruments. One of the original members of the Philharmonic Society, he died in London, aged eighty-two.

11. Herz, Henri. '*Les Favorites ou Les Élégantes.* The First Set of Quadrilles or Contredanses Variées'. 'A Select Catalogue of New Pianoforte Music'. Published by D'Almaine and Co., London. The inscription is 'Miss E. Brontë'.

Henri (Heinrich) Herz (1803–1888) was a pianist and composer born in Vienna. He entered the Paris Conservatoire in 1816 and within two years had won first prize for pianoforte playing. Herz was another pianist who travelled extensively, including to London, where, in 1833, he played duets with Moscheles and Cramer. He went further afield than most, spending six years in the United States, Mexico and the West Indies. On his return, he devoted his energies to pianoforte-making, winning the highest medal of honour at the Paris Exhibition of 1855, and continuing to teach at the Conservatoire until 1874. He wrote a pianoforte 'Method' and much piano music of the drawing room or salon variety. His death in Paris occurred on the day before his eighty-fifth birthday. George Goulding founded his music-publishing house in about 1786. In 1798 he took others into partnership, the new firm being called Goulding, Phipps, D'Almaine and Co., of 45, Pall Mall, and they obtained royal patronage. Further changes of both name and address followed until, about the year 1834, Goulding's name was no longer included and the firm was then called D'Almaine and Co. From 1811 to 1858 the address was 20 Soho Square.

12. Rossini, Gioacchino Antonio. 'Overture to the Admired Opera of *Guillaume Tell*, for the Piano Forte'. Published by Chez D'Almaine and Co., Londres; Chez E. Troupenas, Paris; Chez les Fils de B. Schott, Mayence. Inscribed 'Miss Anne Brontë', the date being illegible.

Guillaume Tell (William Tell) is an opera in four acts to a libretto by Étienne de Jouy and Hippolyte Bis after the 1804 play by Friedrich Schiller based on the Swiss legend. First produced in Paris in 1829, it was Rossini's last opera. The overture is much the most popular part of the opera, often being performed as a concert overture. It is in three parts; the first is an *andante* in 3–4 time, the second is also an *andante*, marked *p, dolce semplice,* being played in the orchestral version on the cor anglais, whilse the well-known third section, with its dramatic trombone entry, is an *allegro vivace.*

13. Herz, Henri. '*Non Piu Mesta,* Cavatina from Rossini's Opera *La Cenerentola,* with Variations for the Piano Forte', opus 60. Dedicated to Miss Anna Kerrison. 'A Select Catalogue of New Pianoforte Music'. Published by D'Almaine and Co., London; E. Troupenas, Paris; Schott, Mayence. The inscription is 'Miss A. Brontë'.

The full title of the opera is *La Cenerentola, ossia la bontà in trionfo,* which translates as 'Cinderella, or Goodness Triumphant'. A two-act opera with libretto by Jacopo Ferretti, it was first performed in Rome in January 1817.

14. Gelinek, Josef. 'A Favourite Air with Variations for the Piano Forte.... No. 26'. Printed by Goulding and D'Almaine, London.

Abbé Josef Gelinek (1758–1825) was a Bohemian priest, pianist and composer. In 1786, after his ordination, he became domestic chaplain and pianoforte teacher in the employment of Prince Ferdinand Kinsky (who was subsequently to become a patron of Beethoven) who took him to Vienna where he studied under Albrectsberger. Gelinek was one of the composers who contributed a variation on Diabelli's waltz, his being in C major, 3-4 time, *presto.* He was also another of those pianists who unwisely took on Beethoven in an improvisation contest. His assorted sets of pianoforte variations were popular in his day. He died in Vienna.

15. Herz, Henri. '*La Parisienne,* National March with Variations for the Piano Forte', opus 58. Published by D'Almaine and Co., London. 'Souvenir des Pianistes No. 28'. There is an inscription 'Miss A. Brontë'.

16. Steibelt, Daniel. 'Pastoral Rondo, in which is Introduced an Imitation of a Storm, Composed for the Piano Forte'. Published for the Proprietors by Metzler and Son, Music Sellers, London. 'New and Superior Edition'.

This is a movement from Steibelt's so-called *Orage* ('Thunderstorm') Piano Concerto, Number 3 in E major. The French composer Charles-Valentin Alkan (1813–1888) subsequently wrote a set of extravagant variations upon the theme. John Field's Piano Concerto Number 5 in C is similarly entitled – *L'Incendie par l'Orage.*

17. Kalkbrenner, Friedrich Wilhelm (Michael). ' "God Save the King", with Eight Variations for Piano Forte', opus 18. Printed by Clementi and Co., London. The inscription is 'Miss A.Brontë', the date being illegible.

In fact, this was not Kalkbrenner's only treatment of the British National Anthem – his opus 99 is a set of *Variazioni di Bravura con Introduzione e Finale per il Pianoforte e Orchestra (ad libitum).* In addition to Kalkbrenner, a number of other composers have used the tune: Beethoven, who wrote a set of seven variations on it, WoO 78, Weber, Paganini, Brahms, Donizetti and Dussek, whose version Emily possessed, to name but a few. Friedrich Wilhelm Kalkbrenner (1785–1849) was a German pianist and composer. Like Herz was to do eighteen years later, Kalkbrenner entered the Paris Conservatoire, in 1798, leaving four years later with a first prize for pianoforte playing and harmony. Between 1814 and 1823 he lived in London before returning to Paris where he attained a reputation as a pianist and teacher. His pianoforte compositions were popular in the mid-nineteenth century. He was another of the composers who contributed a variation on Diabelli's waltz – in C, *allegro ma non troppo*. He died of cholera in Deuil, Seine-et-Oise in his sixty-fourth year.

18. Arne, Thomas Augustine. ' "Rule Britannia", from Dr. Arne's Opera of "Alfred". Variations and an Introduction for the Piano Forte'. Dedicated to Mrs. Fleming by Fred. Kalkbrenner. Printed by Goulding and D'Almaine, London. The inscription is 'Miss A. Brontë'.

Alfred was first produced in 1740 in the garden of Cliveden, Buckinghamshire, then the residence of Frederick, Prince of Wales, as a masque, with words by J. Thomson and D. Mallet. In 1753, it was adapted for production as an opera in three acts. It is based upon the story of the Saxon King Alfred's resistance to the Danish invaders of the ninth century. 'Rule Britannia' is the festive celebration with which the opera ends. Thomas Augustine Arne (1710–1778) was born in Covent Garden, London, the son of an upholsterer. He was educated at Eton. As with Handel, his father intended him for the law, but eventually music prevailed; he was an accomplished harpsichordist and violinist. In composing the music for Dalton's adaptation of Milton's *Comus* at Drury Lane Theatre in 1738, he firmly established his reputation. Two years later came *Alfred.* In 1745, he was engaged as composer to Vauxhall Gardens. His compositional output consisted of operas, masques, serenatas, pantomimes, incidental music and oratorios, plus eight overtures, keyboard and chamber works and songs. He died in London, a week short of his sixty-eighth birthday. Beethoven wrote a set of five variations on 'Rule Britannia', WoO 79, for piano. Ferdinand Ries also used the theme for his 'Grand Variations', opus 116, for piano and orchestra.

19. Weber, Carl Maria von. 'Introduction and Variations for the Piano Forte on C.M. von Weber's Last Waltz'. G(eorge) Kiallmark. Published by D'Almaine and Co., London. 'Books of Instruction and Studies etc.' The inscription is 'Miss A. Brontë'.

Carl Maria von Weber (1786–1826) was born in Eutin in Oldenberg, Germany, the son of an accomplished musician and theatrical impresario, Franz Anton von Weber, who was an uncle to Constanze, Mozart's wife. A fine pianist who was taught as a boy by Michael Haydn, he was another musician of the period who travelled extensively, holding various appointments including those of director of Prague Opera and Court Kapellmeister in Dresden. In 1823 he met Beethoven in Vienna. Three years later he went to London, staying with Sir George Smart, conductor, composer, organist and teacher. However, he was by now seriously ill with tuberculosis, and he died in Smart's house in Great Portland Street in his fortieth year. Weber was an influential composer with a considerable compositional output. He had written his first opera as early as 1800, and his three best-known – *Euryanthe, Der Freishütz* and *Oberon* are performed regularly today. In addition, he composed two symphonies, a number of concertos, of which the two for pianoforte, two for clarinet and one for bassoon are still very popular, along with his clarinet quintet. There are also works for piano, songs and chamber music. It was Weber who established the waltz as a concert piece, most notably with his 'Invitation to the Dance' of 1819. In the form of a rondo, with an introduction and a coda, it is a set of waltzes with contrasting moods, melodies and keys – a bravura pianoforte piece. As has already been noted, Berlioz made an orchestration of this work. (2) As regards Kiallmark, see number 33, below.

20. Klitz, Philip. 'The Princess Victoria's Birth-Day Quadrilles, as danced at Almack's and the Nobilities Balls'. Composed and Dedicated to Her Grace the Duchess of Northumberland. Published by T. E. Purday, Successor (in this branch of the business) to Collard and Collard (late Clementi and Co.), London. Inscription 'Miss A. Brontë', dated September 4th [no year].

Philip Klitz (1805–1854) was born in Lymington, Hampshire, the son of a German-born musician. Although little remembered nowadays, he was a fine pianist, violinist, composer and conductor of his time, as well as a composer of pianoforte pieces, songs and dances for the ballroom. In addition to his musical attainments, he wrote of his Hampshire environment – 'Sketches of Life, Character and Scenery in the New Forest'. Thomas Edward Purday was one of a number of members of his family engaged in the music publishing business, specifically sheet songs, from about 1834 to 1862, at 50 St Paul's Churchyard and 531 Oxford Street. Collard and Collard were also music publishers, afterwards becoming pianoforte makers of high renown.

21. Parry, John. 'The Favourite Air of Laura and Lenza'. Composed by Signor Bossi, arranged as a Rondo for Piano-Forte, and Respectfully inscribed to Miss Bourke. Printed by Goulding D'Almaine Potter and Co., 20 Soho Square and to be had at 7 Westmorland Street, Dublin. The inscription is 'Misses E. (?) and A. Brontë', dated 4th (?) 1833'. There is some fingering in pencil.

John Parry (1776–1851) was a harpist, bandmaster and composer, who was born in Denbigh. He also taught the flageolet, was treasurer of the Royal Society of Musicians between 1831 and 1849, and was music critic to the *Morning Post* for most of that time. He collected, arranged and published a considerable number of Welsh melodies. The flageolet was a type of woodwind instrument in the flute family. Branwell Brontë learnt to play the flute, and wrote out a number of tunes for that instrument in an exercise book. (3)

22. Willis, Edward. 'The Royal Galopades and Devonshire Waltz, with Original Figures, as danced at Almack's and the Nobilities Balls'. Arranged for the Piano Forte. Published by Sykes and Sons, Leeds; Goulding and Co., London. Second Edition. There is some fingering in pencil on the score.

Little seems to be known about Edward Willis other than the fact that he was a pianist and arranger.

23. Fiorini, G.E. 'The Cabinet, A Series of Familiar Rondos on Favourite Airs. No. 6 – "The Jaeger's [Hunter's]March and Chorus" '. Composed and arranged for the Piano Forte. Published by J.B. Cramer, Addison and Beale, London. The inscription is 'Misses E. and A. Brontë', the date being illegible. There is some fingering in pencil.

There are twelve 'popular airs arranged as rondos' in 'The Cabinet', this one being the sixth. It is possible that G.E. Fiorini was related to the composer Giovanni Andrea Fiorini, who was born in Pavia in 1704, and who died in Milan in 1778; otherwise little is known of him.

24. Herz, Henri. 'Waltz Rondino for the Piano Forte'. 'Tyrolese Air'. Published by J. Balls, London. Inscribed 'Misses E. and A. Brontë, 5th August 1833'. There is some fingering in pencil on the score.

This piece is Herz's opus 1, no. 1. James Balls established his firm of music engravers, sellers and publishers at 8, Middle Scotland Yard, Whitehall, London, about the year 1803 .

25. Mazzinghi, Joseph. ' "Huntsman Rest", with Variations for the Piano Forte, and an Accompaniment for Flute'.

Inscribed to the Right Honble. Lady Georgiana Molyneux. Printed by Goulding and D'Almaine, London. The inscription is 'Miss A. Brontë'.

This is a setting of words from Sir Walter Scott's 1810 poem *The Lady of the Lake,* sung by Ellen. It was known to the Brontë children.

'Huntsman, rest! Thy chase is done;
While our slumbrous spells assail ye,
Dream not, with the rising sun,
Bugles here shall sound reveille.

Sleep! The deer is in his den;
Sleep! Thy hounds are by thee lying;
Sleep! Nor dream in yonder glen,
How thy gallant steed lay dying.

Joseph Mazzinghi (1765–1844) was born on Christmas Day in London, the son of a composer and violinist. A count in the papal nobility, descended from an ancient Corsican family, he was a pupil of Johann Christian Bach, the 'London' Bach, and was appointed organist of the Portuguese Chapel at the age of ten. Nine years later he became musical director and composer at the King's Theatre. He was a teacher of the pianoforte, holding the position of Music Master to the Princess of Wales, afterwards Queen Caroline. He composed nearly seventy sonatas for the instrument and made a large number of arrangements. He also wrote numerous songs, a mass for three voices, six hymns and, in collaboration with William Reeve, a number of stage works, including *Chains of the Heart*. He died at Downside, near Bath.

26. Burrowes, John Freckleton. ' "The Admired Air Tyrolien", composed by G. Rossini in His Celebrated Opera *Guillaume Tell'*. Arranged with Variations for the Piano Forte. Published by D'Almaine and Co., London. The inscription is 'Miss A. Brontë'.

John Freckleton Burrowes (1787–1852) was born in London and was a pupil of William Horsley. For nearly forty years he was organist of St. James's Church, Picadilly. An original member of the Philharmonic Society, his opus 13 overture was performed by them. He also wrote and published collections of psalm tunes, songs, Scottish and Irish airs, and sonatas and operatic arrangements for pianoforte, along with two books entitled *The Pianoforte Primer* (1818) and *The Thorough-Bass Primer* (1819), with subsequent 'Companions', still in use today. He was a month short of sixty-five when he died in London after a long illness.

27. Gildon, John. 'March for the Harp or Piano Forte'. 'Books of Instruction, Studies, etc' . Printed by Goulding and D'Almaine, London. Inscribed 'Miss A. Brontë'.

John Gildon was active as a composer and pianist in the late eighteenth and early nineteenth centuries. He wrote extensively for the pianoforte, sometimes giving titles which denoted historical events, such as 'General Jackson's Grand March for Harp or Piano Forte', 'The Jubilee' (probably George III's Golden Jubilee of 1810), and 'The Victory of Salamanca' (which battle of the Peninsula War took place in 1812).

28. Mazzinghi, Joseph. 'Bavarian Air with Variations for the Piano Forte, and an Accompaniment for the Flute'.

Composed for the Rt. Honble. Lady Charlotte Cholmondeley. 'Books of Instruction, Studies, etc.' Published by D'Almaine and Co., London. There is no inscription.

29. Mazzinghi, Joseph. 'Silesian or Copenhagen Air with Variations for the Piano Forte, and an Accompaniment for the Flute'. Composed and Inscribed to the Honble. Miss M.E. Townshend. Printed by Goulding and D'Almaine, London. The inscription is 'Miss A. Brontë, Octr. 1835'.

30. Greenwood, John. '"Burlerian Air". Composed and Arranged with Variations, and Respectfully Dedicated to Miss Clapham'. Published by Sykes and Sons, Leeds; to be had in London of Messrs. Goulding and Co. The inscription is 'Misses E. and A. Brontë, 27th January 1834'. The score contains some fingering in pencil. There is some repaired damage to pages 3–6.

John Greenwood (1795–1837) was a Halifax man, prodigiously gifted on a range of musical instruments from a young age. It was, however, as an organist that he made his name, his first such appointment being at Keighley Parish Church when he was aged sixteen, followed by Leeds Parish Church in 1821 . He travelled in America and France before returning to London where he was a teacher for a while. He was a composer, mainly of church music, including *A Selection of Ancient and Modern Psalm Tunes,* published in Leeds in 1825–6 and '*Modulus Sanctus, a Collection of Sacred Music*', published in Leeds in 1828. His *Psalmody Harmonised in Score* was published posthumously in Halifax in 1838. In 1835 he returned to Halifax to take up the post of organist at South Parade Wesleyan Methodist Church. An interesting footnote to this chapel concerns the funeral of one Samuel Hartley, a Luddite who was killed in the attack on William Cartwright's Mill at Rawfolds in 1812. The minister, the Revd. Jabez Bunting, refused to take the service, which was conducted instead by his assistant. Bunting, who was known to, and disliked by, Patrick Brontë, is held to have been the most likely model for the role of the Revd. Jabes Branderham in *Wuthering Heights.* John Greenwood performed at the concert to celebrate the installation of the organ in Haworth Church in March 1834, an event satirized by Charlotte Brontë, containing the characters of Greenwood as himself, Sudbury Figgs, in reality Abraham Sunderland, the girls' pianoforte teacher, and Benjamin Patrick Wiggins (Branwell Brontë). Greenwood also played at the Wesleyan Methodist Chapel in the same year and was said to have performed 'an astonishing extempore fugue'. (4)

31. Butler, Thomas Hamley. 'Miss Forbes's Farwell [*sic*] to Banff, A Favourite Scottish Air'. Arranged with Variations for Piano Forte, with the Fingering Marked. Engraved and Printed for Ward and Andrews, 18 Spring Gardens, Manchester, by J. Pigot and Son. There is fingering in pencil on the score, which is dated 27th August 1832.

Thomas Hamley Butler (*c*1755–1823) was born in London, the son of a music teacher. As a boy, he was a chorister in the Chapel Royal, and he subsequently studied in Italy for three years. He went to live in Edinburgh for the remainder of his life, where he taught and composed piano pieces, a masque, and the musical drama *The Widow of Delphi.*

32. Knapton, Philip. 'Mrs. Macdonald, A Favourite Scotch Air, with Variations and an Introduction'. Composed and

Dedicated to Mrs. Constable of Wassand. 'New and Improved Edition'. Published by D'Almaine and Co., London.

Philip Knapton (1788–1833) was born in York, the son of Samuel, a music publisher in Blake Street, who carried on the business after the father's death, with a musician by the name of White, until his own death. He was also a pianist, composer and arranger, and an assistant conductor to a number of York Festivals.

33. Kiallmark, George. 'Air' There is no publisher stated, nor caption title, or any inscription.

George Kiallmark (1781–1835) was a violinist and composer who was born in Kings Lynn, Norfolk. He was a prolific composer of pianoforte miniatures and songs, the most popular of which was *The Old Oaken Bucket,* set in 1826 to words by Samuel Woodworth. He died in Islington, London.

34. Powell, Thomas. 'Introduction and Air – "My Love She's but a Lassie yet", with Variations for the Piano Forte'. Respectfully Dedicated to Miss E. Head. Printed by Goulding and D'Almaine, London. There is no inscription.

Thomas Powell was born in London in 1776, and was a harpist, violinist, pianist, composer and played the violincello. He became a member of the Royal Society of Music in 1799 living at various times in Dublin, Edinburgh and London. Most of his compositions involved the violin in some capacity – there were fifteen violin concertos. He died some time after 1863.

35. Kiallmark, George. '"Roy's Wife of Alldivaloch", with Variations and an Introduction for the Piano Forte'.

Dedicated to Miss Anne Douglas. Printed and Sold by S. Chappell, London. The inscription reads 'Miss A. Brontë'.

36. Butler, Thomas Hamley. ' "Lewie Gordon", A Rondo for the Piano Forte'. Published by J.B. Cramer, Addison and Beale, London. At the foot of page 1 is stamped the words 'Sunderland Music Seller Keighley'. Inscribed 'Misses E. and A. Brontë, 27th May 1833'. There is some fingering in pencil on the score.

37. Knapton, Philip. ' "Caller Herring", A Favourite Scotch Air, Arranged with Variations as a Duet for the Piano Forte or Harp'. Printed by Goulding and D'Almaine, London.

Three Bound Volumes of Sheet Music from the 1830s

The music contained within these three volumes is mainly piano music belonging to Emily and Anne. Some of the scores in Volume One are inscribed in pencil with their names, though these inscriptions are not the sisters' own, and dated, and most of them are all but illegible nowadays. Importantly, many of these scores, particularly in Volume One, contain pencil fingering directions. It has already been noted that it might have been Emily and/or Anne who annotated them in this way, in whole or in part, and whenever the numbers 2, 3 and, especially, 4 appear, it could be said that they do bear something of a resemblance to the page numbers written in ink in 'Anne Brontë's Song Book'. However, some of the scores so annotated are technically very demanding, and may have been beyond Anne's capability, and consequently played only by Emily. In any case, it is at least as likely that it was their teacher, Abraham Sunderland, who directed the necessary fingering. Some of the scores are piano duets which the sisters could well have played with each other, or with their teacher. There are arrangements for organ of selections from sacred works by Handel, Mozart and Haydn which might have been of interest to Branwell, and in the third volume there are a number of scores, especially vocal works with pianoforte accompaniment, autographed in ink by Anne, and dated by her November or December 1844, prior to her return to the Robinson family at Thorp Green, where she was governess. These scores are discussed in Chapter Four, page 408 *et seq*. By no means all the pieces in these volumes were originally written for pianoforte; many are transcriptions of orchestral works, and not all of them transfer comfortably to the new idiom. The scores in these three volumes have been grouped here as follows:

Waltzes and Marches
Quadrilles
Transcriptions of Operatic Overtures
Sonatas
Theme and Variations
Fantasias
Studies
Organ Transcriptions
Miscellaneous.

In his book *A Musical Pilgrimage in Yorkshire*, published in 1928, J. Sutcliffe-Smith states 'While on my visit to Keighley, I was fortunate to see some five or six volumes of music which once formed part of the studies of the famous Brontë family of Haworth. These are in the possession of Mrs. Coward … her grandfather, William Summerscales was organist at Haworth church during the time of the Revd. Patrick Brontë', (1) and from 1853 Headmaster of

Haworth Grammar School. He had received them as a gift from Patrick Brontë, with Charlotte's consent, sometime in the 1850s. Sutcliffe-Smith goes on to list some of the works which he saw, describing them as 'ponderous, but interesting: they have title pages whereon we read *Sykes's Favourite Waltzes* (publishers Sykes, Leeds) – *Works from the Classical Authors, Beethoven and Weber;* and what is to us so important, the names 'Miss E. and A. Brontë', written in a fine flowing hand [likely to have been Summerscales's]. We further infer from an inspection of these books, that Charlotte was not musical, [a dubious assertion] as her name never appears, that Anne Brontë was the singer, and that these young ladies were careful students, from the care and neatness with which almost every passage is fingered.' So, Sutcliffe-Smith opts, not necessarily correctly, for the sisters as being the ones who have added the pencil fingerings.

In 1935, it was reported in *Brontë Society Transactions* that the Brontë Parsonage Museum and Library had received a gift from Mrs. Coward and family (Keighley) of:

> 'Folio Music Books (7 volumes), with autographs of Anne and Emily J. Brontë. The Rev. Patrick Brontë gave the volumes to Mr. W.W. Summerscales, formerly organist and choirmaster at Haworth, who was Mrs Coward's grandfather'. (2)

It seems possible that this gift comprised the three volumes of scores discussed here plus the four double-bound volumes of *The Musical Library, Instrumental and Songs*, analysed in the next two chapters. Each sheet was specially treated – conserved – in 1994.

Volume One

Parsonage library reference 1131/2

Transcriptions of Operatic Overtures

1. Mozart, Wolfgang Amadeus. 'Overture to *La Clemenza di Tito*'.

Published by Clementi, London. This transcription also appears in *The Musical Library*, Volume One, number 42, and is discussed there. One of the great composers in history, Wolfgang Amadeus Mozart (1756–1791) was born in Salzburg, the son of Leopold, himself a musician, and, from a very young age, showed phenomenal precocity. Widely travelled as a child, with his sister Maria Anna ('Nannerl'), an excellent keyboard player herself, he was in his early teens when, upon hearing Allegri's *Miserere* in Rome, he wrote it down from memory, much to the chagrin of the Roman Catholic authorities who had myopically regarded it as their own private property. Unhappily employed by the Archbishop of Salzburg, the last years of his life were financially stressful and, when he died in Vienna, he was buried in a grave, the location of which is unknown. Mozart's genius is reflected in his compositional output, catalogued by Ludwig von Köchel. It comprises, inter alia, forty-one symphonies, concertos for a number of different instruments, sonatas for piano and for violin, chamber music, church music, concert arias and songs, and perhaps most outstandingly, operas.

2. Mozart, Wolfgang Amadeus. 'Overture to *Così fan Tutte*', arranged by Joseph Mazzinghi for Pianoforte, Flute and Cello. Printed by Goulding, D'Almaine, London. Another transcription appears in *The Musical Library*, Volume Two, number 31, and is discussed there.

3. Beethoven, Ludwig van. 'Overture to *Men of Prometheus*' [*sic*]. Flute adaptation by J. Parry. Printed by D'Almaine, London. The correct title is *Creatures of Prometheus*. Another transcription appears in *The Musical Library*, Volume One, number 5, and is discussed there.

4. Mozart, Wolfgang Amadeus. 'Overture to *Don Giovanni*, and *Notto e giorno*'. Published by D'Almaine, London. Arranged and inscribed to Her Royal Highness the Duchess of Cumberland by J. Mazzinghi.

The overture is included in *The Musical Library*, Volume One, number 53, and is discussed there. *Notto e giorno faticar* ('Night and day I slave') is the first number of the opera and follows on from the overture without a break, segue subito. Its theme is comprised of unison octaves, with triplet or demisemiquaver motifs inserted, and contrasting dynamics, which serve to illustrate Leporello's sardonic view of his employment in Don Giovanni's service. Beethoven used this theme as the twenty-second of his thirty-three *Diabelli Variations*, opus 120. *Il dissoluto punito ossia il Don Giovanni* (*The Rake Punished*, or *Don Giovanni*) is a *dramma giocoso* in two acts, K527, to a libretto by Lorenzo Da Ponte (1749–1838), composed in 1787, in which year it had its first production, in Prague.

5. Mozart, Wolfgang Amadeus. 'Overture [*sic*] *Le Nozze di Figaro*'. Published by D'Almaine, London.

The designation here ought to be *sinfonia*, not 'overture'. This work is included in *The Musical Library*, Volume One, number 43, and is discussed there.

6. Weber, Carl Maria von. 'Overture to *Preciosa*'. Published by R.W. Keith, London. It is in three sections, and there are a considerable number of pencil fingerings on the score.

The first section is an overture in A minor in 3–4 time, directed to be played *allegro moderato.* This is followed by a *Zigeuner-Marsch (nach einer echten Zigeunermelodie)* ('Gypsy March based upon an Authentic Gypsy Melody') in the relative major, C, in 2–4 time, with an ABA plus coda layout. It is directed to be played *moderato, ma tutto ben marcato.* Grace notes and acciaccaturas feature prominently in the right hand melody. The third section, which is in sonata form and the longest of the three, combines material from each of the first two sections, and is an *allegro con fuoco* in common time. As with the first section, contrasting dynamics feature immediately. *Preciosa,* an opera with dialogue to a libretto by Pius Alexander Wolff, was first performed at the Schauspielhaus, Berlin in 1821. In addition to the overture there are eleven numbers.

Theme and Variations

1. Purcell, Henry. 'Purcell's Ground with Variations' for Pianoforte. Printed by Sykes and Sons, Leeds; sold by Sunderland Music Sellers, Keighley. The score has been marked in pencil for fingering.

The ground in F major is eight bars long, consisting of three two-bar groups descending in thirds, followed by a IV V I cadence, and is repeated; likewise each of the nineteen variations. It is subjected to a variety of treatments, including triplet and semiquaver decoration, and what would subsequently come to be called an 'Alberti' bass. A 'ground', or *ostinato* is a bass which is repeated constantly with changing harmonies while upper parts are constantly varied. Purcell was a master of the genre, his 'Evening Hymn', and especially 'Dido's Lament' from his opera *Dido and Aeneas,* being excellent examples.

2. Broadhead, J. '"Sicilian Mariners' Hymn" for Organ or Pianoforte with Variations'. Printed by Ward and Andrews, Manchester. There are pencil fingerings on the score, and the annotation 'Count 4 beats in a bar'.

In F major and 2–4 time, the theme is of sixteen bars, comprising two eight-bar phrases. There are five variations, the first utilising semiquaver decoration in the right hand, the second right-hand triplet decoration, the third demisemiquaver decoration, again in the right hand, the fourth demisemiquavers in the left hand under the melody in the right, and the fifth broken chords in semiquavers in each hand.

3. Dussek, Jan Ladislav. ' "God Save the Queen" with Variations'. Published by B. Williams, London.

In B flat and 3–4 time, with a wide range of dynamics, there are five variations covering practically the whole range of the keyboard and requiring a considerable technique for performance. As has already been seen, Emily had another working of the National Anthem in her collection of scores, that by Kalkbrenner, listed as number 17 in the 'Parrish Collection'.

Organ

Selected Movements from the Sacred Works of
Handel, Haydn and Mozart,
Arranged as Voluntaries for Organ by H.G. Nixon,
Organist to the Royal Bavarian Embassy in London,
Published by D'Almaine and Company, London

1.	**Mozart, Wolfgang Amadeus.**	Mass Number 2, C
2.	**Haydn, Franz Josef.**	Mass Number 1, B flat
3.	**Mozart, Wolfgang Amadeus.**	Mass Number 12, C
4.	**Haydn, Franz Josef.**	Mass Number 16, B flat
5.	**Haydn, Franz Josef.**	Mass Number 6, B flat
	(Inscribed 'William Summerscales Scott Sr., Keighley')	
6.	**Handel, George Frideric.**	'O had I Jubal's Lyre' (*Joshua*), A
7.	**Mozart, Wolfgang Amadeus.**	Mass Number 3, F
8.	**Haydn, Franz Josef.**	Mass Number 16, B flat
9.	**Mozart, Wolfgang Amadeus.**	Mass Number 3, F
10.	**Haydn, Franz Josef.**	Mass Number 2, C
11.	**Mozart, Wolfgang Amadeus.**	Mass Number 2, C
12.	**Handel, George Frideric.**	Air from *Semele,* B flat
13.	**Haydn, Franz Josef.**	Mass Number 7, G
14.	**Handel, George Frideric.**	'Rushing Tides of Hallowed Zeal' (*Solomon*), F

The numbers of the Haydn masses are those accorded by the publisher Novello. Although described as being 'arranged for organ', these selections are written on two staves, as if for performance on a pianoforte. There is no separate pedal stave, though the abbreviated word 'Ped.' is used frequently. In addition, there are plenty of directions as to which manual is to be used – full organ, great, swell, or choir – and particular stops are often designated, for example, trumpet, diapason, dulcimer and principal. Whether or not Branwell was capable of performing any of them must remain a matter for speculation; there are no pencil fingerings. These same comments apply to the next set.

From the Vocal Works of Handel, arranged with separate accompaniment for the Organ or Pianoforte by
Dr. John Clarke of Cambridge
Published by Clementi, Collard, 26, Cheapside, London

Some title pages are annotated in pencil 'Misses E. and A. Brontë', 25th November, 1833', though not in the sisters' handwriting.

1. Handel, George Frideric. 'He gave them Hailstones for Rain' (*Israel in Egypt*). There are pencil finger markings. A double-chorus for eight voices, *allegro*, it is included in *The Musical Library*, Volume One, number 17, and is discussed there.

2. Handel, George Frideric. 'Comfort ye my People' (Tenor aria from *Messiah*). Number 2 in the oratorio, the text is taken from the book of Isaiah, chapter 40, verses 1–3.

3. Handel, George Frideric. 'Every Valley shall be exalted' (Tenor aria from *Messiah*). Number 3 in the oratorio, the text is taken from the book of Isaiah, chapter 40, verse 4.

4. Handel, George Frideric. 'There were Shepherds abiding in the Fields' (Soprano recitative from *Messiah*). Number 14 in the oratorio, the text is from the Gospel according to St. Luke, chapter 2, verse 8.

5. Handel, George Frideric. 'And lo, the Angel of the Lord' (Soprano recitative from *Messiah*). Number 14 in the oratorio, the text is taken from the Gospel according to St. Luke, chapter 2, verse 9.

6. Handel, George Frideric. 'And the Angel said unto them' (Soprano recitative from *Messiah*). Number 14 in the oratorio, the text is taken from the Gospel according to St. Luke, chapter 2, verses 10–11.

7. Handel, George Frideric. 'And suddenly there was with the Angel' (Soprano recitative from *Messiah*). Number 14 in the oratorio, the text is taken from the Gospel according to St. Luke, chapter 2, verse 13.

8. Handel, George Frideric. 'For unto Us a Child is born' (Chorus from *Messiah*). Number 12 in the oratorio, the text is taken from the book of Isaiah, chapter 9, verse 6. There are pencil finger markings.

9. Handel, George Frideric. 'Pastoral Symphony' (*Messiah*). The 'Pastoral Symphony', number 13 in the oratorio, is included in *The Musical Library*, Volume One, number 21, and is discussed there.

10. Handel, George Frideric. 'Glory to God' (Chorus from *Messiah*). Number 15 in the oratorio, the text is taken from the Gospel according to St. Luke, chapter 2, verse 14.

11. Handel, George Frideric. 'All we like Sheep' (Chorus from *Messiah*). Number 24 in the oratorio, the text is taken from the book of Isaiah, chapter 53, verse 6. There are pencil finger markings.

12. Handel, George Frideric. 'I know that my Redeemer liveth' (Soprano aria from *Messiah*). Number 43 in the oratorio, and the first in Part Three, the text is from the book of Job, chapter 19, verses 25–26. There are pencil finger markings.

13. Handel, George Frideric. 'Hallelujah' (Chorus from *Messiah*). Number 42 in the oratorio, it is included in the 'Parrish Collection', number 6, and was discussed there. There are pencil finger markings.

Miscellaneous

1. Handel, George Frideric. ' "From the Censer" from the Oratorio *Solomon*'. Arranged as a piano duet by Samuel Wesley. There are pencil fingerings on the score. This chorus also appears in *The Musical Library,* Volume Three, number 19, though not as a duet, and is discussed there.

Samuel Wesley (1766–1837) was the son of the Methodist Charles Wesley and nephew of John Wesley. A composer of church music and a celebrated organist, he was an enthusiast of the music of Johann Sebastian Bach, playing a prominent role in the revival of interest in that composer's music in England in the early nineteenth century.

2. Smith, Henry. ' "Morning Bells", A Favourite Russian Air'. Printed by Sykes and Son, Leeds. There are pencil fingerings on the score. In G major, and in common time, there are four sections – a prelude marked *scherzando,* an aria marked *dolce e legato,* a *poco allegro,* and a *con fuoco allegro.* This might have been the first piece of sheet music acquired by Emily.

3. Younge, Mrs. Captain Sophia Elizabeth. 'Sabbath Chimes'.

The first line of the words to this piece in G major, imitative of bells, is 'Hark, hark, hark, the Sabbath's tuneful bells'.

4. Martin, George William. 'Number One of a Collection of Short Anthems for Four Voices (SATB) with Organ or Pianoforte Accompaniment'. Published by J. Alfred Novello.

This piece is written in A major, with a cut-**C** time signature. The words, 'Forsake me not O Lord', are taken from Psalm 38, verse 21. The composer was organist of Christ Church and resident music master of St John's Training College, Battersea.

Volume Two

Parsonage library reference 1131/5

Waltzes and Marches

1. Ries, Ferdinand. 'Grand Triumphal March for Two Performers on the Pianoforte'. It was published by Clementi and Company, London. There are pencil fingering markings on the score.

The key is C major, and the tempo is *allegro*. The march, in common time, *ff*, is preceded by a twelve-bar introduction. By contrast, the trio in A flat is directed to be played quietly, with the march then repeated *DC, senza replica*. According to *The Monthly Magazine*, 'Mr. Ries has furnished a piece which, besides the merit of conveying a well-earned compliment to our victorious countrymen on the continent, exhibits the author's talents and science in a very favourable point of view. The subject, as well as the general cast and spirit of the music, is truly martial, and by the novel manner of opposing the parts in some particular passages, a pleasing and striking effect is produced. The whole is bold, free and flowing; and the connection of the ideas bespeaks a prompt and well-regulated fancy'. (3) Ferdinand Ries (1784–1838) was a talented pianist and a composer who studied with Beethoven. His reminiscences, published in 1838 in conjunction with Dr. Franz Gerhard Wegeler, *Biographische Notizen* über *Ludwig van Beethoven* ('Biographical Notes on Ludwig van Beethoven') are considered to be reliable and valued.

2. Fiorini, G.E. 'Duke of York's Grand March'. This is the fifth in a series of twelve of Fiorini's 'Rondos on Favourite Airs', entitled *The Cabinet*, published by J.B. Cramer, Addison and Beale.

The score contains pencil fingering markings. A three-bar introduction marked *maestoso e legato* leads into the *tempo di marcia* in F major in common time; then follows a trio in C and a repeat of the march. A damaged page has been repaired with tape.

Sykes' Favourite Waltzes for the Pianoforte – Number One
(Third edition)
Selected from the Works of Classical Authors, viz.
Beethoven and Weber, etc., etc.

1. Weber, Carl Maria von. 'Waltz in A flat'. There are pencil fingerings on the score, and an illegible inscription on the title page.

Marked *allegretto,* it is in ternary form with each section containing two eight-bar phrases, each phrase being repeated. The second section includes a modulation to D flat; the third section is a reprise of the first.

2. Beethoven, Ludwig van (attributed). Waltz in F minor, *Schmerzens-walzer,* or *La Douleur* (Pain).

The form is ternary – ABA. Sections A and B each have three parts, each of which is repeated, while the third section is a reprise of the first without its repeats. The tempo is *allegro,* a suggested MM being dotted minim=44.

3. Beethoven, Ludwig van (attributed). 'Waltz in E flat', *L'Espoir* (Hope). The score has pencil fingerings marked

The form is ternary – ABA. Sections A and B each have three parts, each of which is repeated, while the third section is a reprise of the first without its repeats. The tempo is *allegro,* a suggested MM being dotted minim=58. Beethoven left Bonn, his birthplace, for Vienna in 1792, with the injunction from Count Waldstein 'to receive Mozart's spirit from Haydn's hand'. During the next fifteen years or so he wrote numerous short dance pieces – *laendler,* contredances or waltzes – for small orchestral groups, as these were very fashionable in the aristocratic houses of the Austrian capital at the time. Haydn, Mozart, Schubert and others likewise composed a considerable number. Many of Beethoven's pieces of this nature were also published in versions for string trio or as pianoforte arrangements. Although these two pieces are in 3–4 time and designated as 'waltzes', it is not necessarily the case that they were intended as ballroom dances. There is scope for the performer to use contrasting dynamics to emphasise the different aspects of each of the pieces. Presumptively held to have been composed by Beethoven, there is doubt as to their authenticity. Consequently, rather than being allotted one of Beethoven's Opus or WoO numbers – *Werke ohne Opuszahle* ('Work without Opus Number')– they are generally catalogued as *Anhang* ('Appendix') works. There are fingerings marked in pencil on the score.

Sykes' Favourite Waltzes for Pianoforte – Number Two
Selected from the Works of Classical Authors, viz.
Beethoven and Weber, etc., etc.

4. Beethoven, Ludwig van (attributed). 'Waltz in A minor'.

The score is marked in pencil for fingering. In ternary form, the middle section includes a modulation to the relative major. There is an eight-bar coda. The tempo is *allegretto,* and there is a *ppp* marking which is rare in Beethoven's works.

5. Beethoven, Ludwig van (attributed). 'Waltz in A flat'.

Sometimes known as *Sehnsuchtswalzer,* or *Le Désir* (Yearning) it is in ternary form. There is pencil fingering on the score. The doubt as to authorship of these waltzes is most marked in this one which seems to be of a style more akin to Schubert than Beethoven.

6. Weber, Carl Maria von. 'Waltz in D'.

The score is marked for fingering. The tempo is *presto.* Four bars of octave Ds in the left hand lead into section A, *ff*, which comprises two ten-bar phrases, each repeated. Section B is twice as long, and features dynamic contrasts, while section C is a reprise of the first section.

Sykes' Favourite Waltzes for Pianoforte – Number IV
Selected from the Works of Classical Authors, viz.
Beethoven and Weber, etc., etc.

It is considered that the attribution on the title page, as in the above heading, of some or all three of these waltzes to Beethoven is dubious. No composer's name appears on the actual scores. There is pencil fingering marked on all three.

7. Composer not named. 'Waltz in A'.

8. Composer not named. 'Waltz in F'.

9. Composer not named. 'Waltz in B flat'.

Sykes' Favourite Waltzes for Pianoforte – Number Five
Selected from the Works of Classical Authors, viz.
Beethoven and Weber, etc., etc.

Once again, it is considered that the attribution on the title page, as in the above heading, of some or all three of these waltzes to Beethoven is dubious. No composer's name appears on the actual scores. There is pencil fingering marked on all three.

10. Composer not named. 'Waltz in B flat'.

11. Composer not named. 'Waltz in D'.

12. Composer not named. 'Waltz in E flat'.

Three Waltzes by Mozart engraved and printed for Ward and Andrews, Manchester by J. Pigot and Son, Manchester.

1.Mozart, Wolfgang Amadeus. 'Waltz in B flat'.

2. Mozart, Wolfgang Amadeus. 'Waltz in C'.

3. Mozart, Wolfgang Amadeus. 'Waltz in C'.

Three Waltzes for Duet by an Un-named Composer
Published and Sold by Ward and Andrews, Manchester

There are pencil fingerings on the scores of these simple pieces.

1. Composer not named. 'Waltz in D'.

2. Composer not named. 'Waltz in F'.

3. Composer not named. 'Waltz in G'.

Six Waltzes arranged for Pianoforte and
dedicated to Lady Annabella Ramsden by
L. Merveilleux du Plantis, opus 13
Published by Goulding, D'Almaine, London

Cramer and Co., London, Welsh, Novello, Duff and George, London,
Sykes and Sons, Leeds

There are pencil fingerings on the scores of all of these six pieces.

1. **Merveilleux du Plantis, L.** 'The Annabella' in C.

2. **Merveilleux du Plantis, L.** 'The Cecilia' in F.

3. **Merveilleux du Plantis, L.** 'The Isabella' in B flat.

4. **Merveilleux du Plantis, L.** 'The Elizabeth' in E flat.

5. **Merveilleux du Plantis, L.** 'The Adelaide' in F.

6. **Merveilleux du Plantis, L.** 'The Dorothy' in A minor.

Gems de l'Opera
A Selection of the Most Admired Airs, Marches and Waltzes
from the Best Italian, French and German Operas
Pianoforte Duet arranged by M. Corri
Published by Metzler and Son, London

1. **Auber, Daniel.** 'March'.

The march is the fourth in a set of twelve and is an *allegro* in G major in common time. The first page has the instruction 'Count 4 in a bar'. There are fingering marks in pencil on the score.

Daniel Auber (1782–1871) was a French composer who studied with Cherubini, and is best remembered for his forty-nine operas, including *Fra Diavolo* and *Manon Lescaut.* From 1842 to 1870 he was head of the Paris Conservatoire, and, in 1857, he was accorded the dignity of 'maitre de chapelle' by Napoleon III.

Collection of Foreign Marches and Military Movements
Arranged as Duets for the Pianoforte
by Samuel Goedbe

1. Mescery. [No title] Performed by the Bands of the Infantry Regiment in the Prussian Army.

There are pencil fingering markings on the score. In G major, and in common time, this march is headed *tempo di marcia,* and includes a trio in C, the subdominant.

2. Prince Leopold of Sicily. 'March of the Imperial Regiment'.

The score contains pencil fingerings. In C major, and in common time, the performance direction is *marcato.*

Quadrilles

1. Smith, Henry. 'Set of Quadrilles for Pianoforte' composed and dedicated to Mrs. Crossley of Olive Mount, Wavertree, Liverpool, by R. Andrews. Published by Collard and Collard.

The set, which contains fingering markings, comprises *Le Pantalon, L'Été, La Poule, La Trenise, Chassez croisé,* and *Waltz,* and the keys are, respectively, E, E, A, A, F and D.

2. Herz, Henri. *Contre Danses variées Quadrilles* for Pianoforte. Published by Metzler and Company Limited, London.

The dances in the set are as for the previous *quadrille* by Henry Smith, and the keys are E flat, A flat, C, C minor, F and E flat. Technically they are difficult, yet the fact that the score contains pencil fingering marking indicates that Emily, perhaps Anne too, attempted them.

3. Andrews, Richard Hoffman. '"The Manchester Quadrilles", containing the most admired Airs from the compositions of the celebrated Paganini, arranged for pianoforte'. There are five of them, in D, D, G, A minor and C. The first is marked *maestoso,* the second *moderato,* and the last three are all directed to be played *allegretto.* Again, the score shows pencil fingering markings, and a faint inscription on the title page which appears to be the date 1833. Niccolò Paganini (1782–1840), born in Genoa, was a composer whose works include six surviving violin concertos, and a violin virtuoso of the highest order. He commissioned Berlioz's *Harold in Italy,* though he never actually played it in public. His famous *Caprice,* number 24 in A minor, has been the theme for many composers' sets of variations. A great showman, his appearance was said to have resembled that of Mephistopheles – a positive advantage in the Romantic era.

Sonatas

1. Nicolai, Otto. 'Sonata', opus 3.

This Sonata in C is an early work of the composer, and is written for pianoforte with violin accompaniment. There is pencil fingering on the score.

The first movement *allegro,* in common time, is in sonata form. The development passes through G minor and C minor before a passage of dominant preparation leads back to the recapitulation. The *rondo* finale is a *presto* in 6–8 time in an ABACA layout. The first episode is in the relative minor with a section in the tonic, while the second episode is a minuet, marked *staccato.* Otto Nicolai (1810–1849) was a German composer, most notably of opera. His best known work in that category, *The Merry Wives of Windsor,* is based upon Shakespeare's play of that name.

2. (Composer unknown). 'Sonata in C'.

The title page of this piece is missing. Its style is that of the late eighteenth or early nineteenth century, not unlike that of Clementi or Dussek. There are three movements, all with pencil fingering. The first is an *allegro molto vivace* in sonata form. The development section modulates through various keys to C minor where there is some crossing of hands. The recapitulation is varied from the original. The second movement is an *andantino* in the subdominant key of F major in 3–8 time. In ABA form, the episode is in B flat. The sonata concludes with an *allegro vivace* rondo on an ABAC plus coda layout. The first episode is in G, and the second begins in A minor before modulating back to the tonic and the coda.

3. Kotzwara, Frantisek. '"The Battle of Prague" – A Favourite Sonata for the Pianoforte'. Published by G. Walker and Son.

Originally written for pianoforte with violin, cello and drum *ad libitum*, and purporting to portray the Prussian victory over the Austrians at the Battle of Prague in 1757, it is a forerunner of Beethoven's *Battle of Vittoria*, opus 91, also known as *Wellington's Victory*, and was apparently popular in London around the turn of the millennium. Grove, however, takes a different view, describing it as 'that extraordinary and musically quite valueless descriptive piece'. In the key of F major, the first movement, a slow march, is followed by a *largo,* with headings that include 'word of command', 'first signal cannon', 'bugle horn call for the cavalry' and 'the trumpet call'. Then follows 'the attack', an *allegro* designated 'Prussians and Imperialists', including all manner of effects of the battle including cannon, flying bullets, trumpets, attack with swords, light dragoons advancing, heavy cannonade, drums, running fire and, finally, trumpet of recall. The next movement, in the tonic minor, is a *grave,* as befits a section entitled 'cries of the wounded', and a short passage for the right hand only, being the 'trumpet of victory', leads into a rendition of 'God Save the King', followed by a quick step entitled 'Turkish March' in C. Half way through the *allegro* finale is a four-bar *andante,* in the changed time signature of 3–4, consisting solely of eight low octave Cs, designated 'go to bed Tom'! The finale resumes and a coda concludes the whole bizarre piece. There are some faded pencil finger markings and, on page 3, an annotation which appears to contain the words 'With the Girls'. A Bohemian, who lived from c1730–1791, Kotzwara was born in Prague round about the middle of the eighteenth century. The composer's manuscript bears the date 1788, three years before his death, which was said to have occurred in mysterious circumstances (with connotations of sexual perversion) at a 'house of ill fame' in Vine Street, London.

Theme and Variations

1. Handel, George Frideric. '"The Harmonious Blacksmith", A Favourite Air with Variations for Pianoforte'. Printed by Hime and Son, Castle Street and Church Street, Liverpool.

This piece, which has pencil fingerings, also appears in *The Musical Library*, Volume Three, number 17, and is discussed there.

2. Kiallmark, George. ' "Auld Lang Syne" with Variations'. Published by S. Chappell, London. There is an inscription 'W. Summerscales, Haworth', on the first page.

The theme, in F major and in 2–4 time, is an *andante,* and there are five variations. The first makes use of dotted rhythms, the second triplets, the third has semiquavers in the left hand, the fourth is a *minore* in the relative minor, and a cadenza leads to the finale. Anne Brontë, in her *Song Book*, and Branwell in his *Flute Book*, transcribed versions of this popular Scottish song.

3. Herz, Henri. ' "O Mon Cher Augustine". Brilliant and Easy Variations for Pianoforte'. Published by Ward and Andrews, Manchester. A faint inscription on the title page appears to read 'E. J. Brontë'.

An *allegro* introduction in common time precedes a march and four variations in 3–8 time.

4. Composer unknown, except for the initials 'I.G'. 'Mrs. Macdonald's Original Air with Variations'.

The dedicatee of this work is the celebrated pianist, composer and teacher J.B. Cramer, and the publisher is Sykes and Sons. In A major, it is another example of a theme, marked *andantino con espressione,* being preceded by a dramatic introduction, brilliant chromatic figuration, contrasting dynamics, and *ad lib.* passages. There are detailed performance directions including pedalling instructions. The seven variations are marked, respectively, *con delicatezza, dolce, Siciliana, brilliante, minore* in the tonic minor, *allegretto* and *Pollacca.* It is not an easy piece to play.

5. Andrews, Richard Hoffman. 'Introduction and Variations to the Admired Air "Jennie's Bawbee" '.

The piece is in C major, and the score, which contains considerable pencil fingering markings, is initialled 'RA', and inscribed 'Miss E. Brontë'. It was printed by Andrews and Ward of Manchester.

It begins with a dramatic introduction in 3–4 time. Directed to be played *maestoso,* it is thirty-four bars in length, with extremes of dynamics, dotted rhythms and crescendos. A virtuoso written-out cadenza, marked *presto* and *ad lib.* closes into the theme of eight bars, which is marked *adagio con espressione,* and is in common time. The first variation is a peaceful one, the second is marked *brilliante,* the third is an *adagio* in the tonic minor with a modulation by way of cadenza to F sharp in its middle section, *più moto,* the fourth, again *brilliante,* returns to the tonic major and features fast repeated notes requiring a change of finger for each, and the fifth is a *maestoso* march with a cut-**C** time signature and octaves in each hand. The conclusion is by way of a brilliant extended *Polonaise*, cadenza and extended theme in 3–4 time. Richard Andrews (1803–1891) was a composer, teacher and publisher in Manchester.

6. Latour, Théodore. 'Imitations of Many of the Most Eminent Professors in Twenty-six Variations'.

This score consists of twenty-nine pages including the title page, and there is some flute accompaniment. The theme is an *andante* in C major, and in 2–4 time, with the variations being written with a variety of time signatures. Each variation is headed 'à la', followed by the name of the dedicatee, composers and instrumentalists of greater or lesser eminence of the period – Corri, Grassini, Woelfl, Mazzinghi, Saust, Ferrari, Naldi, Pleyel, Mugni, Catalani, Monzani, Cramer, Braham, Dussek, Billington, Ashe, Viotti, Steibelt, Clementi, Von Esch, Salomon, Kramer and Masi. The final *brilliante* variation is headed with Latour's own name. It contains difficult figuration, and the fact that there are pencilled fingering marks throughout raises the interesting question as to the level of performance to which Emily brought this rather inconsequential, though technically demanding, piece.

7. di Monti, H. ' "The Little Bird", A Favourite Air with Variations for Pianoforte', composed and respectfully inscribed to Miss Byne. Published by F. and G. Melville, Glasgow.

There are pencil fingering markings on the score, which consists of an *allegretto* prelude, *andante* theme and seven variations. The key is G major, and a degree of dexterity is required in performance.

8. Hunten, Franz. 'The Fall of Paris' for Pianoforte Duet. Published by Metzler and Company, London.

This piece is Hunten's opus 12. There are pencil fingering markings on the score. It is an *allegretto* in A with three variations and finale, the *primo* part being the more difficult.

Fantasias

1. Rosellen, Henri. 'Fantasie', opus 36.

The score contains pencil fingering markings. A seven-bar *adagio* is followed by a change of tempo to *un poco piu lento,* with an MM of quaver=108, marked *grand espress*, and then a series of sections as follows – *vivace, romanza andante, vivace, allegro, con velocita, vivo ed energico, animato,* and *tempo primo.* Page damage has been repaired with skilful stitching. Henry Rosellen (1811–1876) was a French composer of drawing-room pianoforte pieces, such as fantasias, reveries and rondos.

2. Burgmüller, Johann Friedrich. *Fantasie sur la Romance de Mère et Soeur* ('Fantasy upon the Romance of Mother and Sister').

This is Burgmüller's opus 20. There are pencil fingering markings on the score, which was printed in Brussels, but before Emily studied there. The piece begins with an *introduzione* in F, in common time, and with chromatic writing. Next comes an *andantino* in 6–8 time, and finally an *alla Polacca* in 3–4 time which reaches to the top of the keyboard. Johann Friedrich Burgmüller (1806–1874) studied with Louis Spohr and Moritz Hauptmann. A pianist of note, he wrote numerous salon pieces and, rather more importantly, études, many of which are still in use today.

Miscellaneous

1. Bach, Johann Christian. 'Fourth Concerto' in B flat. Published by Goulding, D'Almaine, Potter and Co., London. The title page indicates the introduction into the score of 'The Yellow-Hair'd Laddie'.

Described by the publishers as 'A Favourite Concerto for the Piano Forte', it is from Bach's opus 13, and is in three movements. The first is an *allegro* in B flat in sonata form which begins with the orchestral *tutti,* the soloist entering at bar (36). The development includes a number of brief modulations. The second movement is an *andante* in the subdominant E flat, and the finale is an *andante con moto,* back in the tonic, and it is this movement that is headed 'The Yellow-haired Lassie'. J.C. Bach (1735–1782) was the eleventh surviving child and youngest son of Johann Sebastian and known as 'the London Bach', owing to the fact that much of his career was spent in the capital. He was composer to the Opera, and it is said that when his opera *Orione* was produced in 1763, it was the first time that clarinets were used in an English orchestra. He is remembered for his operas, pianoforte concertos, sonatas, and chamber music, and was admired by Haydn, Mozart and Beethoven, amongst others.

2. Diabelli, Anton. 'Duet in D' for Two Performers on the Pianoforte. Published by Metzler and Son.

There are pencil fingering markings, *primo* and *secondo* on the score of this piece. The first movement *allegro moderato,* in common time, is in sonata form. The middle movement is a quiet *andante cantabile* in 3–4 time, and the finale is a rondo *allegretto* with an ABC layout plus coda, the episode being in the tonic minor. Anton Diabelli (1781–1858) was an Austrian composer, teacher and, especially, publisher, whose great claim to fame rests upon the set of thirty-three variations, opus 120, which Beethoven wrote upon his simple C major theme.

3. Composer unknown. 'The Fall of Paris' for Pianoforte Solo. Published by Sykes and Son, Leeds.

This piece is another setting of the *allegretto,* this time in C rather than A, as in Hunten's setting, above.

4. Composer unknown. 'Bolden's Extracts on American Airs' for one or two performers on the pianoforte.

There are two Airs – 'Sick a Gettin' Upstairs' and 'Jim Crow'. They are simple pieces, in G major, marked *allegro.*

Volume Three
Parsonage library reference 1131/3

Waltzes and Marches

1. Mozart, Wolfgang Amadeus. 'Twelve Waltzes for Pianoforte with an Accompaniment for a Flute or Violin'. Published by Potter, Drum, Tambourine and Instrument Maker, Westminster'.

The score contains pencil fingering markings. The twelve keys are – C, F, B flat, E flat, G, D, B flat, F, C, F, A and C. Numbers

2, 4, 5, 8, 10 and 11 are in binary form, each part being repeated. Numbers 1, 3, 6, 7, 9 and 12 each have a trio which precedes the reprise of the waltz. They are all very simple; it is possible that Branwell played the flute accompaniment.

Quadrilles

1. Kolner, Andreas. 'Select Quadrilles, Number 26'. Published by B. Williams, London.

The sections are – *Le Pantalon* ('Lucy Neale'), *L'Été* ('The Boatman's Dance'), *La Poule* ('My Skiff is on the Shore'), *La Trenise* ('Ole Aunt Sally'). Then follows a finale, the five titles in which are – 'Old Joe', 'The Monkey's Wedding', 'Lucy Long', 'Buffalo Gals' and 'Railway Overture'. The piece concludes with a coda.

Sonatas

1. Kotzwara, Frantisek. 'The Battle of Prague'.

This is another copy of the piece which first appeared in Volume Two, above. There are no pencil finger markings on this copy.

Theme and Variations

[-] **McGregor.** 'There's nae such Luck', Number 117 of *Select Piano Forte Pieces*, from *Cyclopaedia of Music*, published by B. Williams, London.

The score is marked in pencil for fingering. In D major and in 2–4 time, there are six variations before a reprise of the theme. The usual treatments are used in the variations, but the third is interesting in that the right-hand melody follows the left hand at a distance of a semiquaver.

Fantasias

2. Moscheles, Ignaz. 'Fantasia – "Napoleon's Midnight Review and the Sea" '.

This programmatic piece is fifteen pages long, including the title page, and is in three sections.

'Andante patetico'

In the key of G minor and in common time, with an MM of crotchet=69, it is marked *ff,* until its final bar which is *p.*

'Napoleon's Midnight Review'

Beginning in G minor, *pp, sotto voce,* over a deep rumbling bass, a sudden *crescendo* in bar (17) leads to three *ff* bars, and a close into a *cantabile* melody, *p* and *dolce.* After eight bars, the key signature changes to E flat, and after a further ten to C major. There are detailed performance directions, a change of tempo to *allegro agitato* for pages 5 and 6, and brilliant figuration. The whole range of the keyboard is used.

'The Sea'

Directed to be played *allegro vivace,* with an MM of dotted crotchet=104, in C major and in 6–8 time, initially *ff,* this is the longest of the three sections. There is a brief modulation to E flat on page 9, and another, to D major, at page 13, in which key, rather unusually, the piece ends. There are extremes of dynamics from *ff* to *ppp,* and once again brilliant figuration. There are also some pencil finger markings. Charlotte's friend Mary Taylor, an accomplished pianist, described this piece as 'vulgar', saying, ' "The Sea" is but a simple air. You should admire elaborate fantasies made on elaborate subjects that want three hands or twelve fingers to play them – where you are left to invent now and again a brilliant *appoggiatura,* cadence, *Harfenspiel arpeggio).'* (4)

2. Cramer, Johann Baptist. ' "Beauties of Neukomm" – A Characteristic Fantasia in which are introduced "The Stormy Petrel", "Count Balthazar", and "The Sea Rover" ', arranged for Pianoforte, and dedicated to the Hon. Lady Anna Granville by J.B. Cramer. Published by S. Chappell, London.

The score is marked in pencil with some fingering instructions, and bears the inscription in ink 'E.J. Brontë, August 7th' (without a year). This is Emily's own signature. In D major and in common time, a dramatic *allegro maestoso* introduction, utilising extremes of dynamics, is followed by an aria, initially marked *moderato* then *allegretto moderato.* An ad libitum bridge passage links this to a rondo designated *vivo.* The final page of Emily's copy appears not to be the correct one.

Studies

1. Czerny, Karl. *Cent Exercises.* (One Hundred Exercises).

These technical exercises, numbers 54–76 from opus 139, with plenty of printed fingering, are just some of the many hundreds which Czerny wrote. Numbers 54–61 are from the first volume of opus 139, numbers 62–76 from the second, and number 62 has a few pencil fingerings added. They contain all manner of technical challenges in a wide variety of tempi and keys. A pianist of the first order, Karl Czerny (1791–1857) was a pupil and friend of Beethoven who wrote extensively and authoritatively on the performance of that composer's thirty-two piano sonatas. He was a noted teacher and a composer himself, not just of *études,* but also seventeen beautiful nocturnes. He also knew Hummel and Clementi, and studied the latter's teaching methods which he applied to his own teaching.

2. Czerny, Karl. *Die Schule der Gelaufigkeit auf dem Pianoforte, oder dreissig Uebungstuecke.* The English translation is *The School of Fluency on the Pianoforte or Thirty Practice Pieces.* According to *Grove's Dictionary of Music and Musicians,* Czerny's studies 'may be divided into three classes – scholastic, solid and brilliant' … 'the best of all [being] the scholastic'. This set, opus 299, of which numbers 11–20 are included here, along with opp. 300, 335, 355, 399, 400 and 500, were published in three volumes under the title *Complete Theoretical and Practical Pianoforte School.* There are no pencil fingering markings in Emily's copy, though a considerable number of printed ones, so it is not certain that she worked upon any of these extremely virtuosic exercises.

Miscellaneous

1. [-] **Lupeski.** '*Der Schottisch* and "Lola Montes Polka" of Select Waltzes, Polkas and Galops etc., No. 99' from *Cyclopaedia of Music.* Published by B. Williams, London.

Each of these pieces is in G major in 2–4 time, the second containing a modulation to B flat in its middle section.

'The Musical Library' – 'Instrumental'

The Parsonage edition of *The Musical Library* is dated 1844. The set consists of four volumes of piano music, consisting of pianoforte pieces or orchestral works transcribed for pianoforte, described as 'instrumental' volumes, and four of vocal music, the eight being bound in the form of four double volumes. It was published by Charles Knight and Company of 22 Ludgate Street, London, one instrumental volume and one vocal, in each of the years 1834 to 1837, and printed by William Clowes and Son, Duke Street, Lambeth. The price for each of the four volumes published in 1834 and 1835 was ten shillings and sixpence, and for each of the four published in 1836 and 1837 was twelve shillings and sixpence. *The Musical Library* was the work of the music critic William Ayrton, Fellow of the Royal Society, and one of the founder members of the Philharmonic Society.

In the Preface to the fourth volume of Instrumental music, originally dated March, 1837, the editor wrote the following rather long-winded explanation of his editorial criteria – 'When this publication was projected, the piano-forte music then most prevalent, or most fashionable, had reached the very acme of frivolity. Compositions devoid of feeling and taste, requiring from the performer nothing but a certain degree of manual dexterity, had almost superseded whatever bore the stamp of genius or science. To display a kind of sleight-of-hand was the chief object aimed at, and surprise was the best, if not the only, effect produced. But in the present day a brighter prospect begins to open on the true lover of music. The dealers find that the frothy trash which once had so ready a sale, now reposes undisturbed on their shelves. The public concerts, so far as the season has proceeded, afford undoubted evidence of improved taste in those who frequent them; and one subscription concert has been entirely and well supported by classical sonatas and fugues, executed by a most highly distinguished professor, with no other aid (a few songs excepted) than his own judgement in selection, and his admirable performance of works which it was generally supposed had long ago been consigned to oblivion. In this advancing state of a very important branch of the art, we hope, and have been taught to believe, that the Musical Library has not been quite uninfluential. It has, at least, introduced to a very wide circle, compositions of a superior order, with which few, comparatively speaking, were acquainted, and has brought forward again composers of the highest merit, who were little, if at all, known to many of the present generation. It has enabled thousands who never before had such an opportunity offered them, to form some acquaintance with the great symphonies, quartets etc., of Germany, and has placed the finest overtures of any age or country within reach of nearly all, whether as relates to expense as to obtaining or facility in executing. It has revived several of the beautiful but forgotten works of "the father of the piano-forte", [the reference here is to Muzio Clementi] and of other great though neglected composers. It has, in short, given entire pieces, or extracts complete in themselves, amounting in number to one hundred and seventy [in fact there are one hundred and seventy-six], of nearly all the celebrated writers of Instrumental Music who have flourished from the latter part of the seventeenth century down to the present period; exclusive of a far greater number of vocal compositions, equal in name and character to those to which these prefatory observations apply'. For all its undoubted virtues, however, *The Musical Library* is not without its errors, and a number of the editor's selections, as printed therein, compare unfavourably with urtext editions available today.

The volumes in the Parsonage are 34 centimetres high, hard-backed with leather spine; the present writer's first edition volumes are bound in purple silk with leather spine, which suggests that the Parsonage edition has, at some stage, been re-bound. It is known that a considerable amount of restorative work was done on these volumes by the Brontë Society in 1994, though it is not suggested that that year was necessarily the date of any re-binding. Given that, as has already been noted, the scores acquired by Emily and Anne in the 1830s might well have been bound into three volumes shortly after their being returned to the Parsonage by Mrs. Coward in 1935, and that those bindings are identical to those of *The Musical Library*, a similar date is a possibility. (1) Some of the pages show evidence of foxing, some of stains or fingermarks, and some of having been torn and expertly repaired. Again, it cannot be said with certainty when such repair work was done. It is, though, thought that *The Musical Library* left the Parsonage at some point, perhaps upon the death of Patrick in 1861, when so much of the family's property was disposed of; it has already been noted that an item described as 'Music Books etc.', was disposed of in the sale of 1861. (2) But it has also been seen that music scores were given to William Summerscales in the early 1850s, (3) and, indeed, the first Instrumental volume of *The Musical Library* in the Parsonage bears his signature in ink.

A total of twenty pieces are marked on the contents pages of the four Instrumental volumes, *presumably* by Emily, probably to highlight those to which she was to devote most attention during her practising. Various different marks are used – plus sign, small circle, dash – to denote these pieces, though the significance of there being three different signs is not apparent. (That, at least, is the supposition; it is just possible that these markings were inserted by another person at some date after the volumes left the Parsonage and before their return.) Branwell may also have used some or all of the eight volumes. There are no pencil fingerings in any of the volumes, a distinct contrast to the pre-Brussels scores, it being almost certainly the case that Abraham Sunderland had ceased to be Emily's and Anne's teacher by this time. The works marked on the contents pages are by no means amongst the easiest in the collection.

The contents of each volume are listed with composers' names arranged alphabetically, and the page numbers are quoted, although sometimes incorrectly. The composer most represented in the instrumental volumes is Handel, with twenty-five pieces, followed by Beethoven with twenty, Haydn with nineteen, and Mozart with fifteen.

There was also a *Supplement to the Musical Library*, which was issued in monthly parts between April 1834 and July 1836, the whole making a total of three volumes. The price each month was sixpence. It contained biographical and critical notices, and comments upon many of the pieces included in the Instrumental and Vocal volumes, as well as musical matters of the day. Some of the editor's subjective opinions might not meet with universal approval; in this regard, amongst nineteenth-century musical publications, *The Musical Library* was not unique.

The Musical Library 'Instrumental' – Volume One
1834

CONTENTS:

WITH COMPOSERS' NAMES ALPHABETICALLY ARRANGED.

The Musical Library – Instrumental
(Part of) Contents Page of Volume Three
Emily's Markings (o and +)
(Brontë Society)

SUPPLEMENT

TO THE

Musical Library.

JANUARY TO OCTOBER, 1835.

LONDON:

CHARLES KNIGHT,

22, LUDGATE STREET.

1835.

Supplement to the Musical Library

Volume One

1834

Parsonage library reference 1131/1

53 Pieces – None marked on the Contents Page

Autographed on the Title page by William Summerscales

1. Beethoven, Ludwig van. 'Selection from his Grand Septet, arranged for Pianoforte and Flute' (page 25).

The editor of *The Musical Library* has selected 'rather less than a third of the work ... nearly the whole that is adaptable to the two instruments'. First comes the *andante (con molto) alla marcia* which precedes the finale, then the minuet and trio, followed by the fourth movement theme and variations (numbers two and four being omitted), and finally the *scherzo* and trio. He has used Beethoven's own metronome marks, but advises that the *scherzo* should be played at a tempo no greater than an MM of dotted minim=100, as opposed to the stated 126. The original of Beethoven's opus 20 in E flat is scored for clarinet, horn, bassoon, violin, viola, cello and double bass. It was written in 1799 and received its first performance, along with that of the first symphony, on 2 April of the following year. Publication was by Hoffmeister of Leipzig in 1802. Dedicated to the Empress Maria Theresia, there are six movements: *adagio* (3–4) – *allegro con brio* (2–2) (E flat); *adagio cantabile* (A flat, 9–8); *tempo di menuetto* (E flat, 3–4); *tema con variazioni: andante* (B flat, 2–4); *scherzo: allegro molto e vivace* (E flat, 3–4); *andante con moto alla marcia* (E flat minor, 2–4), *presto* (E flat, 2–2). The theme for the Minuet was taken from the piano sonata in G, opus 49, no. 2.

2. Beethoven, Ludwig van. 'Air and Variations from his Fifth Quartet' (page 44). Piano transcription.

This is the fifth quartet of the set of six which constitute Beethoven's opus 18, composed during the years 1798–1800, and published by Mollo of Vienna in 1801. The dedicatee was Prince Lobkowitz, one of Beethoven's aristocratic patrons. The theme, or air, is sixteen bars long, with each of the eight-bar sections being repeated. The key is D major, and the time signature is 2–4. The editor has selected, in addition to the air which is an *andante cantabile,* the second and fourth variations, with part of the fifth, which includes a brief modulation to the contrasting key of B flat, and the *poco adagio* coda, now back in the tonic, as being 'best suited to the piano-forte and general performer'. A note is added at the conclusion that the *minuetto (sic)*, page 46 [is to] follow at pleasure. (The *minuetto (sic)* thus referred to is number 3, immediately following).

3. Beethoven, Ludwig van. '*Minuetto (sic)* from Sonata III' (page 46).

This is taken from Beethoven's piano sonata in D, opus 10, no. 3, and is the third movement of four, the tempo being *allegro*. Both minuet and trio , which is in the subdominant G, exploit contrasts between *staccato* and *legato* articulation and dynamics. Dedicated to Countess Anna Margarete von Browne, and composed in the winter of 1797–1798, it was published in 1798 by Joseph Eder of Vienna. The editor has made a mistake at the very beginning. The upbeat A, with which the movement begins, should be tied over the bar and should be so articulated as to ensure that the F sharp which begins the alto does not sound as though it is part of the melody.

4. Beethoven, Ludwig van. 'Air, with Variations' (page 145).

Six Easy Variations on an Original Theme, WoO 77, were written in 1800, and published in that year by Traeg of Vienna. The key is G major, the time signature 2–4, and the tempo is *andante, quasi allegretto.* The theme comprises two eight-bar phrases, the first modulating to the dominant, the latter back to the tonic, and each is repeated. The variations are written as follows: (1) with semiquaver decoration in the right hand, (2) with triplet decoration in each hand, (3) with running semiquaver decoration and octaves alternating between the hands, (4) in the tonic minor, (5) with two-part texture in the right hand with split octaves in the left, and (6) with demisemiquaver scales and arpeggio decoration of the melody, with a fourteen-bar coda to conclude.

5. Beethoven, Ludwig van. 'Overture to the "Men [*sic*] of Prometheus" ' (page 102). Piano transcription.

The correct title is *Die Geschöpfe des Prometheus,* which translates as 'The Creatures of Prometheus'. It is Beethoven's opus 43, and its overture begins with a sixteen-bar *adagio* introduction in 3–4 time which, like the opening of the first symphony, starts on a chord of the dominant seventh, the tonic C major not being reached until bar (5). There then follows an *allegro molto con brio* in 4–4 time, written in abridged sonata form. There is no development section. The two-act ballet by the court ballet master, the Neapolitan Salvatore Viganò, already discussed, (4) comprises an overture, introduction and sixteen numbers. Written in the winter of 1800–1801, and first performed on 28 March 1801 at the Burgtheater in Vienna, it was dedicated to the Countess Christiane Fürstin von Lichnowsky. Beethoven himself made a piano arrangement in 1801 which was published in the same year by Artaria of Vienna (Hess 90).

6. Beethoven, Ludwig van. 'March from "The Men [*sic*] of Prometheus" ' (page 108). Piano transcription.

The editor has included only the 'substance' of the march, and has omitted that portion which, out of the theatre, 'would seem unconnected with the march'; in fact, it has been very considerably abridged. It is the eighth number in the ballet, and it comes in the second act (which is substantially longer than the first). In the key of D major, and in common time, the original orchestral version is directed to be played *allegro con brio;* the editor has omitted this direction, merely giving an MM of crotchet=92.

7. Beethoven, Ludwig van. 'Introduction and Air from "The Men [*sic*] of Prometheus" ' (page 109). Piano Transcription.

In the key of B flat the introduction is a *largo* in common time and the air a 6–8 *andante quasi allegretto;* together they constitute the fifth number in the work. The editor has included only the first nine bars of the introduction, which opens with arpeggios played on the harp, the use of which instrument is very unusual in Beethoven, followed by a flute solo. Again there is abridgement, particularly as regards the introduction, which is linked to the air by way of a florid cadenza, notated somewhat differently from the orchestral version in the editor's transcription; in the original it is played by a solo cello. The air is in an ABA format, the editor having stipulated an MM of quaver=108. The solo cello continues with the opening theme. In due course, the flutes then clarinets and bassoons join in, before the whole orchestra takes it up. The middle section includes an interesting modulatory episode to D flat major and B flat minor, before seven bars of dominant preparation lead to a reprise of the first section, though for some reason the editor has shortened it by twenty-two bars. A thirteen-bar coda concludes this attractive movement.

8. Clementi, Muzio. 'Introduction and Rondo' (page 133).

In this selection the editor has combined movements from two of Clementi's piano sonatas. The introduction in G is taken from the Sonata opus 33, no. 2 and is marked *adagio* with an MM of quaver=66. It comprises twenty-seven bars, and contains extremes of dynamics, *ad lib.* scalic runs, and chromatic harmony. The rondo is also in G and is taken from the Sonata opus 25, no. 2. Directed to be played *allegro,* MM=108, its layout is ABACA. The first episode is in the dominant, while the second is in the tonic minor, albeit with a modulation to B flat major in its middle section. In *The Musical Library Supplement* Number VIII of November 1834, Clementi is referred to as 'the father of the piano-forte', which is the description inscribed on his tombstone in Westminster Abbey.

9. Corelli, Arcangelo. 'The *Pastorale*, with the Two Introductory Movements, from his Eighth Concerto' (page 38). Piano transcription.

The concerto referred to is the eighth of Corelli's *concerti grossi,* opus 6 in G minor, published in 1714; it is known as the 'Christmas Concerto' because it was written for Christmas Eve. Directed to be played *largo,* and written in the tonic major with an MM of quaver=100, the *pastorale* is the last of the six movements. The editor has prefaced it with two introductory movements, each in G minor – a seven-bar *vivace* marked *ff*, in 3–4 time, and a twenty-four bar *grave* in common time, the first six bars of which are marked *mez.*, short for *mezzo,* which is taken to mean *mezzo piano (mp).* The forces required to perform the original version are two violins and a cello, comprising the *concertante* (soloists) and two violins, two cellos and continuo, as the *ripieno* (the remainder of the players). The time signature in the original is 12–8, but the editor has divided the bars into two, thereby altering the time to 6–8, which, in his opinion, makes the transcribed score easier for the performer to read. Arcangelo Corelli (1653–1713) can be considered the founder of the *concerto grosso* style. A *pastorale* is an instrumental (or vocal) composition, usually in 6–8, 9–8, or 12–8 time, often on a drone bass, which portrays a pastoral character by way of the imitation of country sounds and shepherd's pipes. Handel's *Messiah* contains a 'Pastoral Symphony' (5) as does Bach's *Christmas Oratorio.*

10. Cramer, Johann Baptist. 'Sketch à *la* Haydn' (page 72).

This is an extraction from the piece written in 1823 for *The Harmonicon,* an influential monthly music journal published in London from 1823 to 1833, and edited by William Ayrton, who, as has already been noted, was also heavily involved with the publication of *The Musical Library.* It was dedicated by Cramer to his friend, the virtuoso double-bassist Domenico Dragonetti (1763–1846). Written in the key of D major in 3–4 time, it is marked *scherzo allegretto,* with an MM of crotchet=100. Again, there is a wide range of dynamics, including *mez.* Johann Baptist Cramer (1771–1858) was a German-born pianist of renown whom Beethoven held in high esteem. Arriving in England at the age of three, he subsequently became a pupil of Clementi. Although his compositions are not often played nowadays, his 'Studies' are still in use. He was a founder member of the Philharmonic Society , and also a music publisher, whose firm was set up, with two partners, at 201 Regent Street, London, in 1824.

11. Dussek, Jan Ladislav. 'Air, *Chantons l'Hymen*, with Variations', (page 22).

Written in 1788, this is the third of Dussek's *Petits Air Connûs Variés (*Little-known Airs) opus 6. It comprises an *allegro* theme and four variations. The theme, in A major and in 6–8 time, is in ternary form, a swift cadenza connecting the second and third sections. The variations, which cover a wide dynamic range, contain much brilliant figuration and require considerable dexterity in performance, although not according to *The Musical Library Supplement*, dated May 1834. It's writer opined that 'there is an elegant vivacity in this air which accounts for its having been so long admired, and will always save it from becoming obsolete. Thus treated, and exhibiting nothing in the shape of difficulty – no harmony or modulation of a *recherché* kind, it may be deemed a bagatelle, but it is a trifle that always does, and always will please persons of unsophisticated taste'. Born in Časlav, Bohemia, in 1760, Dussek was a pianist of renown, said to have been the first to play in profile during his recitals.

He had composition lessons from C.P.E. Bach, wrote thirty-four piano sonatas, fifteen piano concertos and a wide range of other music. Dussek's piano sonatas (along with those of Clementi) had a not inconsiderable influence on the developing Beethoven, and some of them look forward to music of the Romantic period. He died in 1812.

12. Dussek, Jan Ladislav. 'Minuet and Trio' (page 142).

This is the third (and penultimate) movement of Dussek's Piano Sonata in A flat, opus 70 in the Boosey and Hawkes edition, entitled *Le Retour* à *Paris.* In ABA form, the tempo is *scherzoso,* with an MM of crotchet=120, which is interesting in that it was usual to designate such a movement either *minuet* or *scherzo.* Also of interest is the *ff* subdominant chord with which the movement opens, and the unusual chromatic writing of the first six bars. The trio, also in ternary form, which is marked *sempre sotto voce e legatissimo,* is in E major, which is not such a remote key as may be thought, as A flat is the enharmonic of G sharp, the third of the scale of E major. The minuet is then repeated *DC* without its own repeats, the chromatic writing at its beginning not seeming so unusual this time round after the tonality of the trio. The editor, writing in *The Musical Library Supplement*, considered that 'this charming composition will only prove difficult for those who are awestruck by crowds of accidental sharps and flats'.

13. Giornovichi, Giovanni Mane. '*Adagio* and *Andante* from his Concerto' (page 94). Piano transcription.

This is an arrangement from one of Giornovichi's twenty-two violin concertos. In the *adagio,* written in D minor, twelve bars of orchestral writing precede the entry of what, in the original, was the solo violin in bar (13). Brilliant figuration reaching to the upper end of the keyboard follows. The close is on the dominant, in order to enable a smooth transition to the *andante* which is also in D minor, but which has a middle section initially in the tonic major, marked *dolce,* which moves into a passage of triplet notation played in the right hand. The Italian violinist and composer, Giovanni Mane Giornovichi, also known as Jarnowick (1740–1804), was apparently a person of unpleasant disposition, who was wont to fall out with his fellow musicians with a considerable degree of regularity. He died at St. Petersburg, apparently of apoplexy.

14. Handel, George Frideric. 'Overture to "The Occasional Oratorio" ' (page 12). Piano transcription.

This is a French (as opposed to Italian) overture in D major in four sections. It begins with a *maestoso,* with characteristic dotted rhythm, in common time, and with dynamic contrasts. After this is a fugal *allegro,* again in common time. A quiet *adagio* follows in the relative minor (vi), closing on its dominant in order to lead into the final section; this V of vi – I progression is common in Handel. The use of suspensions, as occurs in this movement, is another regular Baroque practice. The final section is a march with a cut-**C** time signature. In binary form, each of its parts is directed to be repeated, though the dynamics are diametrically different – *ff* the first time and *pp* the second. For most of the march the bass is played in octaves. Thomas Morell wrote at least some of the words for the *Occasional Oratorio* from the Psalms of John Milton and Edmund

Spenser. It was probably composed to celebrate the putting down of the Jacobite uprising of 1745, and received its first performance at Covent Garden in February of the following year. It consists of forty-four numbers, and is in three parts.

15. Handel, George Frideric . 'Overture to "Samson" ' (page 78). Piano transcription.

This is another French overture; the first of its three parts, in G major and in 3–4 time, and with characteristic dotted rhythm, is marked *pomposo.* It is in binary form, the first part being marked *f* and the second, *ff*, with each part repeated. There is a brief modulation to the relative minor in the second part. Three-bars marked *adagio* link to a fugal *allegro* in common time. The entries of the voices are given in the strings; subsequently there is a prominent part for the horns. Another three-bar *adagio* precedes a minuet in 3–8 time. This is in ternary form, the three sections comprising sixteen bars, repeated, followed by twelve bars and eight bars, the whole twenty being repeated. The trio consists of two sections, of eight and twelve bars respectively, each section being repeated. The minuet is then reprised *DC*, though without its own repeats. A three-act oratorio, with a libretto by Newburgh Hamilton based upon Milton's *Samson Agonistes*, *Hymn of the Nativity,* and *Lines on a Solemn Musick*, it received its first performance at Covent Garden in February 1743. The original story is contained in the Old Testament book of Judges, chapter 16. The celebrated soprano aria 'Let the Bright Seraphim' is the best-known number in the work. *Samson* was said to have been one of Branwell Brontë's favourite oratorios.

16. Handel, George Frideric. 'Funeral March in "Saul", and in "Samson" ' (page 77). Piano transcription.

Known also as the 'Dead March', it features in each of the oratorios. In C major and common time, the tempo is *grave,* with an MM of quaver=63. It is predominantly a quiet piece, though with *ff* outbursts in the middle and during the last four bars. The editor has made a mistake in that, from bar (6) onwards, he has altered the key signature to one flat. (In bar (6) it is only a B flat accidental on the first quaver in the right hand which is required.) The 'Dead March' comes at the end of Act Three, Scene Four of *Saul.* The words of the oratorio *Saul* are by Charles Jennens, and the first performance was at the King's Theatre, London, in January 1739.

17. Handel, George Frideric. 'The Fourth Plague of Egypt, Chorus from "Israel in Egypt" ' (page 86). Piano transcription.

'He gave them hail-stones for rain,
Fire mingled with rain ran along upon the ground.'

This fourth plague is number seven in Part One of the oratorio, the text being taken from the book of Exodus, chapter 9, verse 23. The symphony (orchestra) begins quietly then, after a *crescendo,* leads into the chorus, *ff,* at bar (22). The tempo is *allegro.* Presumably because of an oversight, the editor has not included this piece in the contents page of *The Musical Library.*

18. Handel, George Frideric. 'The Sixth Plague of Egypt, Chorus from "Israel in Egypt" ' (page 88). Piano transcription.

'He sent a thick darkness over all the land,
Even darkness which might be felt.'

This sixth plague of Egypt is the eighth number in Part One, the text being taken from the book of Exodus, chapter 10, verse 21. This is a *largo* directed to be performed *p sempre.* Beginning in A flat, albeit that there are no flats in the key signature, there is much chromatic harmony, an incursion into the key of E flat minor and a concluding cadence into E major, the dominant of A minor, in which key the seventh plague starts – number 19, following.

19. Handel, George Frideric. 'The Seventh Plague of Egypt, Chorus from "Israel in Egypt" ' (page 88). Piano transcription.

'He smote all the first-born of Egypt,
The chief of all their strength.'

This seventh plague of Egypt is number nine in Part One, the text being taken from Psalm 105, verses 36 and 37. The direction is *tempo giusto e staccato,* the MM being crotchet=80.

20. Handel, George Frideric. ' "But as for His People" from "Israel in Egypt" ' (page 90). Piano transcription.

'But as for his people, He led them forth like sheep,
He brought them out with silver and gold.
There was not one, not one feeble person among their tribes.'

This is number ten in Part One; the text is taken from Psalm 78, verse 52, and Psalm 105, verse 37. Written in D major, a tonality which illustrates the more optimistic nature of the text, it is an *andante quasi allegretto.* Compiled from the

Old Testament and the Prayer Book version of the Psalms, possibly by Handel himself, the first performance of the oratorio *Israel in Egypt* was at the King's Theatre, London on 4 April1739.

21. Handel, George Frideric. ' "Pastoral Symphony", from "Messiah" with Mozart's accompaniments' (page 100). Piano transcription.

The 'Pastoral Symphony', number 13 in Part One of the oratorio and, as such, part of the Christmas music, is here transcribed in the form of a duet. According to the editor this is 'in order to introduce the accompaniments added by Mozart which cannot be compassed by a single performer. Handel has used stringed instruments only; Mozart augmented the score by the addition of flutes, oboes, clarinets, bassoons and horns'. Written in C major in 6–8 time, the direction is *larghetto sempre piano e legato.* Pedal points, a characteristic of pastorals, feature prominently. In ternary form, the middle section modulates briefly to A minor, then to G major, which is the home dominant. It is predominantly a quiet piece with gentle dynamic swells.

22. Handel, George Frideric. 'Selection from "The Water Music" ' (page 111). Piano transcription.

Four movements have been arranged in abridged fashion, the editor considering that he has chosen 'those most recommended by beauty of melody'. The first of these is an overture in D major marked *maestoso,* featuring trumpets and (natural) horns in the original orchestration. It concludes with a characteristic Handelian V of vi chord. Next comes a hornpipe designated *andante quasi allegretto,* and emphasis on the syncopated offbeats, again with trumpets and horns prominent, followed by an aria in the subdominant G major (IV) in binary form. Each part is repeated with contrasting dynamics. The selection concludes with a short *vivace, ff.* Back in the tonic, with a cut-**C** time signature, it consists of a four-bar phrase repeated, followed by an eight-bar phrase also repeated, with the bass being played in octaves. The original work is a series of twenty-one instrumental movements, written at different times, and collected for publication by John Walsh of London in 1740. Some of them may have been used for a river party on the Thames by George I and his entourage in 1717 thereby, according to tradition, effecting a reconciliation between composer and his erstwhile master, who was the Elector of Hanover before he ascended the English throne. The orchestral scoring is for trumpets, horns, oboes, flutes, bassoons, recorders and strings.

23. Handel, George Frideric. ' "The March to Battle", in "Joshua" ' (page 103). Piano transcription.

The editor has considered that 'the effect of [this piece] is much improved by the addition of *fortes* and *pianos,* though the composer does not mark them in the score'. It is a martial piece, marked *maestoso* and written in D major, with a cut-**C** time signature. The fourth of Handel's oratorios based upon a libretto by Thomas Morell, *Joshua* was written within a single month in 1747 and premiered at Covent Garden in March of the following year. It was one of a series of Handel's oratorios which he wrote upon military themes in the years immediately following the Jacobite Rebellion of 1745. The popular chorus 'See the Conquering Hero Comes' was originally written for *Joshua*, before being added to the later work *Judas Maccabeus*.

24. Handel, George Frideric. 'Chorus – "Surely He hath borne our Griefs", from "Messiah" ' (page 159). Piano transcription.

'Surely, He hath borne our griefs and carried our sorrows,
He was wounded for our transgressions,

He was bruised for our iniquities,
The chastisement of our peace was upon Him.'

Number twenty-four in Part Two of the oratorio, this chorus and the two following, are part of the Easter music. The tonality for all three is F – minor for the first two, major for the third. The first is homophonic writing, *largo e staccato,* with a distinctive dotted rhythm – double-dotted in some early editions – and some lovely dissonances; the second is contrapuntal, *moderato,* and the third also contrapuntal, *allegro moderato,* until its conclusion, when it reverts to being homophonic and *adagio*. The editor prints the word *segue* at the end of each of the first two choruses in order to indicate that the next one follows in performance without a break. The words for *Messiah* were selected from Holy Scripture by Charles Jennens, those for this first chorus being taken from the book of Isaiah, chapter 53, verses 4–5.

25. Handel, George Frideric. 'Chorus – "And with His Stripes", from "Messiah" ' (page 160). Piano transcription.

'And with His stripes we are healed.'

Number twenty-five in the oratorio, the text is taken from the book of Isaiah, chapter 53, verse 5. Handel's original time signature is cut-C. The editor has, however, divided each bar into two parts.

26. Handel, George Frideric. 'Chorus – "All we like Sheep", from "Messiah"' (page 161). Piano transcription.

'All we like sheep have gone astray,
We have turned every one to his own way,
And the Lord hath laid on Him the iniquity of us all.'

Number twenty-six, the text is taken from Isaiah, chapter 53, verse 6. Another arrangement of this chorus, for piano or organ, was included in the scores acquired by the young Brontës in the 1830s, already discussed.

27. Haydn, Franz Joseph. 'Slow Movement from the Symphony in A' (page 10). Piano transcription.

Although described by the editors as 'No. 16 of Cianchettini's Edition in Score', this is actually the *largo* second movement from Haydn's Symphony Number 64 in A, written probably during the years 1773–1775. In the subdominant key of D major, it is scored for two oboes, two horns and strings. It is an interesting and dramatic movement with much chromaticism, dynamic contrast, and unusual use of rests. One of the major composers, and one of the most prolific, the Austrian-born Franz Joseph Haydn (1732–1809) was employed as Kapellmeister at the Esterháza palace for thirty years from 1761. He gave some early lessons to Beethoven, although relations between the two were sometimes rather strained. His prodigious output included one hundred and four symphonies, along with piano sonatas, masses and other church music, string quartets, operas, concertos and vocal music.

28. Haydn, Franz Joseph. ' "A Representation of Chaos" Introduction to "The Creation" – arranged as a Duet' (page 68). Piano transcription.

The opening of the oratorio is a *largo,* predominantly quiet, though with periodic violent intrusions. The piece actually finishes *ppp,* which was unusual for the time. There is much chromaticism as the representation of chaos unfolds. In a performance of the whole work, this opening leads directly into a recitative sung by the bass soloist, the archangel Raphael:

> 'In the beginning, God created the heaven and the earth; and the earth was without form, and void; and darkness was upon the face of the deep.'

It is said that the astronomer William Herschel, discoverer of Uranus and himself a composer, was greatly taken with this opening number. Haydn's oratorio *Die Schöpfung* (The Creation) was completed in 1798, and received its first performance in that year at the Schwarzenberg Palace in Vienna. The libretto was by Baron Gottfried von Swieten, after Milton's *Paradise Lost*, and was the first oratorio libretto to be printed in both German and English. It is in three parts and scored for four soloists – two sopranos, tenor and bass – four-part chorus, and an orchestra comprising three flutes, two each of oboes, clarinets and bassoons, double bassoon, two horns, two trumpets, three trombones, timpani and strings. Its most popular number is the chorus 'The Heavens are telling'.

29. Haydn, Franz Joseph. ' "Morning": the Introduction to the Third Part of "The Creation" ' (page 93). Piano transcription.

This is another *largo,* in E major and 3–4 time, beginning with the melody given by three flutes, as the opening to Part Three of *The Creation*. It leads, without a break, into Uriel's recitative:

'In rosy mantle appears,
By music sweet awake'd,
The morning young and fair.'

30. Haydn, Franz Joseph. 'Minuet and Trio from his Eleventh [*sic*] Grand Symphony' (page 97). Piano transcription.

The term 'Grand Symphony', when used to describe Haydn's symphonies, relates to his last twelve, numbers 93–104, written for Johann Peter Salomon's concerts in London in the 1790s. This 'minuet and trio' *allegretto,* given unabridged, is the third movement from the Symphony Number 101 in D known as the 'Clock', which nickname derives from the 'tick-tock' accompaniment to the first subject of the second movement. Accordingly, the symphony ought to be designated the ninth of the twelve, not the eleventh. It was written in 1794. The orchestral scoring is for two each of flutes, oboes, clarinets, bassoons, horns and trumpets, plus timpani and strings, the principal flute being prominent in the trio. The minuet is in ternary form, the repeats being of bars (1)–(28) and bars (29)–(80). The trio begins, *pp,* with a D major chord for four bars leading into a seven-bar theme in the right hand, and the minuet is repeated *DC*, though without its own repeats.

31. Haydn, Franz Joseph. 'Andante, from his Third [*sic*] Symphony' (page 137). Piano transcription.

The symphony here transcribed is the second (not third) of the final twelve 'grand' symphonies written for Salomon's London concerts, Number 94, written in 1791. Numbers 93–98 were written for the first series of Salomon's concerts. In G major, it is known as *Der Paukenschlag* (The Surprise) because of its totally unexpected *ff* chord at the end of the first phrase in bar (16) of this *andante* second movement, written in the subdominant C major. The simple binary theme in 2–4 time is treated in four varied ways. Firstly, the melody appears in the left hand, with decoration in the right hand by way of semiquavers. The *minore* variation, which begins in the tonic minor, modulates to E flat after eight bars, and also involves right-hand elaboration, with a right-hand linking passage to the third variation. The theme is given in repeated notes in the right hand, then without variation in the left, and then it is passed between the hands. The final treatment involves a sextuplet figure in the right hand along with more repeated notes. After a diminished seventh chord, a twelve-bar coda concludes the movement. The orchestral scoring is for two each of flutes, oboes, bassoons, horns and trumpets, plus timpani and strings. In regard to this piano transcription, the editor advises that the effect would be greatly impaired if played fast, and attention should be paid to the *staccato* and *tenuto* directions.

32. Haydn, Franz Joseph. ' "Introduction to Autumn", the Third Part of "The Seasons" ' (page 164). Piano transcription.

This piece is taken from *The Seasons*, not *The Creation*, as stated on the contents page of *The Musical Library*. The

'Introduction to Autumn' is marked *allegretto* and is in 3–4 time. The opening eight-bar phrase is repeated an octave higher, while the middle section features a distinctive dotted rhythm. The reprise of the first section is varied and extended, before overlapping into a short coda which utilises the dotted rhythm in the right hand over a tonic pedal in the left. It took Haydn two years to complete his secular oratorio *Die Jahreszeiten* (The Seasons). As with *Die Schöpfung* (The Creation) the work is bilingual, the text, which exists both in German and English, having been written by Baron Gottfried von Swieten, based upon the English poem *The Seasons* by James Thomson. There are three soloists – soprano, tenor, and bass – and an orchestra which was a large one for the period, including piccolo, contrabassoon, three trumpets, three trombones (alto, tenor and bass), timpani and percussion, in addition to the normal strings and wind. There was also a fortepiano for the recitatives.

33. Himmel, Friedrich Heinrich. 'March' (page 140).

The editor describes this march as being 'spirited and original', but was unable to specify the work from which it was taken. In D major, and directed to be played *maestoso,* with an MM of crotchet=96, it is in common time. There are a number of interesting features, including hands moving in contrary motion, modulations, chromatic harmony and triplet passages in each or both hands. Friederich Heinrich Himmel (1765–1814) was a German composer and pianist who met Beethoven in 1796 when that composer was visiting Berlin. His main compositions were operas and choral works, but he did write for the pianoforte, and his opus 25 was a piano concerto.

34. Hoffmann, P. C. 'March from Mozart's *Zauberflöte,* with Four Variations' (page 64).

This is the Priests' March from Scene One of Act Two of Mozart's *Singspiel.* The editor has made some alterations in the transcription, which is not one of the more valued pieces in *The Musical Library*. The march is an *andante* in F with a cut-**C** time signature. The first variation has quaver decoration in the right hand, and makes much use of appogiaturas, the second also has right-hand variation, this time triplets. The third is of eight bars only, with some chromatic harmony and a close on the home dominant, enabling a smooth transition into the final variation which has an active quaver bass under the right-hand melody.

35. Hummel, Johann Nepomuk. 'Romance for Pianoforte and Flute' (page 41).

Hummel's opus 108 is properly entitled 'Amusement for Violin (or Flute) and Piano' and was published in 1826. The editor explains that the flute accompaniment may be attained by way of a third hand at the keyboard. The key is F major, *andante cantabile,* and the layout is ABA plus coda. Two tonic chords precede the eight-bar theme which is given by the piano and repeated with slight variation by the flute. In the middle section there are modulations to A minor and C major, with some chromatic colouring, before the return of the first eight bars of the opening melody, and a fourteen-bar coda to conclude. Johann Nepomuk Hummel (1778–1837) was born in Pressburg, an important composer and virtuoso pianist who studied piano with Clementi, composition with Albrechtsberger and Salieri, and was well acquainted with Beethoven, at whose funeral he was a pall-bearer. His compositions include stage works and church music, concertos, chamber music, and much fine music for solo piano.

36. Hummel, Johann Nepomuk. *Marche à la Romaine* (page 170).

The 'Roman March' is the first of *Trois pièces faciles,* opus 111, in E flat, with an ABA plus coda layout. The first section, marked *allegro maestoso e pomposo,* is in ternary form, with repeats; dotted rhythms feature throughout. Section B is also in ternary form, though much shorter, with repeats. In the subdominant key of A flat, it is a contrast to the previous section in that it is marked *p, dolce e cantabile.* The first section is reprised, with a four-bar coda to conclude.

37. Hünten, Franz. 'Rondoletto' (page 108).

The rondoletto is preceded by a sixteen-bar introduction in C, directed to be played *andantino,* with an MM of quaver=116. It ends with a dominant seventh arpeggio held on the sustaining pedal, enabling the rondoletto to begin also in C. Marked *allegro,* with an MM of dotted crotchet=104, it is written in 6–8 time. The layout is ABA, the middle section beginning in the relative minor and concluding on another dominant seventh chord, that of the home tonic, C major. Franz Hünten (1793–1878), sometimes referred to as François, was a German pianist, composer and author of *Nouvelle méthode pour le piano-forte.* Hunten's piano pieces were not particularly demanding from a technical point of view, though the editor refers to this one as being 'one of the best specimens, of the light kind, of the piano-forte works of M. Huenten, now a popular composer'.

38. Jommelli, Niccolò. *Chaconne* (page 74). Piano transcription.

This chaconne, opus 5, no. 13, was originally written for small orchestra consisting of strings and timpani. It is an *andante* in E flat in 3–4 time, the ground bass being four bars long. An Italian composer, at one time of the Neapolitan school, Niccolò Jommelli (1714–1774) was most noted for his secular dramatic works, of which there are over eighty. He was friendly with the poet Pietro Metastasio (1698–1782), many of whose texts he set. A chaconne (ciaccona in Italian) is a dance on a ground bass which is repeated with variation above throughout the piece. There are some very famous examples – Bach's D minor chaconne from the second Partita in D minor, 'Dido's Lament', from Purcell's *Dido and Aeneas*, and Beethoven's 'Thirty-two Variations in C minor', WoO 80. The passacaglia is practically identical to the chaconne.

39. Kalkbrenner, Friedrich Wilhelm Michael. 'Nottorno, for Piano and Flute' (page 6).

This *cantabile,* Kalkbrenner's opus 129, is an *andante con moto* in F for pianoforte and flute, though, in a note, the composer states that the 'accompaniment' is also suitable for violin or clarinet in C. Alternatively, it could be played by a third hand on the keyboard. In fact, it is the piano which provides the accompaniment throughout. The layout is ABA plus coda. There is a certain amount of ornamentation in the flute part in the reprise of the first section; one wonders whether Branwell would have been up to the task. The composer is described, at the head of the score, as 'Chevalier of the Legion of Honour and of the Red Eagle'.

40. Kuhlau, Friedrich. 'Rondo' (page 61).

This is a light-hearted movement from the third of Kuhlau's four sonatinas, in A minor, opus 88. Marked *allegretto burlesco,* with an MM of crotchet=92, and in 2–4 time, it is in ABA form. The middle section modulates to the relative major and includes an eight-bar passage with a chain of suspensions, before a passage of dominant preparation leads to a reprise of the first section, with a short coda to conclude. The use of acciaccaturas highlights the humorous nature of the piece. Friederich K uhlau (1786–1832) was a Hanover-born flautist, composer and conductor, who settled in Copenhagen. His compositional output included forty-five operas, much piano music and works for the flute. He visited Beethoven in Baden in September 1825 and extemporised a canon on BACH (B flat ACB in German nomenclature) and Beethoven replied with one of his own in three parts, using the same notes, to the words *Kühl, nicht lau* ('Cool, not warm'), which has the WoO number 191, and was published posthumously.

41. Méhul, Étienne Nicolas. 'Overture to the Sacred Opera of "Joseph" ' (page 34). Piano transcription.

A twenty-five bar *adagio* introduction in 3–4 time, marked *legato sempre,* with an MM of crotchet=66, initially *pp,* precedes an *allegro moderato* in common time, whose MM is minim=66 to begin with, then minim=88 from bar (106). This is a transcription for piano of an orchestral overture and, as such, does not always sit easily beneath the hands. The opera *Joseph,* or *Jacob et ses Fils en Egipte* (Jacob and his Brothers in Egypt), is in three acts, set to a libretto by Alexandre Duval, based upon the biblical story as told in the book of Genesis. It was first produced in Paris in February 1807, and a performance in Brussels ensued the following year. According to the editors, 'it was translated and prepared for representation at Covent Garden theatre during the last Lent, when the Lord Chamberlain, on the showing of the Bishop of London, forbade any dramatic performances, and thus drove many hundreds to seek much less innocent amusement than a well regulated stage affords'. Étienne Nicolas Méhul (1763–1817) is best remembered for his operas, of which there were a considerable number. A friend of Napoleon, he was one of the first Frenchmen to be awarded the Légion d'honneur.

42. Mozart, Wolfgang Amadeus. 'Overture to La Clemenza di Tito ' (page 1). Piano transcription.

The editor has made 'such alterations and additions as the score authorized and as appeared likely to improve its effect and facilitate its performance'. In fact, the transcription is not abridged. Written in C major in common time, the overture is in sonata form, beginning with an eight-bar fanfare. The first subject group includes a carillon-like passage with a distinctive triplet figure in the left hand. Mozart's last opera, K621, based upon Metastasio's drama, was completed just two months before his death. It was written, in remarkably quick time, for the coronation of Emperor Leopold II as King of Bohemia, and was first performed at Prague in September 1791.

43. Mozart, Wolfgang Amadeus. 'Overture [*sic*] to *Le Nozze di Figaro*' (The Marriage of Figaro) (page 50). Piano transcription.

Mozart called the orchestral introduction to this opera 'sinfonia', not 'overture', because its contents do not feature again in the opera. This is in contrast to the later operas *Die Zauberflöte*, *Don Giovanni* and *Cosi fan tutte*, where he uses the word 'overture' because of links with what follows in the opera itself. This sinfonia is in abridged sonata form – there is no development section – in D major, and the tempo is *presto*, with an MM of minim=108. The editor counsels against playing this *presto* piece too fast – 'a fact often proved at the King's Theatre, and sometimes even at the Philharmonic concerts'. The first group is rich in subjects; in the original orchestration the distinctive opening seven bars are given to the bassoons, *pp*. The second group enters at bar (107) and the recapitulation at bar (138). A three-note figure in the bass, first appearing at the fourth beat of bar (45) and comprising the notes A, F# and D, is important, in that it features prominently in the coda. The sinfonia is often included on its own in symphony concerts. *Le Nozze di Figaro*, K492, a four-act *commedia per musica* to a libretto by Lorenzo Da Ponte, after the play by Beaumarchais, was written in 1786 and first performed in May of that year in Vienna.

44. Mozart, Wolfgang Amadeus. 'Air from Grétry's Opera *Les Mariages Samnites*, with Variations' (page 104).

This is number 352 in Koechel's catalogue – a set of eight variations on an air from Gretry's opera, completed in the June 1781. The air, in F major with a cut-**C** time signature, and in binary form with each eight-bar part repeated, is *Dieu d'amour* ('God of Love'). However, the editor has included only the first five variations, placing number three as the final one. In the first of them the air is ornamented, the second makes use of semiquavers alternatively in each hand, the third has lengthy trills alternatively in each hand, effectively dominant pedals, the fourth is a *minore* in the tonic minor, and the last contains broken octaves and *arpeggios*. One of the variations omitted, number six, an *adagio*, is said to be 'rather heavy', while number eight is considered to be 'a mere jig, and exceedingly inappropriate'. There are some similarities with Mozart's best-known set of variations, the first movement of his Sonata in A, K331. André Ernest (Modeste) Grétry (1741–1813) was a French composer of Walloon descent. He was a prolific composer of works for the stage, *Les Mariages Samnites* being an early work, set to a libretto by Pierre Légier after Marmontel, which was first performed in Paris in early 1768.

45. Mozart, Wolfgang Amadeus. 'Minuet and Trio (Opus 14) arranged for Pianoforte and Flute' (page 114).

This movement is the second of the three which comprise Mozart's 'Trio for Pianoforte, Clarinet (or Violin) and Viola' in E flat, K498, known by the nickname *Kegelstatt* ('Skittle alley'), here arranged for piano and flute. It is preceded, by way of introduction, by a few bars based upon the opening of the work's first movement. The minuet is in the key of the dominant of the piece, B flat, the introductory bars having been transposed from E flat. It is in ternary form, the first twelve bars being repeated, with the reprise of the first part being varied. The trio is in the relative minor, G minor, and it includes an interesting chain of secondary dominants. An eight-bar passage links the trio with the reprise of the minuet, and coda to conclude. Some slight changes have been made to the original pianoforte part.

46. Mozart, Wolfgang Amadeus. 'Overture to *Don Giovanni*' (page 153). Piano transcription.

The overture begins with loud D minor chords over a timpani roll. The first thirty bars are a dramatic *andante* which features a wide range of dynamics. The *allegro molto* beginning at bar (31) is in the tonic major, and is in sonata form. An important five-note figure (x), consisting of the notes D descending to G# in octaves, which appears in bars (76)–(77), is the basis for the development section, which visits a variety of keys before the eight bars of dominant preparation leading to the recapitulation. The overture's original ending has been amended by the editor to accommodate the fact that, in the opera, it leads directly into the first act *introduzione,* and Leporello's aria *Notto e giorno,* without a break. (6) *Don Giovanni,* K527 is a *dramma giocoso* in two acts to a libretto by Lorenzo Da Ponte, based on the legend of *Don Juan*. It was completed in 1787 and produced in Prague in that year.

47. Onslow, George. 'Air, *Charmante Gabrielle*, with Introduction and Variations' (page 129).

'Charming Gabrielle' is Onslow's opus 12 which, in its original version, consisted of a *largo* introduction, with extremes of dynamics from *ppp* to *ff*, a very simple *grazioso* air, seven variations and coda. The editor, however, has selected only four variations 'that are most likely to prove generally pleasing'. The first involves quaver movement in each hand and syncopation, the second has semiquaver decoration in the right hand, the third uses right-hand triplets, and the final one has running semiquavers, alternately in left hand and right. A fifteen-bar coda, *pp,* using material from the air, ends the piece with a *smorzando* marking. *Charmante Gabrielle* is also included in the Vocal Section of *The Musical Library*, as number 71 in Volume One. André George(s) Louis Onslow (1784–1853) was an Anglo–French composer, who was born in, and died at, Clermont-Ferrand. He studied piano with Dussek and Cramer during a stay in London, and his compositional output included four symphonies, piano music, and much chamber music, of which the quintets are reckoned to be the best.

48. Paradies, Pietro Domenico. 'Andante' (page 21).

This short, tuneful andante, actually directed to be played *quasi allegretto,* with an MM of crotchet=72, is from one of the twelve keyboard sonatas published in London circa 1750, with a second edition in Amsterdam in 1770. Its form is ABA. At the head of the score is the sentence in parenthesis – 'This may be used as an Introductory Movement to the following Air', the piece referred to being Dussek's *Chantons l'Hymen with Variations*, number 11, above. Both pieces are in the key of A major, the andante concluding on the dominant in order to enable the succeeding air to begin in A. The keyboard works of the Italian composer Pietro Domenico Paradies (also known as Paradisi) (1707–1791) were an influence on many subsequent players, including Clementi and Cramer.

49. Plachy, Wenzel. 'Air, from Bellini's *I Montecchi e Capuleti*, (the correct title is *I Capuleti e I Montecchi)* with Introduction and Variations', opus 60 (page 82).

The air upon which Plachy wrote his four variations is *La tremenda ultrice.* It is preceded by a sixteen-bar introduction in G major and in 9–8 time, marked *andante sostenuto* and *dolce.* The air is in common time with the first eight bars being repeated. The next twelve bars contain some minor tone colouring before the final four bars which allude to the air's beginning. The three variations involve, respectively, right-hand semiquaver decoration, triplet decoration, and octaves, with a short coda to conclude. Bellini's two-act opera is a re-working of the 'Romeo and Juliet' story, with a libretto by Felice Romani, which was first performed at the Teatro La Fenice, Venice, in March 1830. Vincenzo Bellini (1801–1835) was an Italian composer most notably of opera. The most popular, in addition to *I Capuleti e I Montecchi* (The Capulets and the Montagues) are *La Sonnambula* and *Norma.* They are characterised by long florid *legato* vocal lines, requiring considerable agility in performance, and were much admired by, amongst others, Hector Berlioz.

50. Pleyel, Ignaz Joseph. 'Air, with Variations, for Pianoforte and Flute' (page 165).

This is a piece transcribed from the third sonata of six 'dedicated to the Queen of Great Britain'. The sixteen-bar theme is given in the piano and is an andante in B flat and 2–4 time, consisting of two eight-bar phrases, each repeated. The first variation is of running semiquavers in the flute part, the second features right-hand demisemiquaver passage work in the piano part, the third involves a sextuplet dialogue between the piano and flute, and the fourth also uses dialogue between the instruments, much of it imitative. In the final variation, the flute and right hand of the piano give the main melody over a running demisemiquaver bass. Ignaz Joseph Pleyel (1757–1831) was a composer who studied with Haydn, and a pianoforte maker, from a large family of musicians.

51. Rossini, Gioacchino Antonio. 'March, in *Semiramide*' (page 48).

The march comes in Act One of the opera. In C major and in common time, it is an *allegro moderato* with a suggested MM of crotchet=92. *Semiramide* is an opera in two acts, with a libretto by Gaetano Rossi, based upon the tragedy by Voltaire. It had its first performance at the Teatro La Fenice, Venice, in February 1823. (Its overture is much the best-known number in the opera, often being performed as a concert overture.)

52. Steibelt, Daniel. 'Selection from his First Fantasie' (page 57).

Steibelt's *Fantaisie avec neuf Variations sur un Air des Mystères d'Isis (die Zauberflöte)* was considered by the editor to be too long to be included in full. Given instead is part of the *allegro agitato* opening in G minor and principal theme, *O cara armonia,* an *allegretto* in G major consisting of six four-bar phrases. Four variations follow, the first involving triplet decoration and the second syncopation. The third is in the tonic minor and the fourth involves the crossing of hands. The order of the last two is transposed so that a conclusion in the major key might be obtained.

53. Weber, Carl Maria von. 'Introduction and Rondo, opus 65' (page 149).

Popularly known as 'Invitation to the Dance', this important piano piece of 1819, *Aufforderung zum Tanz,* 'Rondo brilliant', has already been discussed. (7) The first movement, in E flat and in 3–4 time, is a thirty-five bar *moderato grazioso* ending on a chord of the dominant seventh enabling an immediate entry to the waltz itself. This is an *allegro,* only part of which is included here, transposed from D flat to E flat. The main eight-bar theme, *ff*, is immediately repeated and followed by sixteen bars which are also repeated. A passage of brilliant right-hand figuration reaching to the highest registers of the piano leads to a reprise of the first eight bars of the waltz. The second strain of the waltz is in ABA form, the first thirty-two bars are repeated, as are the next seventy-two which comprise the middle section and the reprise of the first.

Volume Two

1835

Parsonage library reference 1131/1

41 Pieces – 2 Marked on the Contents Page

1. Bach, Johann Sebastian. 'Introduction and Fugue' (page 162).

Disappointingly, this is the only one of J.S. Bach's works to appear in *The Musical Library.* Actually, this is not particularly surprising given that, in the 1830s, Bach's music was nowhere nearly as universally known as it is today. For example, the first performance since his death seventy-nine years before of his *St. Matthew Passion* was conducted by Mendelssohn in Berlin only in 1829. In this selection, the editor's 'introduction' is, in fact, no more than the first twenty bars of the E flat prelude from Book Two of *Das Wohltemperierte Klavier* (The Well Tempered Clavier) which fact is a disgrace, but at least the complete fugue, which is in four voices, is given. There are twenty-four preludes and fugues in each of the two books, in all the major and minor keys. Bach's object was to demonstrate the advantages of what was, then, the new system of equal temperament for keyboard instruments. The first book was written at Coethen in 1722 and the second at Leipzig in 1744. *The Musical Library Supplement* contains the absurd comment that 'as regards effect, [the 48] are overvalued'. A far more apposite approach would be to quote Hans von Bülow's aphorism that 'Bach's 48 Preludes and Fugues are the Old Testament; Beethoven's 32 Piano Sonatas are the New Testament'. Johann Sebastian Bach (1685–1750) was the master composer, polyphonist beyond compare, and organist, whose works in each of the genres in which he wrote are unsurpassed. Amongst his masterpieces, in addition to the '48', may be listed the St. Matthew and St. John Passions, the B Minor Mass, the Goldberg Variations, the six Brandenburg Concertos, numerous organ and other keyboard works, concertos and cantatas. A number of his sons, particularly Carl Philipp Emanuel, Johann Christian and Wilhelm Friedemann, were also composers of renown.

2. Beethoven, Ludwig van. 'Rondo' (page 48).

This rondo is in C major, with a cut-**C** time signature, directed to be played *moderato e grazioso*. It was written round about 1796–7, despite its having a middle period opus number of 51, no. 1 and was published by Artaria of Vienna. The layout is ABACA plus coda. The usual treatments of the subject are employed – ornamentation, triplet decoration, chromaticism, syncopation, and an episode in the tonic minor. There are also detailed performance directions and an extended coda – portents of things to come in Beethoven's writing,

3. Beethoven, Ludwig van. 'Movement from Seventh Symphony' (page 60). Piano transcription. Marked on the contents page.

This is only an extract – in fact the first one hundred bars (plus an added two-bar terminating cadence) – from the second movement *allegretto.* In Beethoven's original, this opening section is followed by two episodes, one in the tonic major the other fugal, and coda. *Main Themes (A) and (B).* In the key of A minor, the tonic minor of the symphony, and in 2–4 time, the *allegretto* opens with a sombre chord in the woodwind, excluding flutes, plus horns, *f*, with dramatic *decrescendo* to *pp*. The main theme (A) of sixteen bars (8+8) with its relentless dactyl-spondee rhythm, is then given in the violas, with cello and double bass accompaniment, *p*. The last eight bars are repeated, *pp*, with the left hand (in the transcription) playing octaves. At bar (27) the second violins enter with the theme, while the cellos provide an enchanting counterpoint, theme (B). At bar (51) it is the turn of the first violins to give the theme, with the counterpoint now in the second violins, and a distinctive figure in the cellos. From this point on *crescendo poco a poco* is directed, and at bar (75) the full orchestra gives the theme *ff*. At bar (91) the editor marks an *fp* followed by a *diminuendo* until bar (98) when the theme ends *p*. The editor concludes this greatly truncated selection with a simple perfect cadence. The contrasting dynamics have been of considerable importance in bringing out the emotion of the extremely simple theme. The seventh symphony, opus 92, was written during the years 1811–1812, and it received its first performance in December of the following year. Published in 1816 by Steiner of Vienna, it was dedicated to Count Moritz von

Fries. Various piano arrangements exist for both two and four hands. Its importance has already been discussed. (8) According to the nineteenth-century Beethoven scholar, Gustav Nottebohm, in his *Zweite Beethoveniana,* Beethoven intended the opening theme of this movement for the second movement of the third *Razumovsky* string quartet, opus 59, no. 3. (9)

4. Beethoven, Ludwig van. '*Largo,* from Third Sonata' (opus 2) (page 86).

In fact, this movement is the *largo appassionato* of Beethoven's second, not third as the editor states, pianoforte sonata – opus 2, no. 2. Dedicated to Joseph Haydn, and composed in 1795, the sonata was published in 1796 by Artaria of Vienna. There are a number of interesting and innovative features about this second movement, which contrasts with the first; Czerny refers to its 'religious character'. The use of the word *appassionato* is unusual for the period; hitherto, composers had contented themselves with the use of *tempi ordinari.* The sonority is broader than anything found in the piano works of Beethoven's predecessors; the eminent pianist Edwin Fischer hears trombones, *tenuto sempre,* contrasted with the neighbouring tone *pizzicato* double bass, at the opening of the main theme. The musicologist and pianist Charles Rosen thinks that the *staccato* bass will sound even more like a *pizzicato* if it is very rapidly *arpeggiated*, or played very slightly before the tenor part. The layout is ABACA plus coda. It has to be said that the editor has omitted a number of Beethoven's performance directions.

5. Beethoven, Ludwig van. 'Overture to *Fidelio*' (page 116). Piano transcription.

The importance of Beethoven's only opera has already been discussed, (10). Beethoven actually wrote four overtures for his opera, the first three all bearing the name *Leonore*, which was the title originally intended for the opera. The first performance was in 1805, but Beethoven subsequently revised it for a production the following year. Still less than fully satisfied, he revised it for a final time for a premiere on 23 May 1814, although the overture did not receive its own first performance for another three days. While the three *Leonore* overtures are similar in style, and all in the key of C major, the overture *Fidelio* is markedly different. It is in the key of E and in sonata form, preceded by an introduction.

6. Beethoven, Ludwig van. 'March in *Fidelio*' (page 124). Piano transcription.

In B flat in common time, marked *vivace,* the march is a short one in binary form. The eight-bar first part opens with timpani, oboes, clarinets, bassoons and horns, closes in the dominant, and is repeated. The twenty-two-bar second part, back in the tonic, contains two further themes, and is repeated. The March occurs in Act One and is the sixth number in the opera. It heralds the arrival in the prison yard of the evil prison governor Don Pizarro with a group of guards. It is Pizarro who is responsible for Florestan's wrongful imprisonment, deep in the dungeons below. Rocco, the sympathetic jailer, hands Pizarro a letter informing him of the imminent arrival of the minister, Don Fernando, who, having heard that Pizarro is exercising his authority in a tyrannical manner, wishes to inspect the prison himself. Accordingly, Pizarro determines to kill Florestan forthwith.

7. Clementi, Muzio. 'Sonata' (page 10).

There are two versions of this Sonata in E flat, Clementi's opus 11. The first, written in Vienna, consists of two movements, *allegro* and *rondeau: presto,* and is dedicated to Maria Theresia von Hess. The later, London, version has slight amendments to these two movements, and includes a central *larghetto con espressione,* and this is the version selected by the editor. Emily's copy shows signs of wear, probably indicative of the fact that, although not marked by her in the contents, it was a piece which she played. The well-known, and virtuosic, 'Toccata', written for harpsichord or piano-forte, also given the opus number 11, is often coupled with this sonata, though the editor of *The Musical Supplement* expresses the opinion that 'the two together make a piece too long for the patience of most performers, and of all hearers'. The first movement *allegro* is in sonata form, though the second subject group of the recapitulation is much reduced. The exposition concludes with a codetta which includes a prominent flattened sixth, and is repeated, after which the exposition itself is repeated. The development soon modulates to B flat minor, then to A flat major, before concluding in the home dominant. The crossing of hands is necessary in this section. The editor has not directed a repeat of the development and recapitulation, which also includes the codetta, but this is a short movement and a repeat would seem desirable. The *larghetto con espressione* is a quiet movement in B flat and ABA form. The first part consists of eight bars and is repeated. The middle section, also of eight bars, closes in the subdominant. The next bar (17) is silent except for the single crotchet in the bass on the first beat; there is also a fermata. A three-bar coda follows the reprise of the first section. The repeat is from bar (9). The rondo finale is an *allegro di molto,* though some editions have it as a *presto,* with the editor's MM of crotchet=126. The layout is ABACA plus coda, with use being made of different registers of the keyboard, and with the second episode being of minor tonality before closing in the home dominant.

8. Clementi, Muzio. 'Introduction and Rondo' (page 100).

According to the editor, this selection is from the first of Clementi's two sonatas bearing the opus number 5. In actual fact, there are three of them in the set, each comprising two movements, and they are written for violin and piano. This is the first of them, and the key is B flat major. Only a small part of the introduction – twenty-two bars – is included. Marked *larghetto con espressivo,* it features dotted rhythms, ornamentation and syncopation, as well as contrasting dynamics. The rondo is given in full. An *allegro con spirito* tempo, with an MM of crotchet=126, its layout is ABACA plus coda. The second episode has some minor tonality colouring.

9. Corelli, Arcangelo. 'Sonata IX' (page 82). Piano transcription.

The ninth sonata from the composer's opus 5, it was originally written for violin and bass with thoroughbass accompaniment for a keyboard instrument. The editor has inserted harmony where necessary. The complete sonata has been selected. The first movement is a *largo* in common time. In binary form, it includes brief modulations to F# minor and C# minor in the second part. Each part is repeated. Next comes a *giga allegro* in 6–8 time, the modulation again being to C sharp minor, prior to the reprise of its first part. Again, each part is repeated. The third movement *adagio* in 3–4 time is only eight bars long. Initially in the relative minor, it finishes on that key's dominant – a common Baroque practice. The final movement is an *allegro* marked *tempo di Gavotta,* in common time and ABA form, with the middle episode, after a passage of sequential writing, again modulating to the key of C sharp minor.

10. Couperin, François. 'Slow March' (page 89).

Written in the key of A flat in common time, the performance direction for this short piece is *andante quasi larghetto.* Predominantly a quiet piece with short dynamic swells, it is in ABA form, the first six bars being repeated. The middle section comprises fourteen bars, leading into the reprise of the first part, which is extended into a short coda. François Couperin, *Couperin le Grand (*1668–1733) was a French harpsichordist, organist and composer, who was the nephew of Louis Couperin, also a composer of significance. Greatly influenced by Corelli, he wrote four books of *Pièces de Clavecin,* consisting of twenty-seven *ordres* (suites); he also wrote organ works, chamber music and religious works. Equally important was his publication in 1716 entitled *L'Art de toucher le clavecin,* a treatise upon the correct fingering, touch and ornamentation required for playing the harpsichord, which strongly influenced Johann Sebastian Bach.

11. Dussek, Jan Ladislav. 'French Air, *L'Amour est un enfant trompeur,* with Variations' (page 53).

The English translation of the title of this piece is 'Love is a deceitful child'. According to the editor, Dussek's intention in writing this piece was 'to please, rather than surprise'; certainly the air, directed to be played *andantino moderato,* is simplicity itself. It consists of two eight-bar phrases, the second of which is to be repeated, with detailed articulation instructions, two turns and a range of dynamics. The four variations require a certain amount of technical ability. Each is in binary form with each part repeated. The first, marked *mez(zo piano),* makes use of a demisemiquaver figure, and requires the crossing of hands. The second, marked *risoluto,* features triplet semiquavers largely in the right hand. The third is a gentle *con grazia*, again requiring the crossing of hands, while the final variation is an *allegretto*, with demisemiquaver figuration in the right hand.

12. Handel, George Frideric. 'Overture to "Esther" ' (page 1). Piano transcription.

The overture is in three parts. The first is an *andante maestoso* with a spiky dotted rhythm, in common time in B flat major, ending with two bars marked *adagio* on the dominant of G minor, in which key the second movement *larghetto* is written in 3–4 time. This movement, much of which involves a walking bass in octaves, also ends on the dominant of G minor, but the third movement, a fugal *allegro,* is back in the tonic B flat, albeit with some minor tonality colouring, in common time. In the original, the oboes feature prominently throughout. Originally composed as a masque entitled *Haman and Mordecai,* around the year 1720 for the Duke of Chandos's chapel, the score was considerably revised in 1732 to become the oratorio *Esther*. Based upon an Old

Testament drama by Jean Racine, it is considered to be the first English oratorio.

13. Handel, George Frideric. ' "Worthy is the Lamb" and "Amen" from " Messiah" ' (Page 40). Piano transcription.

In fact, these two choruses are treated as one number (53 in the Novello edition), the final choruses in *Messiah*. The text is taken from the Book of Revelation, chapter 5, verses 9, 12 and 13.

(Text line one) Worthy is the Lamb that was slain, and hath redeemed us to God by His blood;
(Text line two) To receive power, and riches, and wisdom, and strength, and honour, and glory, and blessing;
(Text line three) Blessing and honour, glory and pow'r be unto Him, be unto Him, that sitteth upon the throne, and unto the Lamb;
(Text line four) For ever, and ever, for ever, and ever;
(Text line five) Amen.

The key is D major, and the rhythm is common time. Text line one begins *largo,* the editor's MM being quaver=72, *ff*, on the second beat of the opening bar, and ends on the dominant of the relative minor. In bars (7)–(11) text line two is given, *andante,* with an MM of crotchet=60, marked *mez(zo) piano.* Both text lines, which are homophonic writing, are then repeated in bars (12)–(23), this time beginning in the dominant and closing in the tonic. Much of the bass line is directed to be played in octaves. At bar (24) the music becomes contrapuntal. The tempo direction is *larghetto,* with an MM of crotchet=72, and the subject is text line three, given initially in the tenors and basses in unison, with the answer in the soprano, beginning on the second beat of bar (28) and carried on into text line four at bar (33). The altos have entered half way through bar (32). Beginning on the anacrusis at bar (39), the voices enter with the subject *stretto.* There is a brief modulation to F sharp minor in bars (50)–(51) and a switch back to homophonic writing, *ff*, for the first half of text line three in bars (56)–(58/1) before the counterpoint returns for the second half of text line three. There is also much use of the voices singing in thirds. The chorus ends with the words 'For ever and ever', homophonic writing once again, *adagio,* in the dominant; thus, text line five may begin in the tonic D major.

'Amen' begins as a four-part fugue, directed to be performed *allegro moderato.* The six-bar subject is given in the bass, in left-hand octaves in the editor's transcription, with the tenor, alto and soprano entering in that order, *stretto,* after five bars. At bar (21) there is an orchestral interlude of ten bars, the first violins being followed by the seconds, before the bass entry with the subject, under a counter-subject in the other voices, and a further two-bar orchestral interlude in bars (36)–(37). There is another short incursion into F sharp in bars (60)–(61) and much imitation between the voices as the music ceases to be contrapuntal as the chorus nears its end. A C natural in the bass in bar (81) and fermata in bar (84) add drama to the closing stages. However, the editor has omitted the silent bar with fermata (85) which is unfortunate. Once again, the final bars are homophonic writing, *adagio,* and the oratorio ends with a triumphant D major tonic chord with fermata. (In the Novello Vocal Score, the last chord is notated as a breve). The original orchestration utilised oboes, trumpets and timpani in addition to the strings and continuo.

14. Handel, George Frideric. 'Overture to *Acis and Galatea*' (page 56). Piano transcription.

Written in B flat in common time, the overture is marked *presto (non troppo)* with an MM of crotchet=100. It features much sequential writing over a running quaver bass, marked *8vi sempre,* which is probably an unnecessary direction in a transcription of this nature. In the original orchestration, the semiquaver passages in thirds, which first appear in bar (13), are written for a pair of oboes. The editor has brought the piece to a conclusion with a perfect cadence, which is not the case with original, where the overture runs into the first chorus, 'Oh! the pleasure of the plains', without a break. Probably composed during the years 1718–1720, the text was written by John Gay, with additions by Alexander Pope and John Dryden. It has been described, alternatively, as a masque, oratorio, serenata and pastoral opera. There have been a number of adaptations made to the original, notably one by Mozart. The part of Acis is sung by a tenor, that of Galatea by a soprano.

15. Handel, George Frideric. 'Introduction and *Andante* (from the Eleventh Concerto)' (page 135). Piano transcription.

This is a selection from Handel's *Concerto Grosso,* opus 6, no. 11 in A, which was actually the last one of the set of twelve to be composed in 1739. The introduction is an abridged version of the original and is a *largo e staccato,* with an MM of quaver=100, in A major in common time. The last two bars of the fourteen are directed to be played *adagio.* Dotted rhythms and repeated notes in the right hand are a feature.

The close is on the dominant in order to facilitate the entry of the *andante con moto,* also in A; in Italian concerto form, it is the penultimate of the five movements. The deceptively simple ritornello theme alternates with gigue-like passages for solo strings, each reprise of the ritornello being subtly varied, with a number of modulations throughout.

16. Haydn, Franz Josef. '*Andante* and Variations' (page 6). Piano transcription.

The *(larghetto quasi) andante* is the second movement, in the subdominant G, of Haydn's Symphony Number 75 in D. It consists of a simple melody in two sections, of eight and ten bars respectively, each repeated. There are four variations and a coda. The first variation makes use of right-hand decoration, the second portrays the brass instruments, the third has a semiquaver running bass, and the last, along with the coda marked *legato,* uses a sextuplet motif, mostly in an inner right-hand part. The orchestral scoring is for flute *obligato,* two oboes, two trumpets or horns, and strings. The *adagio* prefixed to it is taken from Haydn's Symphony Number 92 in G, known as the 'Oxford', written about 1788. This short extract consists of only fifteen bars, closing on the dominant after three bars of chromatic harmony, to lead into the succeeding *andante.*

17. Haydn, Franz Josef. 'Seventh Quartet' (from 'Seven Last Words from the Cross') (page 37). Piano transcription.

The score is headed with the words *In manus tuas, Domine, commendo spiritum meum,* translated as 'Father, into Thy hands I commend my spirit'. It is a *largo* in E flat in 3–4 time. A quiet movement, it is in binary form. The first part, which contains interesting modulations to F minor and G minor before settling in the dominant, is repeated. In the second part, after a brief reprise of the opening theme, the first violin has a poignant passage of triplet writing, and there is much chromaticism. Haydn's 'Seven Last Words of Our Saviour from the Cross' – *Die sieben letzten Worte unseres Erlösers am Kreuz* – was a work commissioned by Cádiz Cathedral in 1785 as a set of seven orchestral interludes to separate the bishop's sermons at the Good Friday service. The original scoring was for strings, flutes, oboes, bassoons, horns, trumpets and timpani. The seven movements were concluded with a short, furious C minor *presto,* the only section of the work to be played at anything other than a slow tempo, depicting the earthquake which occurred at the moment of Christ's death. The firm of Artaria, Vienna, published the work in string quartet form in 1787. Also in that year, the piano adaptation was made, not by Haydn, but with his approval.

18. Haydn, Franz Josef. '*Pastorale* from the First Sonata' (Opus 41). (Page 75). Piano transcription.

This is the first movement of Haydn's Sonata in G, Hoboken 40, marked *allegretto innocente,* in 6–8 time. It is cleverly constructed, in that there are two themes in the following sequence – theme one in G major, theme two in G minor, theme one varied, theme two varied, theme one varied. The first theme is in ABA form, the repeats being of the first eight bars and bars (9)–(24). The second is in binary form, and consists of two six-bar phrases, each repeated. The variations, which follow the same pattern of repeats, become progressively more technical. The editor is of the opinion that 'the beauty and originality of this almost unknown work of the composer will be at once obvious to all persons of taste'.

19. Haydn, Franz Joseph. 'Slow Movement (from the Symphony in G)' (page 130). Piano transcription.

This selection is the second movement of Haydn's Symphony 92 in G, the 'Oxford', a nickname acquired because the composer chose it to be performed under his direction on the occasion of his receiving an honorary degree of Doctor of Music at Oxford University in 1791, it having been written, however, three years earlier. An *adagio cantabile e legato* it is written in D major (V) in 2–4 time, and is in ABA form with coda. It begins with the tonic chord in second inversion – root position is not reached until bar (4) – with an eight-bar theme (4+4), *p*, which is repeated with variation. New material is introduced before a reprise of the main theme, varied. The middle section provides a contrast in that it is in the tonic minor and juxtaposes *f* and *p* passages. The orchestral scoring is for flute, two each of oboes, bassoons, horns and trumpets, strings and timpani.

20. Himmel, Friedrich Heinrich. 'Divertissement' (page 125).

The 'Divertissement' is selected from Himmel's opus 30. According to the editor 'the metronomic figures show the times in which the three movements were played by the composer himself, but they may be slightly moderated by those who cannot neatly execute the passages with the degree of quickness indicated'. The three movements, all in 3–4 time, are *molto vivace* in C major (70 bars), *allegro moderato* in F (32 bars), and *allegro molto quasi presto* in C (95 bars). The technical difficulties, in the third movement in particular, are considerable; they include the playing of rapid thirds and octaves, and thirds within octaves, the whole range of the keyboard being utilised.

21. Krumpholz, Johann Baptist. 'Romanza' (page 105). Piano transcription.

This *Romanza* is taken from Krumpholz's popular harp concerto, arranged by Dussek, and adapted for inclusion in *The Musical Library* for performance on pianofortes which had developed from the instruments of Dussek's time. Four bars of introduction, in which are included two arpeggios to be sustained on the pedal, lead into the *Romanza,* marked *larghetto,* which is in three sections. The first is in D minor in ternary form, respectively of sixteen, eight and eight bars, numbers (17)–(32) being repeated. The second section, again in ternary form, is in the tonic major with much use of the upper notes of the keyboard, and a cadenza, and the third is a reprise of the first, breaking off into a short coda. The elder of two brothers, Wenzel being the younger, Johann Baptist Krumpholz (1742–1790) was a Bohemian composer and harpist who wrote for that instrument. A member of Prince Esterházy's chapel, he took composition lessons from Haydn. . Later he lived in Paris as a teacher and virtuoso. His wife was also an accomplished harpist who, however, was unfaithful to him, which fact apparently caused him to drown himself in the Seine. According to *The Musical Library Supplement*, 'Madame K's conduct after [her husband's death] was not marked by discretion, and she died a few years ago, in circumstances which the admirers of talent could not but deplore'. It is thought that it was Wenzel Krumpholz who introduced the young Carl Czerny to Beethoven in 1799.

22. Kuhlau, Friedrich. 'Brilliant Rondo' (page 156).

This piece is described by the editor as a 'Brilliant Rondo' on an air in Hérold's opera *Marie*, opus 97. The libretto is by Louis Joseph Hérold, and the air is *Batelier, dit Lisette,* which translates as 'Boatman, says Lisette'. The editor goes on to say that 'the introduction and latter part of the rondo are here abridged'. The introduction, marked *allegro brilliante,* consists of just three bars, containing an arpeggio flourish which closes into a *marcato* cadence ending on a dominant chord in first inversion, with fermata. The rondo begins with as an *allegro moderato,* with the editor's MM of dotted crotchet=80, in 6–8 time, over a drone bass. Midway through its first thirty-three bars, the tempo briefly slows. At the thirty-fourth bar, however, it increases to *più allegro,* the new MM being dotted crotchet=88. There is much brilliant figuration in this section, with most of the upper range of the keyboard being used. A cadenza-like passage leads to a brief reprise of the beginning of the opening *allegro moderato,* but the tonality soon changes, first to the tonic minor then to C major. A *presto* coda concludes the piece.

23. Lindpaintner, Peter Josef von. 'Romance and Rondo' (page 31).

The 'Romance and Rondo' comes from Lindpaintner's ballet *Zephir et Rose.* The romance is an *andante* in 6–8 time, marked *dolce,* and, but for a short passage towards its end, is predominantly quiet. Dotted rhythms are a feature. Its opening four bars appear three times. The rondo, in ABA form, is a short *allegretto grazioso un poco lento* in 2–4 time, ending in a ten-bar coda, the final four bars of which are marked *fff*. A German violinist and conductor, Kapellmeister to the King of Würtemberg, whose conducting skills were admired by Mendelssohn and Berlioz amongst others, Lindpaintner is best remembered for his opera *Der Vampyr* (The Vampire).

24. Marin, Marie-Martin Marcel, Vicomte de. 'Slow Movement' (page 150).

Marin's *Nouvelle grande sonata,* opus 31, originally written for the harp, and adapted for pianoforte by Clementi, opens with a slow introductory *adagio.* Marked *un poco adagio cantabile,* in 3–4 time, it is an unremarkable piece in three sections, the outer two in A major the middle one in the tonic minor. It is little more than an étude. The Vicomte, born in 1769, was a French harpist, violinist and composer of Venetian descent, whose compositions for harp, some of which were published by Clementi, were regarded by the musicologist and critic François-Joseph Fétis as 'truly classical'.

25. Martini, Giuseppe San. 'First and Last Movements of the Ninth Trio', opus 111 (page 26). Piano transcription.

These two movements are the first and, according to the editor, last from the ninth of *xii Sonate a due Violioni e Cembalo, se piace, Opera 3za* (opus 3), published in London about the year 174 . The first movement is an *allegro* in A minor in 3–4 time, with some characteristic violin figuration in the right hand. The finale, also in 3–4 time, is an *andante grazioso* rondo, ABA plus coda. The opening section comprises sixteen bars, while the middle section has an episode in the tonic minor. After the reprise of the first section, the movement closes with a twelve-bar coda. In bars (13)–(14), and in the equivalent bars in the third section, there is a chain of trills in the right hand which requires a sound technique in performance given that a series of inner notes must also be played by the same hand. Giuseppe san Martini, more often known as Sammartini, was born in Milan about the year 1693, but lived much of his life in London where he was an oboist and teacher, as well as a composer of trio sonatas such as the one included here. He died probably in 1750.

26. Mendelssohn-Bartholdy, Felix. 'Canzonetta à Quatre Mains', opus 12 (page 44). Piano transcription.

The *Canzonetta* à *Quatre Mains* is an arrangement for pianoforte duet of the third movement of Mendelssohn's String Quartet in E flat, opus 12, completed in September 1829. Although not designated as such in *The Musical Library,* it is really a scherzo and trio. The tempo of the scherzo is *allegretto con moto,* and the time signature is 2–4. Written in G minor, it is in binary form. The two parts, each of which is repeated, consist of, respectively, fourteen and sixteen bars. The trio, in the tonic major, is marked *piu mosso, pp, staccato*. It, too, is in binary form, again with the two parts being repeated. A bridge passage leads to a reprise of the scherzo without its repeats. Towards the end, the original scoring includes *pizzicato* writing. It is typical Mendelssohn, and by no means easy to play at the correct tempo. One of the major composers of the nineteenth-century's Romantic era, Felix Mendelssohn was born in Hamburg in 1809. A child prodigy as pianist, organist, and composer – his remarkable Octet for strings was written when he was just sixteen years of age, and his 'Overture to *A Midsummer Night's Dream*' a year later – he had four years earlier begun a friendship with the poet Goethe, sixty years his senior. His compositions include five symphonies, the oratorio *Elijah*, much piano music, including his set of *Lieder ohne Worter* (Songs without Words), chamber music and songs. He died at Leipzig in November 1847, six months after the sudden death of his sister Fanny, herself an accomplished pianist and composer.

27. Moscheles, Ignaz. 'Divertissement (Opus 28)' (page 153).

The tempo is *andantino con moto quasi allegretto,* and the time signature is 2–4. In rondo form, the key is E flat, with a middle section in the subdominant A flat. The main theme consists of two eight-bar phrases, each repeated. The middle section is the longest; an eight-bar phrase is answered by one of similar length, leading to a sequential passage, and then a reprise of the first sixteen bars, ornamented and extended to close into a reprise of the opening section. A twenty-six bar coda, much of it over a tonic pedal, concludes the piece. The word *divertissement* translates as 'amusement'. There are six *Divertissements ou Caprices* which constitute Moscheles' opus 28, of 1814; another one is to be found as number twenty-seven in Volume Four, below. According to the editor, the original of this piece has been revised and enlarged by the composer for *The Musical Library.*

28. Mozart, Wolfgang Amadeus. 'Air, with Variations' (page 21).

The editor states – 'This is an abridgement of the original, and adapted to the modern piano-forte'. The air is a simple eight-bar *allegretto* in A major in common time. Beginning on the third beat of the bar, a four-bar phrase is answered by one of similar length, the eight bars being repeated. A further four-bar phrase (2+2) is answered by a repeat of bars (4)–(8). Bars (9)–(16) are then repeated. There are seven variations. The first three all involve right-hand decoration of the melody, respectively in triplets, semiquavers and quavers. The cross rhythms in the first variation require a sound technique. The fourth, in the tonic minor, consists largely of running semiquavers passed between the hands, the fifth reverts to the major key and makes use of distinctive semiquaver figuration in the right hand with some crossing of hands, and the sixth, marked *un poco piu lento,* uses right-hand turns and trills as ornamentation. The final variation begins *allegro,* with semiquaver arpeggios in the right hand and octaves in the left, for seven and a half bars. The next bar is silent and, *tempo primo,* the air returns for four bars in its original form, then with triplet decoration, and a short coda *ff.*

29. Mozart, Wolfgang Amadeus. 'Tema, with Variations and Rondo, for Piano-Forte and Violin' (page 63).

The editor states – 'The accompaniment, slightly altered, may be played on the flute'. The need for slight alteration arises partly by virtue of the fact that the violin part occasionally drops below middle C, the lowest note normally obtainable on the flute, and partly because it would not be possible to reproduce the violin's occasional double stopping. This is the second movement of Mozart's Sonata for Violin and Piano, K377. The theme is an *andante* in D minor in 2–4 time, syncopated and ornamented with turns. The first eight bars are given by the piano and repeated by the violin with piano accompaniment. The piano then resumes the theme, at first imitated a bar later by the violin a perfect fifth lower, in a delightful eight-bar phrase which is then repeated, with the violin this time having the upper part. There are five variations, each in binary form, with each part being repeated. The first involves further imitative dialogue between the instruments, while in the second the theme is decorated with triplets by the violin. In the third variation the theme is given by the violin over a piano accompaniment of demisemiquavers, and in the fourth, which is in the tonic major, there is further skilful counterpoint and imitation between the instruments. The violin and piano play in octaves for much of the fifth variation over a bass of fuller texture, before a sixteen-bar coda brings this delightful and beautifully constructed movement to a close.

30. Mozart, Wolfgang Amadeus. 'Rondo' (page 69).

The finale to Mozart's Sonata for Violin and Piano, K377, is a minuet in F. The title 'rondo' is given by the editor, who does not actually name the composer at the head of the first page. The relatively simple violin part can be played on the flute, albeit that allowances have to be made for four bars of double-stopping in the bridge passage which leads to the return of the main theme and six bars in the coda. In each case, the upper notes are the ones that should be played by the flautist. The layout is ABCA plus coda. The movement, in 3–4 time, is directed to be played *un poco allegretto.*

31. Mozart, Wolfgang Amadeus. 'Overture to *Cosi fan tutte*' (page 145). Piano transcription.

The overture is written in C major with a cut-**C** time signature. It opens with a fourteen-bar *andante* by way of introduction, a solo oboe, *p*, answering the *f* orchestral chords. Then the tempo increases to *presto,* the MM being minim=112, for the rest of the overture which is in sonata form. The development section begins in the relative minor and passes through a number of modulating sequences, before fourteen bars of dominant preparation lead to the recapitulation and a coda. Woodwind solo passages feature throughout. A transcription of this overture was also included in the scores acquired by Emily in the 1830s.

32. Plachy, Wenzel. 'Air *Non v'ha sguardo* from Donizetti's *Anna Bolena,* with three Variations' (page 140). Piano transcription.

The air is sung by Anna Bolena in Act Three. The correct title of Plachy's variations is: *Variations pour le Piano Forte sur la Cavatina de l'Opera, Anna Bolena,* opus 61, and, according to the editor, there are three variations. The work begins with a seven-bar introduction, *andante maestoso,* in 2–4 time, linked by a short cadenza to the air. This is a simple sixteen-bar melody in binary form, the first eight bars closing in E minor (iii). There is an interrupted cadence in bars (13)–(14), followed by a diminished seventh chord and a 6–4, 5–3 cadence to conclude. Each part is repeated, the tempo being *moderato.* The first variation is marked *poco piu moderato.* The second is in two parts, a *scherzando* followed by a *cantabile* beginning in G marked *poco piu lento,* which includes a modulation to B minor, at which point there is a florid *presto* cadenza, and there is another much longer one, *vivace,* leading into the final variation, back in C major, marked *animato.* It is not clear why the editor has regarded the second variation as being in two parts, rather than designating these parts as distinct variations in their own right. Donizetti's opera *Anna Bolena,* with a libretto by Felice Romani, received its fist performance in Milan in December 1830. Gaetano Donizetti (1797–1848) was an Italian composer most noted for his operas, of which he wrote seventy-five.

33. Ries, Ferdinand. 'March' (page 18).

This march in C major was composed for the *Harmonicon.* Marked *maestoso,* and with much use being made of dotted rhythms, it is in three sections, the first of which contains an interesting modulation to E minor (iii), and is repeated. The second section begins in the subdominant, modulates briefly to D minor, before the dominant preparation, involving some crossing of hands, leads to a reprise of the first part of the march. Then follows a trio which also starts in the subdominant, but soon modulates to A major, then A minor, in which key the first part closes, and is repeated. F major tonality is soon restored, but there is an unusual switch to A flat for one bar only – bar (15). Finally the march is repeated *DC,* but without its own repeats.

34. Rossini, Gioacchino Antonio. 'March, *Tancredi*' (page 62). Piano transcription.

In D major, common time, and directed to be played *maestoso*, this march is in binary form, with the first part ending in the dominant, and being repeated. The opera *Tancredi* has already been discussed. (11)

35. Rossini, Gioacchino Antonio. 'Overture to *Demetrio e Polibio*' (page 94). Piano transcription.

The overture is in C major and it begins with an eight-bar adagio in common time. This is followed by a twenty-four bar andante in 6–8 time, in the nature of a melody, which in the original orchestration is a solo for bassoon subsequently joined by an oboe, and which ends on the dominant, thereby enabling a close into an allegro in C. An eight-bar theme is repeated an octave higher, and after a transition the second subject group enters in the dominant, G major, with another bassoon solo. The twenty-two bar development is in E flat with further material on the oboe prior to the recapitulation, and a twenty-two bar coda to conclude. This was Rossini's first opera, composed in 1806, with a libretto by Vincenzina Viganò-Mombelli. It was first performed in Rome in 1812; hence, it was not the composer's first staged opera. Polibio is King of Parthia and his part is sung by a bass, while Demetrio is King of Syria, his role being taken by a tenor.

36. Ruppe, Christian Friederich. 'Rondo' (page 108).

Taken from Ruppe's Sonata in D minor, opus 26, this is an *allegretto mosso,* with an MM of quaver=152, and a time signature of 2–4, in an ABACA layout. Section A comprises an eight-bar phrase (4+4) answered by one of the same length, and concluding with one of six-bars (2+2+2). Section B begins in D minor but soon modulates to the relative major. It comprises right-hand triplets and some crossing of hands to introduce a new melody in a lower register. Section A is then repeated. Section C is written in the tonic major, with a new theme added in the local dominant, thereby providing a bright contrast to the previous sections, before section A returns to conclude the movement. Ruppe, who lived from 1753–1826, was a Dutch composer and organist, and Maitre-de-Chapelle at the University in Leiden. This rondo, published in Amsterdam, is typical of the piano pieces he wrote.

37. Schobert, Johann. 'Sonata (Op. 10)' (page 78). Piano transcription.

In sonata form in E flat major and 3–4 time, this unexceptional movement is marked *allegro assai*. The exposition, which comprises much unison playing between the hands and the use of pedal points, is repeated. The development modulates to G minor, then B flat major, the home dominant, to close into the recapitulation in the tonic. There is a resemblance to the first movement of Mozart's Sonata in C minor, K457 in bars (94)–(97). Only the first subject of the exposition is given in the recapitulation, with a coda concluding the movement. Schobert's three opus 10 works are properly called 'Symphonies for Harpsichord, Violin and two Horns *ad lib*'. This first one was transcribed for keyboard. The editor has omitted the second movement on the grounds that 'it is unequal to the first'. Most of Schobert's compositional output was written for harpsichord, on which instrument he was accomplished, within a small chamber ensemble. He was a German composer, born round about the year 1720. According to Grove, his death in 1767, along with those of his complete family, except for one small child, a friend and his servant, was caused by eating poisonous mushrooms.

38. Schröter, Johann Samuel. 'Rondo'(page112). Piano transcription.

This Rondo is taken from Schröter's Piano Concerto number 2, opus 5. In F major, and marked *tempo di minuetto,* it is in ABA form. The episode begins in the tonic minor before modulating to its relative major, A flat. Ultimately, twenty bars of dominant preparation lead to a return of the main theme (A), initially in a higher register, plus a short coda, with a *ff* ending. Johann Samuel Schröter (*c*1752–1788) was a pianist and composer from a German musical family, though he was born in Warsaw. He was also a teacher, one of whose pupils was Johann Baptist Cramer. His *oeuvre* consisted mainly of pianoforte music, both sonatas and concertos.

39. Steibelt, Daniel. 'Selection from the 19th Pot-Pourri' (page 90).

The editor's selection from Steibelt's nineteenth 'Pot-Pourri' in D major begins with an *andante con espressione* in common time, with the editor's MM of crotchet=60, leading straight into an *air Russe,* marked *allegro moderato,* now with an MM of quaver=126, in 2–4 time. The two sections consist of, respectively, nineteen and eighteen bars, which is rather unusual. Based upon the material of this opening section are six short variations featuring brilliant figuration, but little in the way of instructions as to performance direction. Each variation follows the previous one without a break. The first is dominant/tonic based, while the second features demisemiquaver arpeggios in each hand, sometimes together in contrary motion. The third employs dotted notation and the skilful use of semiquaver rests. Double-dotted rhythms and an extensive use of the upper range of the keyboard feature in the fourth variation, while the fifth uses right-hand triplets, and the sixth has the theme picked out in inner parts in a fuller texture.

40. Composer unknown. 'Marquis of Granby's March (for Flute and Piano-Forte)' (page 134).

The march is a short one consisting of only twenty bars, marked *maestoso,* with an *ad lib.* flute part. In B flat major in common time, its harmony is largely tonic/dominant, the dotted rhythm being appropriate for its purpose. The editor was unable to name the composer of this piece; it is likely to have been played originally by a military band.

41. Woelfl, Joseph. 'Adagio from a Sonata (Opus 25)' (page 34). Marked on the Contents page.

Taken from Woelfl's opus 25 Sonata in C minor, published in 1803, the *adagio* is the penultimate movement, written in the key of A flat major, in 3–4 time. It is in the form of a rondo with an ABA layout. The main theme (A) consists of eight bars, *p*, closing in the dominant. Two sequential two-bar phrases follow, and a third overlaps in its second bar with a five-bar phrase with minor tonality colouring, which closes with a V7-I cadence into E flat major. The episode (B) begins at bar (19) with a new phrase involving a figure (x) sequentially in E flat, but this is interrupted abruptly by repeated chords in C flat, alternatively *f* and *p*, with the figure in the left hand, before closing into E flat. However, after a further six bars another modulation leads to a very brief incursion into G minor, which key is abruptly vacated, three further bars leading into the key of D flat major at bar (37) which is much closer to A flat, the key in which the movement started. A modulating sequence now begins, proceeding in two-bar steps from D flat major to E flat minor to F minor then, with the addition of an extra bar, back to D flat. Ensuing chromatic harmony leads to V of F minor, but the resolution is, instead, into the tonic major key of A flat. The main theme (A) returns at bar (52), this time over a florid bass line of semiquavers and demisemiquavers. At bar (60), the equivalent of bar (9), the music necessarily stays in the tonic, though with some minor colouring, remote tonalities, and some change in notation before the movement closes *pp*. For some reason this piece appears again in *The Musical Library* – in Volume Four at page 151. On that occasion, the editor has added to the end of the piece the words 'The Minuet and Trio to follow at pleasure'. Joseph Woelfl (1773–1812), pianist and composer, was born in Salzburg, and studied there under Leopold Mozart and Michael Haydn. He was another pianist to come off second best in a piano duel with Beethoven. A tall man with huge hands, his contemporary, the pianist Johann Wenzel Tomaschek, wrote that Woelfl could stretch a tenth. His compositional output, which is of little intrinsic value, included two symphonies, operas, six piano concertos, chamber music and music for the pianoforte, including this sonata. He died in London, in which regard 'The Musical Supplement' had this to say – 'unfortunately, this able musician divided his attentions equally between Apollo and Bacchus; and to his libations in honour of the son of Semele his premature departure from this world is to be mainly attributed.'

Volume Three
1836
Parsonage library reference 1131/4
42 Pieces – 6 Marked on the Contents Page

1. Bach, Carl Philipp Emanuel. 'Rondo' (page 6).

This is a rondo *andantino* in E flat, the layout being ABA, with a 2–4 time signature. It is Wq.61/1 in Alfred Wotquenne's catalogue. Section A is itself in ternary form, its first part consisting of sixteen bars, the second thirty, and the third, which is a reprise of the first this time closing in the dominant, is also of sixteen. Section B develops the material in a variety of different keys – D flat, A minor and, after a two-bar diminished seventh arpeggio, C minor. The reprise is of only the first sixteen-bar part of A, closing into a twenty-nine-bar coda to conclude. This is a movement which looks forward to the keyboard works of Dussek and Clementi. *The Musical Library Monthly Supplement* has this to say: 'In the opinion of all music critics, this is the best instrumental work that ever proceeded from the pen of the composer'. Carl Philipp Emanuel Bach (1714–1788), the second son of Johann Sebastian Bach, was another composer who was originally intended for a career in the law. Cembalist at the court of Frederick the Great, and subsequently successor to Telemann as director of church music at Hamburg, his greatest achievement was his development of sonata form, as evidenced in his considerable output of keyboard sonatas, sinfonias and concertos. He wrote choral music for the church, and an important treatise on klavier-playing, *Essay on the True Art of Playing Keyboard Instruments.* Mozart said of him, 'He is the father, we are the children'.

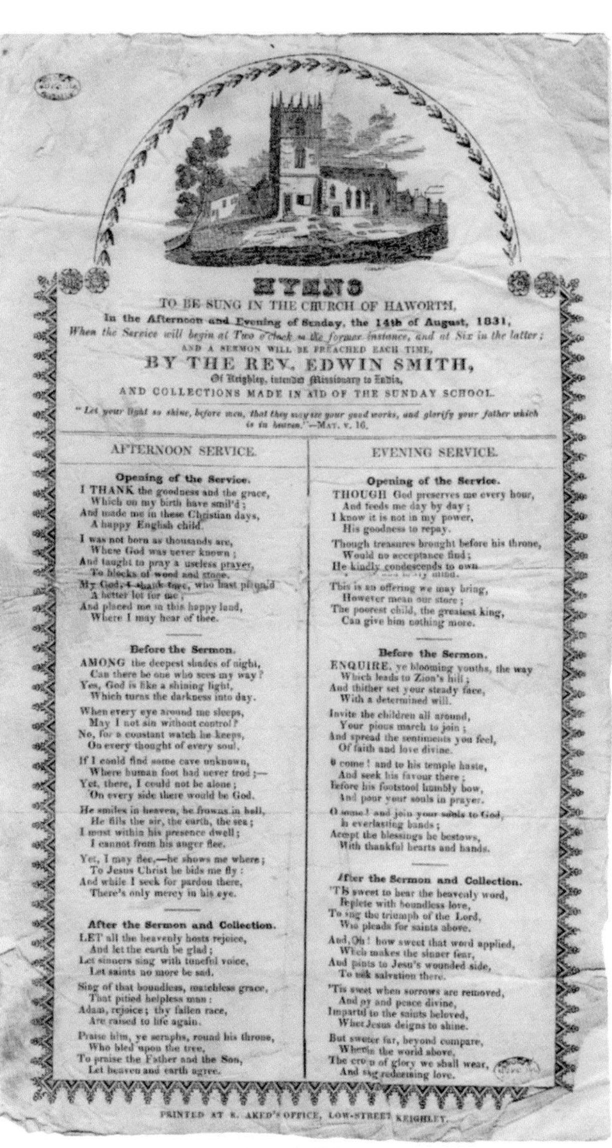

HYMNS

TO BE SUNG IN THE CHURCH OF HAWORTH,

In the Afternoon and Evening of Sunday, the 14th of August, 1831,

When the Service will begin at Two o'clock in the former instance, and at Six in the latter;

AND A SERMON WILL BE PREACHED EACH TIME,

BY THE REV. EDWIN SMITH,

Of Keighley, intended Missionary to India,

AND COLLECTIONS MADE IN AID OF THE SUNDAY SCHOOL.

"Let your light so shine, before men, that they may see your good works, and glorify your father which is in heaven."—MAT. v. 16.

AFTERNOON SERVICE.

Opening of the Service.

I THANK the goodness and the grace,
Which on my birth have smil'd;
And made me in these Christian days,
A happy English child.

I was not born as thousands are,
Where God was never known;
And taught to pray a useless prayer,
To blocks of wood and stone.

My God, I thank thee, who hast plann'd
A better lot for me;
And placed me in this happy land,
Where I may hear of thee.

Before the Sermon.

AMONG the deepest shades of night,
Can there be one who sees my way?
Yes, God is like a shining light,
Which turns the darkness into day.

When every eye around me sleeps,
May I not sin without control?
No, for a constant watch he keeps,
On every thought of every soul.

If I could find some cave unknown,
Where human foot had never trod;—
Yet, there, I could not be alone;
On every side there would be God.

He smiles in heaven, he frowns in hell,
He fills the air, the earth, the sea;
I must within his presence dwell;
I cannot from his anger flee.

Yet, I may flee,—he shows me where;
To Jesus Christ he bids me fly:
And while I seek for pardon there,
There's only mercy in his eye.

After the Sermon and Collection.

LET all the heavenly hosts rejoice,
And let the earth be glad;
Let sinners sing with tuneful voice,
Let saints no more be sad.

Sing of that boundless, matchless grace,
That pitied helpless man:
Adam, rejoice; thy fallen race,
Are raised to life again.

Praise him, ye seraphs, round his throne,
Who bled upon the tree,
To praise the Father and the Son,
Let heaven and earth agree.

EVENING SERVICE.

Opening of the Service.

THOUGH God preserves me every hour,
And feeds me day by day;
I know it is not in my power,
His goodness to repay.

Though treasures brought before his throne,
Would no acceptance find;
He kindly condescends to own
[illegible]

This is an offering we may bring,
However mean our store;
The poorest child, the greatest king,
Can give him nothing more.

Before the Sermon.

ENQUIRE, ye blooming youths, the way
Which leads to Zion's hill;
And thither set your steady face,
With a determined will.

Invite the children all around,
Your pious march to join;
And spread the sentiments you feel,
Of faith and love divine.

O come! and to his temple haste,
And seek his favour there;
Before his footstool humbly bow,
And pour your souls in prayer.

O come! and join your souls to God,
In everlasting bands;
Accept the blessings he bestows,
With thankful hearts and hands.

After the Sermon and Collection.

'TIS sweet to hear the heavenly word,
Replete with boundless love,
To sing the triumph of the Lord,
Who pleads for saints above.

And, Oh! how sweet that word applied,
Which makes the sinner fear,
And points to Jesu's wounded side,
To seek salvation there.

'Tis sweet when sorrows are removed,
And joy and peace divine,
Imparted to the saints beloved,
When Jesus deigns to shine.

But sweeter far, beyond compare,
When in the world above,
The crown of glory we shall wear,
And sing redeeming love.

PRINTED AT R. AKED'S OFFICE, LOW-STREET KEIGHLEY.

Hymn Sheet for Service in Haworth Church
14 August 1831
(Brontë Society)

The gold-painted panel on the Parsonage piano (Ken Forrest)

Emily's painting of a Merlin Hawk (possibly Nero) dated 27 October 1841
(Brontë Society)

The Organ, Haworth Old Church

Ponden Hall
(John Hennessy – permission of Julie Akhurst)

Ludwig van Beethoven
Miniature in Ivory by Christian Hornemann, 1803
(Beethoven-Haus, Bonn)

The Parsonage Piano
without its silk-pleated screen in Ken Forrest's workshop
(Ken Forrest)

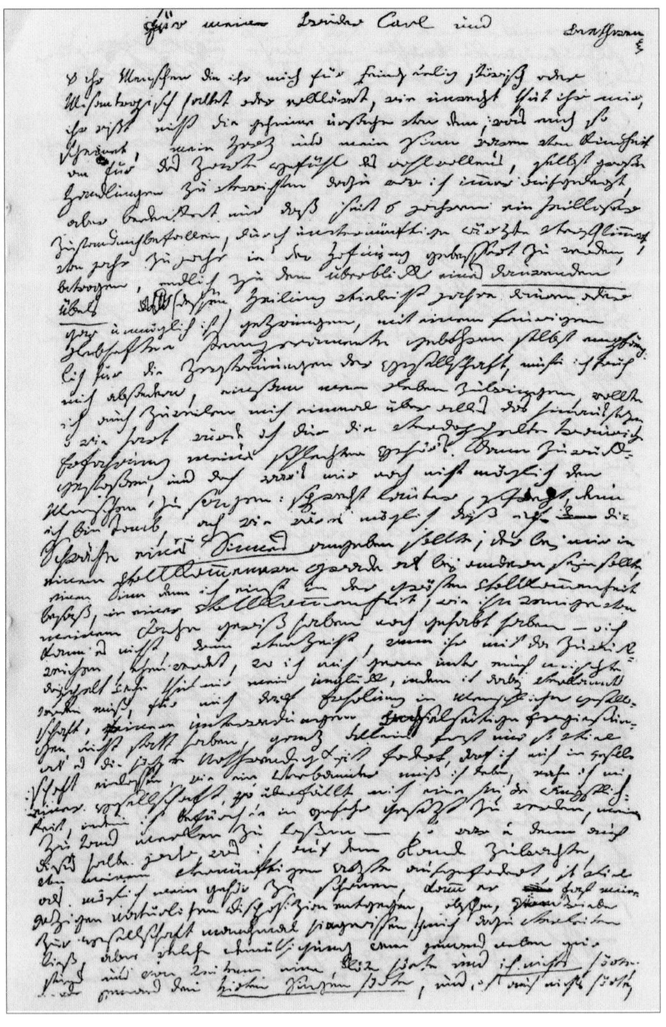

The Heiligenstadt Testament (First page)
(Original in the National and Universal Library, Hamburg)
'The only thing that held me back [from suicide] *was art. For indeed it seemed to me impossible to leave this world before I had produced all the works that I felt the urge to compose.'*

2. Beethoven, Ludwig van. 'Serenade for Flute and Pianoforte' (page 1). Piano transcription.

This selection is a hybrid, consisting of parts of two of Beethoven's works. The *poco adagio* is the first fourteen bars (of seventeen) of the middle movement of Beethoven's Sonata for Horn and Piano, opus 17. The key is F minor and the time signature 2–4. It concludes with a dominant seventh chord plus fermata, thus enabling the next movement to start in F major. The *andante quasi allegretto* and *allegro* are two sections of the final movement of the Serenade for Violin, Viola and Cello in D, opus 8, here transposed up a minor third to F major. The first part consists of a sixteen-bar binary theme, each of the eight bars repeated, and four variations. In the first variation, the melodic decoration is provided by the flute (violin in the original), and in the second by the piano (viola in the original). The third is in the tonic minor and involves syncopation, while the fourth reverts to the major with the piano having the theme (cello in the original), and the flute providing an accompaniment. This section is followed by an *allegro* in 6–8 time, with the piano and flute taking it in turns to vary the theme, before an interesting modulation to D flat leads to a coda, with a *tempo primo* direction, once again in 2–4 time. The editor has declined to include the march with which the original serenade ends. Not for the first time in his comments on pieces in *The Musical Library*, he suggests that, in the absence of a flute or violin, the accompaniment could be taken by a third hand on the keyboard.

3. Beethoven, Ludwig van. 'Pastoral Symphony (A Portion of)' (page 61). Piano transcription. Marked on the Contents page.

The editor's choice is the exposition of the first movement together with the third movement *scherzo* and trio. The titles of the movements are not given in *The Musical Library* transcriptions. (12) Tovey describes the harmony of these two movements, plus the finale, as being of 'rustic simplicity'. (13) The analysis which follows is based upon the full orchestral score, not just the piano transcription. The first movement, which is in sonata form, is entitled *Angenehme, heitere Empfindigung, welche bei derAnkunft auf dem Lande im Menschen erwachen* which translates as 'Awakening of happy feelings on arrival in the country', and is directed to be played *allegro ma non troppo,* Beethoven's 1817 MM being minim=66. The key is F major. The first subject group of the exposition opens with a four-bar theme in the first violins, beginning after a quaver rest on an offbeat, *p*, over a double pedal in the violas and cellos, and with a fermata over the fourth bar. It is answered by the second violins and violas, with the first violins supplying a countersubject. The five notes in the first violins in bar (2) constitute an important figure. A third four-bar phrase is immediately repeated. At bar (16), a five-note figure of distinctive rhythm enters and is repeated for thirteen bars, initially in the first violins latterly in the seconds, over a dominant pedal, with a dynamic swell. (This repetition of short phrases will occur throughout the movement.) At bar (29), the main theme enters given by the oboes, but without the first quaver rest. This material is developed by the whole orchestra, with grace notes in the first flute redolent of birdsong, until bar (53). The transition consists of a bar of triplets in the clarinets and bassoons, followed by a three-bar figure given in the first violins, *p*, then woodwind triplets and pizzicato lower strings for eight bars. The second subject group begins at bar (64) with, in

Beethoven's original score, a new eight-bar theme given in the cellos under a quaver countersubject in the first violins for four bars and the second violins for the next four. However, from here, and for the next seventy-four bars, the editor's piano transcription is not an accurate representation of the original. He rounds off his selection with a further twenty-five bars using material from the end of the movement.

The third movement is entitled *Lustiges Zusammensein der Landleute,* the English translation being 'Joyous gathering of country folk'. It is a boisterous scherzo in 3–4 time, *allegro,* Beethoven's 1817 MM being dotted minim=108. Once again the key is F major. The main theme consists of sixteen bars, the first eight being given in the strings, *pp*, answered by a phrase of similar length with the first flute added and then the first oboe joining in, closing on the dominant of G major. The sixteen bars are repeated. This material is used amongst the different orchestral instruments until bar (52/3) when the whole orchestra gives the first six bars of the main theme, *ff*, before progressing to a new eight-bar phrase of broad writing with *sf* emphasis, which is repeated, to close into a four-bar cadence phrase, itself repeated, the last two bars being twice insisted upon. Four further bars, *diminuendo,* lead to a new theme given in the first oboe, *pp*, beginning at bar (91/2), over an incessantly repeated figure in the violins, and short, though important, contributions from the second bassoon and first clarinet. At bar (122) the first clarinet takes over the solo before handing over to the first horn at bar (133). The final twenty-four bars are used to prepare for the entry of the trio.

The trio opens with a change of time signature to 2–4 and a new tempo, *allegro.* A rustic four-bar theme is given in the violins four times, with much *sf* emphasis. Then, while the bassoons and cellos continue with the theme, the violins now add a four-bar countersubject; these four bars are repeated, to be followed by a further four bars, themselves repeated, slightly varied. A further eight bars, *sempre più forte,* bring the trio to a conclusion, the huge chord in bar (203) being marked *ff* followed by *diminuendo* and fermata over the rest, with the final chord plus fermata being marked *p*, although the editor does not include all these directions in the piano transcription. The coda uses the original material, and a new tempo of *presto* halfway through, until the movement terminates suddenly and dramatically, leading without a break into the fourth movement *Gewitter, Sturm* (Tempest, Storm). The editor, of necessity, has to conclude his selection with a contrived perfect cadence.

Beethoven wrote his Symphony Number 6 in F, opus 68, in 1808, and dedicated it to Prince Lobkowitz and Count Razumovsky. It had its first performance in December of that year and was published by Breitkopf und Härtel in the following year. The orchestral scoring is for piccolo, two each of flutes, oboes, clarinets, bassoons, trumpets, trombones, with timpani and strings.

4. Beethoven, Ludwig van. 'Variations on Paisiello's Air *Quanto e Bello*' (page 121). Marked on the contents page.

Dedicated to Count Karl Lichnowsky, these variations, WoO 69, were written in 1795, and published in the same year by Traeg of Vienna. The theme is taken from Paisiello's opera *La Molinara.* Entitled in full *Quanto è bello' l'amor contadino,* the air is Rachellina's response in the quintet beginning *Il villan che coltiva il Giardino.* For some reason, only seven of the nine variations have been included by the editor, numbers six and eight being omitted. *La Molinara* was popular with composers who wrote variations on its arias. Beethoven wrote a further set in 1795, on the aria *Non cor più non mi sento,* WoO 70; so, too did Paganini, whose 'Introduction and (Seven) Variations' on the same aria, written in 1821, is a virtuoso violin piece requiring astonishing technical skill. Giovanni Paisiello (1740–1816) was an Italian composer, largely of opera, one of which was *Il Barbiere di Siviglia. La Molinara* was completed in 1788.

In A major, the theme is an *allegretto* in 2-4 time. An eight-bar phrase which modulates to the dominant is answered by one of identical length returning to the tonic. The second of these phrases is repeated, slightly ornamented by way of acciaccaturas, with a 6–4, 5–3 cadence to close, but the editor's direction that it should be played an octave higher in the right hand is incorrect. His dynamics range from *p* to *f*. In variation one, the theme is varied by the use of triplets in the right hand. The contrast in articulation, between *staccato* and *legato*, is important. In the second variation, the theme is decorated by way of semiquavers in the right hand. The editor's registration is wrong – for the first sixteen bars, quite unjustifiably, he has pitched the music an octave too high. Variation three has sextuplet figures in the left hand underlying an outline melody in the right. The fourth variation is a *minore* variation in the tonic minor, though following diminished seventh harmony there is a modulation to the relative major in bars (14)–(15). The right hand is written in octaves throughout, while there is new harmony, again including a diminished seventh chord, in bars (21)–

(22). Variation five is back in the tonic major, new figures appearing in the bass. Again, the contrasting articulation is important. The seventh variation has a two-bar phrase in the right hand, which includes the important figure comprising the four semiquavers in bar (1), which is worked upon throughout. In variation nine, the time signature changes to 3–4, because this final variation is marked by Beethoven as *tempo di menuetto,* though the editor does not designate it as such. He gives a tempo of *più moto,* and an MM of crotchet=96, as opposed to crotchet=76 hitherto. There is new figuration in the right hand at bar (9) and syncopation in bar (11). The second beat of bar (24) overlaps with a twenty-eight-bar coda, which elaborates existing material by such means as broken octaves in bars (39)–(42), a version of an 'Alberti' bass between bars (39) and (48), and the crossing of hands in the last three bars, which are marked *pp*, with the editor having added the direction *e calando*.

5. Berger, Louis (of Berlin). 'Introduction and Rondo *Pastorale*' (page 128).

The introduction is a fourteen-bar *moderato* in common time in C major with a three-bar incursion into E flat major. The rondo, also in C but in 3–4 time, contains two episodes, in the tonic minor and relative minor, respectively, with modulations leading back to the tonic. A coda concludes this uninspiring movement which the editor states has been slightly abridged for inclusion here. Louis (Ludwig) Berger (1777–1839) was a German composer, pianist, and pupil of Clementi; he was himself a noted teacher, whose pupils included Felix Mendelssohn, Adolf von Henselt and Karl Taubert. His pianoforte studies are important.

6. Bierey, Gottlob Benedikt. 'Overture to *Rosette, das Schweizerhirtenmaedchen*' (page 154). Piano transcription.

The Overture to *Rosette, the Swiss Shepherdess* begins with an *andantino* in C in 6–8 time, followed by an *allegro molto* rondo in common time. Another piece of little intrinsic worth, it is nonetheless one of the longest in the whole collection. Gottlob Benedikt Bierey, born in Dresden in 1772, was a composer of music for the church and theatre.

7. Boccherini, Luigi. 'Rondo, Minuet and Trio' (page 74).

These two movements are taken from the second of a set of six sonatas for violin and pianoforte. The rondo is an *allegro molto* in D minor in 2–4 time. The first section, which contains a seven-bar passage in the tonic major, is repeated. The middle section begins in the relative major before reverting to D minor, and the movement concludes with a coda. The minuet is in ABA form comprising, respectively, eight, twelve and eight bars. Bars (1)–(8) are repeated, as are bars (9)–(28). The trio is also in the tonic major, consisting largely of tonic/dominant harmony. The Italian composer and cellist Luigi Boccherini (1743–1805) was prolific in a number of fields – operas, thirty symphonies, eleven cello concertos, and a considerable quantity of trios, quartets and quintets, for various string combinations often including guitar.

8. Carpentier, Adolphe Le. 'Variations on Rossini's *Non piu mesta*' (Op. 4). (Page 146).

This well-known air is taken from *La Cenerentola* (Cinderella), and is preceded by a short eight-bar introduction. In G major and in common time, the air is a simple sixteen-bar melody directed to be played *moderato.* There are three variations and a finale. The first makes use of right-hand triplets which leap up from the middle of the keyboard to its upper reaches, while the second features right-hand semiquaver decoration. The third is a slower *andante con moto, semplice,* in 3–4 time which requires some crossing of the hands; it ends on the dominant, closing into the expanded *allegro* finale in 2–4 time which concludes the piece, *ff.* Adolphe Le Carpentier (1809–1869) was a French composer, winner of the Second Grand Prix de Rome in 1833, and a professor at the Conservatoire de Musique.

9. Clementi, Muzio. 'Sonata in E flat, opus 7' (Page 53). Marked on the contents page.

Muzio Clementi journeyed from Paris to Vienna in 1781, arriving there on 19 December, and bearing a letter of introduction to the Emperor Joseph II from the emperor's sister, Marie Antoinette, for whom Clementi had recently played. The following year saw the publication by Holle and Litolff of the three opus 7 sonatas in, respectively, the keys of E flat, C and G minor, dedicated to Mme. de Hess, *née* de Leporini. The editor's selection is the first of them, opus 7, no. 1; there are three movements. This is the only complete three-movement piano sonata included in *The Musical Library*. It is typical of the period and ideal for performance on the John Green cabinet piano. Emily marked it on the contents page; an assured performance of this work would indicate an accomplished pianist. A full analysis follows.

1. Allegro assai: Sonata Form – E flat

The movement is in sonata form, *allegro assai,* with a cut-**C** time signature, featuring a wide dynamic range from *pp* to *ff*. It should be remembered that the pianos of the time were much quieter than modern instruments; consequently, there was less scope for gradation of tone, and fewer dynamic levels were generally recognised – usually *pp*, *p*, *f*, and *ff*, though sometimes a variation such as *fp* followed by *crescendo* might be used. *Sforzando (sf)* markings were common; occasionally *mezzo*, which can be read as *mp*. The first subject group of the exposition begins with three four-bar phrases, *legato,* and *p* until the second beat of bar (10) when a *f* dynamic is marked – it would have been preferable for this marking to have been placed one beat later, to apply to the semiquaver run which ends in the dominant. The transition begins at bar (12/4), *p*, with material clearly derived from the opening phrase of the movement; eight bars (4+2+2) with *f* emphasis on the off-beat minims in bars (16) and (18), lead to new material in the dominant. The editor's attempt to introduce contrast by raising the right hand notes in bars (18)–(20) by an octave is unjustified. The second subject group begins at bar (20/3), *pp*, with a new four-bar theme entering with the hands being crossed for four beats from (22/4) to (23/3); the last four beats of the phrase are insisted upon and close into an imperfect cadence, *f*, consisting of eight-note and seven-note chords. The four-bar *pp* phrase is repeated but this time the cadence is perfect. A new two-bar phrase with off-beat *sf* emphasis (32/2)–(34/1) is repeated twice, closing into a semiquaver run, at first upwards then down, with *crescendo*, closing into a final three bars of big chords, *ff*, in the dominant. The exposition is repeated.

The development begins on the anacrusis in bar (43), *p*, with a four-bar phrase including a figure derived from the opening phrase of the movement, but with immediate minor inflections, and Neapolitan harmony in bar (45). A new four-bar phrase enters at bar (47/4) in C minor. A single-bar phrase from (50/3) featuring a dissonant minor ninth is repeated immediately. The five bars from (49) have all been over a dominant pedal. From bar (53/3) a right-hand sextuplet figure enters. From the third beat of bar (54), this figure is given over left-hand octaves, initially *f*, then *ff* from the third beat of bar (56). This phrase closes at bar (57) on to an F major chord, *p*, but the tonality is really minor as the one-bar phrase is given again, a tone lower than hitherto, and immediately repeated, closing into the sextuplet phrase which, on this occasion, however, closes into a two-bar, three-octave upward scale beginning on middle C, which in turn closes into a perfect cadence in F minor, *ff*. (This C minor scale seems rather dubious; other editions of the Clementi sonatas have a two-octave chromatic scale, which does sound more convincing). On the second beat of bar (65), *sf* – the editor has placed the *sf* marking one beat early – the six-bar phrase (32/2)–(38/1) from the exposition re-enters, thus emphasising the unity of the movement, but this time, instead of closing into a semiquaver run, the four-bar sextuplet phrase enters, *ff*, with some initial filling out of the bass chords. This, in turn, closes into an extended version of the upward scale which, once again, would sound more convincing if it was written chromatically, beginning as before on middle C, but carrying on to reach top F, before cascading downwards in an F minor tonic arpeggio, and crescendo, to close in a perfect cadence of full chords in F minor, *f*. But this key is remote from the tonic of the movement – E flat major – in which the recapitulation must begin. In the last chord of bar (79), however, the tonic (i) in F minor is the supertonic in E flat major (ii) – it is a pivot chord. A simple diatonic progression from here through V7b7 (of E flat) to V7, with fermata over the second of the two crotchet rests, leads seamlessly to the recapitulation. This begins on the anacrusis of bar (81), *pp*. The opening is as before, although bar (91) is subtly different from bar (10). Again, however, the editor has unnecessarily raised the right-hand melodic line by an octave from the last beat of bar (89) to the first beat of bar (93). Bars (12/4)–(16/1) are omitted, the transition comprising just the four bars (93/2)–(97/1). Yet again, the raising of the right-hand melodic line in bars (95)–(97) is unjustified. The second subject group is now in the tonic, continuing as before up to and including bar (118). Bars (117)–(118) are repeated, *ff*, to form a short coda, closing with a perfect cadence –V7-I at bars (120)–(121), with full chords in the lower register of the piano.

2. Mesto: Abridged Sonata Form – A flat

This is an interesting movement, especially in regard to Clementi's treatment of the link between the exposition and the recapitulation. A useful comparison can be made with Beethoven's Sonata in C minor, opus 10, no. 1. The slow middle movement in that sonata is also in abridged sonata form, in the same key of A flat. But, whereas Beethoven effects the link in a purely conventional way by using a chord of the dominant seventh in root position in one single bar, Clementi uses a four-bar cadence theme, and begins the recapitulation with a tonic chord in first inversion, following two quaver rests and a dominant-seventh chord in third inversion, which was highly unusual for the period.

The tempo given in later editions of the sonata was *maestoso,* not *mesto.* The thin tone of the fortepianos of Clementi's day meant that composers sometimes felt inclined to fill out the bass chords of the left hand, as happens here. As with the first movement there is crossing of hands – sopra – and a wide variation in dynamics. The first subject group begins with a four-bar phrase (2+2), each of the two bars ending with a quaver rest in the right hand, closing into another four-bar phrase, ending in an interrupted cadence at bars (7)–(8). This phrase begins to be repeated, but branches out in high right-hand octaves to close in the dominant in bar (12), after a *crescendo* from *p.* There being no transition, the first two bars of the second subject group are based upon material from bars (1)–(2), but at bar (15) a new three-bar phrase in three-part counterpoint, with crossed hands and contrasting *piano* dynamics, enters. This closes into a two-bar phrase at bars (18/3)–(20/2). Bars (13)–(20) are repeated. At bar (20) the cadence theme referred to above enters, once again with the need for the hands to be crossed. In bar (23) syncopated diminished seventh chords, *ff,* close into the next bar with the dominant seventh in third inversion on the final

Bars 21–24 of the Second Movement
Linking the Exposition to the Recapitulation

quaver beat, which has been preceded by two highly effective quaver rests, leading to the first chord of the recapitulation, in first inversion, on the first beat of bar (25). In addition to the highly innovative writing above, the bass underlying the theme of the first four bars is continually moving in quavers. At bar (29) material from bars (5)–(6) enters for two bars, but soon digresses for another four bars with delightful chromaticism, to hang uneasily suspended, with fermata in bar (34). Eight cadential bars, syncopated for the first five, initially *pp* with *crescendo* rising to *ff* then *diminuendo* back to *pp*, and then in bars (40)–(41) using material from bars (32–33), lead to the second subject group. The first eight bars of the second subject group are given in the tonic, again with contrasting dynamics, and repeated, though with lower registration. A three-bar coda, beginning on the anacrusis of bar (58), brings the movement to a close, *calando* and *pp*. This movement, like the first, closes in the lower registers of the keyboard.

3. Allegro: Rondo – E flat

The finale is a short rondo, based on a simple A, B1, A, B2, A structure. Each of the two episodes contains the most technically demanding feature of the whole sonata – the quaver fragment over the extended inner trill all to be played in the right hand. Some amateur pianists might decide to play the right-hand upper notes an octave lower in left-hand thirds. (One wonders how Emily would have reacted to such a suggestion.) The main theme (A) opens with a four-bar phrase, *p*, and is answered by another of four bars, the last two of which are marked *f*. The next two bars (8/2)–(10/1) are immediately repeated an octave higher in the right hand, though this again suggests undue editorial licence, and close into four bars of downward syncopated octaves. Bars (8/2)–(16/1) are then repeated, but the final two bars are chromatically varied, *ff*. The first episode (B1) begins with a two-bar phrase which is repeated a tone lower, closing into a new figure (x) in bars (29)–(30). These two bars are repeated and close into four more bars (33)–(36) of downward semiquavers under right-hand octaves. The following two-bar phrase, based upon material from the first two bars of the movement, is immediately repeated, answered by two bars of figure (x), themselves repeated, and followed by a four-bar phrase consisting of a rising semiquaver scale which closes in a perfect cadence in the dominant at bar (48). Then follow the nine bars of extended trill referred to above, plus a silent half-bar (58), which closes the episode. The main theme (A) then returns. The second episode (B2) begins in similar style to the first but soon digresses. Four two-bar phrases, the first two identical, the second two sequential, close into a four-bar phrase, the first two bars of which are sequential and the last two cadential, closing in the tonic. Bars (72/2)–(74/1) are immediately repeated to close into a repeat of bars (68)–(71), this time extended by the interpolation of an extra bar (79). Bars (80)–(82/1) are a repeat of bars (70)–(72/1), while bars (82/2)–(91) are a repeat of (58/2)–(67). Three further bars, the second with fermata, lead into the nine bars of extended trill, plus the silent half-bar, and a final return to the main theme (A) to close the sonata.

10. Clementi, Muzio. '*Arioso*' (Op. 9) (page 176).

Clementi's Sonata in B flat, opus 9, no. 1 (of 3), was written during his time in Vienna and published about the year

1782. Placed between a frantic opening *allegro assai* and a rondo *prestissimo* finale, the *arioso,* as the editor calls it, is a short *larghetto* in E flat, the subdominant of the key of the sonata. Written in an ABA layout, it consists of just thirty-eight bars. Section A comprises the first eight bars (4+4) closing in the tonic. The middle section is twice as long and modulates to the dominant, while the first section is reprised with an overlap into a short coda.

11. Corelli, Arcangelo. 'The Seventh Concerto' (page 96). Piano transcription.

This is the seventh of the important opus 6 set of *Concerti Grossi,* in D major, published posthumously, probably in 1714, a year after Corelli's death in Rome. The editor has omitted one movement, the *allegro* fifth – 'as being the least attractive part of the work' – an inaccurate judgement. There are six movements including the omitted one. The first is an introductory nine-bar *vivace (moderato)* played by the full orchestra ending on the dominant, and this leads straight into a fugal *allegro* with the opening ascending arpeggio figure given by the solo violin in the original orchestration, and sequential writing subsequently. After forty-three bars, the tempo slows to *adagio* for nineteen bars. There follows another *allegro,* in binary form, with each of the seventeen-bar parts repeated. Over a running bass, the movement opens with the whole orchestra, before *concertante* and *ripieno* indulge in dialogue. Next comes an *andante largo* in the relative minor. This concludes with a characteristic Baroque cadence, leading without a break into the fifth movement fugal *allegro,* which is the one omitted by the editor. Consequently, in his selection, the concerto ends with the sixth movement, a dance-like *vivace (allegretto moderato),* again with skilful dialogue between soloists and orchestra.

12. Dejazet, J. 'Chorus in Bellini's *Norma,* with an Introduction, a Variation, and a Finale'. (Op. 18) (page 168). Piano transcription.

In F major, the introduction, marked *adagio risoluto,* containing some diminished seventh harmony and a *strepitoso* (noisily) marking in bar (12) leads directly, after a 6–4, 5–3 cadence and a silent final bar, into the chorus. This is an *allegretto,* marked *dolce, e ben legato il canto.* In ABA form, the first part consists of eight bars, repeated an octave higher, the second is just four bars long, and the reprise of the first part is written over a different rhythm in the bass, marked *staccato.* The variation is marked *lusingando* (alluringly), directed to be played slightly faster – an MM of crotchet=120, as opposed to 112 – and its first part is a dialogue between the hands, the five-note figure in the left hand being prominent. The upper register of the keyboard is used in bar (7). In the second part, the chromatic semiquaver notation in the right hand is written over a rhythmic bass in the left. The repeat is *dal segno,* at bar (9). Resuming the tempo of the original chorus, the finale is marked *allegremente,* laid out as ABA plus coda. The first section consists of two four-bar phrases, the whole being repeated. The second section develops the material of the first with some pleasing chromatic harmony before, *ritenuto un poco,* the first section is reprised without its repeats. An eight-bar coda, repeated, concludes the piece, about which the editor states that he has chosen such of the variations as 'are worth reprinting'. *Norma* is a two-act opera, with the libretto by Felice Romani, composed in 1831, with its first performance in Milan in that year. The eponymous heroine is a Druid priestess.

13. Döhler, Theodor. 'Introduction and Theme, from Bellini's *I Montecchi e Capuleti* (the correct title is *I Capuleti e Montecchi)*' (Op. 3) (page 104). Piano transcription.

The fourteen-bar *introduzione* is marked *andante* and, ending on a chord of the dominant seventh, leads straight into the *tema,* a sixteen-bar air in ABA form. The first eight bars are repeated; likewise bars (9)–(16). The four-bar middle section has some minor colouring. The first variation comprises right-hand semiquaver decoration reaching to the top of the keyboard and the second has the theme decorated in the right hand over a bass of triplets and sextuplets. The third is a *vivace* marked *marziale,* dotted rhythms featuring prominently, with the fourth being an *andantino alla Siciliano* in the relative minor, D minor, that does not require a repeat of each part. A cadenza leads into the *vivace* finale, with just the first part being repeated, and an extended coda to finish. The Capulets and Montagues are the families in *Romeo and Juliet.* Although born in Naples, Theodor(e) Döhler (1814–1856) was an Austrian pianist and composer, most usually of drawing room pianoforte pieces like this one.

14. Dussek, Jan Ladislav. 'Rondo' (Op. 35) (page 10).

This rondo is the finale of the second of the opus 35 set of piano sonatas, dedicated to Clementi, the first movement of which is an *allegro.* In the key of G major, with the time signature of 6–4 (the only occasion when any of the pieces in the Instrumental section of *The Musical Library* has this time signature), it is directed to be played *molto allegro con espressione;* the MM of dotted minim=60 indicates a genuinely fast tempo. The layout is ABACA plus coda; the dynamic range varies throughout, from *ff* to *pp.* The theme (A) of the first section is in ternary form; the first four bars, *pp,* are repeated, the next ten (6+4) are not. Section B begins with an eight-bar theme over a strident bass, *ff,* which is repeated immediately an octave higher. Interesting modulating sequences lead to a variation of theme (B) in the dominant, *dolce* and *legato,* though with different figuration, and then a passage containing chromatic harmony in the upper registers of the keyboard, closing into a repeat of theme (A). The second episode, in the tonic minor, is a stormy one, beginning *ff* and involving rapid scales passages and modulations, first to E flat major then, after a big *arpeggio,* initially descending then ascending, to C minor. Then, after another *arpeggio,* diminished seventh this time, the tonality of D – initially minor then major – which is the home dominant, is reached, leading subsequently to the second reprise of section A. This time, however, the first four bars are not repeated, and there are some subtle changes of movement in the lower parts in the succeeding ten bars. The coda involves more scales, in unison this time, and highly effective syncopation. A dramatic F natural in the right hand, six bars from the end, followed by some chromatic harmony and the direction *largo* for the final two bars, brings this interesting movement to an end, *pp.* The editor is of the opinion that '[this piece] is composed much more with a view to fame than profit', whatever that is supposed to mean. It was published in 1797, and it is a distinct possibility that this sonata was known to Beethoven. There are obvious thematic and structural similarities to be found in his sonatas opp. 10 no.3 (first movement), 28 (fourth movement) and 53 (third movement).

15. Gluck, Christoph Willibald von. 'Religious March from "Alceste" ' (page 81). Piano transcription. Marked on the contents page.

This transcription is of the march of Alceste, accompanied by the priests, to the temple of Apollo, to implore the restoration of life to her consort, Admetus, King of Pherae in Thessaly. In G major with a cut-**C** time signature, it is an *andante* with an MM of crotchet=84, dignified and predominantly quiet throughout. A simple flute part has been added. An eight-bar theme, *p,* is answered by a further eight bars an octave higher, initially similar, but which digress to close in the dominant at bar (16). The melody continues for a further eight bars, briefly touching on A minor, with a *crescendo* between bars (21)–(24), to close into a final twelve bars, *mez(zo piano),* consisting of three four-bar phrases, the last two bars being marked *diminuendo. Alceste*, or *Il Trionfo dell' Amor Conjugale (*The Triumph of Married Love) with a libretto by Ranieri de Calzabigi, based on the play *Alcestis* by Euripides, rececived its first performance at the Burg Theater, Vienna, on Boxing Day 1767. The title role is taken by a soprano, with the part of Admetus being sung by a tenor. The 'Religious March' is in Act One. Calzabigi's publication of the text contained a preface signed by Gluck, in which composer's and librettist's ideals for operatic reform were set down. These included no *da capo* arias, no room for vocal improvisations, no melismas, but instead a more predominantly syllabic setting of the text, far less repetition of the text, less recitative, simpler, more flowing melodic lines, an overture which is linked to the ensuing action, and a more prominent role for the chorus, rather after the fashion of classical Greek drama. Gluck was an important figure in the development of opera or musical drama.

16. Gollmick, Carl. 'German Air, *Denkst du daran* with an Introduction and Variations' (page 41).

This is Gollmick's opus 39. The air is a popular duet from the opera *Dem Alten Feldhorn* (The Old General), and it is preceded by a thirteen-bar *adagio* introduction in G minor. The air is a sixteen-bar *andante,* the editor's MM being given as crotchet=76, in G major and in common time. The first eight bars (4+4) are repeated. A middle section of four bars is then followed by a reprise of bars (5)–(6) of the air; bars (9)–(16) are also repeated. The first variation is of right-hand semiquaver decoration over a *marcato* bass, and the second is a *scherzo ma a tempo,* it being important to observe the *staccato* markings. The third is marked *piu vivace* and *amarevole* ('with bitterness') , while the fourth is an *adagio con espressione* in the tonic minor, with a change of time signature to 6–8. There is an increase in tempo to an MM of crotchet =100 for the final variation, a *polonaise* in 3–4 time, and the concluding coda which contains detailed performance directions. Carl Gollmick (1796–1866) was a German writer and composer.

17. Handel, George Frideric. 'Air, "The Harmonious Blacksmith" with Variations' (page 38).

This well-known piece is the fourth and final movement of Handel's fifth *Pièces de Clavecin* (Suite for Harpsichord) of the set of eight published in London 1720. The air in E major and in 2–4 time is an *andante,* also marked *legato sempre.* In binary form, with each half repeated, there are five variations. In the first there is semiquaver decoration in the right hand, and in the second it is in the left hand. Likewise in the third variation the triplet decoration is in the right hand, and in the fourth in the left hand. The final variation makes use of demisemiquaver scalic runs in each hand. There is a sense of things speeding up as the movement progresses. The editor has this to say: 'We have affixed the true *signature.* In Handel's early days it was the absurd custom to put three sharps or three flats at the clef, though the key required four. This was done to *cheat* the performer with an appearance of ease, while the difficulty, of course, remained'. The piece's nickname relates to a story, perhaps apocryphal, that Handel heard the basic tune being sung by a blacksmith named Powell who lived in his locality.

18. Handel, George Frideric. ' "The Nightingale Chorus" (from *Solomon*)' (page 132). Piano transcription.

The final chorus of Act One, 'May no rash Intruder', is usually known as 'The Nightingale Chorus', with birdsong effects being provided by the flutes. The editors state that Handel's flute part, *ad libitum,* is preserved in 'an almost unaltered state … though the pianoforte arrangement provides a very good effect of the accompaniment'. The words of the chorus, sung as Solomon and his Queen are leaving the stage are as follows:

'May no rash intruder disturb their soft hours;
To form fragrant pillows, arise fragrant flowers!
Arise, oh ye flow'rs,
Ye zephyrs, soft-breathing, their slumbers prolong,
While nightingales lull them to sleep with their song.'

As may be discerned from the words, this is a peaceful chorus, following on from an orchestral introduction (symphony). In G major and in common time, it is an *allegretto moderato* The oratorio *Solomon* was written in less than six weeks in 1748. There is doubt as to the librettist, though it might have been Newburgh Hamilton . It is based upon the Old Testament story. Its first performance was at Covent Garden in March 1749, the role of Solomon being sung by an alto. Interestingly, one of the characters is Zadok the Priest, but the name apart, there is no connection with Handel's well-known 'Coronation Anthem'. There are three acts preceded by an overture. The best-known piece in the whole work is that which opens Act Three – 'The Arrival of the Queen of Sheba'.

19. Handel, George Frideric. 'Chorus, "From the Censer" (From *Solomon)*' (page 136). Piano transcription. Marked on the contents page.

The double chorus 'From the Censer' is the first number in Act Two of the oratorio.

'From the censer curling rise
Grateful incense to the skies;
Heaven blesses David's throne,
Happy, happy Solomon!
Live, live for ever, pious David's Son;
Live, live forever, mighty Solomon.'

This is a typically Handelian chorus, with prominent wind instruments and timpani giving forth joyously in both harmonic and contrapuntal writing. Its piano transcription is not easily played, portraying the orchestral writing rather more than the vocal. In D major and in common time, it is an *allegro moderato*. The chorus enters in the twelfth bar after the orchestral *tutti* in which trumpets are prominent. It is the middle section which is contrapuntal, choral writing being punctuated by orchestral interludes. The *crescendos* are important in that they are meant to give the impression of incense rising from the censer (a pan or vessel in which incense is burned).

20. Handel, George Frideric. 'March' (page 150). Piano transcription.

The March is arranged from the second sonata in the second set of Handel's Sonatas and Trios for violins (or oboes or flutes) and cello published in 1739. In D major and in common time, it is directed to be played *con spirito*. It is in binary form with each part, of twelve and sixteen bars respectively, being repeated. The first part closes in the dominant and there is sequential writing in each. On its first playing the dynamic is *f*, while contrastingly, the second time it is *p*.

21. Haydn, Franz Josef. 'Minuet and Trio (from the Eleventh [*sic*] Grand Symphony)' (page 36). Piano transcription.

This piece is the third movement from Haydn's Symphony Number 102 in B flat; accordingly, the editor should have designated it as the tenth, not eleventh, of the final twelve 'Salomon' or 'London' symphonies of Haydn. (In fact, in

The Musical Library Supplement it is referred to as the ninth Grand Symphony). The minuet, *allegretto,* is in ABA form. In the first section, *f,* an eight-bar phrase is answered by one expanded to twelve bars, and the twenty bars are repeated. The short middle section contains interesting modulations, first to C minor then, following an interrupted cadence, to a V7 of V chord in first inversion (though the editor has omitted the natural before the E in the bass) with fermata, and finally the home dominant. The third section is a reprise of the first, but expanded to a total of thirty-two bars. The repeat is from bar (21). The trio is also in B flat, in ABA form, but is marked *p* in contrast to the minuet. An eight-bar phrase is answered by one of like length and repeated. The middle section, also of eight bars, ends on the dominant, leading to a reprise of the first section, though this time with some interesting chromatic colouring in its final bars. The repeat is from bar (17). Thereafter, the minuet is repeated *da capo* without its own repeats.

22. Haydn, Franz Joseph. 'Introduction to "Winter" (from *The Seasons)*' (page 60). Piano transcription.

Die Einleitung ('The Introduction') to 'Winter' is by way of a thirty-one bar overture, and is the opening to the last part of *Die Jahreszeiten* (The Seasons). In C minor, with a cut-**C** time signature, it is marked *adagio ma non troppo,* the MM being crotchet=54. There is a touch of Neapolitan harmony in bar (25). Apart from two *f* directions, the second one inserted in order to emphasise the interrupted cadence in bar (20), it is largely a quiet piece.

23. Haydn, Franz Joseph. '"The Austrian Hymn", with Variations' (page 101). Piano transcription.

Haydn's String Quartet in C, opus 76, no. 3, was probably written in 1799, and this is the slow movement from it. In G major and in common time, the tempo marking is *poco adagio cantabile.* The melody comprises twenty bars – the first four are repeated, and so are numbers (12/3)–(16/2) with the important addition of a grace note on the first beat of the melody in bar (17). There are four variations. In the first, *sempre piano,* the melody is given in the left hand with semiquaver decoration in the right for the first eight bars (four repeated) then vice versa for the remaining twelve. In the second, it is in the left hand, briefly the bass then an inner part, while in the third it reverts to the right hand, initially in an inner part then in the upper part, *p e legato.* The final variation is in the relative minor (four bars repeated) for the first eight bars, *pp,* then the tonic for the remaining twelve, with some chromatic colouring. A short coda which includes some diminished seventh colouring concludes the movement. The hymn is very well known, the English title being 'Glorious Things of Thee are Spoken'. (14) Anne Brontë included it in her *Song Book*, as number 9, 'God is love: His mercy brightens all the path'. It is also the German National Anthem – *Gott Erhalte Franz, den Kaiser!*

24. Haydn, Franz Joseph. 'Adagio' (page 151). Piano transcription.

Said to be from the tenth Grand Symphony, although 'seventh' would be a more accurate description, this G major *adagio cantabile* is the second movement of Haydn's Symphony Number 99 in E flat major. Written in 3–4 time, it is in ABA form, with the first section repeated. In the original orchestration the woodwind features prominently.

The middle section modulates briefly to C major, and after a passage featuring a distinctive triplet rhythm, *staccato,* ends in B major, *ff*. The first section is reprised with variation and expanded to include a reference to the initial material of section B and a final entry of the main theme. The orchestral scoring is for two each of flutes, oboes, clarinets, bassoons, horns and trumpets, with timpani and strings. According to *The Musical Library Supplement,* 'the composer thought [this symphony] the best of the twelve written for Salomon's concerts',

25. Herz, Henri (Heinrich). 'The Gavotte of *Vestris* with Variations' (page 78).

The full title of Herz's opus 28 is *Variations non difficile pour le Piano Forte sur la Gavotte de Vestris.* As with so many pieces of this nature it begins with an introduction, a twelve-bar *andante* in common time, which leads straight into the *tema,* an *allegretto moderato* in C major and 2–4 time. A simple tune in binary form, over an equally basic left hand, each part is repeated. The first of four variations, *p e leggiero,* has semiquaver decoration in the right hand, while the second, *f* and *con fuoco,* has the theme in the right hand over arpeggiated triplets in the bass. The third is in the tonic minor, *sostenuto; più moderato, ed espressivo,* and contains a brief modulation to E flat, the local relative major, and a touch of Neapolitan harmony, while the fourth uses right-hand triplets to decorate the theme within the whole range of the keyboard. *The Harmonicon* commented on this work as follows: '(Herz) has succeeded in producing a few extremely agreeable pages which none need scorn to perform as drawing-room music'. (15) The editor of *The*

Musical Library has this to say: 'The variations by M. Herz, selected from others because simple and adapted to the subject, were written in one of his rational moments, and are not only practicable by those who bestow a reasonable portion of time on the piano-forte, but calculated to please, in a moderate degree, all who have not been taught to believe that musical beauty consists only in difficulties which people of sense will never attempt to conquer, and in extravagances which true taste must ever contemn'. Monsieur Vestris is described as the '*dieu de danse*', who charmed all Paris and all London, by his grace and agility, some sixty or more years ago' (during the 1770s).

26. Himmel, Friedrich Heinrich. 'Grand March' (page 46).

Directed to be played *vivace,* in C major, in common time, this march is a simple one in binary form with each part repeated. The first part ends in the dominant, then follows an equally straightforward trio, with the left hand playing basic primary chords, and a repeat of the march *da capo* but without its own repeats. The editor states that this march is 'much used in continental regiments, but very little known in this country'.

27. Hummel, Johann Nepomuk. 'Romanza' (page 172).

This Romanza is an early work of Hummel's, written for flute and piano. Beginning with a ten-bar *maestoso introduzione* in common time for which, according to the editor, the composer is not responsible, the romance itself is a *poco andante* in C major in 3–4 time. In ABA form, the first section consists of an eight-bar phrase (4+4) which is repeated, except that the close in bar (16) is in the tonic not the dominant of bar (8). The middle section soon modulates to the dominant though, and also has some attractive minor tonality colouring. The reprise of the first section includes some variation in the flute part and the piano's left hand. A tranquil piece, neither piano nor flute part is difficult.

28. Kuhlau, Daniel Friedrich Rudolph. 'Rondo, on Mozart's *Non più andrai*' (page 68). Piano transcription.

Non più andrai (Now, no more) is sung by Figaro to Cherubino, and is the final number in Act One of Mozart's opera *Le Nozze di Figaro* (The Marriage of Figaro). This arrangement has been transcribed from the original C major to G. All the different themes of the original are used in various ways, and with a number of modulations. It is probably one of Kuhlau's better-known pieces.

29. Kalliwoda, Johann Wenzeslaus. 'Rondoletto Pastorale' (Op. 40) (page 84).

One of the longer pieces in Volume Three, this is an *allegretto* in G and in 2–4 time. In ABA form, the first eight bars are repeated, while the next twelve are for the most part sequential and lead to a reprise of the first eight. Bars (9)–(29) are repeated. There are episodes in D and C. Jan Kalliwoda (German version of his surname) was a prolific Bohemian composer (Kalivoda). He lived from 1801–1866, writing in many different categories, and was highly regarded by his contemporaries such as Robert Schumann.

30. Kalkbrenner, Friedrich Wilhelm Michael. 'Nocturne, *les Soupirs de la Harpe Eolienne*' (Op.129 No.1) (page 21).

The English translation is 'The Sighs of the Aeolian Harp'. There are two nocturnes in the set – this first one in A flat is the more difficult. Directed to be played *adagio di molto; cantabile e legatissimo,* the time signature, after three bars of huge arpeggios, is 12–8. An eight-bar phrase (4+4) is repeated with some minor tonality colouring in bars (15)–(16). A further four bars lead into a passage of six bars of chromatic harmony, the remote key of B major being reached at bar (21) before a reprise of the first eight bars, marked *p* and *les deux peds.* A fifteen-bar coda concludes the piece. Large broken chords in the left hand feature throughout, and the whole range of the keyboard is used, as is the sustaining pedal. The Irish composer John Field was the first to use the name 'nocturne' regularly for piano pieces of this type – he wrote eighteen of them. Karl Czerny wrote seventeen but the most popular are those by Chopin.

31. Lock, Matthew. 'Symphony (or Overture) to the Music in "Macbeth" ' (page 120). Piano transciption.

According to the editor, 'The music in *Macbeth* is a lasting monument of the author's creative power and judgement', which seems a rather generous assessment for this thirty-six bar *allegretto* in F in 6–4 time. There is a short modulation to the subdominant to provide a little relief from the tonic/dominant harmony. An acceptable alternative spelling of the composer's surname is 'Locke'. His date of birth is uncertain, but was probably between 1621 and 1630. He is remembered as being the first composer to write music of a high standard for the English stage, including his *Incidental Music to Macbeth*, produced by William Davenant in 1663. He also wrote church anthems and 'Musick for His Majesty's

Sackbutts and Cornetts' – he was composer-in-ordinary to Charles II – and he died in London in 1677.

32. Méhuel, Étienne Nicolas. 'Overture (à *la Chasse)* to *Le Jeune Henri*' (page 24). Piano transcription. Marked on the contents page.

The Overture à *la Chasse* (Hunt) to *Le Jeune Henri* in D major begins with an *andante* in 2–4 time, switching to *allegro* in 6–8 at bar (44). There are considerable performance directions throughout this overture descriptive of a hunt, with passages portraying horn calls and horses galloping. It is one of the longest pieces in *The Musical Library. Le Jeune Henri* was written to a libretto by Jean-Nicolas Bouilly, and it received its first performance at the Opéra Comique in May 1797. The overture was described by the editor as being 'one of the stock pieces of the Philharmonic Society, where it is frequently performed and cordially welcomed'.

33. Mozart, Wolfgang Amadeus. 'Rondo' (Op. 26) (page 48). Piano transcription.

This is an abridged and much-adapted arrangement of the third movement of the composer's Duo for Violin and Viola in G, K423, written in Salzburg in 1783. On an ABACA plus coda layout, the first section consists of an eight-bar phrase, repeated an octave higher with slight variation in the last bar, overlapping with a further four bars which close into the first episode. There is soon a modulation to the dominant and new triplet material. After a reprise of section A, the second episode begins in the tonic minor and includes diminished seventh arpeggios which close into the second reprise of section A. An extended coda concludes the movement.

34. Mozart, Wolfgang Amadeus. 'Opening and Finale of the Fourth Grand Symphony' (page 110). Piano transcription.

The editor has included just the first nineteen bars of the first movement *adagio* of Mozart's Symphony Number 36 in C, K425. In 3–4 time it touches upon a number of keys, both major and minor, with contrasting *f* and *p* dynamics, ending on the dominant in order that the following *allegro con spirito* may start in the tonic. The finale is a *presto non troppo* in 2–4 time, with an MM of crotchet=116 and, fortunately, the whole movement is included. In sonata form, the exposition is repeated. The development section, which is relatively short, includes brief modulations to A minor and F major, before a passage containing diminished seventh harmony leads to the recapitulation, with a coda to conclude the movement. Mozart composed this symphony at Linz in 1783. The orchestration comprises two each of oboes, bassoons, horns and trumpets, with timpani and strings.

35. Mozart, Wolfgang Amadeus. 'A Selection from the First Quintet' (page 161). Piano transcription.

This is not, as the editor states, Mozart's 'first' Quintet. It is, in fact, his C minor Quintet, K406, one of three which he completed in Vienna in the spring of 1787. His first, K174 in B flat, had been written in 1773. The editor has adapted 'the best parts of the quintet' – which actually means the second, third and fourth movements. It might be that the first movement was omitted on the basis of its length – it constitutes nearly half of the complete work. The instrument added to the conventional string quartet in order to make the quintet is a second viola. The second movement *andante* is in the relative major, E flat, in 3–8 time. The layout is ABA, with the middle section containing minor tonality colouring and, after a brief modulation to A flat major, a return to the home dominant leads to a reprise of the first section. Next comes an interesting *minuetto in canone* at one bar in C minor and 3–4 time. The *trio, al rovescio* (reversal), is in the tonic major. In four voices, much use is made of inversion of the parts. The *minuetto* is repeated *da capo* without its repeats. The finale is an *allegro* in C minor, given here in an abridged form. An eight-bar phrase, repeated, is answered by another of like length, also repeated. It is followed by five variations. Mozart actually wrote eight, but the editor has chosen to omit three of them and alter the order of the remaining ones. The first makes use of a prominent triplet motif, the second decorates the melody with right-hand triplets, while the third, in the editor's selection, is a quiet one in the relative (E flat) major. The fourth, which is the third in the original, reverts to the tonic minor and is syncopated, while the fifth, marked *più moto,* is in the tonic major and closes into a short coda.

36. Oginski (spelt Oginsky by the editor) Comte D'. '*Polonaise,* arranged as a Duet' (page 34).

Originally composed as a solo piano piece, in *The Musical Library* it is arranged as a duet. The *Polonaise* is written in F major, directed to be played *moderato* with an MM crotchet=104, and is in 3–4 time. In ABA form, the first part is repeated; so, too, are the middle four bars and the reprise of the first eight, bars (9)–(16). The sixteen-bar trio is in the tonic minor, with a brief modulation to A flat major, and it, too, is repeated, prior to a reprise of the *Polonaise* without its own repeats. Comte Michael D'Oginski, a high-ranking Russian official, was an amateur pianist and violinist. According to *The Musical Library Supplement*, the Comte wrote this *Polonaise* for a woman with whom he was infatuated, but who turned him down for a rival. After having danced it with her at the nuptial ball, he ran outside and shot himself.

37. Plachy, Wenzel. 'Air from Bellini's opera "Norma", with an Introduction and Variations', opus 62 (page 16). Piano transcription.

The air is preceded by a *maestoso* introduction in G minor of twelve bars, the penultimate one of which is a florid right-hand cadenza. The final bar comprises a low arpeggiated dominant seventh chord, *pp,* with fermata, which facilitates the entry of the air in G major. This is a sixteen-bar *andante* in common time in ABA form. The first eight bars are repeated; so, too, are the middle four bars (9)–(12), and the next four bars which are a reprise of bars (5)–(8). A five-bar codetta is added at the end of the repeat of the second part. There are two variations. The first is marked *risvegliato* ('awakened') and has a middle section *più moderato* in the key of B flat which alludes to the material of the introduction towards its end. Another cadenza leads into the second variation, a *scherzando* of the same tempo, back in the home key of G major with some initial syncopation, and a short coda. The editor states 'We have stripped the original of such parts as, apparently, were written to swell out the piece to a size better calculated to aid the mercantile views of the music dealer than to add to the effect of the work'. Just visible on the bottom left of the front sheet, below, are the words 'Entered at Stationers' Hall'. The Copyright Act, 1709, protected proprietors of music and books who gave a copy to the Company of Stationers in London.

38. Ricci, Luigi. '*Preludio e Balletto*, from the *Opera-buffa Un Avventura di Scaramuccia*' (page 92). Piano transcription.

The prelude is an *allegro risoluto* in E flat. This leads, after a silent final bar, into an eighteen-bar *larghetto* in A flat, a simple melody ending with a bar which is marked *ad lib,* which permits a short improvised cadenza, and closes into a final *allegro moderato.* In 3–8 time, it is a dance-like movement in ternary form with a short coda. Luigi Ricci (1805–1859) was an Italian opera composer. His opera buffa *Un'avventura di Scaramuccia,* from which this piece is taken, was first performed at La Scala, Milan in March 1834. Scaramouch is a character in Italian comedy.

39. Spohr, Louis. 'Minuet from the opera *Faust*' (page 82). Piano transcription.

This minuet (and trio) is the beginning of the opera, called *tanzmusick* (dance music) by the composer. During the latter part of it, Faust enters and delivers a *recitative,* to which the remainder of the minuet serves as an accompaniment. It is in F major and in binary form, though the tonic in root position is not reached until bar (3). The first half consists of ten bars and the second of twelve, which are directed to be repeated. The trio is in C major, the dominant key, and is in a distinctive dotted rhythm, with its first eight bars repeated. There are brief modulations to E minor. The minuet is repeated *DC* but without its own repeats. Spohr's opera 'Faust', opus 60, with the libretto by Joseph Karl Bernard based upon the traditional legend, was first produced in

Prague in September 1816. Louis (Ludwig) Spohr (1784–1859) was a German composer, violinist and conductor, said to have been one of the first to use a baton. He is especially remembered for his chamber music.

40. Steibelt, Daniel. 'Selection from a *Pot-Pourri*' (page 141). Piano transcription.

This selection comprises a number of sections beginning with a *moderato* in E flat and 2–4 time marked *dolce, pp.* In ABA form, it includes the use of grace notes. At bar (40) the time signature changes to 6–8 and the tempo is made subject to various changes. At bar (65) there is a return to 2–4 time for the original *moderato* which is varied. A new theme, *andante,* enters at bar (89) in F minor, *con espressione,* but at bar (129) the original theme returns briefly in F major before new material is introduced. At bar (173) the theme returns, in its original key of E flat, *tempo primo,* and a subsequent *accelerando* leads into a short coda concluding the movement, which has been in the form of a rondo. Steibelt wrote twenty *potpourris,* medleys or short pieces like this, for pianoforte.

41. Szymanowska, Madame Maria. *Polonaise* (page 174, not 170 as listed in the Contents).

A *Polonaise* is a Polish dance in simple triple time, in this case 3–4, played at moderate tempo. Chopin was the greatest exponent of the genre. This one in A minor is preceded by a simple six-bar introduction, marked *resoluto*. The *Polonaise* comprises ten bars, repeated, followed by a section of eight bars, and the first section played again. It is followed by a trio in the relative major, C, consisting of twelve bars, repeated, and ten bars which lead into a reprise of the *Polonaise*, though without its repeats. Maria Szymanowska (1790–1831) was a Polish pianist of high reputation, and composer of pianoforte pieces of the drawing-room variety. It is said that Goethe was inspired by her. In 1818, Beethoven wrote a *Klavierstück* in B flat, WoO 60, marked *ziemlich lebhaft* ('fairly lively'), 'written upon request on the afternoon of August 14th 1818 by Beethoven'. It is believed that the person making the request was Maria Szymanowska. She died of cholera while on tour in St. Petersburg, although the editor of *The Musical Library* gives the cause of death as 'decline'.

42. Weber, Carl Maria von. 'Grand March (from the *Konzert-Stück*)' (page 126).

In C major, *tempo di marcia,* with an MM of crotchet=126, this is an abridged version of Weber's original, which includes a wide dynamic range and a *glissando* half way through. It is difficult to reconcile this brief extract with the editor's opinion that 'this military movement is unquestionably the most original and striking portion'. The *Konzertstück,* opus 79, was completed in 1821. It is a single-movement work for piano and orchestra in four sections: F minor, *larghetto affetuouso* – F minor, *allegro passionate* – C major, *tempo di marcia* – F major, *presto giocoso.* The whole work is one which requires a brilliant technique in performance. There are three upward octave *glissandi,* one in the third movement and two in the fourth. Liszt made an arrangement of the *Konzertstück* for solo piano.

Volume Four

1837

Parsonage library reference 1131/4

40 Pieces – 12 Marked on the Contents Page

1. Arnold, Dr. Samuel. '*El Fandango,* arranged as the Overture to "The Spanish Barber" ' (page 141). Piano transcription.

This is an *allegro* in D minor and in 6–8 time which works particularly well on the harpsichord. There is a modulation to the relative major in the middle. A fandango is a lively Spanish dance of ever increasing speed. Samuel Arnold (1740–1802) was an English composer who held the post of organist at both the Chapel Royal and Westminster Abbey, where he is buried. Only a small amount of his music has survived, including six overtures, opus 8, an overture to *Polly,* the sequel to *The Beggar's Opera*, and his *Incidental Music to Macbeth*, comprising eight numbers. He was the father-in-law of William Ayrton, music critic and publisher of *The Harmonicon* and *The Musical Library.*

2. Beethoven, Ludwig van. 'A Selection from the Fourth *(sic)* Symphony' (page 1). Piano transcription. Marked on the contents page.

The editor of *The Musical Library* has made a glaring mistake – this is Beethoven's Second, not Fourth, Symphony, in D major; he has, however, got the opus number, 36, correct. He has selected the second movement *larghetto,* in the dominant A major, and the third movement *scherzo*, but unfortunately has prefaced the *larghetto* with an eight-bar *adagio* introduction based on the opening of the first movement of the symphony. Nor is that the end of his editorial meddling. He cuts off the exposition at bar (78) to jump into the development, which here consists of only a few of Beethoven's phrases, randomly cobbled together. A brief allusion to the recapitulation of the opening theme, and a contrived ending, bring to a close the unsatisfactory transcription of this movement which, in its original version, is a long lyrical one with a series of melodies which follow each other seamlessly. At the bottom of the last page of the *larghetto* in the Parsonage copy, where the pianist would turn over for the *scherzo,* a sizeable piece, having been torn off, has been expertly repaired. The *scherzo,* in the tonic D major, is the third movement of the symphony, and the editor has given the full score, except to the extent that he has not called for the repeat from bar (17). The oboes feature prominently in the trio. This was the first time that Beethoven used the word *scherzo* (the literal translation from the Italian being 'joke') in a symphony, though he had used it in earlier works, for example the piano sonata opus 2, no. 3, and the first of the opus 18 string quartets. The characteristics of this lively movement are its light textures and much use of *staccato* articulation. The tempo is *allegro*; in 1817, having become enamoured of Maelzel's newly invented metronome, Beethoven gave the movement a marking of dotted minim=100. Dedicated to Prince Karl Lichnowsky, Beethoven's second symphony was written during the years 1801 to 1802, and received its first performance at the Theater an der Wien on 5 April 1803. (16) Its orchestral parts were published in 1804 by the Bureau des Arts et d'Industrie, Vienna, and the first German edition of the score was produced in 1822 by Nikolaus Simrock of Bonn. (An edition of the score had been published in London by

Cianchettini and Sperati in 1808, but this had nothing to do with Beethoven.) It is scored for double woodwind, two trumpets, two horns, strings and timpani.

3. Beethoven, Ludwig van. Welsh Air, 'Of noble race was Shenkin', with three Variations (page 44).

The editor has attributed this piece to Beethoven. While it is the case that Beethoven set a total of one hundred and sixty-eight folk songs, mostly British and Irish, for the Edinburgh publisher George Thomson, 'Of noble race was Shenkin' was not one of them, and Thomson's were not set with variations as this one is. The twenty-six Welsh settings included in the one hundred and sixty-eight, which Beethoven did set, were arranged for voice accompanied by piano, violin and cello; they bear the WoO number 155. This setting, which has an easy flute accompaniment, in C minor and in common time, is a sixteen-bar *allegretto scherzoso,* the last four bars of which are repeated to make twenty bars in total. There are three variations. The first involves a dialogue in the piano between the hands, the second running semiquavers, largely in the left hand, while the last is in the tonic major, closing into a twenty-bar coda, back in the tonic minor, with an increased tempo of *allegro.* A feature of the coda is the eighteen-bar right-hand trill on G, which is in effect a dominant upper pedal. Beethoven often used lengthy trills in his piano writing, not merely as ornaments, but as a structural part of the work.

4. Beethoven, Ludwig van. '*Marcia Funèbre,* from the *Sinfonia Eroica*' (page 81). Piano transcription.

The *Eroica* Symphony, already discussed, (17) is one of the great works of music, worthy to be ranked with its successors,

Wagner's *Tristan und Isolde* and Stravinsky's *Sacre du Printemps* (Rite of Spring) as three of the most definitive and ground-breaking works in the one hundred and fifty years dating from the end of the Baroque period to the new musical world of the twentieth century. Composed in 1803, its first public performance was not until 1805 at a benefit concert for the violinist and composer Franz Clement at the Theater an der Wien. Its eventual dedicatee, after Beethoven had changed his mind about Napoleon, was Prince Lobkowitz, and it was published by the Bureau des Arts et d'Industrie, Vienna, in 1806. The movement is in rondo form, with a layout of ABA (contrapuntally developed) CA plus coda. However, as was the case with the slow movement of the Second Symphony, the editor has severely abridged this movement. He has included only the first one hundred and four bars, comprising sections A and B, plus the final nine bars of the movement, thereby greatly reducing it from its original two hundred and forty-seven bars. In the key of C minor, the relative minor of the key of the symphony, the second movement of *Eroica* is a slow funeral march, marked *adagio assai.* Beethoven's metronome marking of 1817 was quaver=80, and this has been adopted by the editor. The opening theme, given in lower register violins over a distinctive figure in the double basses, is of eight bars, and repeated by the first oboe. A second theme enters and is developed, leading to a new section (B) in the tonic major, C. In the piano transcription, *ff* tremelos in each hand replace the fast repeated notes possible only on the stringed instruments. These thirty-six bars are given in full by the editor, who then concludes by adding the final nine bars of the movement *pp* and *p*.

5. Beethoven, Ludwig van. '*Air Russe,* with Variations' (page 128).

This is Beethoven's 'Variations on the Russian Dance from the ballet *Das Waldmädchen*', in A major, by Paul Wranitzky, WoO 71, written around 1796–7, dedicated to the Countess von Browne, and published by Artaria, Vienna. The theme is an *allegretto* in 2–4 time, *dolce,* in two unequal parts of, respectively, ten and nine bars, only the second part being repeated. Beethoven actually wrote twelve variations; for some reason the editor has omitted numbers four, seven and nine together with the coda, substituting a contrived ending. All the usual methods of variation are employed – new melodic figures, running bass, triplet decoration, tonic minor, broken chords, free treatment of the theme and, in the final variation, change of time signature (to 6–8) and tempo (to *allegro).* Beethoven wrote a number of sets of piano variations, which reached their apotheosis in his *Diabelli Variations,* opus 120. Paul Wranitzky (1756–1808) was an Austrian violinist and composer of Moravian origin. He became acquainted with Haydn upon joining the orchestra of Prince Esterhazy and was later appointed leader of the Court Opera in Vienna. His prolific compositional output included operas, ballets, symphonies and many chamber works.

6. Beethoven, Ludwig van. 'Selection from his Sonata (Opus 26)' (page 161).

Again, this selection can be said to be rather unsatisfactory in that it consists of the theme and just two of its five variations in the first movement of opus 26, followed by the *scherzo* and trio. The dedicatee is Prince Karl Lichnowsky. Sketches for this sonata survive in the *Landsberg 7* sketchbook in Berlin which dates from the winter of 1800–1801, and it was published in March 1802 in Vienna by Giovanni Cappio. Opus 26 is the first of Beethoven's sonatas where none of the movements is in sonata form; he was challenging the established ideas concerning the structure of the piano sonata. It is said to have been Chopin's favourite Beethoven sonata, and it is the first for which the manuscript has survived. From it can be seen Beethoven's use of pedal markings in a piano sonata for the first time. The opening movement's theme and variations is not the first piano sonata to begin in this way; Mozart's A major Sonata, K331, had also started with such a movement.

The first movement is headed *Andante con Variazioni* and is in the key of A flat major. Beethoven has not indicated a change of tempo for any of the variations. A feature of this movement is the extensive use of *(subito) p* dynamics – a *crescendo* followed by a sudden drop to *p*. In the theme alone, this marking appears six times, while on a further three occasions a *crescendo* rises to a *sf*, to be followed by a *diminuendo* hairpin to *p*. The editor has not transcribed Beethoven's markings accurately in this regard. Each variation is based upon various facets of the theme, which is a lyrical melody in three strains. The first strain is a symmetrical sixteen-bar tune incorporating a half close at bar (8), varied repetition of the first eight bars, and a full close at bar (16). The second strain, beginning on the upbeat F in bar (16), *sf*, consists of two bars in the supertonic sequentially repeated in the tonic. This is followed by a four-bar phrase modulating to the dominant, with an interrupted cadence at bar (23) leading to a two-bar echo closing into the third strain, which is in the tonic and comprises a repeat of bars (9)–(16), not the whole of the first strain. In the first variation, a series of arpeggios is woven into the framework of the theme; there is a feeling of lift. For example, instead of a suspension in bar (2) the downbeat is released in an upward direction. The harmony in the inner parts of bar (32) of this variation is fuller than in its equivalent bar (14). The fourth variation is in the tonic major, and considerable use is made of different registers and rhythmic displacements. For the most part it moves in a two-note slur pattern anticipated by a tied upbeat. The bass rises for the first six bars, *sempre staccato,* against the *legato* right hand, *pp,* and the first eight bars are repeated with variation in the bass. Again, the middle strain provides a contrast, including *sf* emphasis, and the third strain repeats the second half of the first one. The *scherzo* is a light and humorous movement in A flat major, with complex accentuation. It is placed second in the scheme of the sonata so as to separate the last slow variation of the opening movement from the funeral march of the third movement. It is in three strains, while the trio, which is based upon trochaic figures in single bars, a minim followed by a crotchet, is in two, and written in D flat.

7. Clementi, Muzio. 'Sonata' (Opus 6) (page 56).

These movements are taken from the second of Clementi's opus 6 sonatas, in E flat, written for piano and violin. The first movement has a cut-**C** time signature and is marked *presto,* with an MM of minim=100. It has prominent split-octave passage work in the left hand. In ABA form, the first part is repeated, and the reprise begins in the subdominant.

The second movement is a gentle *andante con moto, ma con espressione* in 3–4 time. In three short sections, the first, marked *mez.*, which means *mezzo piano,* is repeated. The middle section contains some contrasting dynamics, while the reprise of the first section is written out and expanded to twice its length to incorporate a short coda. The *prestissimo* has been omitted.

8. Clementi, Muzio. 'First Movement of Sonata IV' (Op. 12) (page 136).

This opening movement of Clementi's Sonata in E flat, opus 12, no. 4, was published in London in 1784. It has a cut-**C** time signature, and is in sonata form. There are technical difficulties throughout, particularly in the right hand, in regard to the rapid octaves as well as big chords approached by leap. There is a wide dynamic range, from *pp* to *ff*. The exposition is repeated. The development section is in contrasting minor tonality and contains a two-bar passage between the hands in semiquavers at an interval of a sixth. The development and recapitulation are repeated.

9. Corelli, Arc(h)angelo. 'Second Concerto (abridged)' (page 84). Piano transcription.

The editor has selected the first and last of the five movements of Corelli's *Concerto Grosso* Number Two in F, opus 6, written for two violins and cello with strings and bass continuo, and published in 1714. The movements omitted are a *largo,* an *allegro,* and a *grave-andante largo.* The first movement, which is abridged, juxtaposes a variety of tempi. It opens with an eight-bar *vivace,* and is followed by a fugal *allegro.* The technical difficulty in this section involves the playing of passages in thirds in the right hand at rapid speed. Next comes an *adagio* which begins in the tonic minor and leads into a reprise of the *vivace,* this time in the dominant. This in turn precedes a return of the *allegro,* which in its eight bars, however, digresses into a sequential passage modulating to the relative minor before returning to the tonic. A two-bar cadence marked *adagio* is where the editor concludes this movement. The ending is on the dominant, *ff,* which facilitates a smooth entry into the finale. This is an *allegro* with a cut-**C** time signature. In ABA form, it consists largely of groups of four-bar phrases (2+2). The first part, which contains a brief modulation to the relative minor, is repeated. The second part also begins in D minor and modulates in ten sequential bars to A minor, prior to a reprise of the first part in the tonic, considerably varied. The repeat is from bar (27).

10. Dussek, Jan Ladislav. 'Rondo on the Air, "Oh dear, what can the matter be?" ' (page 6).

The popular and simple eight-bar tune, in F major and in 6–8 time, is in ternary form. The layout of the movement is ABA plus coda. There is crossing of hands and semiquaver decoration in the first episode, while the second is in the relative minor. In each, the theme appears in outline in the left hand and, once again, there is a wide range of dynamics. Dussek wrote his Rondo on this tune, number 99 in Howard Craw's 1964 catalogue, in 1793.

11. Dussek, Jan Ladislav. ' "The Consolation" (With an Introduction), Op. 62' (page 61).

La Consolation is a rondo, *andante con moto,* preceded by an eighteen-bar introduction. In the key of B flat, it was written by Dussek in 1807, and is number 212 in Craw's catalogue. It is a considerable disappointment that the editor has abridged this piece by the omission of the second episode and the second return of the main theme. There appears to be no good reason for this. As it is, what Dussek wrote as an ABACA plus coda rondo has been reduced to a layout of ABA plus coda. The introduction is marked *adagio, non troppo; con affetto,* and contains the rather unusual direction of *ppp* in bar (15). The theme of the rondo, *andante con moto,* is itself in ternary form, each part consisting of eight bars, with the third being a reprise of the first, albeit concluding in the tonic rather than the relative minor. Bars (1)–(8) are repeated; so too bars (9)–(24). There are a number of interesting features in the only episode selected, which begins in the tonic minor, *sotto voce,* and includes a section in D flat major; it has extremes of dynamics, from *pp* to *ff,* and an unusual number of other performance directions – *sotto voce, dolcissimo, con anima,* and *rinforzando.* The (only) reprise of section A has right-hand sextuplet and triplet decoration, *legatissimo,* while the coda is written largely over a tonic pedal demisemiquaver figure, and concludes with a five-octave arpeggio, marked *morendo* ('dying away'). (In Dussek's original, the second episode was written in the subdominant E flat with demisemiquaver decoration, and new, syncopated, material over an extended 'Alberti' bass was introduced. Its conclusion was a long descending scale passage, *diminuendo poco a poco,* leading to the second return of the theme.)

12. Dussek, Jan Ladislav. *Rondo Spagnola* (page 118).

'The Spanish Rondo' is an *allegretto* in A minor in 2–4 time, beginning with a three-bar introduction, *ff*. The theme is of twenty-four bars length (12+12), initially *pp*, then *f* for the second half. The episode modulates to the relative major in its middle section, and features triplet decoration, semiquaver notation, first in the right hand then the left, and finally broken chords, closing on the dominant to enable the return of the theme in the tonic. The movement concludes with a twenty-bar coda.

13. Geminiani Francesco. 'Concerto Number 1' (page 48). Piano transcription. Marked on the contents page.

This is a selection from the first of Geminiani's *Concerti grossi*, opus 3, written in 1732 – the editor suggests 'about 1734'. It comprises the first three bars of the opening *adagio*, the slow movement *largo*, and the rondo *allegro* finale. The *adagio, f*, is included here purely as a short introduction, its three bars closing on the dominant in order to facilitate a smooth entry of the next movement. (The original second movement, an *allegro*, has been omitted by the editor.) It is followed by the *largo*, a gentle movement with a lilting rhythm in 6–8 time. The *allegro* is in the form of a rondo, with the time signature 6–8, and the MM dotted crotchet=96. There are technical difficulties to overcome in the right hand – rapid thirds and held inner notes. Born in Lucca, Francesco Geminiani (1687–1762), a violinist and composer who studied under Corelli, spent some time in London, arriving in 1714, and it was here that he met Handel. He died in Dublin.

14. Gluck, Christoph Willibald. 'Overture to *Iphigénie en Aulide'* (page 101). Piano transcription.

The overture begins with an *andante sostenuto* in C minor, before leading into the main section, an *allegro,* with a suggested MM=126, after nineteen bars. Ten bars of unison writing between the hands, theme (A), lead to a passage of orchestral writing involving left-hand arpeggios. Further themes (B) and (C) are introduced, at bars (39-40) and (62) respectively, and these are worked upon in various ways and in different keys throughout. In the original orchestral version the overture leads without a break into the first sung number. The editor has attempted to accommodate this problem by substituting a not very convincing ending of his own. *Iphigénia en en Aulide* is an opera in three acts to a libretto by Le Bland du Roullet after Jean Racine's play based on Euripides. It received its first production in Paris in 1774.

15. Handel, George Frideric. 'Overture to the Opera of *Alcina'* (page 17). Piano transcription. Marked on the contents page.

The overture to the opera *Alcina* is in the French style, comprising an *andante maestoso, allegro, musette* and *minuetto.* A three-act *opera seria,* it was first produced at Covent Garden in 1735. The *andante maestoso* is in B flat with a common time signature, dotted rhythms, as is the case with French overtures, figuring prominently. The fugal *allegro ma non troppo* is based on a two-bar theme given initially in the right hand with the second bar imitating the first a tone lower. There follows the *musette,* a type of gavotte over a drone bass, which is an *andante* marked *pia(no) sempre* in B flat and in common time, and the piece concludes with a *minuetto,* an *allegretto* in 3–8 time.

16. Handel, George Frideric. 'Musette from his Sixth Grand Concerto' (page 76). Piano transcription. Marked on the contents page.

The sixth of Handel's *Concerto Grossi,* in G minor, consists of five movements, the *musette* being the third one, written in E flat. It is a pastoral of one hundred and sixty-three bars, elegiac in nature, with a distinctive drone bass redolent of bagpipes. Dotted rhythms are a feature of the *musette.* The editor has chosen approximately half of the original, closing it about half way through. The *Concerti Grossi,* or 'Twelve Grand Concertos', opus 6, were written for a *concertante* of two violins and a cello, and a *ripieno* comprising a four-part string orchestra with harpsichord continuo. They were published by John Walsh in London in 1739, and were originally intended for performance between the movements of the various masques and oratorios produced at Lincoln's Inn Theatre.

17. Handel, George Frideric. 'Minuet, from the Overture to *Berenice*' (page 127). Piano transcription.

The editor states – 'This is transposed [to D major] from E flat, that it may be used as an additional movement to the preceding overture', which is in fact the Abbé Vogler's, 'Overture to *Herrmann von Unna*' (number 37, below).The well-known minuet appears in Handel's overture. An *andante* in 3–4 time, it is in three sections, the first section of which consists of four four-bar phrases, ends in the dominant, and is repeated. The middle section is also of sixteen bars, and it includes a modulation to the relative minor. In the reprise the first and fourth phrases only are given, the last four bars being insisted upon. The repeat is from bar (17). *Berenice* is a three-act opera to a libretto by Antonio Salvi. Based upon the life of Cleopatra Berenice, daughter of Ptolemy IX, it was first performed at Covent Garden in 1737.

18. Handel, George Frideric. 'Gavotte, from the Overture to *Semele*' (page 170). Piano transcription.

This piece is the final one in the Instrumental section of *The Musical Library*. An *allegretto* in C minor and in common time, it opens with a 'one-off' C minor chord, *ff*; the gavotte proper begins on the third beat of the bar, *mez(zo) piano.* Three two-bar phrases and one of six bars make up the first part which is repeated. The middle section modulates immediately to the relative major, E flat, before reverting to minor tonality after twelve bars. A passage of sequential writing over a steadily rising bass follows before a final four bars close with a *tierce de Picardie* dominant chord. The whole section is repeated from bar (13) prior to a reprise of the first section, though without the initial C minor chord, and without its repeats. Contrast is provided in the left hand by the periodic doubling of the bass line. Handel originally presented his opera *Semele* as an oratorio. First performed in London in 1744 , the text was adapted from William Congreve's libretto for John Eccles' opera of the same title. Semele was the mother of Dionysius. The most popular number in the opera is the aria 'Where'er you walk', which is included in *The Musical Library* – 'Vocal' section, Volume Four, at page 170.

19. Haydn, Franz Joseph. 'Opening and Finale of Symphony, Number 18' *(sic)* (page 21). Piano transcription. Marked on the contents page.

This transcription is not of Haydn's eighteenth symphony, but his seventy-fifth. (The editor has taken the number from Cianchettini's edition). Written round about the year 1780, it is scored for flute *obligato,* two oboes, bassoon, two trumpets or horns, and strings. The first twenty-three bars are directed to be played *grave.* The piece opens with a three-bar phrase, the first unison D being marked *ff,* the remainder *p,* ending with a dominant seventh in second inversion with fermata. The answer is initially in similar fashion, but extended to six-bars, with the dotted rhythm so typical of a French overture, to close with a unison tonic at bar (10). Then in the tonic minor, with diminished seventh colouring, the home dominant is reached at bar (15) with a further eight bars of dominant preparation to follow, *pp,* closing into the next section, which in the full orchestral score is marked *presto,* but which the editor does not include in his selection. Accordingly, the next section is a rondo with an ABACA plus coda layout, *vivace,* with an MM of minim=108, and a cut-**C** time signature. The main theme comprises three sections. An eight-bar phrase, *p,* is immediately repeated. A middle section opens with a four-bar phrase which is answered by one of six bars closing on the dominant. A repeat of bars (1)–(8) follows, with bars (9)–(26) then being repeated.

The first episode (B), in the tonic minor, *f,* begins with a four-bar phrase, with the theme in the bass for the first two bars then in the right hand for the next two, closing on the dominant, and answered by another phrase of four bars which closes in F major. The eight bars are repeated. The next eight-bar phrase, beginning with diminished seventh harmony, and in which the first two bars are repeated sequentially a tone higher, closes in the dominant of D minor at bar (42) into another eight-bar phrase. The first four of these bars are a repeat of the opening phrase of the episode, though under a dominant *tremelo* this time, and the second four remain in the tonic minor, in which key the episode closes at bar (50). The main theme (A) returns with some thickening of texture as it progresses, and the use of the upper registers of the piano. The second episode (C) begins at bar (76) the material of bars 4/(4)–(6) being given in an inner part in the right hand, with the first eight-bar phrase closing on the dominant of B minor, the relative minor. Over repeated left-hand chords, further modulations, to F# minor after ten bars, and finally to the home dominant seventh in second inversion four bars later, lead to another two bars of dominant-seventh harmony, this time in root position, *pp,* with a fermata over a crotchet rest, and a final return of the main theme. While the first ten bars are given unaltered, there is considerable variation of the remainder of the second part, which is extended by four bars on a dominant pedal, after which five bars of V7 of V harmony, the last three bars and one beat of which are unaccompanied in the right hand, close into a single G natural, the seventh note of the home dominant. The movement ends with a coda which uses material from the main theme; the last two bars are marked *ff.*

20. Haydn, Franz Joseph. '*Andante from his Symphony in D*' (page 78). Piano transcription. Marked on the contents page.

This is Haydn's Symphony Number 53 in D, *L'Impériale,* composed round about 1775. The *andante* in the key of the dominant, A major, and in 2–4 time, is the second movement of four. It is in the form of a theme and five variations. The editor states that this symphony was composed for the concerts [at the King's Concert Rooms, Hanover Square] of (Johann Christian) Bach and (Karl) Friedrich Abel. The theme is a simple one, consisting of an eight-bar phrase, *p,* closing in the tonic and repeated, and answered by another eight-bar phrase also closing in the tonic and repeated. The first variation begins in the tonic minor, *legato.* The first eight bars close in C major and are repeated. The second part soon modulates back to A minor, aided by a little diminished seventh harmony. The second variation is back in A major; the first half of the melody is given unaltered, then decorated in the right hand with demisemiquavers for its repeat. The second eight bars are also decorated. Because each of the two eight-bar repeats is varied, the full thirty-two bars are written out. Variation number three is in the tonic minor with a rhythmic bass. The modulation after the first eight bars is to C major, the relative major of A minor. The next eight bars, which in the original orchestration feature a bassoon solo, are given under semiquaver decoration. There is a modulation back to A minor, along with syncopation, in the second half. Running semiquavers in the right hand feature in the fourth variation with each part being identically repeated. For the final variation the original theme is given, largely in octaves, in the right hand over a chordal bass in the left, and with chromatic variation at the cadence which ends the first part. Each part having been repeated, the movement ends with a final iib V7-I cadence, *ff.*

21. Haydn, Franz Joseph. 'Finale from his Fourth Quartet. (Op. 76)' (page 108). Piano transcription.

Haydn completed his last set of six string quartets in 1797 following his second visit to London. As with so many of Haydn's compositions, it has acquired a nickname – 'The Sunrise' – which relates to the quiet opening against a sustained tonic triad with which the work begins . The second movement is an *adagio,* and the third a *menuetto: allegretto.* It is the finale which is included here, an *allegro* with an MM of crotchet=132 in the form of a rondo, with the layout ABA plus coda. For some reason the editor has included a two-bar introduction which is not part of the original work. In the key of B flat, the main theme (A) is itself in three parts of, respectively, eight bars (4+4) which are repeated, sixteen bars and ten bars, these last twenty-six then being repeated. The episode (B) is in the tonic minor with a modulation to its relative major, D flat, at its eighth bar. The main theme returns at bar (72/4), varied with touches of syncopation and imitation, and leads into a lengthy cadenza-like coda, initially a single line passing between the instruments, marked *più allegro.* Then, when the sonority has built up to full quartet texture again, the tempo increases to *più presto.* The movement ends with full *ff* chords.

22. Haydn, Franz Joseph. 'Opening and Finale to the Second Grand Symphony' (page 156). Piano transcription.

In fact, this is Haydn's Symphony Number 93 in D, the first of the last twelve of his works in the genre the 'London' Symphonies written for Salomon's concerts of the 1790s, this one for the 1792 season. The editor's selection begins with the first movement's opening twenty-bar *adagio.* In

3–4 time it begins *ff*, but there are *p* markings as well, and there is a brief incursion into the key of E flat, before a close in the dominant, necessary to facilitate the *allegro assai* of the original, or in the editor's choice, the finale, which is a rondo, *presto ma non troppo,* in 2–4 time.

23. Haydn, Franz Joseph. 'Romance from his Quartet. (Op. 74)' (page 168). Piano transcription.

The movement, which the editor calls a 'Romance', with the tempo marking of *adagio* is, in fact, the second movement, *largo assai*, of Haydn's String Quartet in G minor, opus 74, no. 3, the 'Rider', written in 1793. This movement is in D major with a cut-**C** time signature, and in ABA form. The three string quartets opus 74 were dedicated to the Count Apponyi. The Haydn scholar H.C. Robbins Landon has suggested that they, and the opus 71 set, were the first string quartets by any of the great Vienna-based composers to have been intended for the concert hall rather than for an intimate gathering in a private house.

24. Hoogstraaten, P.B van. *'Polonaise'* (Op. 4) (page 52).

This *Polonaise* comes from Hoogstraaten's Piano Sonata in C, opus 4, written in about the year 1819, and published by H.C. Steup of Amsterdam. It is preceded by a six-bar introduction, marked *spiritoso,* which includes an immense dominant-seventh *arpeggio.* Directed to be played *allegretto,* it is written in 3–4 time, and has a first episode which modulates to G major, and a second which is in F major with a brief modulation to D minor. The piece concludes with a thirteen-bar coda. P.B. van Hoogstraaten was a Dutch composer who lived from 1766 or 1768 to 1828, and was an accomplished organist.

25. Koch, Charles. '*Rondeau à la Allemande* (opus 55)' (page 12). Marked on the contents page.

In this 'German Rondo' an eight-bar *moderato* introduction, featuring a flamboyant arpeggio, precedes a rondo *allegro ma non troppo* – ABA plus coda – containing much chromaticism. Charles Koch was an early nineteenth-century German composer, especially of pianoforte pieces like this one.

26. Meyerbeer, Giacomo. 'Solemn March, from the opera of *Emma von Roxburgh*' (page 134). Piano transcription.

Marked *molto moderato*, in C minor and in common time, a two-bar *tremelo* drum roll, introduces the eight-bar theme, *p* and *staccato*. It is a dotted rhythm, in unison between the hands, and is repeated. A further eight-bar phrase in similar style concludes the first section in the tonic. By way of contrast, the middle section is in A flat major and is directed to be played *ppp,* a rare marking in *The Musical Library*. A four-bar phrase is answered by one of equal length, which modulates to the dominant; each of these phrases has a distinctive drumbeat figure in the left hand. Another four-bar phrase, which begins on an offbeat and continues the bass drumbeat figure, is answered by another of equal length which closes in the tonic. Four cadential bars conclude the section. The first four bars of the first section are reprised unaltered, but thereafter two further bars close into five of dominant/tonic harmony, *ff*, two more consisting of the drum roll *tremelo* of bars (1)–(2) with dynamic swell, and a single bass note C, *f*. Meyerbeer's opera *Emma von Roxburgh* correctly titled *Emma di Resburgo,* was written to a libretto by Gaetano Rossi, and first performed in Venice in 1819. Giacomo Meyerbeer (1791–1864) was a German composer who lived and worked mainly in Paris. Remembered largely as a composer of operas, including *Robert le Diable* to a libretto by Eugène Scribe based upon the medieval legend, he was born of Jewish parents, and as such was bitterly attacked by Wagner.

27. Moscheles, Ignaz. 'Divertissement' (Op. 28) (page 30).

Another movement from this work was included in Volume Two of *The Musical Library* at page 153. In D major and in 2–4 time, marked *allegro con fuoco,* it is in ABA form with coda. The middle section begins in the tonic minor and includes modulations to it relative major – F.

28. Mozart, Wolfgang Amadeus. 'Overture to *Idomeneo*' (page 66). Piano transcription. Marked on the contents page.

The three-act opera *Idomeneo, Re di Creta* (Idomeneo, King of Crete), was composed during the years 1780–1781, to a libretto in Italian by Giovanni Battista Varesco. It was first produced in Munich in 1781. The overture is an *allegro* in D in common time. It is in the form ABA plus coda.

29. Mozart, Wolfgang Amadeus. ' "German Air", with seven selected Variations' (page 112).

The 'German Air' is *Unser dummer Pöbel meint* (Our dumb Poebel reckons), K455, completed in Vienna in 1784. The title comes from Gluck's *Pilgrimme von Mecca.* The twelve-bar theme makes use of bare octaves as a descriptive way of illustrating the title character; a performance direction of *pesante* (ponderous) might be deemed appropriate. The repeats are of bars (1)–(4) and (5)–(12). In fact, Mozart wrote ten variations, the editor having for some reason decided to omit numbers two, six and nine, and considerably curtail numbers eight and ten. The devices used in the variations, numbered as per the editor's selection not Mozart's original, include semiquaver decoration in the right hand in variation one, triplet decoration in variation two, the theme in the left hand in variation three, tonic minor writing in variation four, chromatic harmony and syncopation in variation five, the crossing of hands in variation six, and the increase of tempo to *allegro* in variation seven. At the end, the *allegretto* theme is brought back, *tempo primo,* although it, too, has been greatly shortened here.

30. Mozart, Wolfgang Amadeus. 'Overture to *Die Zauberflöte*' (page 144). Piano transcription.

Mozart finished work on *The Magic Flute*, K620, in July 1791, some five months before his death. The German text was written by Emanuel Schikaneder, and the first performance was given at the Theater auf der Wieden, Vienna, on 30 September; the composer himself conducted and Schikaneder played the role of Papageno. A highly dramatic work, it is a *Singspiel,* combining music and spoken text. Particularly stunning are the two coloratura arias sung by *Die Königin der Nacht* (The Queen of the Night) who sings as high as top F. It is also a work which embraces Enlightenment ideals – the spirit of eighteenth-century French philosophers, believing in the concepts of reason and human progress, rather than tradition and authority – and Masonic principles; both composer and librettist were Masons. Goethe was highly impressed and wrote a second part to it. The Queen of the Night is considered to be anti-Masonic, while Sarastro is portrayed as the enlightened sovereign who rules by reason, nature and wisdom. The popular overture is often performed as a separate concert work. Interestingly, Branwell Brontë was a Mason, a member of the Three Graces Lodge in Haworth. The overture in the key of E flat, considered to be a Masonic key, opens with a fifteen-bar *adagio*. The three *ff* orchestral chords contained in bars (1)–(3) are reckoned to be the Three Masonic Pillars (or the Pillars of the Three Officers); they appear again immediately before the development section (and frequently during the opera itself). After the introduction there is an *allegro* in sonata form. The main theme, which contains an important figure (x) in the four right-hand semiquavers comprising the final beat of bar (1) of the *allegro*, is treated contrapuntally. The exposition ends in the dominant, in which key the three chords are given, prior to the development which modulates through a number of keys including C minor and G minor, figure (x) being prominent throughout. In the recapitulation, both subject groups are in the tonic. A short coda concludes the overture.

31. Pinto, George Frederick. 'Romance' (Op. 3) (page 41). Marked on the contents page.

It is heartening to know that Emily studied this beautiful piece. It is a rondo in 2–4 time, *larghetto quasi andantino, affettuoso e sempre legato,* with an ABA layout. The lovely thirty-six bar melody, which would not be out of place in Mendelssohn's *Lieder ohne Worter,* is skilfully, and sometimes unusually, harmonised. However, this 'romance', as the editor calls it, is not a free-standing piece; it is in fact the middle movement of Pinto's 'Grand Sonata for the Piano Forte' in A major, opus 3, no. 2, dedicated to Miss Griffith. In D major, it is in the subdominant key of the sonata. Right from the start there is a surprise. Although the melody (A) starts with the tonic note in the right hand, the harmony for the first bar is a chord of the dominant seventh, the tonic note not being played in the left hand until the second bar. In fact, the first two quavers of the right hand in bar (1), D and B, may be regarded as *appogiaturas.* The opening four-bar phrase, *p,* is answered by one of identical length, descending chromatically with dynamic swell, to close on the dominant. Bars (1)–(4) are then repeated with a slight thickening of texture, to be answered with three strident chords, the last two *arpeggiated, f,* and, after a crotchet rest, a close into the dominant at bar (16). The melody continues, with imitation between the hands in bars (17)–(18), over a dominant pedal, *crescendo,* for four bars, to be answered by another four which include a clever enharmonic change – A sharp = B flat – in bars (22)–(23) and a close into a reprise of the opening of the melody, again beginning on the dominant-seventh chord, but this time with an *f* marked in the second bar, further thickening of texture and chromatic harmony. The melody is interrupted in bar (32) prior to the final four bars, *p,* with *crescendo* to another *(subito) p,* the first two of which are directed to be played *staccato.*

Episode (B). Beginning at bar (37) the episode is conveniently placed in B flat and, until its final eight bars, comprises a flowing melody with a rippling triplet accompaniment in a middle part and a bass in octaves. The first four bars are answered by another four which modulate to the key of A flat. However, the next two bars, which are immediately repeated, take the music into that key's relative minor, F minor, for four more bars marked *crescendo.* The next two bars remain in F minor, but when the melody is repeated there is a lovely surprise in the harmony, A major seamlessly intruding with a *crescendo* directed, this being regarded as the dominant of D minor, which key is reached at bar (57), overlapping at bar (60) into eight bars of dominant preparation, *ff*, with offbeat *sf* emphasis, and *diminuendo* in the last two bars to close into a return of melody (A). Apart from a slight variation in bar (68), where there is no seventh in the harmony and the final quaver in the melody is an octave higher than hitherto, the first eight bars are given unchanged. At bar (76) the A# in the bass brings the key of B minor four bars earlier than in the first section. There is some decoration of the melody and further alteration of harmony which adds interest, until at bars (102)–(103) an interrupted cadence leads into a seven-bar coda, which concludes this delightful piece.

George Frederick Pinto (1786–1806) took his maternal grandfather's surname as his own – his actual name was Sanders. A violinist, who studied with Johann Peter Salomon, and a pianist, he wrote three violin sonatas and three piano sonatas, in respect of which latter works the entry in the *Oxford Dictionary of Music* states that they are 'works of extraordinary merit, which could easily be mistaken for mature Schubert'; high praise indeed. It is certainly true that Pinto is a much neglected composer, whose work was innovative and is deserving of a revival. Upon Pinto's death, Salomon wrote – 'If he had lived, and been able to resist the allurements of society, England would have had the honour of producing a second Mozart'.

32. Pinto, George Frederick. 'Minuet and Trio' (page 154).

The editor of *The Musical Library* states that this minuet and trio is from the *Harmonicon*, and that the trio is by the editor of that work, presumably William Ayrton. In bar (4) the last chord in the right hand is dubious; it ought perhaps to consist of the notes E flat and D flat (not F and E flat). An *allegretto* in A flat, the minuet is in ternary form, with the three sections each consisting of sixteen bars. The first ends in the tonic, while the second, which begins in the dominant, has some Neapolitan harmony in bar (22). The return of the first section is interestingly altered chromatically in bars (40)–(44). The repeats are of bars (1)–(16) and bars (17)–(48). The trio is in binary form, with the first eight bars repeated. Marked *sempre legato e piano,* it is in the key of E major, which key is not as remote as may appear at first sight, the harmonically important third note, G sharp, being the enharmonic equivalent of A flat. In fact, the first note of the trio in the right hand is G sharp. By its nineteenth bar the music is back in A flat, enabling a reprise of the minuet *DC,* though without its repeats.

33. Pleyel, Ignace. 'A Selection from his *Concertante*' (page 26). Piano transcription. Marked on the contents page.

There are three movements. The first is an aria and variations, *andante grazioso,* in E flat and in 2–4 time, and it is a simple melody in ternary form of tonic/dominant harmony. The first eight bars are repeated. Bars (9)–(12) begin in the dominant, and bars (13)–(16) are a reprise of bars (5)–(8), slightly varied. Bars (9)–(16) are repeated. The first variation has semiquaver movement in each hand, the second involves right-hand triplet decoration with *appogiatura* emphasis, while the third decorates the aria with demisemiquaver figuration. Each half of each variation is repeated. There is in an error in the notation of the right hand of the ninth bar of the third variation – the first four notes should be demisemiquavers, not semiquavers. The aria is directed to be repeated, *D.C. e poi adagio*. There follows an *adagio* in 2–4 time, also a simple ternary piece. The first eight bars are repeated. The next four are in the dominant, while the final four bars are a reprise of the first four, this time diverted to close in the tonic. Bars (9)–(16) are repeated. The final movement is a *menuetto and trio,* also in ternary form. The first section of eight bars closes in the tonic. The first four bars are given in unison between the hands, and the remaining four are of dominant/tonic harmony; the eight bars are repeated. The second section is of twelve bars, largely dominant, while the reprise of the first part is back in the tonic. Bars (9)–(28) are repeated. The *trio* is also in ternary form. A twelve-bar theme of basic simplicity, starting and finishing in the tonic, is repeated, and followed by six bars in the dominant and a reprise of bars (7)–(12). Bars (13)–(24) are then repeated. The editor does not direct that the *menuetto* be repeated, but it would be good musical practice to do so, though without its own repeats. It is not easy to imagine what Emily found interesting in this trite selection, which is wholly tonic/dominant based. Nor is it other than a surprise that it was included in *The Musical Library* in the first place.

34. Pleyel, Ignaz Joseph. 'Romance, for Piano-forte and Flute; or for Three Hands' (page 94).

In C major and 3–4 time, both piano and flute parts are simple. An eight-bar melody for the flute closes on the dominant, and is repeated on the piano with decoration in the right hand. The middle section consists of two eight-bar phrases (4+4), the first in the dominant and the second modulating back to the tonic, while the third is a varied reprise of the first with the last four bars repeated as a duet between the piano and flute playing in thirds. A twelve-bar coda concludes the piece.

35. Righini, Vincenzo. 'Dance of Warriors, in the Opera *La Selva Incantata*' (page 72). Piano transcription. Marked on the contents page.

This is an *allegretto ben marcato* in D minor and in 2–4 time. It is in rondo form with the layout ABACBA plus coda. The main theme (A) is an eight-bar phrase, *p*, ending on a dominant minor chord, and is repeated. It is answered by another eight-bar phrase with Neapolitan harmony in its fifth bar, which closes on to a dominant major chord in bar (17). Seven bars on a dominant pedal close into a reprise of the main theme (A) which, however, is altered chromatically in its second four-bar phrase, the last two bars of which are insisted upon, overlapping into three cadential bars (33)–(36). The first episode (B), beginning at bar (37), is in the tonic major, *mez(zo) piano*, and consists of eight bars of tonic/dominant harmony which are repeated. These are followed by another eight bars of dominant/tonic harmony which are also repeated. The main theme (A) returns at bar (53). There is much variation of the original material, by way of decoration of the theme, added chromaticism in the left hand, and dynamic contrast. The second episode (C) begins at bar (92). A four-note motif, first heard in the inner parts of bar (7), enters in the right hand, and this forms the basis for the second episode. The eight-bar phrase in bars (92)–(99) is repeated. The next four bars, which begin with the motif and are in unison between the hands, are also repeated, very slightly varied. Bars (108)–(109) revert to harmony and are immediately repeated, while in bars (111)–(113) the motif rises in unison steps, closing six bars later in the tonic at bar (120). Bars (121)–(141) are a repeat of (100)–(120), except for a much fuller texture in bars (131)–(132), *ff*. The first episode (B) now returns. The right hand is decorated in semiquavers, and a four-note semiquaver motif also appears three times in the left hand. A four-bar single-note linking passage leads to a final return of the main theme (A). The first eight bars are unchanged, though a modified version of the linking passage is added in before the repeat. The remainder is also unchanged until seven bars from the end. The piece concludes with a coda wherein the four-note motif is insisted upon for a further four bars, in tonic/dominant harmony. The final five cadential chords, the last of which is with fermata, are marked *ff*. The Italian Vincenzo Righini (1756–1812) was a composer and operatic tenor. Beethoven wrote Twenty-four Variations for Piano on his arietta *Venni amore*, WoO 65. The two-act opera *La selva incantata* (The Enchanted Forest) with libretto by Filistri da Caramondani, was completed in 1803.

36. Romberg, Andreas. 'Minuet and Trio, from his Symphony in D' (page 166). Piano transcription.

This short, though interesting, movement begins with an *allegretto vivace* in D in ternary form. The twenty-two bar first section ends in the dominant and is repeated. The middle section begins with the C# of the dominant chord flattened, and in three two-bar phrases touches briefly upon E minor and G major before returning to the tonic at bar (34). At bar (42) the third section begins, initially in the same way as the first. However, it soon digresses before closing into an eight-bar codetta which concludes the minuet. The trio is also in ternary form and in D major. Its sixteen-bar first section, which ends in the tonic, is repeated. The middle section begins in the relative minor and on the first quaver in the left hand of each of its seventh to twelfth bars, *appogiaturas,* emphasised with *fp* markings, are used to underline the sense of momentum. By the end of this passage the music has modulated back to the tonic for a final eight bars of a modified and reduced first section. The minuet is repeated, though without its own repeats. Andreas Romberg (1767–1821) was a German violinist and composer. As a member of the court orchestra in Bonn, in 1790, he met the twenty-year-old Beethoven. His compositions include chamber works and some liturgical music.

37. Rossini, Gioacchino Antonio. 'Overture and Introduction to the opera of *Ricciardo e Zoraide*' (abridged) (page 88). Piano transcription.

The selection is in four parts with much abridgement. The overture begins with a *largo* section, MM of quaver=80, in C minor and in common time, with a wide range of dynamics and detailed performance directions. There is a modulation to the relative major midway through and some interesting chromatic harmony towards the end. Right-hand suspensions over a walking bass are a prominent feature. Then follows a short ternary form *tempo di marcia* in 2–4 time in the tonic major. The MM is quaver=112. The *andante grazioso* that follows is in F major and in 6–8 time, with an MM of quaver=120, and much elaboration of the melody in the right hand, while the final part is a reprise of the march, this time in a much extended ABA layout, the middle section featuring right-hand sextuplet decoration, and a coda concluding the whole. Rossini's opera *Ricciardo e Zoraide,* written to a libretto by Francesco Berio di Salsa, was written in 1818 and first performed in Naples in that year.

38. Vogler, Abbé Georg Joseph. 'Overture to *Hermann von Unna*' (page 121). Piano transcription.

The overture, in D minor, begins with a fourteen-bar introduction ending on the dominant, with the dynamic range stretching from *pp* to *ff*. The following *allegro* is interrupted halfway through by a short, contrasting eight-bar *largo cantabile* in the dominant, A major, which is repeated. The arpeggios and broken octaves in the left hand give the piece a sense of forward movement. Ultimately a coda, with detailed directions as to tempo changes, concludes the piece, though it has already been noted that the editor considers that Handel's Overture to *Berenice* can be followed 'at pleasure' (number 17, above). The opera *Hermann von Unna* is generally considered to be Vogler's most noted work, comprising an overture, choruses, songs and dance music. It was produced in 1800, originally with a Swedish libretto. He also wrote an opera *Castor and Pollux*; Weber wrote a set of piano variations based upon an air in it (number 39, following). Georg Joseph Vogler (1749–1814) was a German composer, organist, teacher and theorist, who was ordained a priest while at Rome, and appointed chamberlain to the Pope. He travelled widely and lived for a while in both Sweden and Denmark. His new method of fingering for the harpsichord was criticised by many, including Mozart. The Austrian conductor and composer Johann Gänsbacher (1778–1844) relates the rather remarkable story that, upon the occasion of a musical soirée given by Joseph Sonnleithner in honour of Vogler, that composer improvised at the piano upon a theme of Beethoven, who was also in attendance, and in return gave Beethoven a short theme upon which he was to improvise. Gänsbacher's opinion was a follows – 'Beethoven's excellent pianoforte playing, combined with an abundance of the most beautiful thoughts, surprised me beyond measure, but could not stir up the enthusiasm in me which had been inspired by Vogler's learned playing, which was beyond parallel in respect of its harmonic and contrapuntal treatment'.

39. Weber, Carl Maria von. 'Variations on an Air in the opera of *Castor and Pollux*' (page 96). Piano transcription.

This is a set of variations on an *air de ballet* from Vogler's opera *Castor and Pollux,* briefly mentioned in selection number 37 above. It is Weber's opus 5, written in 1804. The simple *andante theme* is in F major and in 2–4 time, marked *dolce* and *staccato*. It comprises three eight-bar sections, the third being a reprise of the first, with the repeats being of bars (1)–(8) and (9)–(16). The variations are fairly conventional for the time, the first, marked *con grazia legato,* utilising right-hand semiquaver decoration, and the second expanding the harmony and texture with quaver chords in each hand. The third, marked *mezza voce, sempre legato,* switches to 6–8 time and involves right-hand octave playing over quavers in the left. Reverting to 2–4 time, the fourth variation uses a distinctive broken octave semiquaver figure in the right hand, while the fifth is in the tonic minor, *sempre legato*. The sixth variation, back in the major key, features octaves in the left hand, again *sempre legato*. There follows a *mazurka* marked *moderato*, in 3–4 time and in ternary form, comprising three eight-bar sections, the third being a reprise of the first. The first section is repeated, so too are bars (9)–(24). A mazurka is a traditional Polish dance in triple time, with accentuation on the second beat of the bar. Chopin wrote in excess of fifty of them.

40. Winter, Peter von. 'Overture to *Marie von Montalban*' (page 34). Piano transcription. Marked on the contents page.

The overture was known to Berlioz who commended it. *Marie von Montalban* was written to a libretto by Karl Reger, based upon Johann Nepomuk Komareck's tragedy, and first performed in Munich in January 1800. The overture begins with a thirty-two bar *grave*, the editor's MM being crotchet=69. Interestingly, the unison notes, though not the exact rhythm, are identical to those with which Mozart opens his final, C major, Symphony, K551, written in 1788, a dozen years before Winter's opera which, in fact, has a C minor key signature. The introduction concludes with six bars of dominant preparation to facilitate the move into a sonata form *allegro*, MM minim=66, in the tonic major. This orchestral piece does not easily transcribe for the piano. There is considerable use of tremelos, broken octaves, and arpeggios, the movement concluding with a six-bar coda. German-born Peter von Winter (1754–1825) was a violinist and prolific composer for the stage who studied with Salieri and, in 1775 was appointed Director of the Orchestra to the Theatre at Mannheim. His *The Labyrinth* or *The Battle with the Elements* was a sequel to Mozart's *Die Zauberflöte*.

The Musical Library – 'Vocal'

As was the case with the pianoforte music in the Instrumental section, there are four volumes of songs in *The Musical Library*, 'Vocal' section, double-bound, one volume of the four being published in each of the years from 1834 to 1837. It is quite possible that Emily played some of the songs while Anne sang. While a number of these songs are of the 'drawing-room' variety by lesser composers, a fair number are anything but. Beethoven's *Adelaide* is a classic, and there are transcriptions from his opera *Fidelio,* and Goethe settings. There are songs, arias, canzonets and duets by Handel, Haydn, Mozart, Mendelssohn, Purcell and Weber, along with madrigals by John Dowland, Orlando Gibbons, Thomas Morley, Thomas Weelkes and John Wilbye. Nor should the less well-known composers be overlooked; the unfortunate (younger) Thomas Linley, who drowned in 1778 aged twenty-three, was a close friend of, and highly regarded by, Mozart. Sadly, Schubert is only represented twice; his music was so little known for many years after his death, especially in this country, while Schumann's great song-writing years, particularly 1840, were yet to come. The writers include Goethe, Byron and Scott. None of the titles on the contents pages has been marked by Emily as being noted for special attention, as had been the case with a number of the pianoforte pieces, and there are no fingering annotations.

In the preface to the fourth volume, the editor states, 'The pianoforte accompaniments to nearly all the vocal compositions have been added or newly arranged; and we beg leave to mention particularly those to Purcell's cantatas, to the madrigals and glees, as well as to Jackson's duets, to the songs of ancient date, and those from the English operas. The canzonets of Haydn are, we need hardly say, left unaltered. To this statement we must add, that where we have found the notation inconvenient or unnecessarily difficult, we have modified it; that we have, without hesitation, transposed such pieces as are beyond the compass of most voices, general utility having been our aim; and that we have occasionally, but very cautiously, made what we see to be corrections of errors that had escaped the notice of the composers, or the editors of the original editions'.

The following list contains a brief description of each of the types of vocal piece which are included in *The Musical Library*.

Air A term which is synonymous with 'song';
Aria Used in opera and oratorio to describe elaborate song forms;
Ariette A short air;
Ballad A drawing room song, often of a sentimental nature;
Bolero A song having the characteristics of the Spanish *bolero* dance;
Cantata Dramatic madrigal or recitative and aria;
Canzonet(ta) A short song of a light character;
Catch A type of humorous round;
Cavatina Solo aria in one section rather than three;
Dirge Song of a funereal nature – a burial song;
Duetto/Duettino A piece for two singers;
Elegy/Elegia A lament for a deceased person, or a melancholy event;
Glee Unaccompanied vocal piece for at least three voices, usually male;
Madrigal Vocal piece for several voices, usually unaccompanied;

Modinha Portuguese or Brazilian song;
Quartet(to) Song for four voices;
Recitative Declamatory speech-like preface to an aria or chorus;
Romanza Song which implies a tender, amorous or personal quality;
Rondo In opera, an aria with a slow section followed by a faster one;
Round Short unaccompanied canon, the voices entering in turn;
Roundelay Country song or ballad with recurring first verse;
Scena Elaborate concert aria in several sections;
Serenade Open-air evening music, often a love song;
Terzettino/Trio A piece for three singers.

Volume One
1834
Parsonage library reference 1131/7
75 Pieces

1. Anonymous (1834). Round, 'Call Philip Flat-nose' (page 97).

This four-bar round in common time is for three voices with simple piano accompaniment. According to *The Supplement to the Musical Library*, this 'whimsical equivoque' from a volume of 'Satyrs and Epigrams' published in 1620 is by Henry Fitz-Geffry, whose father, Charles Fitz-Geffry, also a poet, is mentioned at some length in Wood's *Athenae Oronienses.* The music is 'an impromptu written to fill up a spare corner in the page'.

'Call Philip flat nose, straight he frets thereat;
And yet this Philip has a nose that's flat'.

2. Arne, Thomas. Pastoral Ballad, 'Hebe' (page 144).

Part of the words of this five-verse ballad are taken from a four-part work by William Shenstone, written in 1743. In this setting by Arne, the first verse is an adaptation of a stanza from the first part of Shenstone's work, entitled 'Absence', the second from half a verse in the second part, headed 'Hope', and the third from the third part, 'Solitude'. The remaining two verses are by an unknown author. In Greek mythology, Hebe was the daughter of Hera, and the wife of Herakles, and cup-bearer of Zeus. William Shenstone (1714–63) was a poet and landscape gardener born near Halesowen in Worcestershire, who was educated at Pembroke College, Oxford.

3. Asioli, Bonifacio . *Arietta, Ah! Non lasciarmi, no* (page 61).

A sixteen-bar arietta, the English translation of the title of which is 'Ah! Leave me not'. It is in 6–8 time, marked *adagio.* Bonifazio Asioli was born at Corregio in 1769. A child prodigy, he subsequently held positions in Turin, Venice and Milan, and wrote instrumental music, particularly for the mandolin and guitar, as well as operas and much church music, along with several theoretical treatises. He attended the wedding of Napoleon and Marie Louise in Paris in 1810, and died in his home town in 1832.

4. Atterbury, Luffman. Round, 'Sweet Enslaver' (page 128).

An eight-bar round with simple piano accompaniment in common time, this is one of a number of catches, glees and rounds written by this composer, whose date of birth is not known, but who is known to have died in London in 1796. Originally a carpenter, he was a singer who became one of the musicians-in-ordinary to George III. According to *The Supplement to the Musical Library*, 'his compositions display much taste, but are more influenced by agreeable melody than by vigour or science'.

5. Baildon, Joseph. Glee, 'Adieu to the Village Delights' (page 168).

The words to this glee are by Lord Lyttleton. An unaccompanied glee in 3–4 time, transposed to C major from the original key of E, it is set for three voices, although the score is annotated 'but may be sung by one only'. An organist and singer, as well as composer of songs, glees and catches, Joseph Baildon was born about 1727 and died in London in 1774.

6. Beethoven, Ludwig van. Canzonet, 'My Wife's a Winsome wee Thing' (page 62).

The music is Beethoven's WoO 123, but the words are not. Those that he set were by Karl Friederich Herrosee – *Zärtliche Liebe* (Tender love), written sometime during the mid-1790s, and published by Traeg of Vienna in 1803 . These words are by Robert Jamieson. The editor has inserted a bar containing a G major chord at the beginning of the song which is not Beethoven's. Ignoring this bar, and numbering the bars from Beethoven's first, there is a mistake in the vocal line in bar (29) – the F sharp should be F natural.

7. Beethoven, Ludwig van. May Song, 'Now Nature Shines' (page 136).

The words are by Goethe, translated from the German by John Oxenford. This is the fourth of eight songs which comprise Beethoven's opus 52 set; the original German title is *Wie herrlich leuchtet mir die Natur* (With glory Nature brightens again). The set was compiled during the years 1803–5, and published by Bureau des Arts et d'Industrie, Vienna in 1805. However, the songs were written much earlier, during the 1790s, perhaps even before Beethoven left Bonn in 1792.

8. Beethoven, Ludwig van. *Aria, Per pieta non dirmi addio* (page 146).

Beethoven's opus 65 is a *Szene und Aria für Sopran und Orchester,* 'Ah! Perfido', written early in 1796, to a text of Pietro Metastasio (1698–1782) and published by Hoffmeister und Kühnel of Leipzig in 1805. The dedicatee is the Countess Josephine de Clary. Only the first part of the aria, the seventy-two bar *adagio* section, has been included by the editor. The English translation of the title is 'For pity's sake do not leave me'.

9. Blow, John. Song, 'The Self Banished' (page 104).

This beautiful single-verse song of thirty-two bars, directed to be performed *andante,* has some interesting chromatic harmony in its middle section. The words are by Edmund Waller —(1606-1687), an interesting character who became an MP at the age of eighteen, was involved in a conspiracy against Parliament on behalf of Charles I in 1643, expelled from the House, fined and banished. In his eightieth year however, he returned as a member in the first parliament of James II. John Blow (1649–1708) was an important composer of over one hundred church anthems, thirteen services, and the masque *Venus and Adonis.* He was also organist of Westminster Abbey from 1668–79, when he was succeeded by his pupil Henry Purcell.

10. Boieldieu, François-Adrien. Duet, 'When the Moonlight streaming' (page 141).

This two-part song is founded on the French air *Le clair de la lune.* It is unusual in that each of the four verses is directed to be performed at different speeds – respectively, *andante, allegretto, largo, allegretto.* The second verse is extended from sixteen bars to twenty-four. Adrien Boieldieu (1775-1834) was a French composer, notably of comic operas, the son of the better-known François Adrien, under whom he studied at the Paris Conservatoire.

11. Callcott, John Wall. Glee, 'Forgive, Blest Shade!' (page 12).

The score is annotated with the words 'An Epitaph in a churchyard inthe Isle of Wight'. A glee, set for two sopranos and bass, directed to be performed *largo,* and quietly throughout, it is in two sections, of sixteen and twenty bars respectively, each section being repeated. *The Supplement to the Musical Library* describes it as being 'set to music with great feeling, and in the purest taste', yet considers that the pianoforte accompaniment 'is given only for the convenience of those who require the aid of an instrument, and ought not to be used by such as do not feel the necessity of support. A glee properly so-called should, whenever possible, be sung without accompaniment'. John Wall Callcott (1766–1821) was a distinguished writer of glees, and a Doctor of Music at Oxford University, who studied under Haydn when that master was in this country in 1791.

12. Callcott, John Wall. Glee, 'The May Fly' (page 56).

The words are by Mrs. Mary Robinson. An *allegretto* in 2–4 time, for two sopranos with piano accompaniment, it is in three sections, the first two of which are repeated. The piano accompaniment does not seem unduly out of place here.

13. Callcott, John Wall. Glee, 'The Fairies' (page 129).

Set for two sopranos, the features of this glee are the changes of tempo in the middle sections, and the range of dynamics, from *f* to *pp*.

14. Camera, Gago da. Portuguese Modena, 'Those Lovely Lips'. (page 120).

According to the score, the words have been translated and adapted. A *modhina* is described as 'a song à la mode – a fashionable song'. Set for high voice with piano accompaniment, there are two verses of sixteen bars; each is sub-divided into eight, four and four-bar sections, and each of these sections is repeated. *The Supplement to the Musical Library* states of the composer – 'the music [is] by Gago da Camera, of whom we know only that he is, or was, a Brazilian'.

15. Cherubini, Luigi. Air, 'Sweet are the Banks' (page 96).

The interest in this two-verse air, or aria, is that it is taken from one of the most famous of 'rescue' operas, *Les deux journées* (The Two Days), also known as *Le porteur d'eaux* (The Water Carrier). The libretto was by Jean-Nicolas Bouilly, and both Beethoven and Goethe thought highly of it, Beethoven having kept a copy of it on his desk while writing *Fidelio,* with which plot there are similarities. The action takes place in 1647 in the time of Cardinal Mazarin, with whom Cardinal Armand has fallen out of favour. He arranges with Mikeli, a water-carrier, to escape from Paris in a barrel, and it is Mikeli's aria – *Guide mes pas, o providence* – translated into English by William Woty, which is included here. Woty (c1731–1791) was a law clerk and poet of no great consequence. Luigi Cherubini, born in Florence in 1760, was a composer most notably of opera, initially influenced by Gluck, and masses. He spent time in Paris, Vienna, where he met Haydn and Beethoven, and London, and returned to Paris where he held various posts at the Conservatoire, dying in the French capital in 1842.

16. Cooke, Benjamin. Glee, 'Hark! The Lark at Heaven's Gate sings' (page 38).

The words are taken from Shakespeare's *Cymbeline,* Act Two, Scene Three. Cooke's setting is a glee for two sopranos, alto and bass with *tempo Siciliano* in 6–8 time. The first four lines are directed to be repeated, similarly the last three. Benjamin Cooke (1734–93) was an organist, and composer of canons, glees, rounds and duets. His musical doctorate was conferred by Cambridge University in 1775, with an identical award from Oxford University following in 1782.

17. Corfe, Joseph (harmonised by). Glee, 'Tweed-Side' (page 138).

Harmonised by Corfe as a glee for soprano, alto, tenor and bass, and directed to be sung *larghetto,* the words are by Robert Crawford. Joseph Corfe (1740-1820) was for many years a chorister and organist at Salisbury Cathedral and a Gentleman of the Chapel Royal. He was a composer of church music and wrote a treatise on thorough bass.

18. Dowland, John (1597). Madrigal, 'Awake, sweet Love!' (page 1).

This two-verse madrigal for soprano, alto, tenor and bass is in 3–2 time and marked *andante*. It is printed with a piano accompaniment. In fact, it is number 19 in the *First Book of Songs or Ayres*, of 1597 with the original accompaniment being for lute. According to *The Supplement to the Musical Library* it is 'an elegant piece of vocal harmony'. However, the editor continues 'we have not discovered the author of the words, which in truth are not worth the trouble of research, or the space which they would occupy if reprinted'! John Dowland (c1563–1626) was a virtuoso lutenist and an important composer of songs with lute accompaniment. Eighty-seven of them were printed in four volumes with lute tablature – *Books of Songes or Ayres*, of 1597, 1600, 1603, and *A Pilgrim's Solace,* 1612 – with a further three included in his son Robert's *Musical Banquet* of 1611. He also wrote twenty-one instrumental works, published in *Lachrimae* of 1604, and pieces for solo lute.

19. Dowland, John. Madrigal, 'Now, o now, I needs must part' (page 93).

A four-part madrigal in 3–2 time, *andante,* the score is annotated 'the words of line two are to be sung at the repeat'.

The date of composition is given as 1590, and it appeared in the *First Book of Songs and Ayres* of 1597. The words portray the poet's feeling of love and loss.

20. Drobisch, C.L. Song, 'The Hermitage' (page 53).

According to the score 'the words are imitated from the German', the original title being *Die Einsiedler*. Beginning in E major, an eight-bar (4x2) *adagio* verse is interrupted by a *quasi recitative* in C which, in its ninth bar, leads to a return of the original eight bars, *tempo primo*. Carl Ludwig Drobisch (1803–1854) was Kapellmeister of the Protestant Church in Leipzig, and a composer of many choral works including a requiem. He was best known as a teacher and influential writer on the subject of the mathematical determination of musical pitch.

21. Gail, Madame. Nocturne, *Ni jamais, ni toujours* (page 48).

This three-verse nocturne for two voices with piano accompaniment in A minor, with a brief modulation to the relative major included, is directed to be played *moderato*. The English translation of the title is 'Neither never, nor always'. Sophie Gail, *née* Garre (1775–1819) was a singer who toured Europe and composer. She divorced her husband after seven years of marriage and died in Paris, the city of her birth.

22. Gastoldi, Gio Giacomo. Madrigal, 'Out upon it'(page 162).

This five-part madrigal for two sopranos, alto, tenor and bass, with piano accompaniment is in common time and marked *allegretto.* The words are Sir John Suckling's, and the score indicates that it was written in 1581.There are two eighteen-bar sections, the second of which is directed to be repeated. Giacomo Gastoldi (1554–1609) was an Italian composer, most notably of the madrigal form known as the 'ballett' for five voices, which he published in Venice in 1591. Sir John Suckling (1609–42) was a poet and dramatist born in Middlesex and educated at Trinity College, Cambridge. Involvement in political intrigue led to his flight from England, and his subsequent death, allegedly by his own hand, in Paris. Some have said that he invented the game of cribbage.

23. Gibbons, Orlando. Madrigal, 'The Silver Swan' (page 118).

Gibbons' most popular madrigal, composed probably in 1611, is set for soprano, alto, tenor and two basses in common time, *tempo giusto.* The words are by Sir Christopher Hatton (c1579–1619) Chancellor to Elizabeth I, and portray the legend that a swan never sings until death is approaching. Orlando Gibbons (1583–1625) was a noted organist and one of the foremost early English composers, particularly of church music (anthems and motets), madrigals, and works for keyboard and viols. 'The Silver Swan' is included in the composer's *First Set of (twenty) Madrigals and Mottets,* which he dedicated to Hatton. A Doctor of Music at Oxford University, *The Supplement to the Musical Library* records that, 'in 1625, while in attendance at the marriage of Charles I at Dover, he took the small-pox and died'. Grove's *Dictionary of Music and Musicians,* however, records the cause of death as being an apoplectic fit. He was buried in Canterbury Cathedral.

24. Gluck, Christoph Willibald. *Aria, Non vi turbate, no!* (page 160).

This aria is taken from Gluck's opera *Alceste,* sung by the title character when she pleads with the infernal deities. With a *larghetto* tempo, Gluck used muted strings and English horns in order to achieve the required aura of pathos. The opera was first performed in Vienna in 1767. The libretto is by the Florentine poet Ranieri de' Calzabigi (1714–1795), who also collaborated with Gluck on his opera *Orfeo e Euridice.* Branwell Brontë wrote to the Halifax organist Joseph Henry Frobisher, probably in early 1845, to the effect that he had composed English words (eight stanzas) to this aria 'on the recent stirring events in India', and enquiring whether Frobisher would 'make what use you think best of it – or publish it as Gluck's air adapted to English words by myself – or arranged by yourself – or under any title if it would deserve a title at all'. The events referred to were the Anglo–Sikh Wars which resulted in Britain annexing the Punjab. In a second letter, dated 21 March 1845, Branwell writes that 'I leave the song and its subject entirely in your hands'. Joseph Henry Frobisher was organist of Halifax Parish Church from 1838 to 1862 and, as with so many who held that post, contributed tunes, anthems and chants to *Chetham's Psalmody and Supplements.*

25. Harrington, Henry (M.D.). Round, 'How great is the Pleasure!' (page 92).

This eight-bar round is set for three voices in 3–4 time, *poco allegretto.* The words, which are supposed to be by the composer read:

'How great is the pleasure, how sweet the delight,
When soft love and music together unite.'

Henry Harrington (1727–1816) was a surgeon from Somerset , his doctorate of medicine having been obtained at Queen's College, Oxford.

26. Hayden, George. Duet, 'As I saw fair Clora walk alone' (page 126).

This ten-line verse is set as a duet for tenor/soprano and bass/contralto. There are four sections of differing lengths, each repeated, the first two *andante,* the last two *allegretto.* According to *The Supplement to the Musical Library*, 'we have not been able to trace the author of these verses' which, given their very trite nature, is of no great consequence. George Hayden, who lived during the late eighteenth and early nineteenth centuries, was an organist and minor composer, as this piece, which is probably his best known effort, confirms.

27. Haydn, Franz Joseph. Song, 'Forgive me' (page 4).

The score is annotated – 'Composed to German words by Haydn, and never before published in England. The English words by P.L. Courtier'. This is a single verse song, *adagio cantabile,* with piano accompaniment, containing some interesting modulations.

28. Haydn, Franz Joseph. Canzonet, 'Recollection' (page 25).

The second of the six canzonets published in 1794, Hob. XXVIa 25–36, with words by Mrs. John (Ann) Hunter

(1742–1821) to whom the set is dedicated. She was a minor poet married to a surgeon. Written in F, *adagio,* there are two verses.

29. Haydn, Franz Joseph. 'The Mermaid's Song' (page 41).

This is the first of the six canzonets published in 1794 – there were six more the following year – with words by Mrs. John (Ann) Hunter (1742–1821) to whom the set is dedicated. It is a sprightly *allegretto* in C, of two verses. *The Supplement to the Musical Library* says about it – 'it's gaiety and strongly marked rhythm please all, even those who have not taste enough, or are not sufficiently accustomed to music, to enter into its other beauties. If from nervousness, or actuated by a desire to display nimbleness of finger, the accompanist hurries this, the effect will be seriously injured'.

30. Haydn, Franz Joseph. Canzonet, 'My Mother bids me bind my Hair' (page 64).

The third of the canzonets written in 1794, with words by Mrs. John (Ann) Hunter (1742–1821) to whom the set is dedicated, it is probably the most popular of them all. An *allegretto* in A, there are two verses. It is also referred to by its alternative title 'A Pastoral Song'.

31. Haydn, Franz Joseph. Air, 'With Verdure Clad' (page 72).

The words of this well-known aria from *The Creation* are translated from the German of Baron von Swieten. This is Gabriel's air in Part One of the oratorio, and makes considerable demands upon the singer, with florid runs and notes as high as top B flat. Gottfried van Swieten (1733–1803) was a diplomat, librarian, and government official, best remembered for his being a patron of a number of composers including Haydn, Mozart and Beethoven, whose First Symphony was dedicated to him. He was Haydn's librettist for the oratorios – *The Creation* and *The Seasons.*

32. Haydn, Franz Joseph. Canzonet, 'Pleasing Pain' (page 82).

The fifth of the canzonets published in 1794, with words by Mrs. John (Ann) Hunter (1742–1821) to whom the set is dedicated, it is a three verse *allegretto* in G in 6–8 time.

33. Haydn, Franz Joseph. Canzonet, 'Despair' (page 101).

The fourth of the canzonets published in 1794, with words by Mrs. John (Ann) Hunter (1742–1821) to whom the set is dedicated, it is a four verse *adagio* in E in 6–8 time.

34. Haydn, Franz Joseph. Canzonet, 'Fidelity' (page 122).

The sixth of the canzonets published in 1794, with words by Mrs. John (Ann) Hunter (1742–1821) to whom the set is dedicated, it is a through-composed *allegretto* which begins in F minor and, after a modulation to A flat, concludes in the tonic major.

35. Haydn, Franz Joseph. Air, 'The Husbandman' (page 132).

This aria is from the oratorio *The Seasons* with libretto by Baron van Swieten, translated by the Revd. John Webb,

M.A. It is the fifth number of the first section, Spring, sung by Simon. An interesting feature concerns the piano accompaniment which includes quotations from the *andante* of Haydn's Symphony number 94, *The Surprise.*

36. Haydn, Franz Joseph. Canzonet, 'Sympathy' (page 149).

The third of the six canzonets published in 1795, with words by Pietro Metastasio (1698–1782) translated by John Hoole, it is dedicated to the Rt. Hon. Ladie *(sic)* Charlotte Bertie, and is an *andante* in E.

37. Haydn, Franz Joseph. Canzonet, 'The Wanderer' (page 165).

The second of the six canzonets published in 1795, with words having been selected by Mrs. John (Ann) Hunter (1742–1821), it is dedicated to the Rt. Hon. Ladie *(sic)* Charlotte Bertie, and is a solemn piece in G minor, directed to be played *poco adagio.*

38. Hayes, Dr. William. Round, 'Winde, gentle Evergreen' (page 45).

An eight-bar round for three voices with piano accompaniment, the words, translated from the Greek, are:

> 'Winde, gentle evergreen, to form a shade
> Around the tomb where Sophocles is laid'.

William Hayes (1708–77) D.Mus., was organist at Magdalen College, Oxford. An enthusiast of Handel, particularly his oratorios which he conducted regularly, he too composed in that genre, along with cantatas, instrumental and vocal music. He was instrumental in the building of Holywell Music Room, said to be the oldest purpose-built music room in Europe.

39. Himmel, Friedrich Heinrich. Song, 'Ada to Alexis wih a Rose'. (page 152).

A short song in A flat, *allegretto,* in rondo form with piano accompaniment.

40. Jackson, William (of Exeter). Duet, 'Love in thine Eyes forever plays' (page 33).

A duet for two sopranos, the editor has transposed it down a tone from E major in order to 'bring it within the compass of every soprano voice'. The directed tempo is *allegretto.* In binary form, each section is repeated. The first verse is adapted from words by Abraham Cowley and the second is by Jackson himself. William Jackson (1730–1803) was born in Exeter where he received organ lessons at the Cathedral, later becoming organist and master of the choristers there. He was a composer of songs and other vocal music, as well as sonatas for harpsichord.

41. Jackson, William (of Exeter). Duet, 'Time has not thinned my flowing Hair' (page 69).

Set for two sopranos in common time in G, *allegro,* this song is in binary form, with both sections directed to be repeated. *The Musical Library Supplement* considers that it was 'long the favourite of all amateurs, and never has lost any part of its value in the opinion of competent judges'.

42. Linley, Thomas (Senior). Song, 'The Woodman' (page 80).

The first four verses of this song are directed to be performed *moderato,* in common time, but for the fifth there is a change of rhythm to 3–8 time, with the tempo increased to *vivace.* The words are by William Pearce who, according to *The Supplement to the Musical Library,* was 'a successful dramatic writer at the end of the last [18th] century'. Thomas Linley (1733–1795) was a teacher and entrepreneur who was at one time joint manager and part owner of Drury Lane Theatre, London. As a composer he wrote music for plays, songs, madrigals and cantatas. His eldest son, Thomas junior, was also a composer, noted violinist and friend of Mozart. He died in a boating accident, aged twenty-two.

43. Linwood, Miss Mary. Canzonet, 'Pretty Fairy!' (page 88).

The composer has set her own words in this canzonet marked *allegretto e scherzando. The Supplement to the Musical Library* has this to say about the composer [who is] – 'Miss Mary Linwood, concerning whom our information only enables us to state that she is the younger sister of the justly-celebrated artist. But we may venture to add that these two highly gifted ladies are not more closely united by the tie of relationship, than by their love for the sister arts of poetry, painting and music'.

44. Lock, Matthew. Glee, 'Ne'er trouble thyself with the Times' (page 78).

This glee in 3–4 time is set for soprano/alto, second soprano/ tenor and bass. A note on the score states – 'when sung by equal voices, the upper staff of the accompaniment [is] to be played an octave lower'. According to *The Supplement to the Musical Library*, 'this first appeared in Playford's "Musical Companion", published in 1673, from which we have extracted and scored it. The glee is there printed in single parts, that for the second voice being reversed – turned upside down, to enable a performer on the opposite side of the table to sing from the same book'. The author of the words is not mentioned.

45. Loewe, Carl. Song, 'How Deep the Slumbers of the Floods' (page 20).

This song is to be performed *adagio con espressione* and *sempre pp*. The piano accompaniment is a succession of chords, with much use of the sustaining pedal directed. The words have been translated from the German. Carl Loewe, sometimes referred to as Johann Carl Gottfried Loewe (1796–1869) was a German singer, conductor and composer, most notably of over five hundred ballads and lieder published in seventeen volumes.

46. Loewe, Carl. Song, 'Jephtha's Daughter' (page 22).

The five verses of this song are taken from Byron's *Hebrew Melodies*, and Loewe's setting is in common time, *andante maestoso*.

47. Mendelssohn, Felix. Song, 'The Kiss, dear Maid! Thy Lip has left' (page 11).

Mendelssohn set Byron's two verses to a simple *andante* melody with piano accompaniment.

48. Mornington, Earl of. Glee, 'Here in Cool Grot' (page 66).

The first line of the first verse is set to a four bar *largo* introduction in common time; then follow the remaining five lines *vivace* in 6–8 time, the whole being repeated. There is no initial *largo* for the second verse, which is also repeated, but the final two bars of the repeat are so designated. The words are by William Shenstone (1714–1763), described in *The Supplement to the Musical Library* as being 'the elegant pastoral and elegiac poet', and are 'the first two stanzas of verses written "On a Tablet against a Root-house" at the Leasowes, in Worcestershire'. Another score of this piece was acquired by Emily and Anne in the 1830s. Garret, First Earl of Mornington (1735-1781) was a member of the Wellesley family and father of the Duke of Wellington, the Brontë family's hero. An accomplished violinist, who also played the harpsichord and organ, his compositions were mainly vocal. According to the *Harmonicon,* 'Lord Mornington devoted all his leisure hours to music, and such was the success attending his favourite pursuit, that small indeed is the number of professors who by their works have arrived at the same rank in the art as that so fairly gained, and so incontestably possessed, by the noble Earl'.

49. Mozart, Wolfgang Amadeus. Serenade, 'Good Morrow' (page 21).

This delightful and popular two-verse song is an *allegretto* in 3–4 time. The words, not the original ones, are by Thomas

Heywood written in 1638, three years before his death. The original German title is *Die Kleine Spinnerin* (The Little Spinner-woman) K531.

50. Nares, James, Dr. Glee, 'Fear no more the Heat of the Sun' (page 108).

This glee is a transposition from the original for male voices, now set for two sopranos and a bass who sings the bottom line of the piano accompaniment. The first part of twenty-one bars is an *andante* in A minor, while the final sixteen bars are a *larghetto* in the tonic major. The words are taken from Shakespeare's *Cymbeline*, Act Four, Scene Two, spoken by Guiderius. James Nares (1715–1783) was an accomplished organist and composer of church music, glees and canons.

51. Neukomm, The Chevalier. Song, 'Thy Voice is Sweet, is Sad, is Clear' (page 36).

The music is a simple four-verse *andantino* in 6–8 time of a song by Neukomm, the German words of which have been replaced by the editor of *The Musical Library* with these English words, the title being 'To a Nightingale at Midday', taken from a volume of *English Songs and Other Small Poems* by Barry Cornwall, published in 1832. 'Cornwall' was a pseudonym; his real name was Bryan Waller Procter (1787–1874) and his occupation was as a lawyer. Sigismund Neukomm (1778–1858) was a minor composer, born in Salzburg. An organist and student of Michael Haydn, he spent time in St. Petersburg, Paris and London, in the latter as a diplomat.

52. Neukomm, The Chevalier. Canzonet, 'To my Boat' (page 105).

An *allegretto* in 6–8 time, 'the words are by permission of Mr. Mori'.

53. Pacini, Giovanni. Song, 'Beneath the Ocean's Swelling Wave' (page 6).

Taken from Pacini's opera *Niobe,* this two verse aria is an *andante cantabile.* The words are taken from the 'New York Mirror'. Giovanni Pacini (1796–1867) was an Italian composer, principally of operas, of which he wrote over seventy. *Niobe,* with its libretto by Andrea Leone Tottola, was premiered at the Teatro San Carlo, Naples in 1826.

54. Paisiello, Giovanni. Aria, *La Rechalina* (page 98).

From Paisiello's comic opera *La Molinara,* the English translation of the aria's title is 'the Maid of the Mill'. It was introduced by Stephen Storace as 'Whither my Love', in *The Haunted Tower*, the words being written by James Cobb, and both versions, Italian and English, are included in the score, the Italian as the first verse, the English as the second. Storace was known for borrowing material from other composers for use in his own work.

55. Palestrina, Giovanni Pierluigi da (1590). Madrigal, 'When flow'ry Meadows deck the Year' (page 28).

Set for soprano, alto, tenor and bass, with piano accompaniment (which ought not to be used in performance) this is a beautiful madrigal despite its banal words, which are a translation from the Italian original.

56. Paxton, Stephen. Song, 'O, sing unto my Roundelay' (page 32).

A *larghetto* in A minor, the two verses are sung quietly throughout. The words are by Thomas Chatterton (1752–1770) from his *Aella.* Stephen Paxton (1734–87) was a cellist and composer of glees, for many of which he won prizes.

57. Piantanida, Giovanni. *Bolero, Son Gelsomino* (page 170).

Son Gelsomino is florid aria, directed to be performed *allegretto grazioso.* The author of the words is unknown. Giovanni Piantanida (1705–1782) was a violinist and composer of romances and ariettas such as this one.

58. Pollini, Francesco Giuseppe. *Arietta, Bella Ciprignia* (page 113).

A short arietta, in two sections each directed to be repeated, the score is marked *sostenuto.* Francesco Giuseppe Pollini (1763–1846) was an Italian composer and virtuoso pianist, albeit born in Ljubliana, Slovenia. He was a pupil of Mozart. Most of his compositions were for piano, but he also wrote an opera, a cantata and a *Stabat Mater.* Highly thought of by his contemporaries, Bellini dedicated his opera *La Sonnambula* to him.

59. (Portuguese composer unknown). *Modhina,* 'As fades the Morn' (page 164).

The words of this simple eighteen-bar modinha are translated from the Portuguese.

60. Purcell, Henry. Siren's Duet, 'Two Daughters of the aged Stream are we' (page 17).

King Arthur, Z628, from which this song is taken, is a semi-opera or masque in five acts with words by John Dryden, which had its first performance at the Queen's Theatre, London in 1691. The two sirens' duet is the first number in Act Four, Scene Two. A pastoral *andante* in common time, there is an increase in tempo towards the end.

61. Purcell, Henry. Cantata, 'Mad Tom' (page 46).

This is one of Purcell's three 'mad cantatas', a popular genre in the seventeenth century, John Eccles also having written a number of them. They were distinguished by rapidly shifting effects and delusions of grandeur coupled with *double entendres.* Hence, 'Mad Tom' begins in A major, *maestoso,* but switches to an *allegro* section in the tonic minor after twenty-two bars – a Jacobean masque tune – before a four-bar *largo* leads into a final *allegro* in the major key. The words were by the poet William Basse (c1583–c1653) and the three masques were published in *Orpheus Britannicus* after the composer's death.

62. Purcell, Henry. Cantata, 'Mad Bess' (page 114).

This is the first of Purcell's three 'mad cantatas', displaying all the usual features detailed in the previous entry. Hence the tempi are – *mesto, vivace, andante, mesto, andante, agitato, allegretto, agitato, andante, vivace, andante.* The true title of the work is 'From Silent Shades (Bess of Bedlam)'.

63. Reissiger, Karl Gottlieb. Song, 'Adieu, ye Streams!' (page 77).

The words of this two-bar song are a translation of the German. Set in common time in E flat, there is a modulation to G flat towards the end. Karl Gottlieb Reissiger (1798–1859) was a German conductor and composer of operas, church and instrumental music.

64. Reissiger, Karl Gottlieb. Canzonetta, *Cara Lisa* (page 112).

A simple three verse canzonetta in common time in E flat. The melodic line has some interesting ornamentation.

65. Righini, Vincenzo. Duet, 'Come Opprima' (page 8).

Righini's opera *Enea nel Lazio,* from which this duet is taken, was written for Friedrich-Wilhelm II, and received its first performance at the Berlin Opera House in 1793. The duet, sung by Lavinia and Enea, begins as an *andantino* then increases tempo to *allegretto* half way through.

66. Rossini, Giaocchino. Aria, *Deh calma, O Ciel* (page 44).

The aria is Desdemona's in the last scene of the opera *Othello*, the English translation of the title of the aria being 'O calm, kind heavens'. *Othello* is a three-act opera which received its first performance in 1816. The librettist was Francesco Mario Berio di Salsa.

67. Rossini, Giaocchino. Invocation, *Giusto Ciel! In tal periglio* (page 91).

This short aria, *andantino,* was written for the opera *Maometto Secondo,* and transferred to *L'Assedio di Corinto* which, according to *The Supplement to the Musical Library,* is only an alteration of the former work, concerning the Turkish siege of Corinth under Mahomet II. The English translation of the title is 'Gracious Heaven! In such dread danger'. The melodic line is ornamented in typical style.

68. Spofforth, Reginald. Glee, 'Health to my Dear!' (page 154).

Set for two sopranos, alto and bass, with piano accompaniment, *vivace*, the dynamics range from *f* to *pp*. Written in A major, 'the music has been transposed from C to suit female voices'. The words are by Mrs. Barbauld. Reginald Spofforth (1770–1827) was a minor composer of songs and glees.

69. Storace, Stephen. Song, 'Toll, toll the Knell' (page 14).

According to *The Supplement to the Musical Library*, the words, which are by Prince Hoare, Esq., from the opera *Mahmoud*, 'though passable on stage where lyric poetry has not been in a very palmy state during the present century, have not sufficient merit to tempt us to insert them here; but the music to which they are united will long preserve them from oblivion'. The opening phrase illustrates the editor's opinions – 'Toll, toll the knell, Ding, ding dong bell'! The song is a *larghetto* in 2–4 time. In fact, the opera, whose alternative title is *The King of Persia*, was left incomplete at the composer's death but was made fit for performance by his sister Ann Selina, also known as Nancy, a well-known soprano, and her friend, the distinguished tenor Michael Kelly (a close associate of Richard Brinsley Sheridan, Mozart and Paisiello amongst others.). Stephen Storace, also known as Sorace (1763–1796) was English of Italian descent. A composer, particularly of operas, violinist and harpsichordist, he lived for some time in Vienna where he knew Mozart, whose influence can be discerned in much of his work.

70. Storace, Stephen. Quartet, 'Five times by the Taper's Light' (page 85).

An *andante* in common time with a distinctive piano accompaniment, this quartet is scored for two sopranos, alto and bass. It is taken from Storace's three-act opera *The Iron Chest*, with a libretto by George Colman (1762–1836) and first performed on 12 March 1796, just seven days before the composer's death.

71. (Unknown composer). Air, *Charmante Gabrielle* (page 121).

The words are ascribed to Henri IV. The editor has stated that the composer is unknown. However, the air appears with an introduction and four variations in a piano arrangement in Volume One of *The Musical Library* – Instrumental section, at page 129, and is attributed there to George Onslow.

72. (Unknown composer). Duet, 'Could a Man be Secure' (page 157).

This short *allegretto* is set for soprano or tenor and bass. The score directs – 'when the upper part is sung by a tenor, the accompaniment, if any, should be confined to the real notes of the two voices'.

73. Webbe, Samuel. Air, 'The Mansion of Peace' (page 75).

A two-verse *air affetuoso,* preceded by a *recitative,* it comprises two eight-bar sections, each of which is repeated.

74. Weber, Carl Maria von. Romance, 'Oh! Cease in Pity' (page 54).

The words were written by Robert Jamieson, and appeared in a two-volume collection of *Popular Ballads, Tradition, Manuscripts and Scarce Editions etc.* published by him in two volumes in 1806. The music adapted to the words is the Romance *Unter blühenden Mandelbäumen* (Under blossoming almond trees) from Weber's opera *Euryanthe,* written for a tenor in B flat, but transposed to G to suit soprano voices. The opera was first performed in Vienna in 1823.

75. Wilbye, John (1598). Madrigal, 'As fair as Morn, as fresh as May' (page 50).

Included in Wilbye's *Second Set of [thirty-four] Madrigals* of 1609, this delightful setting is for two sopranos and tenor. It is in two sections, the first of which is repeated. John Wilbye (1574–1638) was a composer, largely of madrigals, his first of two sets having been published in 1598, and he was one of the greatest composers in that genre of any nationality.

Volume Two

1835

Parsonage library reference 1131/7

59 Pieces

1. Arne, Thomas and Linley, Thomas (Senior) Air, 'Blow, blow thou Winter Wind' (page 42).

This is a setting of the song from Shakespeare's *As You Like It*, sung by Amiens in Act Two, Scene Seven. The first two verses, without refrain, are sung *andante* in common time. Then follows the refrain, in 6–8 time, marked 'cheerfully'.

2. Asioli, Bonifacio. Arietta, *Se resto sul lido* (page 80).

An *allegretto* in binary form, the two sections, respectively of eight and sixteen bars, are each directed to be repeated. The words are by Metastasio, the English translation of the title being 'If you rest on the shore'.

3. Atterbury, Luffman. Glee, 'Tell me then the Reason why' (page 150).

Set for two sopranos (or soprano and alto) and bass, the editor of *The Supplement to the Musical Library* states 'we know not the author of these rather silly lines; the music is exceedingly melodious and graceful, and may be said to be wholly unknown'.

4. Attwood, Thomas. Canzonet, 'Go, lovely Rose' (page 73).

A note on the score states – 'Composed for this Work'. A *larghetto* in 6–8 time, the words are by Edmund Waller. Thomas Attwood (1765–1838) was a composer and organist, who studied in Naples before becoming a pupil of Mozart. Subsequently he was a friend of Mendelssohn. As a composer he is best remembered for his theatrical and church music. One of the first professors at the Royal Academy of Music, he was also a founder member of the Philharmonic Society.

5. Beethoven, Ludwig van. *La Marmotte,* or 'The Savoyard Boy's Song' (page 20).

Goethe wrote the words which were set by Beethoven as the seventh of his opus 52 set of songs, compiled during the years 1803–5, though written a decade earlier, and published by Bureau des Arts et d'Industrie, Vienna, in 1805. The first line in the original German is *Ich komme schon durch manches Land* (From land to land I freely roam).

6. Beethoven, Ludwig van. Song, 'Young Spring-Gods around us flying'. Words by Goethe, translated by J. Oxenford (page 53).

Beethoven's opus 83, written in 1810, published a year later by Breitkopf und Härtel in Leipzig, and dedicated to Princess Kinsky, comprises settings of three Goethe songs. This is the third of them, entitled *Kleine Bluemen* (Little flowers).

7. Beethoven, Ludwig van. Quartet, 'How strange does all appear', from *Fidelio.* Translated from the German by J. Oxenford (page108).

This wonderful quartet, *Mir ist so wunderbar* (To me he is so Wonderful) is the third number in Act One of Beethoven's only opera, (1) the four singers being Marzelline, Leonore, Rocco and Jaquino, each of whom sings different words to the same music. It is an accompanied canon and is sung quietly throughout, until the final *ff* perfect cadence.

8. Beethoven, Ludwig van. Cavatina, 'Joy has fled, and all is cheerless', from *Fidelio.* Translated by J. Oxenford (page 112).

Florestan's aria *In des Lebens Frühlingstagen* (In life's springtime) follows his opening recitative at the beginning of Act Two of the opera. The editor has restricted his choice to the twenty-six bar *adagio cantabile.*

9. Beethoven, Ludwig van. Duet, 'Oh more, far more than mortal Pleasure', from *Fidelio.* Translated by J. Oxenford (page 114).

The number immediately preceding the finale, this is the duet between Leonore and Florestan which celebrates the latter's rescue. Marked *allegro vivace,* the editor has transposed it down a tone from G major.

10. Bellini, Vincenzo. Song, 'The Parting' (page 102).

The words are by 'the late F. Townsend, Esq.', and they have been adapted to an air from Bellini's opera *La Straniera,* first performed in Milan in 1829. The song is a two-verse *andantino* in 3–4 time.

11. Berg, Georg(e). Glee, 'Lightly tread, 'tis hallowed Ground' (page 17).

Written for three voices, *andante,* this glee is in two sixteen-bar sections, each to be repeated. The author of the words is unknown. George Berg (1720–75) was an organist and a writer of songs and glees, for some of which he won prizes, often for performance in Ranelagh or Spring Gardens.

12. Boyce, William. Song, 'Tell me, Lovely Shepherd' (page 136).

A two-verse song, *andante* in *tempo di Siciliana,* each verse is to be repeated. The words are by the dramatist Edward Moore (1712–1757). William Boyce (1711–1779) was an organist and important composer, especially of church anthems and services, masques, odes, trio sonatas and eight symphonies.

13. Callcott, John Wall. Glee, 'Harold the Valiant' (page 76).

Set for two sopranos and bass in common time, this glee is in three sections, the third being a repeat of the first. A seven-bar *larghetto e dolce* in the first section interrupts the *allegro* tempo. The writer of the words is not known.

14. Carey, Henry. Ballad, 'Sally in our Alley' (page 14).

According to *The Supplement to the Musical Library* both the words and music 'are from the prolific pen of the famous Henry Carey'. There are five verses, *andante,* the score bearing the rather gratuitous instruction that 'the five stanzas [are] to be sung as numbered'.

15. Carter, Charles Thomas. Song, 'O Nanny, wilt thou gang with me' (page 56).

A four-verse song, *andante ed espressivo,* with piano accompaniment, of which *The Supplement to the Musical Library* states – 'public opinion has so long stamped a value on these verses that it were now superfluous to dwell on their tenderness, simplicity and beauty'. The author was Thomas Percy, D.D., Bishop of Dromore, who, among other things was, apparently, capable of translating Chinese and Icelandic poetry. Charles Thomas Carter (c1735–1804) was an Irish composer of songs, catches and glees, this one being his most popular. *The Supplement to the Musical Library* again – '... he came to London, where imprudences counterbalanced the advantages that rarely fail to attend talent and social qualities'.

16. Cimarosa, Domenico. Duet, *Deh! Ti conforta o car* from *Il Matrimonio Segreto* (page 138).

The famous duet from the final scene of Cimarosa's most celebrated work is a *larghetto* sung by Paolino and Carolina who, when they are actually singing together, do so in thirds. The opera had its first performance in February 1792 in Vienna. The libretto was by Giovanni Bertati, and was based upon *The Clandestine Marriage* by George Colman (1732–94) and David Garrick (1717–79).

17. Danby, John. Glee, 'The fairest flowers the vale prefer' (page 105).

This glee won a gold medal for the composer – he wrote nearly one hundred of them. A *larghetto, quasi andante,* in common time, it is set for two sopranos and tenor/baritone. John Danby (1757–1798) was a London-born organist and composer of glees, such as this one, masses and motets. Apparently he died during the performance of a concert which his friends had got up for his benefit, he having long lost the use of his limbs by sleeping in a damp bed at an inn.

18. Eberwein, Traugott Maximilian. German Song, *Ich liebte dich.* (page 89).

Adapted to Lord Byron's Stanzas, the music is a German song by Traugott Maximilian Eberwein (1775–1831) referred to in *The Supplement to the Musical Library* as 'a clever composer, but little known'. There are two simple verses, performed *larghetto.*

19. Ford, Thomas (1620). Madrigal, 'Since first I saw your face' (page 160).

A madrigal set for first soprano, second soprano/alto, tenor, and bass, *andante,* in four verses, it was composed in 1620. It is not known who was the author of the words. Thomas Ford (c1580–1648) was a lutenist, viol player, poet and an important composer, particularly of madrigals, like this one. In 1607 he published *Musicke of Sundrie Kindes.* ('Since first I saw your face' was set again, in 1942, by Roger Quilter).

20. Giordani, Tommaso. Song, 'O gentle maid' (page 28).

A simple *larghetto,* set originally to Italian words, *Caro mio ben,* it is the composer's most popular work. Tommaso Giordani (c1730–1806) was an Italian composer, mainly of opera, who spent much time in London and Dublin, where he taught John Field.

21. Graeff, Johann Georg. Canzonet, 'I told my Nymph' (page 162).

A five-verse *pastorale allegretto* in 6–8 time, this is one of six canzonets which are reckoned to be the composer's most important works. The third verse is in the tonic minor and the fifth has some melodic ornamentation. Johann Georg Graeff was a German composer born in 1762, but who lived in England from the age of twenty-two. At one time, he studied with Haydn. The words are by William Shenstone.

22. Grétry André Ernest Modeste. Air, '*La Danse ne pas ce que j'aime*' (page 124).

An air from Act One, Scene Two of Grétry's most popular work, the opera *Richard Coeur-de-Lion,* there are three verses sung in French, each one ending with an identical refrain. The libretto is by Michel-Jean Sedaine (1719–97). André Ernest Modeste Grétry (1741–1813) was a French composer, albeit born in Liege, Belgium, who wrote some fifty operas, along with church and instrumental music.

23. Gyrowetz, Adalbert. Song, 'When I roved a young Highlander' (page 132).

The three verses are part of a song by Lord Byron, adapted to Gyrowetz's original with German words. It is a simple *allegretto* in 2–4 time. Adalbert Gyrowetz (Vojtěch Matyáš Jírovec) (1763–1850) was a Bohemian-born German composer whose works, according to *The Supplement to the Musical Library* 'have not obtained the notice out of his own country to which their merits entitle them'. A prolific composer in all genres, he was much travelled, knew Mozart and Haydn, and was a pall-bearer at Beethoven's funeral.

24. Handel, George Frideric. Air, 'Where'er you walk' (page30).

This popular air is from Handel's three-act opera *Semele,* adapted from the libretto by William Congreve (1670–1729) for John Eccles' opera of the same name. The plot details Semele's love for Jupiter, and the first performance was at Covent Garden in 1744. Written in three sections, *largo,* the third is a repeat of the first.

25. Handel, George Frideric. Aria, *Rendi'l Sereno al Ciglio* (page 52).

This aria is from the opera *Sosarme,* first performed at the King's Theatre, London in 1732. Sung in Italian, it is a *largo* in 6–8 time. In three sections, the third is a repeat of the first. The libretto is by Matteo Noris adapted from his *Alfonso Primo,* and based upon an earlier libretto by Antonio Salvi. Sosarme was a king of Media, and in the original performance, the title role was sung by an alto castrato.

26. Handel, George Frideric. Air, 'Love in her Eyes sits playing' (page 60).

This air is the seventh number in *Acis and Galatea,* and is sung by Acis. A *larghetto* in lilting 6–8 time, it has been transposed to C from E flat 'to suit soprano voices'. The words are attributed to John Gay with additions by John Dryden, Alexander Pope and John Hughes, and the work received its first performance at Cannons, Edgware, sometime between 1718 and 1720.

27. Handel, George Frideric. Trio, 'The Flocks shall leave the Mountains' (page 62).

The seventeenth number from *Acis and Galatea,* described as a masque, serenata, pastoral, or secular choral work, this trio is sung by Acis (tenor), Galatea (soprano) and Polyphemus (bass). The performance direction is *andante e staccato.* The words are attributed to John Gay with additions by John Dryden, Alexander Pope and John Hughes.

28. Handel, George Frideric. Air, 'Heart, the Seat of soft Delight' (page 66).

The penultimate number in *Acis and Galatea*, sung by Galatea, *larghetto e piano,* it is characterised by much use of a dotted rhythm. The words are attributed to John Gay with additions by John Dryden, Alexander Pope and John Hughes.

29. Handel, George Frideric. Aria, *Verdi Prati* (page 94).

Taken from the opera *Alcina,* this famous aria is sung by Ruggiero, and although written for a castrato, is nowadays sung by a counter tenor or mezzo soprano. It is a *larghetto quasi andante.* The libretto is by Antonio Marchi from Ariosto's *Orlando furioso.*

30. Haydn, Franz Joseph. Cavatina, 'Winter' (page 1).

Number thirty-six in the oratorio *The Seasons,* the first line of this short cavatina reads 'Light and life dejected languish'. It is a *largo* sung by Jane. The English words are translated from the German libretto of Baron von Swieten who had presented the German version to Haydn as a translation of an English poem by James Thomson (1700 – 1748).

31. Haydn, Franz Joseph. Canzonet, 'Piercing Eyes' (page 18).

This is one of the six canzonets published by Haydn in 1795, and dedicated to the Rt. Hon. Ladie *(sic)* Charlotte Bertie. Mrs. John (Ann) Hunter is believed to have selected the poems. A sprightly *allegretto* in 6–8 time, it is one of the shorter of Haydn's canzonets.

32. Haydn, Franz Joseph. Canzonet, 'She never told her Love' (page 38).

This is one of the six canzonets published by Haydn in 1795, and dedicated to the Rt. Hon. Ladie *(sic)* Charlotte Bertie. The words are Shakespeare's and are taken from Act Two, Scene Four of *Twelfth Night,* spoken by Viola.

33. Haydn, Franz Joseph. Cavatina, *Il Pensier sta negli orgetti* (page 81).

Haydn composed his *opera seria Orfeo ed Euridice* in 1791, to a libretto by Carlo Francesco Badini. This cavatina is sung by King Creonte in Act One, Scene Two. The performance direction is *andante.*

34. Haydn, Franz Joseph. Chorus, 'Come gentle Spring' (page 125).

The third number from *The Seasons* is a four-part chorus. An *allegretto,* it is one of the longest selections in the Vocal volumes. The English words are translated from the German libretto of Baron von Swieten (see note under 30, above).

35. Haydn, Franz Joseph. Canzonet, 'O Tuneful Voice' (page 145).

One of the canzonets published in 1795 with words selected by Mrs. John (Ann) Hunter, it is to be performed *un poco adagio.* It contains interesting harmonies and a distinctively rhythmic piano accompaniment.

36. Home, (Anne), Miss. 'The Death Song of the Cherokee Indian' (page 45).

The Supplement to the Musical Library refers to Anne Home (not Ann as previously) as being 'the sister of the late Sir Everard Home [and] afterwards the wife of the justly-celebrated John Hunter, [commenting also upon the] many elegant poetical effusions of the same lady'. Mention has already been made of her in regard to Haydn's canzonets, as poet and dedicatee. As regards this song, she explains: 'this simple melody was brought to England ten years ago by a gentleman named Turner who had (owing to some singular events in his life) spent nine years among the natives of America. He assured the author that it was peculiar to that tribe or nation called the Cherokee, and they chanted it to a barbarous jargon implying contempt for their enemies in the moments of torture and death. The words here annexed have been thought characteristic of the spirit and sentiments of those brave savages. We look upon the fierce and stubborn courage of the dying Indian with a mixture of respect, pity and horror; and it is to those sentiments in the breast of the hearer that the Death Song must owe its effect'. It is likely that the original 'simple melody' has been modified to equate more with European tastes, perhaps by Anne Home herself, a fact which the score seems to bear out with the words 'the symphonies and accompaniments are new additions'.

37. Horsley, William. Glee, 'The Sun shines fair on Carlisle Wall' (page 32).

These seven verses are taken from Sir Walter Scott's *Lay of the Last Minstrel*, Canto VI, stanzas 11 and 12, a work which was known to the Brontë children. It is set for two trebles and bass, with accompaniment *ad libitum,* and directed to be performed moderately fast. There are changes of tempo and a number of performance directions, including a wide range of dynamics. Sir William Horsley (1774–1858) was an organist and composer, particularly of glees. At the head of the score it is stated that he was a B.Mus [Oxford] and Member of the Royal Academy of Music, Stockholm. He was also a founder member of the Philharmonic Society in 1813.

38. Horsley, William. Glee, 'Go happy Heart' (page 134).

A four-part glee – soprano, alto, tenor and bass – performance is directed to be 'with expression but not too slow'. The words are by John Fletcher (1579–1625) taken from his tragicomedy *The Mad Lover*, published in 1647.

39. Hummel, Johann Nepomuk. Romanza, *L'ombrosa Notte vien!* (page 37).

This romance is taken from Act Three of Hummel's best-known opera – strictly a *Singspiel* – *Mathilde von Guise,* first performed in Vienna in 1810, and is sung by the eponymous character. A *larghetto* in two verses, each with an identical refrain, it is written in Italian, and towards its end it includes an extraordinary downward leap of two octaves for the singer to negotiate.

40. Jackson, William. Canzonet, 'Go, gentle Gales' (page 129).

A two-verse canzonet in E major, marked *andante affettuoso,* with piano accompaniment, the words are taken from the third pastoral of Alexander Pope (1688–1744). According to *The Supplement to the Musical Library* Jackson's music 'may, as a song, be considered his *chef-d'oeuvre.* We have adapted it from the composer's score, and believe that, like many compositions which have already appeared in our work, it will be new to ninety-nine one hundredths of our subscribers'.

41. Leveridge, Richard. Ballad, 'Black-eyed Susan' (page 86).

The words are by John Gay (1685–1732), written under the title of *Sweet William's Farewell to Black-eyed Susan.* Only six of the eight verses are included in the score, the whole eight being printed in *The Supplement to the Musical Library*, which goes on to state that 'the music is commonly ascribed to Handel, who possibly altered and improved the original melody, but it appears to us quite clear that the composition is by the famous singer Leveridge'. Richard Leveridge (1670–1758) was a singer and composer of 'convivial songs'.

42. Mäyer, Simone. *Scena e Duetto, Parto! Ti lascio, addio!* (page 9).

The *scena* is from Mäyer's opera of 1800, *Lodoviska,* and comprises a thirty-two bar *recitative* beginning *allegro,* then incorporating *andante, allegro* and *andante* sections, before leading into *Duetto, andante grazioso,* the whole being sung by Lodoviska and Lovinski. Simone Mäyer, sometimes spelt Mayr (1763–1845) was an Italian composer of German origin, who wrote over sixty operas and church music. Also a teacher, one of his students was Donizetti. In his later years he became blind.

43. Méhuel, Étienne Nicolas. Romance, *Ah, lorsque la mort* (page 142).

This romance is taken from Méhuel's opera *Joseph*, first performed in Paris in 1807, and is based on the biblical story of Joseph and his brothers. The libretto is by Alexandre Duval, and this romance is sung in the original French, by Benjamin. It is a three-verse *allegretto poco andante* in 3–8 time.

44. Mercadante, Giuseppe Saverio Raffaele. Cavatina, '*Soave imagine d'amor*' (page 152).

Taken from Mercadante's 1821 opera *Andronico,* the English translation of the title of this cavatina is 'Sweet Picture of Love'. An *andante* in 6–8 time, there is much ornamentation in the melodic line. Saverio Mercadante (1795–1870) was an Italian composer, most notably of opera, and another to become blind in later life.

45. Morley, Thomas. Madrigal, 'Now is the Month of Maying' (page 69).

This very well-known madrigal dates from 1595, and is set for treble, counter tenor, tenor, and two basses. It is of two verses with the familiar fa-la-la refrain, each line of each verse being repeated, and is thus the type of madrigal known as a ballett. The words are full of *double entendres.* Thomas Morley (1557–1602) was an organist and composer, especially of madrigals, of which he was one of the greatest exponents. A pupil of William Byrd, he also wrote instrumental *Books of Consort Lessons* and *Books of Ayres* for lute and bass viol. It is said that he worked as a government spy.

46. Mornington, Earl of. Madrigal, 'Return, return, my lovely Maid' (page 24).

Set for two sopranos, alto and bass, this madrigal is to be performed *moderato.* It is possible that it was Francis Hutcheson (c1722–1780) not Mornington, who was the composer. The author of the words is not known.

47. Nares, James. Duet, 'Why should Mortals sigh for Gold' (page 96).

The first two lines of this duet are sung *allegretto* and repeated, likewise the next two. Lines five and six are given *andante,* and finally the first two lines are repeated *allegretto. The Supplement to the Musical Library* has this to say: 'We know not the author of these lines; and in truth they are unworthy of the music, which is among the many admirable compositions which we have undertaken to rescue from oblivion'.

48. Rossini, Gioacchino. *Canzonetta, Nizza, je puis sans pain* (page 21).

A two-verse *canzonetta* for soprano, each verse beginning in E minor before switching to the tonic major, the words are French by É. Deschamps.

49. Salomon, Johann Peter. Canzonet, 'Say not that Minutes swiftly move' (page 84).

The last canzonet of the second set published by Salomon in 1804, the first verse is repeated, while the second contains some interesting chromatic harmony.

50. Shield, William. Song, 'The Streamlet', from 'The Woodman'. (page 100).

This is a simple two-verse *andante* sung quietly throughout from the opera *The Woodman* (1791) by the Revd. Sir Henry Bate Dudley, Bart., who for many years was the proprietor and editor of *The Morning Herald.*William Shield (1748–1829) was a violinist and composer, particularly of stage pieces, songs and string quartets, who studied with Charles Avison and made the acquaintance of Haydn.

51. Spohr, Louis (Ludwig). Song, 'What makes this poor Bosom'. (page 2).

The words of this two-verse song are translated from the German by Friedrich Kind. Directed to be played *appassionato ma non troppo lento,* this is the first of Spohr's *Sechs Deutsche Lieder*, opus 41, and is a soulful piece with a gently moving piano accompaniment.

52. Spohr, Louis (Ludwig). Duet, 'Still confiding' (page 46).

From Spohr's *Singspiel Faust*, this duet is sung, *andante,* in Act One by Faust and Rosa. The contents page of *The Musical Library* states: 'Words by Goethe, translated by J[ohn] Oxenford', but in fact the libretto of the opera was by Joseph Karl Bernard, based upon the traditional legend. The opera had its first performance in Prague in September 1816, with Weber conducting. The original German title of the song is *Folg dem Freunde.*

53. Storace, Stephen. Song, 'Down by the River' (page 50).

Another song taken from *The Iron Chest*, with words by George Colman the Younger, produced in 1796 just a week before Storace's death, this is a two-verse pastoral *larghetto.*

54. Travers, John. Canzonet, 'Soft Cupid, wanton amorous Boy' (page 4).

This six-verse canzonet, titled *Cupid's Promise*, is a paraphrase of a French *chanson* by Matthew Prior (1664–1721) set to music by Travers in his set of *Eighteen Canzonets.* Its performance, by two sopranos and either tenor or bass, features regularly changing *tempi – largo, andante, più moto, largo, andante, vivace, larghetto, allegretto, larghetto* – and the editor has transposed it from C minor to G minor, 'to suit female voices'. John Travers (c1703–1758) was an organist and composer who, in addition to his *Eighteen Canzonets*, wrote church music, and voluntaries for organ and harpsichord.

55. Travers, John. Canzonet, 'Haste my Nanette' (page 154).

A canzonet for soprano and bass it is in a number of sections – *moderato* in E major, common time, *Siciliano* in E minor, 6–8 time, *largo* in B minor, common time, *andante* in E major, 3–4 time, and *vivace* in E major, 6–8 time. It is taken from Travers' *Eighteen Canzonets,* with the words by Matthew Prior.

56. Webbe, Samuel. Glee, 'You gave me your Heart' (page 40).

This is a five-part glee, set for soprano, soprano or alto, two tenors and bass, *andante,* in 3–4 time, published in the fifteenth of *Warren's Collection of Catches, Canons and Glees* of 1776. The words are said to be by Joseph Craddock.

57. Weber, Carl Maria von. 'May-Song' (page 58).

A simple song for two sopranos, *allegretto,* the opening line of which, translated from the German by W.J. Walter, is 'Hail! All hail! Thou merry month of May', it is taken from Weber's *Volkslieder.*

58. Wilbye, John. Madrigal, 'Flora gave me fairest Flowers' (page 90).

This madrigal was published in Wilbye's *First Set of Madrigals* of 1598, not 1609 as is stated on the score, that year being the date of publication of the second set. It is written for five voices – two sopranos, alto, tenor and bass – to be performed *allegretto.*

59. Winter, Peter. *Aria and Coro, Lieti fiori, ombrosi piante* (page 70).

Taken from *Il Ratto di Proserpina (*'The Rape of Proserpina') with libretto by Lorenzo Da Ponte, this aria is sung, *andante,* by the title character, during the absence of her mother, Ceres, during which time Pluto takes advantage of the situation. A two-part female chorus also features. The opera premiered at the Haymarket Theatre in 1804.

Volume Three

1836

Parsonage library reference 1131/6

60 Pieces

1. Arne, Thomas. Song, 'Gentle Youth, ah! tell me Why' (page 70).

The seventh number in Act One of the opera *Love in a Village* is a gentle *larghetto* in common time. The opera is a ballad opera in three acts, a pastiche arranged by Arne, comprising five musical numbers newly composed by him, thirteen taken from his earlier works, a newly written overture by the composer and entrepreneur K.F. Abel (1723–1787), and a further twenty-three by a whole string of other composers. The libretto, based upon Charles Johnson's play of 1729, *The Village Opera,* is by Isaac Bickerstaff, which name is, in fact, a pseudonym used by Jonathan Swift. Probably the best-known song in the opera is 'The Miller of the Dee'.

2. Arnold, Samuel. Song, 'The Hardy Sailor' (page 56).

A single-verse song of eight lines, *grazioso* in a gentle 6–8 time, the first four lines are repeated after the whole eight have been sung. It is taken from the comic opera *The Castle of Andalusia*, the words being by John O'Keeffe (1747–1833).

3. Arnold, Samuel. Duet, 'Idalian Queen' (page 58).

Another song from *The Castle of Andalusia*, this one being an *andante grazioso* in 2–4 time. For the majority of the time the two voices are singing in thirds.

4. Arnold, Samuel. Song, 'An Address to a Locket' (page 124).

The words are taken from the novel *Emma Corbett, or the Miseries of Civil War* by Samuel Jackson Pratt (1749–1814), and the three-verse song is an *affetuoso* in common time.

5. Arnold, Samuel. Glee, 'The Seasons' (page 164).

This is a two-verse glee set for soprano, second soprano or alto, tenor and bass, initially *allegretto,* then *vivace* with a distinctive dotted rhythm illustrating the word 'laugh', and a short *largo* to finish. The words are by Dr. Stanley.

6. Attwood, Thomas. Dirge, 'He is gone to the Mountain' (page 71).

Taken from Canto III, XVI of Scott's *Lady of the Lake*, written in 1810, a work known to the Brontës, this is a Gaelic *coronach* (dirge or funeral song) in three verses, set to suitably sparse music by Attwood.

7. Beethoven, Ludwig van. Canzonet, 'The fortunate Land' (page 90).

The English words are translated by J.W. Walter, the original German title being *Das glücklische Land.* The first of Beethoven's opus 75 set of six songs, the first three of which are settings of Goethe, this one taken from his *Wilhelm Meister.* (2) The set was compiled in 1809 and published the year after by Breitkopf und Härtel of Leipzig. The dedicatee was Princess Kinsky. Known as 'Mignon's Song', the first line of the original German text is *Kennst du das Land* (Knowest thou the land), and the performance direction is *larghetto.*

8. Bellini, Vincenzo. Cavatina, *Con sorriso d'innocenzo* (page 6).

The cavatina is taken from Act Two of *Il Pirata* (The Pirate), Bellini's three-act opera, with libretto by Felice Romani, which had its first performance in Milan in 1827. Sung *andante sostenuto* in common time, the melodic line is in typically florid Italian style. The English translation of the title of the song is 'With an innocent smile'.

9. Bellini, Vincenzo. Terzettino, *Angiol de pace all' anima* (page 101).

The three singers in this trio, *largo sostenuto,* are the tenor Ornabello, and the two sopranos Agnese and Beatrice, the two women singing together in thirds. It is taken from the opera *Beatrice di Tenda,* with libretto by Felice Romani, which was first performed in Venice in 1833.

10. Bertoni, Ferdinando Giuseppe. Rondo, *La Verginella come la rosa* (page 51).

A note on the score states that this rondo is 'Introduced as "Love, soft illusion" in *The Castle of Andalusia*, while, according to *The Supplement to the Musical Library*, it comes from the opera *La Governante,* an adaptation of Sheridan's *Duenna,* made for the King's Theatre by [Carlo Francesco] Badini. Ferdinando Giuseppe Bertoni (1725–1813) was an Italian organist and operatic composer.

11. Callcott, John Wall. Glee, 'Desolate is the Dwelling of Morna' (page 1).

Set for three voices, various tempi are used, respectively *larghetto quasi andante, allegro, maestoso, con spirito.* The words are taken from Ossian.

12. Callcott, John Wall. Glee, 'Oh! tarry, gentle Traveller' (page 126).

This glee is set for two sopranos and bass. It is an *allegretto,* with a *larghetto* middle section. The author of the words is unknown.

13. Cook, Benjamin, Mus.D. Glee, 'In the Merry Month of May' (page 109).

As is usual with this type of composition, there are a number of different tempi used – lively, quick, slow, quick and sprightly and distinct. There are some interesting modulations in the slow section. The words are by poet and dramatist Nicholas Breton (1545–1626), taken from *England's Helicon*, published in 1600, and it was awarded a gold medal from the Catch Club in 1773.

14. D'Alary, (Forename unknown). *Elegia, Sulla tomba di Bellini, l'Amico dolente* (page 121).

An elegy 'on the tomb of Bellini', in other words, a homage. Beginning, *lento,* in A minor, the middle section is in the relative major, *più animato.* Little seems to be known about the composer D'Alary, although 'Scene and Romance from *Rosamunde*' by 'Alary' was the final item in the concert which Charlotte attended in Brussels in October 1843.

15. Dibdin, Charles. Duet, 'The neighb'ring Convent's Bell' (page 118).

The duet is sung by Leonora and Leander, with piano accompaniment depicting the peeling of the bells, *andante con moto*, in D major, 'transposed from F'. The words, from *The Padlock*, are by Isaac Bickerstaff (Jonathan Swift). Charles Dibdin (1745–1814) described in *The Supplement to the Musical Library* as 'original and sensible', was the youngest of eighteen children. Also a dramatist, actor and entrepreneur, as a composer he is best remembered for his songs, of which he wrote over six hundred.

16. Fitzherbert, Thomas, Esq. Glee, 'In holiday Gown' (page 74).

A three-part glee – two sopranos and tenor or bass – it is an *allegretto* in 2–4 time. The words are by the Irish poet John Cunningham, and it was composed and presented to *The Musical Library* by Thomas Fitzherbert Esq., of whom little is known other than that he was of an ancient Staffordshire family.

17. Geary, Timothy (Thomas Augustine) Duet, 'Soft is the Zephyr's breezy Wing' (page 170).

A single-verse canzonet, *poco allegretto,* it is in G, 'transposed from B flat'. The author of the words is unknown, but the composer is described in *The Supplement to the Musical Library* as 'a native of Dublin, and a most promising genius who died at an early age, just as the great superiority of his talent was beginning to manifest itself'. In fact, he was found drowned in a canal, his death possibly being suicide. Timothy Geary (1775–1801), who adopted the forenames Thomas Augustine, probably as a homage to Arne, was an accomplished organist and pianist who performed a Dussek concerto at a concert in Dublin in 1792, at which this duet was also sung.

18. Giardini, Felice de. Song, ''Tis not Wealth, it is not Birth' (page 84).

Taken from Arne's pastiche *Love in a Village*, where it is sung by Rosetta, the words are by Isaac Bickerstaff (Jonathan Swift). Giardini is one of the many composers whose music features in the opera. It is in three sections, *andante grazioso*, the third being a repeat of the first. Felice Giardini (1716–1796) was a violinist and prolific composer, particularly for the violin and the string quartet. He travelled widely, spending much time in England, and died in Moscow.

19. Handel, George Frideric. Duetto, *Caro! Bella!* (page 32).

From *Giulio Cesare*, this is the final duet of the opera, sung by Cesare and Cleopatra, *allegro ma non troppo*. The libretto is by Nicola Francesca Haym, one of several libretti that he wrote for Handel, and the opera had its first performance at the King's Theatre, London, in 1724.

20. Handel, George Frideric. Recitativo. *Alma del gran Pompeo!* and Aria, *Piangero* (page 61).

This number from the opera *Giulio Cesare* is sung by the title character, the aria being a *largo* in 3–8 time. The libretto is by Nicola Francesco Haym.

21. Horsley, William. (M.B.Oxon.). Round, 'Here, in Sweet Sleep' (page 51).

A ten-bar round for three voices, it is to be performed *dolcemente sempre, sempre pp*.

'Here in sweet sleep the son of Nicon lies,
He sleeps, for who shall say the good man dies.'

22. Howard, Samuel. Song, 'O had I been by Fate decreed' (page 86).

Another song from Arne's pastiche *Love in a Village*, it is a *Siciliana* in 6–8 time, sung by Young Meadows, with words by Henry Baker, 'and inserted without any acknowledgement in the opera by Isaac Bickerstaff' (Jonathan Swift). Samuel Howard (1710–82) was a minor composer of opera and songs.

23. Hummel, Johann Nepomuk. Romance, 'O forebear to bid Me slight Her' (page 28).

This twenty-bar, two-verse romance is directed to be played *larghetto molto espressivo,* with a rippling piano accompaniment consisting of triplets. The words, by Aaron Hill (1685–1750) have been adapted by the editor to Hummel's German air 'Neidisch trennen Tal und Hügen'. Hill provided the libretto for Handel's opera *Rinaldo,* and was also a theatre manager at Drury Lane and Covent Garden.

24. Jackson, William (of Exeter). Elegy, 'Ye Woods and ye Mountains' (page 24).

Transposed from the key of E flat to B flat, 'to suit female voices', this four-verse elegy, the fifth of six in Jackson's opus 3, is written for two sopranos and bass, *larghetto ed amoroso.*

25. Keller, Carl. Rondo, 'Down a thousand Fathom Deep' (page 98).

To be performed *allegro non troppo,* in D minor, the final verse is in the tonic major. The piano accompaniment consists of repeated chords throughout. Set originally in German, the English words are adapted by Mrs. Radcliffe. Carl Keller (1784-1855) was a German flautist, and composer, mainly of music for his instrument, and songs such as this one.

26. Linley, Thomas (senior). Song. 'No Flower that blows' (page 29).

This popular song is taken from the opera *Selima and Azor,* described as a 'Persian Tale'. The libretto is by Sir George Collier, from Marmontel's *Zémire et Azor,* and the opera had its first performance at Drury Lane in 1776. According to *Grove*, 'it utilises to some extent Grétry's music'. It is an *allegretto* in common time.

27. Martini, Vincenzo. Quartet, *Pieta di noi* (page 12).

Taken from Martini's comic opera *L'Albore di Diana* (The Tree of Diana) the singers are Silvio and Endimione (tenors), Doristo (bass) and Diana (soprano). The quartet is an *andante con moto* in 3–8 time, the last twelve bars requiring virtuoso singing from the soprano. The opera received its first performance in Vienna in 1787, and was one of three by this composer set to libretti by Lorenzo Da Ponte, better known for his work with Mozart. Vincenzo Martini, whose real name was Vicente Martín y Soler (1754–1806), was an organist and composer, mainly of operas. Born in Valencia, he travelled widely, working in Madrid, Naples, Vienna and St. Petersburg, where he died.

28. Martini, Vincenzo. Cavatina, *Piu Bianca di giglio* (page 104).

From Martini's opera *La Cosa Rara* (A Rare Thing) this is a *cavatina, andante amoroso.* The first verse is sung in English, the second in Italian. It also appears in Stephen Storace's pastiche opera *The Siege of Belgrade* as 'The Rose and the Lily'. The English words are by James Cobb.

29. Martini, Vincenzo. Round, *Se placar volete Amore* (page 140).

This round is a simple *allegretto* for three voices, sung to Italian words.

30. Méhul, Étienne **(Nicolas).** Ariette, *Le Doux Mal* (page 54).

Described as an *ariette,* and composed by Méhul, according to *The Supplement to the Musical Library*, 'it is now copied from [Jean-Baptiste Matho's opera] *Arion*'. This was a five-act tragic opera, based upon the myth of the Greek poet of that name, first performed in Paris in 1714. There are two verses, *andante*, sung in French.

31. Mendelssohn, Felix. Spring Song, *Frühlingslied* (page 134).

The English translation of 'Spring Song' is by John Oxenford. An *andante* in 2–4 time, the first verse comprises the English translation, the second, the original German.

32. Mendelssohn, Felix. Romance, 'Expectation' (page 174).

Three short verses, translated from the German by John Oxenford, to be performed *allegro con moto, ff,* comprise this romance from Mendelssohn's *Zwölf Lieder,* opus 9.

33. Mercadante, Giuseppe Saverio. Cavatina, *Sgombra I miei dubbi, O Cielo!* (page 161).

The three-act opera *Ismalia* was first performed at La Scala, Milan in 1832. The libretto is by Felice Romani (1788–1865) and the English translation of the title is 'Clear my Doubts, O Sky!' A cavatina, it is an *andante* in 9–8 time.

34. Meyerbeer, Giacomo. Cavatina, *Tu sai qual' oggetto* (page 150).

From Meyerbeer's opera *Romilda e Costanza,* which received its first performance in Padua in 1817, this *andante grazioso cavatina* is one with a heavily ornamented melodic line. The libretto is by Gaetano Rossi (1774–1855) who wrote for many of the major Italian composers of his time, including Rossini, Donizetti and Mercadante.

35. National. A Brazilian Air, 'And are these the Mountains' (page 8).

The words are 'feely translated from the Portuguese for this work', the author being the neoclassical Brazilian poet, Tomás António Gonzaga (1744–1810). Beginning *larghetto,* the tempo increases to *allegro agitato* for the last eight bars.

36. National. Russian Air, 'You are a Tulip, Seen Today' (page 87).

The words of this six-bar air, *allegretto moderato,* are those of Robert Herrick (1591–1674) from his *Meditation for his Mistress*, adapted to a Russian tune.

37. Neukomm, Sigismund Chevalier von. Song, 'Come dear Maria' (page 146).

The words are by Miss Whatley, printed in *Ritson's Collection*, and they have been adapted to Neukomm's music, a simple *allegretto* in common time.

38. Paer, Ferdinando. Duet, *Dolce dell'anima* (page 41).

This duet from the heroic drama *Sargino, ossia L'allievo dell'amore,* is a heavily-ornamented *larghetto* sung by Soffia and Sargino. The libretto is by Giuseppe Maria Foppa, and the first performance took place in Dresden in 1803. Fernandino Paer (1771–1839) was an Italian composer of Austrian descent. This was one of his fifty-five operas, and he was another to have set the 'Leonore' ' story – Beethoven was said to have been impressed by him.

39. Purcell, Henry. Cantata, 'From Rosy Bowers' (page 14).

'The Song of the Swan' is taken from part three of what was largely Purcell's setting of Tom D'Urfey's *Don Quixote,* one of the first stage dramatisations of Miguel Cervantes' novel, and it is probably one of the last songs the composer wrote. It is a dramatization of the scene where Altisidora tries to seduce Don Quixote into leaving his beloved Dulcinea. As was common with cantatas of this nature it alternates recitative and aria, and makes use of different tempi. Purcell wrote the music for *Don Quixote* in three stages during

1694–95. Tom D'Urfey (1653–1723) – he himself added the apostrophe – was an English writer and wit who was involved in the development of the ballad opera, ten of the sixty-eight songs in *The Beggar's Opera* being his. He wrote thirty-two plays and over five hundred songs, many of them between 1698 and 1720, and published in his collection *Wit and Mirth; or, Pills to Purge Melancholy*. They evince a distinct tendency towards bawdiness.

40. Purcell, Henry. Cantata, 'Let the dreadful Engines' (page 152).

Another one of the 'mad songs' which Purcell set, this one is sung by Cardenio in D'Urfey's *Don Quixote*. It is a cantata, alternating recitative and aria, with contrasting tempi – *largo, allegretto, agitato, affetuoso, andante, largo* – and a wide dynamic range. The editor of *The Supplement to the Musical Library* considered that 'the words of the latter part [are] unfit for modern ears, however relished'.

41. Ravenscroft, Thomas (1611). Canzonet, 'Can'st thou Love and Live Alone?' (page 141).

According to *The Supplement to the Musical Library*, 'the author of these words is unknown; they are most likely the production of one of the numerous poetasters of the day whose names speedily sank into oblivion'. The editor goes on to call the composer, Thomas Ravenscroft (c1590–c1633) a 'bigot'. In fact, he was an English theorist, musical editor and composer who, in 1611, published a volume entitled *Melismata. Musicall Phansies: Fitting the Court, Citie and Countrey Humours. To 3, 4, and 5 Voyces (sic)*, in which this canzonet appears. Set for four voices – two sopranos, alto and bass – it is in two sections, the first being an *andante affettuoso* in G major, the second an *allegretto* in the tonic minor, each section then being repeated.

42. Reissiger, Karl Gottlieb. Ballad, 'The Brook's Lullaby' (page 48).

The words are translated from the German by John Oxenford. A four-verse ballad, *moderato,* it is sung quietly throughout – *pp* and *ppp,* which later direction is unusual in *The Musical Library.* Karl Gottlieb Reissiger (1798–1859) was a German conductor and composer, particularly of operas, including *Turandot.* He succeeded Weber as the Director of the Dresden Court Opera in 1827 , conducted the first performance of Wagner's *Rienzi* in 1842, and appointed that composer as second conductor the year after.

43. Ricci, Luigi. Arietta, *Or son d'Elena invaghito* (page 78).

This arietta is taken from Ricci's comic opera *Un'avventura di Scaramuccia,* which received its first performance at La Scala, Milan in 1834. The librettist is Felice Romani. It is a single verse *moderato,* sung in Italian.

44. Rousseau, Jean-Jacques. Air *(de trios notes), Que le jour me dure* (page 20).

The words to this simple air are by the composer. An *andantino* in 3–8 time, the whole sixteen bars are written on just three notes – G, A and B. The English translation of the title is 'How the day drags, spent far from you'. Jean-Jacques Rousseau (1712–1778) was the celebrated French political philosopher, educationist and author, born in

Geneva. His masterpiece was *Du contrat social,* published in 1762, with its English translation *A Treatise on the Social Contract,* following two years later. His theory of education was also published in 1762, in the form of a novel – *Émile, ou de l'éducation.* As a composer, he left unfinished *Daphnis et Chloé,* and wrote approximately one hundred songs.

45. Rousseau, Jean-Jacques. Duettino, *Tendre fruit des fleurs d'Aurore* (page 80).

This simple two-verse duet is an *andantino* in 3–4 time, sung in French to words by M. Bernard. The English translation of the title is 'Soft fruit of Aurora's Tears'.

46. Sacchini, Antonio Maria Gaspero Gioacchino. Song, 'Henry culled the Flow'rets Bloom' (page 138).

The words of this simple, single-verse song are by Mrs. Frances Brooke, and are taken from the opera *Rosina,* first produced in 1798. In fact, the music is nearly all by William Shield (1748–1829), but he introduced into it two Scottish melodies and this air, composed by Sacchini. Antonio Maria Gaspero Gioacchino Sacchini (1730–1786) was an Italian composer, who was influenced by the operatic reforms of Gluck. Another who travelled widely – Naples, Venice, Rome, London and Paris. *Rosina* is one of over forty operas which he wrote.

47. Schnyder von Wartensee, Franz Xaver. Romance and Duet, 'If in that Breast' (page 132).

The words by Sir John Moore, Bart. are translated from the French, *L'amour timide,* and were published in an edition of his *Poetical Trifles* about the year 1780. The music to which these words are adapted is from a German opera, the English translation of the title being *Fortunatus with the Purse and Wishing Cap,* performed at Frankfurt in 1832. The composer was the Swiss, Xaver Schnyder (1786–1868), a minor composer, who was active in Vienna, where he met Beethoven and Czerny amongst others.

48. Schubert, Franz Peter. 'The Letter of Flowers' (page 116).

One can only wonder if, and hope that, Emily accompanied Anne in this lovely Schubert *lied,* D622 in Otto Deutsch's catalogue. It was written in 1818, to words by Aloys Schreiber (1761–1841). A beautiful melodic line is supported by Schubert's inimitable harmony, *moderato con espressione.* Both German text and English translation by John Oxenford are included in the score. Franz Peter Schubert (1797–1828) is one of the greatest figures in the history of music. Born in Vienna, he was unsurpassed as a composer of *lieder,* of which he wrote hundreds, including three song-cycles *Die Schöne Müllerin, Winterreise* and *Schwanengesang.* His output of symphonies, piano music, chamber music and church music was also prodigious, as to both quality and quantity. For various reasons, some of his music was left unfinished, and much of it was not performed during his lifetime. Ill-health, probably brought on by dissolute living, dogged his short life. He revered Beethoven, was a torchbearer at his funeral, and was, himself, buried near to Beethoven at Währing.

49. Schubert, Franz Peter. Air, *Le Secret* (page 144).

The original German words are by Goethe, from his *West-östlicher Divan, Buch des Liebes,* the title of the *lied* being

Geheimes. Schubert's setting is his D719, a *poco allegro* sung quietly throughout.

50. Smith, John Christian. Song, 'The Owl is Abroad' (page 136).

The editor of *The Supplement to the Musical Library* states: 'This is from "The Tempest"; not Shakespeare's nor that drama as altered by [John] Dryden or [Sir William] Davenant, but from a second metamorphosis made by [David] Garrick, and so performed at Drury Lane in 1756, when the whole of the lyrical poetry introduced by Shakespeare in the play, also what was added by the bold innovators in 1670, together with the present song, which does not appear in what is called Dryden's "Tempest", was set by John Christian Smith'. It is a short single-verse song, a sprightly *moderato* in common time, wrongly attributed to Henry Purcell. In fact, the words first appeared in Ben Johnson's *Masque of Queens* of 1609.

51. Storace, Stephen. Song, 'The Sapling Oak' (page 176).

A song composed and introduced into *The Siege of Belgrade* by Storace, with words by James Cobb, this is a simple one verse *andantino* in common time.

52. Storace, Stephen. Song, 'Peaceful slumb'ring on the Ocean' (page 176).

A short two-verse song in common time, *soave* (sweetly or tenderly), this song is taken from Storace's opera *The Pirates*, which received its first performance at the Haymarket Theatre in 1792. The libretto is by James Cobb.

53. Webbe, Samuel. Prize-Glee, 'Swiftly from the Mountain's Brow' (page 64).

The words of this prize-glee are by John Cunningham. The first verse is an *allegretto,* initially in 2–4 time, then 6–8, while the second is an *andantino* in common time.

54. Webbe, Samuel. Terzetto and Chorus, 'O come, O Bella' (page 158).

These Italian words of 1729 are by Paulo Antonio Rolli (1687–1767). Set as a trio for two sopranos and bass with chorus and piano accompaniment, the third verse is sung unaccompanied by the two sopranos, while the first two lines of the fourth verse are for the bass.

55. Weber, Carl Maria von. Four-part Song, 'Enjoy Thyself, however Thou art' (page 88).

The English words to this short two-verse, four-part song are translated from the German lied *Ermunterung* (Encouragement). It is to be performed *moderato con moto.*

56. Weelkes, Thomas. Madrigal, 'The Nightingale' (page 94).

Set for two sopranos and bass in the key of F, it having been transposed from D, this single-verse madrigal is to be performed *moderato.* Probably written in 1600, it was the penultimate of twenty-six madrigals included in *Ayres or Phantasticke Spirits, for three voices, made and newly published by Thomas Weelkes, Gentleman of His Majesty's Chapell, Bachelor of Musicke, and Organist of the Cathedral*

Church of Chichester, Lond[on]. The date of publication was 1608. Thomas Weelkes (c1576–1623) was an organist and one of the foremost composers of madrigals in three, four, five and six voices.

57. Wilbye, John. Madrigal, 'Sweet Honey-sucking Bees', Part One (page 36), Part Two (page 41).

This lovely madrigal was published in Wilbye's second set, in 1609, and is set in G minor for two sopranos, alto, tenor and bass.

58. Winter, Peter von. Arietta, 'The Country Wedding' (page 148).

The words to this four-verse ballad, the author of which is unknown, are taken from from *Ritson's Collection of English Songs*. The arietta is from a German *burletta* by Winter, and is an *allegro* in 3–8 time for solo voice with piano accompaniment.

59. Zelter, Carl Friedrich. Aria, *In Felice in tanti affanni* (page 21).

An aria in common time in A flat, *andante,* the English translation of which is 'Unhappy with so many worries', it is in three sections, with the middle one containing some interesting chromatic harmony. Carl Friedrich Zelter (1758–1832) was a German conductor, teacher and composer, who was best known for his friendships with Goethe, many of whose verses he set and with whom he carried on a lengthy correspondence, and Mendelssohn. He was involved with the latter in the celebrated production in 1829 of Bach's *St. Matthew Passion.*

Volume Four
1837
Parsonage library reference 1131/6
58 Pieces

1. Arne, Thomas. Recitative and Air, 'On every Hill in every Grove' (page 58).

The libretto is by John Dalton (1709–1763), and this recitative and air are taken from his masque *Comus,* based on John Milton's of the same name of 1634. It had its premiere at the Theatre Royal, Drury Lane in 1738. A recitative, *largo* in E major, leads into an air in the tonic minor, two verses, *amoroso.*

2. Arnold, Samuel. Song. 'On board of the Valiant' (page 132).

This three-verse song is taken from Arnold's comic opera *The Shipwreck.* It is sung in Act One by the character Dick. *Andante con moto,* the piano accompaniment is intended to reflect the interplay between clarinet and bassoon in the original orchestration.

3. Bach, John (Johann) Christian. Duet, 'Io lo so' (page 161).

A duet for two sopranos, sung *andantino,* written by the 'London Bach', the English translation of the title is 'I Know'. It is the second of one of the two sets of six Italian canzonettas of 1765–6. As is often the case with Italian duets of this era, the duettists frequently sing in thirds.

4. Battishill, Jonathan. Round, 'I loved thee Beautiful and Kind' (page 124).

A simple round for three voices, *andante, piano sempre.*

'I loved thee beautiful and kind,
And plighted an eternal vow.'

Jonathan Battishill (1738–1801) was an English composer, especially of church music, but also of glees, catches, madrigals and part-songs.

5. Baumgarten, Karl Friedrich. Song, 'Her Image ever rose to View' (page 112).

A song which he contributed to William Pearce's operatic farce *Netley Abbey,* it is one of the very few works of this composer to have survived. It is a simple *grazioso* in 3–4 time. Karl Friedrich Baumgarten (c1740–1824) was a German violinist, organist and composer, whose list of publications included stage and instrumental works.

6. Beethoven, Ludwig van. Canzonetta, *Vita Felice* (page 21).

Although the text in *The Musical Library* is given in Italian, this song was set by Beethoven in his native German with the title *Das Glück der Freundschaft* (The Good Fortune of Friendship). The author is unknown. Written and published, by Löschenkohl of Vienna, in 1803, it is Beethoven's opus 88.

7. Beethoven, Ludwig van. Canzonetta, *In questa tomba oscura* (page 56).

This setting of Beethoven's is unusual in that it was written as a contribution to a collection of sixty-three settings of a text by Giuseppe Carpani, by a total of forty-six composers. Written sometime in the years 1806–7, it was published by Mollo of Vienna, who dedicated it to Prince Lobkowitz. Its WoO number is 133.

8. Beethoven, Ludwig van. (Aria) Song, 'Adelaide'(page 81).

One of the most delightful of all German *lieder,* it is, despite its opus number 46, an early work of Beethoven's, composed around about the mid-1790s to words by Friedrich von Matthisson, and published by Artaria of Vienna. Written in B flat for high male voice, its two sections are marked *larghetto* and *allegro molto.* Schubert also set these words (D95), in 1814. Friedrich von Matthisson (1761–1831) was a German poet, four of whose poems Beethoven set, one of them, *Opferlied,* no less than four times.

9. Bononcini, Giovanni. Round, *Chi mai d'iniqua stella* (page 103).

This simple round, sung in Italian, *andante,* is of eight bars length. It is probable that the composer is Giovanni Bononcini (1670–*c*1755) from an Italian family of musicians. He spent time in England where his operas and madrigals were popular, He also wrote church music.

10. Callcott, John Wall. Glee, 'Peace to the Souls of the Heroes!' (page 96).

The words are from Ossian's *Fingal,* Book One. The score is headed as follows: 'Originally written for three equal voices in G, in which state this glee is much to be preferred; the only motive for transposing it is to enable ladies to sing it in the absence of more appropriate voices'. The new key is E flat, and it is set for two sopranos and tenor or barytone *(sic)*. There are extremes of dynamics, from *pp* to *ff*. Ossian was a legendary Irish poet and warrior living probably in the third century AD.

11. Cavendish, Michael (1598). Madrigal, 'Every Bush new Springing' (page 141).

A madrigal set for two sopranos, alto, tenor and bass, it is to be sung *allegro*. Michael Cavendish (c1565–1628) was an English composer who, in 1598, published his *Ayres in Tabletorie*, dedicated to his second cousin, Lady Arabella Stuart, and this madrigal is the seventh of the eight included therein, intended to be performed with lute accompaniment.

12. Cooke, Dr. Benjamin. Round, 'The Dumb Peal' (page 13).

A simple four-bar round for four voices, with the performance direction 'slow and expressive', the score bears the annotation 'the pauses indicate the final pause'.

13. Croce, Giovanni. Madrigal, 'Cynthia! The Voice and Chanting' (page 32).

This madrigal is set for five voices – two sopranos, alto, tenor and bass – in common time. It was written in 1590, and published in the composer's *Il secondo libro di madrigali a 5 voci* in 1592. Giovanni Croce (c1557–1609) was a Venetian composer of secular music, particularly madrigals, and liturgical music, often for double choirs used antiphonally. It is likely that he was an influence on English madrigalists, particularly Thomas Morley. (The date 1560 on the score is probably a reference to the approximate date of Croce's birth).

14. Danby, John. Prize Glee, 'Awake! Aeolian Lyre' (page 70).

These words by Thomas Gray (1716–71) are the first stanza of his *The Progress of Poesy,* a Pindaric Ode, completed in 1754. This prize glee was written in 1783, and is set for soprano, alto, tenor and bass. It begins *largo e sostenuto,* then changes to *andante, tempo, largo sostenuto* again, then finishes *spiritoso.* The dynamic range is from *p* to *ff.* A Pindaric ode is ceremonius in nature, and named after the 5th century BC lyricist Pindar. Its structure is triadic, consisting of strophe, antistrophe, being of the same stanza form, and an epode as the final which is different.

15. Danby, John. Catch, 'Let the Merry Peal go on' (page 125).

This is an eleven-bar catch, of which Danby wrote many, for three voices, to be sung *moderato.* The score bears the annotation 'the first and second voices omit the five bars between the asterisks, until the third voice joins; then the whole is sung'.

16. Dibdin, Charles. Rondo, 'When the Lads of the Village' (page 92).

Sung by the character Steady, a middle-aged Quaker, in the opera *The Quaker,* this is an *allegretto* in the form of a rondo. Dibdin also wrote the libretto, based upon Charles Shadwell's *The Quaker of Deal*. The first performance was at Drury Lane in 1775.

17. Donizetti, Gaetano. Romanza, *Una furtive lagrima* (page 138).

The English translation of the title of this Romanza is 'The Furtive Tear', and it comes from Donizetti's opera *L'elisir d'amore* (The Elixir of Love) which was premiered in Milan in 1832. The libretto is by Felice Romani, based upon Eugène Scribe's *La Philtre*. This number comes in Act Two, Scene Eight of the opera, and is sung by the tenor Nemorino when he finds that the love potion which he has bought in order to win the lady of his dreams does actually work. It is a *larghetto* in 6–8 time, beginning in G minor, but ending in the tonic major, with a short cadenza for the soloist. Gaetano Donizetti (1797–1848) was an important Italian composer, principally of operas, of which he wrote seventy-five.

18. Ford, Thomas. Madrigal, 'Fair! Sweet! Cruel! Why dost thou fly me?' (page 88).

This two-verse madrigal is set for two sopranos, tenor and bass, in A minor. The date given on the score is 1636.

19. Handel, George Frideric. Duetto, *Uno a un puro affetto* (page 25).

Teseo (Theseus) is Handel's only five-act opera, and this duet is sung by the soprano Clizia and the alto Arcane in Scene Four of the final act. First produced at the Queen's Theatre, London in 1713, it features a number of dramatic magical effects, including flying dragons, on stage. The libretto is by Nicola Francesco Haym. It is in three sections, the third being a repeat of the first, with the middle one in the relative minor. There is much singing in thirds, sometimes to a distinctive dotted rhythm.

20. Handel, George Frideric. Duetto, *Amor gioie mi porge* (page 150).

With words by Abbate Hortensio Maura, this is the first movement of the fourth of Handel's thirteen Chamber Duets of 1711. The editor has changed the time 'from three minim to three crotchet' – 3–4 time – *andante con moto.*

21. Haydn, Franz Josef. Duet, 'O what various Charms unfolding' (page 1).

This duet, sung by the soprano Jane and the tenor Lucas, is the penultimate number in 'Spring' from Haydn's oratorio *The Seasons.* An *andante,* it has been considerably abridged compared with the original score, which involves the entry of the chorus.

22. Haydn, Franz Josef. The Spirit Song, 'Hark! What I tell to Thee' (page 77).

An *adagio* in F minor with a modulation to the relative major in the middle section the words are by Shakespeare.

23. Haydn, Franz Josef. Duetto, *Guarda qui, che lo vedrai* (page 126).

The English translation of the Italian words is 'Look here, who will see him'. It is a duet for soprano and tenor with piano accompaniment, which Haydn wrote in 1800. There are changes in tempo and rhythm – *allegro* with a cut-**C** time signature, *allegretto* 6–8, *adagio* and *allegretto* again.

24. Hayes, William. Glee, 'Melting Airs soft Joys inspire' (page 20).

With words by John Hughes from his *Ode in Praise of Music,* this is a four-part glee, *affettuoso,* in two sections, of eight and twelve bars respectively, each section being repeated.

25. Huber, Ferdinand Fürchtegott. Swiss Air, *Le Chasseur de Chamois* (page 114).

The title of this Swiss air translates as 'The Chamois Hunter', and it is an arrangement by Huber of an air from *Sur les Alpes, quel delice* of 1833 by Berlioz. It is a simple *andante* in C for solo voice and piano accompaniment. Ferdinand Huber (1791–1863) was a Swiss composer, notably of songs in the Swiss tradition.

26. Jackson, William (of Exeter). Song, 'Encompassed in an Angel's Frame' (page 48).

Taken from the opera of *The Lord of the Manor,* which received its first performance at Drury Lane in 1780, the words being by General Burgoyne, this single-verse song is an *andante affettuoso* in common time.

27. Labarre, T. (Théodore). Romance, *Ma belle Ange* (page 6).

Paroles de (words by) Emile Barateau, the English translation of the title is 'My Beautiful Angel'. The romance is an *andantino con moto* in 6–8 time. Théodore Labarre (1805–1870) was a French harpist and composer, mainly of romances and melodies such as this.

28. Linley, Thomas. Elegy, 'While Grief and Anguish rack my Heart' (page 154).

Another song taken from *Selima and Azor,* with Sir George Collier's libretto, this elegy is a trio for two sopranos and bass, *andantino.*

29. Linley, Thomas. Roundelay, 'In my pleasant Native Plains' (page 94).

From Linley's comic opera *The Carnival of Venice*, which was first performed at Drury Lane in 1781, with a libretto by Richard Tickell, this roundelay is an *allegretto* sung by Mrs. Cargill.

30. Linley, William. Song, 'Fair Leila' (page 158).

Both words and music are by Linley; this is a two-verse *affettuoso* in 3–4 time. William Linley (1771–1835) was a son of Thomas, above. He was a minor composer, mainly of songs. He was also, along with his brother-in-law Richard Brinsley Sheridan, involved for a while in the management of Drury Lane Theatre.

31. Moscheles, Ignaz. Trio, 'An Argument' (page 64).

This trio, with words by Leigh Hunt (1784–1859), the critic, essayist, poet and writer, is said to have been 'composed for this work by I. Moschelles'. It is set for two sopranos, or two tenors, and bass.

32. Mozart, Wolfgang Amadeus. Song, 'How hardly I concealed my Tears' (page 24).

The words are said by the editor to be 'by Mrs. Wharton, first wife of Thomas, afterwards Marquis of Wharton', adapted to the German song *Das Traumbild* (K530) composed by Mozart. It is a two-verse *andantino* in 6–8 time.

33. Mozart, Wolfgang Amadeus. Aria, '*Per pietà, non ricercate*' (page 146).

Mozart wrote this aria (K 420), along with two others, for insertion into the opera *Il curioso indiscreto* by the Italian composer Pasquale Anfossi (1727–1797) in a 1784 performance given by Haydn at Esterháza. However, for some reason it was not included in the actual performance. Written for the tenor Valentin Adamberger singing the role of the Count, iòt is a rondo, *andante,* in common time.

34. Mozart, Wolfgang Amadeus. Ariette, *Oiseaux, si tous les ans* (page 164).

This *ariette* (K307) was written in Mannheim in 1777, with words by Antoine Ferrand (1678–1719). The tempo is *allegretto.*

35. Müller, George. Canzonetta, *Aure amiche* (page 41).

This is an *allegro vivace* for solo voice with a distinctive chordal piano accompaniment. Georg Gottfried Müller (1762–1821) was a German composer, mainly of vocal music.

36. Paisiello, Giovanni. Song, 'No! 'twas neither Shape nor Feature' (page 4).

According to an old English custom, a flitch of bacon could be awarded to a married couple who could swear that they had no regrets for having been married for a year. William Shield's opera *The Flitch of Bacon*, upon this very theme, was first produced at the Little Theatre in the Haymarket, London, in 1778. The libretto was by Sir Henry Bate Dudley. This song was introduced into Act One, Scene Three of the opera, the music, according to the editor of *The Musical Library,* having been written by Giovanni Paisiello . It is a two-verse *andante con moto,* with a little ornamentation in the melodic line towards the end.

37. Pasquali, Niccolò. Duettino, 'When first I saw Thee graceful move' (page 145).

A duet for two sopranos, it is a sixteen-bar *andantino* in two sections, each one being repeated. Niccolò Pasquali was an Italian violinist and composer, mainly of songs, who wrote a treatise entitled *The Art of fingering the Harpsichord.* He died in Edinburgh in 1757.

38. Pepusch, Johann Christoph. Cantata, 'Alexis' (page 14).

Set to poetry by John Hughes (1677–1720) this cantata alternates recitative and air, varying major and minor tonalities. Johann Christoph Pepusch (1667–1752) was a German organist and composer of operas and masques who settled in London in 1704. He probably wrote the overture to John Gay's *The Beggar's Opera.*

39. Piozzi, Gabriele Gabriel. Canzonetta, *La Contradizzione* (page 67).

This *andantino* in 3–8 time – the time signature is wrongly given as 3–4 in the treble clef in *The Musical Library* – was written about 1782 for solo voice and piano accompaniment. Gabriele Piozzi (1740–1809) was an Italian-born musician who lived for much of his time in England, having, in 1784, married 'the celebrated Mrs Thrale', a widow, which occurrence, according to Grove, 'drew down upon the lady the wrath of Dr. Johnson, who had been for twenty years the cherished guest of [Mr.] Thrale and herself'. Little seems to be known of Piozzi as a composer.

40. Purcell, Henry. Duet, 'Hark! My Daridcar!' (page 104).

Taken from the 1694 tragedy of *Tyrannic Love* or *The Royal Martyr*, with words by John Dryden, it is one of the longer works in *The Musical Library*, Songs volumes. A short recitative by the bass leads into the duet for soprano and bass in C major, *allegretto* initially, increasing in tempo to *vivace*. An *andante* section in the tonic minor follows before a return to *vivace* in C major, with the last page written for two-part chorus.

41. Purcell, Henry. Song, 'What shall I do to show her how much I love her' (page 143).

This song is from the opera of *The Prophetess, or the History of Dioclesian,* with the libretto by Thomas Betterton, adapted from Beaumont and Fletcher. It received its first performance at the Queen's Theatre, Dorset Garden, London, in 1690. An *andante* in B minor, there is a modulation to the relative major in the middle section.

42. Rossini, Gioacchino. Quartetto, *Dal tuo stallato soglio* (page 43).

Rossini's opera *Mosè in Egitto* (Moses in Egypt) was written in 1818 to a libretto by Andrea Leone Tottola, and produced in that year in Naples. This quartet is in Act Three and is sung, *andantino,* by Elcia (soprano), Amenofi (alto), Aronne (tenor) and Moses (bass). The singers are assisted by a piano accompaniment involving considerable triplet movement in the bass. Beginning in G minor, the piece ends in the tonic major.

43. Sarti, Giuseppi. *Cavatina, Lungi del caro bene* (page 101).

Taken from the opera of *Giulio Sabino,* which received its first performance in Venice in 1781, the cavatina is for solo voice and piano accompaniment of distinctive triplet rhythm, *andante quasi larghetto.*

44. Savile, Jeremiah. 'The Waits' (page 166).

The last selection in *The Musical Library* Songs volumes, this is a trite sixteen-bar *allegretto* in C consisting solely of the words 'Fa la la la'. Written in 1667, it is 'to be sung four times – 1st *f*; 2nd *p*; 3rd *pp*; 4th *ff*. A note at the head of the score states: 'With this piece every meeting of the Madrigal Society concludes'. It was printed in Playford's *Musical Companion* (1667), but other than this piece, and 'Here's a Health unto His Majesty', little is known of this seventeenth-century composer.

45. Shield, William. Song, 'Ere around the huge Oak' (page 66).

This is a simple three-verse ballad from Shield's opera of 1787, *The Farmer,* with words by John O'Keefe. The editor of *The Musical Library* says of the composer: 'His songs will never cease to please those whose taste is unsophisticated'.

46. Shield, William. Song, 'Light as Thistle-down' (page 156).

With the words by Mrs. Brook, this song is taken from Shield's 1782 opera, *Rosina.* Sung by the title character, it is an *allegro* in A. *Rosina* is the work by which Shield is best remembered today.

47. Smith, John Stafford. Prize-glee, 'Return, blest Days' (page 134).

With words by Dr. Percy, this four-part glee is set for alto, two tenors and bass. Written in 1777, the editor states that 'as a glee writer he had no superior'. John Stafford Smith (1750–1836) born in Gloucester, was a singer, organist and composer, particularly of songs and glees. He studied under William Boyce.

48. Spofforth, Reginald. Glee, 'Mark'd you her eye of heavenly Blue' (page 29).

The words to this glee are by Richard Brinsley Sheridan. An *andante,* it has been arranged for three voices – soprano and mezzo soprano, who start with a long duet, and bass – the original having been set for five men's voices.

49. Spohr, Louis. Cavatina, *Si, lo sento* (page 11).

This cavatina is taken from Spohr's opera *Faust*, with libretto by Josef Karl Bernard, which received its first performance in Prague in 1816. A *larghetto con moto,* there is a cadenza towards the end, and a top B flat for the soloist to negotiate.

50. Spohr, Louis. Song, 'What makes this poor Bosom' (page 61).

The words are 'imitated from the German of Friedrich Kind', and the music is the first of Spohr's *Sechs Deutsche Lieder,* opus 41. The song is of two verses, *appassionato ma non troppo lento.*

51. Storace, Stephen. Song, 'With lowly Suit, and plaintiff Ditty' (page 38).

Taken from the two-act opera of 1790, *No Song, No Supper*, with libretto perhaps by Prince (a given name) Hoare, or, according to the editor *of The Musical Library,* James Cobb, a librettist who collaborated with Storace on a number of occasions, this song is performed in Act One by Margaretta. It is a two-verse *larghetto espressivo* in 3–4 time.

52. Storace, Stephen. Song, 'There the Silver'd Waters roam' (page 118).

Another song from the opera *The Pirates* of 1792, one of Storace's most popular works, it is an *andantino* in common time.

53. Travers, John. Canzonet (for four voices), 'I, my Dear, was born today' (page 49).

The words of this canzonet, are by Matthew Prior (1664–1721) entitled 'On my Birthday, July 21st'. The setting is for tenor or treble and bass. Beginning in A major, *vivace,* the long middle section is in the tonic minor with contrasting tempi – slow and *tempo primo* – before the conclusion in the major, which includes a change of time signature to 6–8, and a direction that it be performed 'tenderly'.

54. Webbe, Samuel. Prize-glee, 'A gen'rous Friendship no cold Medium knows' (page 116).

The words are taken from Alexander Pope's translation of Homer's *Iliad,* Book ix, Verse 725. A prize-winning glee of 1768, the setting is for soprano, alto, two tenors and bass, *andante affettuoso.* It is in two sections, each repeated.

55. Webbe, Samuel. Song, 'From glaring Show and giddy Noise' (page 121).

The words of this song are by the poet William Hayley (1745–1820). Directed to be performed *amoroso,* it is a rondo with the outer sections in F major, and the middle one in the relative minor. The editor has added the word *Violoncello* to the bass line of the piano accompaniment.

56. Weber, Carl Maria von. *Schlummerlied* (page 140).

A *Schlummerlied* is a lullaby, and this one is a sixteen-bar, three-verse *andante* in E. Written in 1822, it is one of six part-songs for four-part men's chorus comprising Weber's opus 68, although the version in *The Musical Library* is for solo voice with piano accompaniment. Liszt wrote a set of piano variations on it.

57. Winter, Peter. Duet, *Doppo cento affanni* (page 74).

Winter's opera *La grotta di Calipso* received its first performance at the Haymarket Theatre, London, in 1803. The libretto is by Lorenzo Da Ponte. This duet is sung by Calypso and Telemacho. It is a virtuoso piece, with florid writing, much of it in thirds, and a top C# for Calypso at the conclusion.

The Musical Library – 'Vocal'
Volume Three – First Edition, 1836

58. Unknown (according to the editor) Trio, 'When the rosy Morn appearing' (page 8).

The score is headed with the following: 'This is an adaptation of the round "Care, thou canker of our joys", the composer of which is unknown'. It is sung in William Shield's opera *Rosina* by the title characters, Phoebe and William, the words being by Mrs. Brooke.

'Anne Brontë's Songbook' And Vocal Scores

Prima facie, Emily Brontë's younger sister's collection of assorted hymns, sacred music and songs ought to have no place in an assessment of Emily's music. Yet, there are good reasons for including a listing of the contents of *Anne Brontë's Song Book*, and her other music scores here, with brief comments appended to each piece. It is clear that Emily and Anne were very close – Ellen Nussey described them as being 'like twins, inseparable companions in the very closest sympathy'. (1) They are known to have played duets together and shared a love of the emotions and importance of music. Little matter that Emily was the more accomplished musician, the Parsonage was where they made music; accordingly, Anne's interests are recorded here. The same reasoning applies to Branwell and his *Flute Book* (2).

Anne Brontë's Song Book bears the inscription 'Thorp Green, June 1843' under her signature. Housed now at the Parsonage Museum, it is MS 133 in the Bonnell Collection. Anne held the position of governess to the children of Edward and Lydia Robinson, at Thorp Green, ten miles north-west of York, from May 1840, when she was twenty years old, to June 1845. It was a difficult period in her life culminating in Branwell's dismissal from his post as tutor

Inscription in Anne Brontë's Song Book(Brontë Society)

as a result of his apparent misdemeanours regarding the mistress of the house. However, despite problems with the children and homesickness, she does appear to have coped stoically, and was able to use her experiences, both there and at her previous position at Mirfield Hall with the Blake family, to good effect when writing her novels, *Agnes Grey* and *The Tenant of Wildfell Hall.*

From June 1843, when she bought a music manuscript book printed by J. and F. Harwood of London, price three shillings and sixpence, to at least 13 October 1844, which date is written on page 72, eight pages before the end of the book, she copied into it, not with complete accuracy and often with simplified harmonies, a total of thirty-four hymns, sacred pieces, songs and melodies, requiring none too technical an ability for performance. Her index shows that half of the entries were hymns, seven more were sacred pieces, and eight were a miscellany of songs. In fact, two melodies (without words) are omitted from the index; these are number 16, *Sul margine d'un rio*, and number 18, 'Waltz'. The purpose of the book was probably twofold – firstly, to be used as a teaching aid, and secondly to be just for her own enjoyment. It was acquired by the collector J.H.

Dixon of Harrogate and, after his death, sold at Sotheby's in 1916. It has already been noted that Anne's inscription is on many of the scores now in the 'Parrish Collection' (3) and on a number of vocal pieces (4) and it seems likely that at least some of them accompanied her on her return to Thorp Green in January 1845. These will be discussed later in this chapter.

It is also likely that Anne started to learn the piano sometime during the years 1832–1834, meaning that she had been playing for at least six years before taking up her appointment and, accordingly, had reached a tolerable level of ability on the instrument, though probably not to the same level of accomplishment as Emily. According to Ellen Nussey, whereas Emily played with 'precision and brilliancy, which was not often if other than the family circle were within hearing', Anne played also 'but she preferred soft harmonies and vocal music. She sang a little; her voice was weak, but very sweet in tone'. (5) Her love of music was sometimes reflected in her writing as, for example, in her poem *Music on Christmas Morning*, which begins with the words 'Music I love', and which was one of the twenty-one poems of hers which were published in the 1846 edition of *Poems* by 'Currer, Ellis and Acton Bell'.

The method adopted for describing each of the hymns is as follows –

First line;
Author;
Date (if known);
Title of tune;
Metre;
Composer (if known);
Comments.

Contents of 'Anne Brontë's Songbook'

1. Hymn – 'Oh! for a heart to praise my God'. Charles Wesley, from his *Hymns and Sacred Poems* (1742). *Celestial Concerts.* C.M. Charles Rider. There are five verses, and Anne has written out only two voices – treble and bass.

The words have been set to a number of tunes other than this one, which are included in *Hymns Ancient and Modern, Standard Edition* (number 549) and *The Methodist Hymn Book* (number 550). Charles Wesley, born in Lincolnshire in 1707, was the brother of John Wesley, founder of Methodism. Also an evangelist, he wrote an extraordinary number of hymns, including 'Hark, the herald angels sing' and 'Love divine, all loves excelling'. He died in 1788. Charles Rider published *A Selection of (336) Hymn Tunes for the use of the Sunday School in Elm Street, Manchester* in 1816. There was also a later edition. Anne had a certain sympathy with Methodism.

2. Hymn – 'Oh! where shall rest be found'. *Watchman.* S.M. James Leach (ed.) from the *Second Sett [sic] of Hymns and Psalms.* There are two verses.

In the *Methodist Hymn Book* this tune accompanies the words of the hymn 'Rise up, O men of God' (585). James Leach (1762–1798) published his *Second Sett [sic] of Hymns and Psalms*, probably in 1794, his *New Sett [sic]) of Hymns and Psalms* having appeared in 1789, published by Preston of London. The tune 'Watchman' is number 48 in the second volume, though set to different words. He had the misfortune to die from a stagecoach accident.

3. Hymn – 'I love the Lord: He heard my cries'. Isaac Watts from *The Psalms of David* (1719). *New Cambridge.* John Randall. CM. There is just one verse.

Dr. John Randall (c1715–1799) was appointed organist of King's College, Cambridge, in 1743 . Isaac Watts (1674–1748), born in Southampton, was a prolific writer of hymns – in excess of five hundred of them. He is described in *Historical Companion to Hymns Ancient and Modern* as 'the real founder of English hymnody'. In 1707, he published *Hymns and Spiritual Songs,* and in 1719, *Psalms of David.* Upon his death in 1748, a monument to him was erected in Westminster Abbey.

4. Hymn – 'O God, our help in ages past'. Isaac Watts (1719), from *The Psalms of David. Cheltenham.* CM. (According to Anne) Milgrove. One verse.

The composer to whom Anne refers could have been the Benjamin Milgrove (1731–*c*1810) who lived in Bath. Anne's notation, however, is incorrect. The crotchets in bars (1), (8) and (10) should be minims, while the repeat of the words 'Our shelter from the stormy blast' is surely superfluous, and disruptive of the common metre. This is a very popular hymn which nowadays is always sung to William Croft's tune 'St. Anne' of 1708. The hymn features in Chapter 24 of *Shirley*, when Caroline Helston asks Mrs. Pryor to sing it for her.

5. Hymn – 'My God, my everlasting hope'. Isaac Watts. *Oldham.* CM. James Leach (ed.) *New Sett [sic] of Hymns and Psalms* (1789). There are three verses. Again, Anne's copying seems to be at fault.

6. Hymn – 'Christ the Lord is risen today'. From *Lyra Davidica* (1708), based upon an anonymous Latin hymn *Surrexit Christus hodie.* 'Easter Hymn No. 2', also from *Lyra Davidica.* 7 7 7 7 and Alleluias. One verse.

Nowadays, the title of this Easter hymn is 'Jesus Christ is Risen Today'.

7. Hymn – 'How beauteous are their feet'. Isaac Watts (1707). *Zion.* SM. Composer not known. Three verses.

On page seven Anne has omitted the B flat in the key signature, and there are errors in the notation. Only two voices have been copied out – treble and bass. This hymn appears in a variety of hymnals, such as *Hymns Ancient and Modern Standard Edition* (number 755) and *The Methodist Hymn Book* (number 778) but with different tunes in each case, 'Venice' in the former and 'Day of Praise' in the latter.

8. Hymn – 'Worthy the Lamb of boundless sway'. 'Portuguese Hymn'. Nowadays it is better known as the popular Christmas hymn *Adeste fidelis* ('O, Come All Ye Faithful). According to *Hymns Ancient and Modern Standard Edition* (number 59), it is a 'traditional melody' of irregular metre. There are five verses.

9. Hymn – 'God is love: His mercy brightens all the path'. John Bowring. *Austria.* Haydn. 8 7 8 7. 8 7 8 7.

This famous melody, written in 1799, was originally the theme of the slow movement of Haydn's String Quartet, opus 76, no. 3, nicknamed *Kaiserquartett* ('Emperor' Quartet) upon which a set of variations was written. Also the German national anthem, it was included in *The Musical Library*, and has already been discussed. (6) The hymn is in *The Methodist Hymn Book* (53), but set to two different tunes, 'Sussex', and *Unser Herrscher*. 'Austria' is, however, twice in *Hymns Ancient and Modern Standard Edition*: 'Praise the Lord! ye heavens adore Him' (292) and 'Glorious things of Thee are spoken' (545).

10. Hymn – 'Through the day thy love has spared us'. Thomas Kelly. *Communion.* 8s and 7s. Two verses.

Although Anne does not name either the author of the hymn or its composer, the writer is Thomas Kelly (1769–1855) who was an Irish judge who took holy orders in 1792. His *Hymns on Various Passages of Scripture* was first published in 1804. By the time of its final edition in 1853, it had expanded to include seven hundred and sixty-five hymns. In 1815, he published a companion volume containing tunes composed by himself suited for every metre in his hymnal.

11. Hymn – 'Does the Gospel word proclaim?' *Ephesus.* Beethoven. John Newton. 7 7 7 7. Two verses.

The melody is a much simplified version of the theme of Beethoven's Romance for Violin and Orchestra in G, opus 40, written sometime during the years 1800–1802, and published by Hoffmeister of Leipzig in 1803. Anne has written out only the first of the three of Newton's eight-line verses. John Newton (1725–1807) was actively engaged in the slave trade for many years, even after turning to Christianity. He became an ordained minister of the church, taking the curacy of Olney and, four years later, become friendly with the poet William Cowper, with whom he published the

Olney Hymns, of which this is one. His most popular hymn is, however, 'Amazing Grace (how sweet the sound)'.

12. Melody – 'Has sorrow thy young days shaded'. Thomas Moore.

This was one of a large number of songs by the Irish poet and musician Thomas Moore (1779–1852) written between 1808 and 1834, and grouped under the title *Irish Melodies.* Their publication was by William Power of Dublin, and was entitled *Selection of Irish Melodies, with Symphonies and Accompaniments by Sir John Stevenson, Mus. Doc., and characteristic words by Thomas Moore, Esq.* Stevenson, like Moore born in Dublin, lived from 1761–1833. Anne has written out only the first of four eight-line stanzas of this song. Another of Moore's *Irish Melodies* is entitled 'The Meeting of the Waters'; this was the name given by the sisters to one of their favourite places on the moors above Haworth, which strongly suggests that they were aware of Moore's work some years before Anne's time at Thorp Green.

13. Sacred Song – From the Oratorio of 'Saul' (numbers 21–23). Handel. Recitative: 'Already see the daughters', Chorus 'Welcome, welcome mighty king', and *Accompagnato* (orchestral, rather than continuo, accompaniment) 'What do I hear?'

Handel completed the oratorio *Saul* in a few days over two months in 1738. It received its first performance at the King's Theatre, London, on 16 January 1739. The text was written by Charles Jennens, based upon the First Book of Samuel, chapters 18–20 and 31, and the Second Book of Samuel, chapter 1. The recitative is the final number (21) of Scene

Two, sung by Michal, the chorus (of women) is the first number (22) in Scene Three, followed by the *accompagnato,* sung by Saul.

14. Song – 'I remember'. Anne Brontë attributed this song to Mrs. Ed. Fitzgerald. It is an *Andantino* in E flat, marked *piano espressivo.*

15. Song – 'Ye banks and braes o' bonny Doon'. Robert Burns. One of the most popular of all Scottish folk songs by Scotland's revered poet.

Ye banks and braes o' bonnie Doon
How can ye bloom sae fresh and fair
How can ye chant, ye little birds
And I sae weary fu' o' care?
Thou'lt break my heart, thou warbling bird
That wantons thro' the flowering thorn
Thou mind'st me o' departed joys
Departed – never to return!

This song features in Charlotte's *Shirley,* and as number eleven in *Branwell Brontë's Flute Book.*

16. Melody – *Sul margine d'un rio.* (On the bank of a river). A popular Italian song, *andante* in A major and 2–4 time.

17. Song – 'Night at sea'. Henri Hertz [*sic*]. The correct spelling of the composer's surname is 'Herz'. In A major, in 3–3 time, there are six verses.

18. Melody – 'Waltz'. Anne Brontë has attributed this short waltz to Beethoven, but it is considered that this is doubtful. It comprises three eight-bar phrases in 3–4 time in A major.

19. Song – 'The Troubadour'. According to Anne, this piece is by Thomas Haynes Bayly. A troubadour was a lyric poet in France during the eleventh to thirteenth centuries. Anne has given this piece the unusual time signature of 4–8. The key is E flat major.

20. Sacred Song – 'Thou art gone to the grave'. Words by Reginald Heber, music by William Henry Havergal.

Reginald Heber (1783–1826) was, prior to his death, Bishop of Calcutta, and is best known nowadays for his hymns 'From Greenland's Icy Mountains' and 'Holy, Holy, Holy'. William Henry Havergal – Anne has misspelt the name by adding a second 'l' – (1793–1870), also a clergyman, set the first of the two as an anthem. He undertook to improve psalmody by the publication of a reprint of Ravenscroft's *Psalter* in 1847.

21. Sacred Song – 'The bird let loose'. Words by Thomas Moore, music by Beethoven.

The melody is adapted from the Bagatelle, opus 33, no. 4, transposed down from A to F. The set of seven bagatelles was written sometime during the years 1801–1802, and published the following year by *Bureau des Arts et D'Industrie*, Vienna.

22. Sacred Song – 'Oh! thou who dry'st the mourner's tear'. Words by Thomas Moore from *Sacred Songs* (full title *A Series of Sacred Songs Composed and Selected by Sir John Stevenson and Mr. Moore)* of 1816, music by Joseph Haydn.

Marked *larghetto*, a seven-bar keyboard introduction leads into the song, the format of which is three sections, ABA, each of eight bars. The piece concludes with a four-bar keyboard postlude.

23. Sacred Song – 'As down in the sunless retreats'. The words are by Thomas Moore from *Sacred Songs*, with the music being an air by Haydn. Marked *andante con espressione*, there are two verses.

24. Sacred Song – 'Thou art, O God!' The inscription is 'Air supposed to be by Mrs. Sheredan'. The words are by Thomas Moore from *Sacred Songs*.

25. Sacred Song – 'But who shall see'. The words are by Thomas Moore from *Sacred Songs*, and the music is an air by Sir John Stevenson. There are two verses.

26. Song – 'In summer when the hay was mawn'. Words by Robert Burns (1759–1796).

The title of this poem is 'Country Lassie', and the first verse gives an indication of the Scottish dialect so beloved of the Brontë siblings –

In simmer when the hay was mawn,
And corn wav'd green in ilka field,
While claver blooms white o'er the lea;
And roses blaw in ilka bield;
Blythe Bessie in the milking shiel
Says 'I'll be wed, come o't what will;
Out spak a dame in wrinkled eild,
'O' guid advisement comes nae ill'.

Simmer – summer
Mawn – mown
Ilka – every
Claver – clover

Blaw – blow
Bield – shelter
Shiel – hut
Spak – spake
Eild – age

27. Song – 'Come beneath the linden tree'. The music is by Mozart, from his opera *Die Zaueberflöte* (The Magic Flute), Act One finale, the duet between Pamina and Papageno. Anne has attributed the words to J. (or I.) M. Wade.

Marked *andantino*, an eight-bar keyboard introduction precedes the song, the layout of which is ABA. The piece concludes with an eight-bar postlude. There are two verses.

28. Song – 'Auld lang syne'. Robert Burns. A very popular Scottish folk song, it is also number five in *Branwell Brontë's Flute Book.* The words of the first verse which Anne transcribed vary slightly from those sung nowadays on New Year's Eve, and indeed Burns' original.

Should auld acquaintance be forgot,
And never brought to mind?
Should auld acquaintance be forgot
[And days] of auld lang syne?
For auld lang syne my dear
For auld lang syne

We'll take a cup of kindness yet
For the sake of auld lang syne.

29. Hymn – 'My God! Oh let me call thee mine'. Anne Brontë. *Justification.* L.M.J. Eagleton. Four verses.

More than one hymn has been set to this tune, including 'Praise ye the Lord!' and 'Arm of the Lord, awake, awake' both in the *Methodist Hymn Book* (numbers 79 and 486, respectively). The composer, the Revd. John Eagleton, was born in Coventry in 1785, and died in 1832.

Anne's manuscript is dated 13 October 1844, and is number 34 in Edward Chitham's *Poems of Anne Brontë*. The text is as follows –

'A Prayer'

My God! O let me call Thee mine!
Weak wretched sinner though I be,
My trembling soul would fain be Thine,
My feeble faith still clings to Thee.
My feeble faith still clings to Thee.

Not only for the past I grieve,
The future fills me with dismay;
Unless Thou hasten to relieve,
I know my heart will fall away,
I know my heart will fall away.

I cannot say my faith is strong,
I dare not hope my love is great:
But strength and love to Thee belong,
O, do not leave me desolate!
O, do not leave me desolate!

I know I owe my all to Thee,
O, take this heart I cannot give.
Do Thou my Strength my Saviour be:
And make me to Thy glory live!
And make me to Thy glory live!

30. Hymn – 'There is a land of pure delight'. Isaac Watts. *Prospect.* CM.

This tune is most popularly used to accompany the words of Ben Johnson's song of 1616 'Drink to Me only with Thine Eyes'. It appears that only the first four-line stanza, of a total of six, is by Watts; the name of the author of the remainder is unknown, though Anne herself is a possibility.

31. Hymn – 'A saint, oh would that I could claim'. John Marriot. *Daniel.* 8 8. 8 8. 8 8. Four verses.

This hymn was number XIV in Mrs. Frances Sara Fuller-Maitland's *Hymns for Private Devotion* of 1827. The Revd. John Marriott (1780–1825) held various curacies in Derbyshire and Devon.

32. Hymn – 'Time by moments steals away'. John Newton. *St. Philip.* T (?) Mather. 7 8 7 8. Two verses.

The composer's initial could conceivably be 'I', 'J', or 'T', but it does seem to be identical to the first letter of the first word of Anne's written text – 'Time'. This is another of the *Olney Hymns*, Book Two, number 4, of 1779, although Anne has written out only the first of five verses.

33. Hymn – 'What shall the dying sinner do'. *Jubal.* Isaac Watts. LM. William Mather. Six verses.

34. Hymn – 'Hark the Song of Jubilee'. James Montgomery. *Resurrection.* 7 7 7 7. Thomas Pettman. Four verses.

The hymn is entitled 'The New Missionary Hymn'. The words were written by Montgomery (1771–1854) in 1818, and the tune by Pettman (1807–1844) in 1841. Thomas Pettman was a professor of music and singing from Ramsgate.

Vocal Scores

1. Moore, Thomas. 'Come Chase that Starting Tear away', from a *Selection of National Airs arranged with Symphonies and Accompaniment by Henry R. Bishop.* Published by J. Power, London.

2. Webbe, Samuel. *Solfeggio.* Designed to assist young pupils to sing at sight. Newly arranged by J.B. Sale.

There are twenty-eight such exercises in a variety of major and minor keys, and many pencil annotations. *Solfeggio* is an Italian term meaning exercise(s) for the voice using only vocal sounds such as tonic sol-fa notation. According to Ellen Nussey, Anne's musical forte was singing. The title page has been autographed in ink by Anne, and dated November 19th, 1844. There is much pencil handwriting of the tonic sol-fa scale on the score. Samuel Webbe (1740–1816) and his son, also named Samuel (c1770–1843), were English organists and composers of unaccompanied choral music, including catches, glees and canons.

3. Marlborough, His Grace the Duke of. 'Tho' Cruel Fortune binds me now', with an accompaniment for Harp and Violin in E flat.

4. Traditional. 'Poor Mary Anne'. The tune is the Welsh folksong *Ar hyd y nos* (All through the Night). Described as 'a dirge for two sopranos and a bass', there are three verses. The key is B flat. It is also the third piece in *Branwell Brontë's Flute Book*. The title page has the initials 'A.B.', in ink, and on the back cover is a geometric drawing in pencil.

5. Bolden, T.M.L. ' "'Tis not the Eye of the Softest Blue", a Favourite Ballad'. The composer also wrote the words and autographed the score on the title page. There are four verses, the last marked *marziale.*

6. Rimbault, Edward F. 'Happy Land – Tyrolienne'. The words are by J. Bruton. The title page is autographed in ink 'A. Brontë, Dec. 1844'.

7. Field, Ellen J. 'Britannia's Brave'. The words are by Miss Harrison; there are six verses. The title page is autographed in ink 'Anne Brontë, November 19th 1844'.

8. Russell, Henry. 'The Old Oak Tree', or 'Woodman spare that Tree'. The title page is autographed in ink 'Anne Brontë'.

9. Devereaux, L. 'O'er the Bonnie Clyde'. The title page is autographed in ink 'Anne Brontë, November 19th 1844'. Number one of *Vocal Beauties of Caledonia,* it is a duet.

10. Traditional. ' "Scots Wha Hae Wi' Wallace Bled", or "Bruce's Lament", as sung by Mr. Braham in *Guy Mannering*

(Sir Walter Scott). Words by Robert Burns. The blank first page is autographed in ink 'E. Nussey'.

This is an arrangement for pianoforte and flute, with words. It is also the fourth piece in *Branwell Brontë's Flute Book.*

11. Bayly, T. 'Isle of Beauty, Fare thee Well', from the composer's *First Volume of Songs to Rosa*. Melody by Charles Sharpland Whitmore; 'symphonies and accompaniments' by T.A. Rawlings. Published by D'Almaine and Co, London. The title page is autographed in ink 'Anne Brontë, Nov. (no year)'

12. Mozart, Wolfgang, Amadeus. ' "The Parting Hour", written by D. Thomson, adapted to the music of W.A. Mozart'. The title page is autographed in ink 'Anne Brontë'.

Arranged from the original score by Muzio Clementi, and published by Chappell of London, it is written for two female voices with pianoforte accompaniment. The first line reads 'Time around his dial stealing'. The original is the aria *Ah, perdona al primo affetto,* from the opera *La Clemenza di Tito.*

13. Mornington, Lord. Glee – 'Here in Cool Grot'. Arranged for four voices with Pianoforte accompaniment, by E.I. Westrup. It is also in *The Musical Library*, Vocal Section, Volume Three, number 48.

Anne was the youngest of all the Brontë children. She was deeply religious, in a conventional sense – the antithesis of Emily's spirituality – perhaps as a result of her having, from a very early age, come under the influence of her pious

Methodist Aunt Branwell more than her elder siblings ever did. In addition to her Bible and Prayer Book, inscribed 'Miss Outhwaite to her goddaughter Anne Brontë, Feb. 13, 1827', she owned a copy of Clare's *Sacred Harmony*, which is a collection of thirty-five psalms and hymn tunes, published in 1841. It is thought that Anne was in love with her father's curate, William Weightman, and was deeply affected by his death from cholera in 1842, while she was at Thorp Green.

A number of Anne Brontë's religious poems have been set to music as hymns. Probably the best known is 'The Narrow Way', which was written in April 1848, some eight months before Emily's death, and thirteen months before Anne's own. It is included in the *Methodist Hymn Book* as number 591, and *Songs of Praise*, as number 453. It was not written into her *Song Book*, but it is quoted here as a testament to the struggle she had to sustain her faith.

Believe not those who say
The upward path is smooth.
Lest thou should stumble in the way,
And faint before the truth.

It is the only road
Unto the realms of joy:
But he who seeks that blest abode
Must all his powers employ.

Arm – arm thee for the fight!
Cast useless loads away;
Watch through the darkest hours of night:
Toil through the hottest day.

To labour and to love
To pardon and endure,
To lift thy heart to God above,
And keep thy conscience pure.

Be this thy constant aim,
Thy hope thy chief delight;
What matter who should whisper blame
Or who would scorn or slight?

If but thy God approve,
And if, within thy breast,
Thou feel the comfort of His love,
The earnest of his rest.

Also included in the *Methodist Hymn Book* are 'Oppressed with Sin and Woe' (number 352), and 'I hoped that with the Brave and Strong' (number 592). In more recent times, a number of Anne's verses have been set by the former organist of Haworth Parish Church, Jack H. Rhodes.

Anne Brontë died on 29 May 1849 in Scarborough, where she had travelled, in the company of Charlotte and Ellen Nussey, in the vain hope of finding an improvement in her consumptive condition. Charlotte decided that it would be less stressful to her father to arrange for her sister's burial in St Mary's churchyard on Castle Hill, Scarborough. Over the years the wording on the original headstone became considerably weather-worn. In 2011, rather than altering the original stone, the Brontë Society placed a slab on the grave itself –

Anne Brontë
1820–1849
novelist and poet

The original headstone reads

Here lie the remains of Anne Brontë
Daughter of the Revd P Brontë
Incumbent of Haworth Yorkshire
She died Aged 28 May 28th 1849

The text contains one error
Anne Brontë was aged 29 when she died.
This plaque was placed here in 2011
By the Brontë Society

Emily's drawing of herself and Anne in her Diary Paper of 26 June 1837.
She has depicted herself as sitting on the nearside of the table with her quill pen beside her left hand, while Anne's is to her right-hand side.
Does this suggest that Emily was left-handed?
(Brontë Society)

Branwell Brontë's Flute Book

As was noted in the introduction to the chapter on *Anne Brontë's Song Book*, discussed above, *Branwell Brontë's Flute Book* is, in a sense, peripheral to the study of Emily's music. Yet, they all made music together in the Parsonage, and it is not inconceivable that Emily accompanied Branwell's flute on occasion. On a more sombre note, it is perhaps sadly accurate to say that, as Branwell's dissolute lifestyle spiralled out of control, Emily was the only one in the household who, even to a limited extent, could handle him.

Branwell wrote frequently to his friend, the sculptor John Bentley Leyland, and this knowledge was used by Leyland's brother Francis A. Leyland in his 1886 book *The Brontë Family, with Special Reference to Branwell Brontë*, as the following passage illustrates. '[Branwell] was acquainted with the works of the great composers, and although he could not perform their elaborate compositions well, he was always so excited when they were played for him by his friends that he would walk about the room with measured footsteps, his eyes raised to the ceiling, accompanying the music with his voice in an impassioned manner, and beating time with his hand on the chairs as he passed to and fro'. (1) Leyland goes on to relate that, on a visit to Liverpool in 1839, he prevailed upon one of his companions, a Mr. M…, [Hartley Merrall, son of a local mill owner] 'an accomplished musician', to buy the score of Handel's oratorio *Samson.* In return Branwell, a talented artist, painted his friend's portrait in oils during sittings in the Parsonage. Furthermore, he 'painted the names of Johann Sebastian Bach, Mozart, Haydn and Handel at each corner of the canvas respectively'. (2) A further reference reveals that, during his ultimately disastrous time at Thorp Hall as tutor to the young Edmund Robinson, 'Branwell was found to be a thorough musician, for he had further cultivated this taste and acquired considerable skill in performance'. (3) And in a letter dated 20 February, 1834, written by Charlotte to Ellen Nussey, who was then visiting London, a postscript asked 'Will you be kind enough to inform me of the number of performers in the King's Military Band? Branwell wishes for this information.'

Branwell had learned to play the organ – he played the instrument at a Freemason service on Christmas Day 1837 (4) – and it has already been seen that a number of transcriptions for organ of sacred works by Handel, Haydn and Mozart were included in the sheet music acquired for the Parsonage during the 1830s. (5) He also learned to play the flute. The flute upon which Branwell played would have been made of wood, not metal as is the case with modern instruments. It would have been transverse with a thumb hole and eight finger holes. The modern fifteen-hole metal instrument with twenty-three keys and levers was not invented by the German flautist Theobald Boehm until 1847, although his ring-key system had been in existence for fifteen years before that.

Branwell began compiling his collection of twenty-one flute pieces in November 1831 and completed the task in little more than three months. The set is MS 56 in the Bonnell Collection. On the inside front cover is the inscription 'P B Brontë November 1st 1831 – for flute'. It is a slim volume, smaller in all respects than *Anne Brontë's Song Book*. Branwell's spelling and grammar leave a certain amount to be desired; like Anne, he also made errors in notation. In the original manuscript neither the pages nor the individual pieces are numbered. The pieces in the collection are of no great technical difficulty.

Patrick Branwell Brontë (1817–1848) was an intrinsically talented person, with abilities in music, literature and art. A deep-rooted personality defect, of whatever nature, resulted in a descent into drug and alcohol abuse, and consequently not only the non-fulfilment of his aspirations, but also his early death, in 1848.

Contents

1. 'Old Hundredth' Psalm.

The opening line of this popular hymn tune is 'All people that on earth do dwell'. The words are to be found in *Day's English Psalter* of 1561, and are by William Kethe. The music is by the French composer Louis Bourgeois (*c*1510–*c*1561); according to the *Methodist Hymn Book* it appeared in the *French Psalter* of 1551. In G major in common time, the manuscript is dated November 1831, one bar being heavily scored out.

2. 'Old Fortieth' Psalm.

Written in D major in common time, the manuscript is dated November 1831.

3. 'Poor Mary Tune'.

This is the well-known Welsh air '*Ar Hyd Y Nos*', the English translation of which is 'All Through the Night'. In D major and common time, the manuscript is dated November 1831.

4. 'Scots wha hae wi' Wallace bled'.

The words are by Robert Burns and the music is by Sir Henry Rowley Bishop (1786–1855). In D major and common time, marked *maestoso,* the manuscript is dated November 1831. Consisting of six verses, it is Robert Bruce's address to his army before the Battle of Bannockburn on 24 June 1314. The first of the six stanzas reads –

'Scots, wha hae wi' Wallace bled,
Scots, wham Bruce has aften led,
Welcome tae yer gory bed,
Or tae victorie.'

5. 'Auld Lang Syne'.

In D major in 2–4 time, the manuscript is dated November 1831. Robert Burns wrote words to this much loved old Scottish folk tune. It is also number 28 in *Anne Brontë's Song Book,* and was discussed there.

6. 'Glorious Apollo'.

The manuscript is dated November 1831; the piece is written in common time in the key of E flat. Branwell has written on the manuscript 'the A flat is fingered thus 12.4 – or 123 and G key'. The words and music are by Samuel Webbe (1740–1816) more than half of whose compositions, such as this one, were catches, glees and canons; six of them appear in *The Musical Library* 'Vocal' Section.

7. A March.

In G major and in common time, the manuscript is dated December 1831.

8. 'Martin Luther's Hymn'.

The manuscript is written out beautifully. In D major, in common time, it is the only piece in the book which includes words. Dated December 1837, it includes the initials 'JR'. The tune probably first appeared in *Geistliche Lieder* of 1529. The words which Branwell has copied are as follows:

'Great God, what do I see and hear?
The end of things created,
The judge of mankind doth appear
On clouds of Glory seated.
The trumpets sound the graves restore
The dead which they contained before
Prepare, my soul, to meet him.'

Martin Luther lived from 1483 to 1546. A German priest and religious reformer, he is considered to be the founder of the Reformation. On 31 October 1517, he drew up a list of ninety-five theses on papal indulgences which he nailed to the door of the church in Wittenburg, at which town's university he was a lecturer in philosophy. During the years 1521–1534, he translated the Bible into German.

9. 'Home Sweet Home'.

Branwell omitted the first 'Home' in his manuscript. This well-known setting of words is by Sir Henry Rowley Bishop (1786–1855). In G major and 2–4 time, the manuscript is dated December 1831, and includes the initials 'JR', along with Bishop's surname.

10. 'Jessy of Dumblain'.

A Scottish folk song with a distinctive jerky offbeat rhythm, it is ideally suited to being played on the bagpipes. It is written in 6–8 time in D major. The manuscript is dated January 1832, and it too has the initials 'JR'.

11. 'Ye Banks and Braes o' Bonny Doon'.

Robert Burns' popular Scottish song; it was also number 15 in *Anne Brontë's Song Book.* In C major and 6–8 time, marked *andante,* the manuscript is dated January 1832. Branwell has added a footnote to his score: 'there should have been added to the end of the prelude [the notes] crotchet C quaver C and crotchet C'.These are in fact the notes of bar eight, the last bar of the prelude to the song, which he has omitted to write out. The dynamics range from *f* in the prelude to *p* in the song. In the aftermath of his doomed love affair with Mrs. Lydia Robinson, Branwell went on a trip to Wales with his friend, the Haworth sexton John Brown, during which, in a letter to the sculptor John Bentley Leyland dated 25 November 1845, he related that, as he was writing his poem, 'Penmaenmawr', on board a steamer in the Menai Strait, the band struck up 'Ye Banks and Braes'. (6) Charlotte has Mrs. Pryor singing the first stanza in Chapter Twenty-four of *Shirley*. (7)

12. 'Dunois the Young and Brave'.

A French romantic legend, translated into English by Sir Walter Scott, the music is by Hortense, Queen-consort of

Louis, King of Holland and brother of Napoleon. In F major, in common time, and similar dynamics to the previous piece, the manuscript is dated January 1832.

13. 'Loyal Carmarthen Fusiliers Dead March'.

In D minor, and in common time, six bars have been crudely scored out. The manuscript is dated January 1832.

14. 'Blue Bonnets over the Border'.

The words are from Sir Walter Scott's 'Border March', one of the poems from chapter xxv of the novel *The Monastery* of 1820. There are varied dynamics – *f* to *p* – and a direction of *allegretto* in this manuscript which is dated January 1832. The key is D major, and the time signature 6–8.

15. A Funeral March.

The manuscript is dated January 1832 and the key is G, in common time.

16. 'Jock o' Hazledean'.

The key is D, the time signature 2–4, and the manuscript is dated January 1832. With exception of the first stanza, which is ancient, this is one of Scott's *Miscellaneous Poems*, written in 1816.

17. 'Oh! No – We Never mention Her'.

This is another of Sir Henry Rowley Bishop's song-settings. The first two lines read:

'Oh! no, we never mention Her,
Her name is never heard.'

In chapter 47 of Anne Brontë's *The Tenant of Wildfell Hall,* Fergus teasingly uses (all bar the first two of) these words in conversation with his brother. In D major, in 2–4 time, the performance direction is *andante, p.* The manuscript is dated January 1832.

18. 'The Swiss Hymn'.

Dated January 1832, in D major and 2–4 time, there is some crossing out in the final bar.

19. 'When Order in this Land Commenced'.

The subject matter in this song by Joseph Mazzinghi (1765–1844) is King George III who reigned from 1760 to 1820. Again, the manuscript is dated January 1832. The key is C, the time signature is cut-**C,** and the direction is that the piece is played *con spirito.* The dynamic range is from *f* to *ff* and back.

20. 'The Wreath'.

Described on its original title page as an 'admired glee', this popular song was written by Joseph Mazzinghi. Marked *larghetto, p*, with *crescendo* to *f,* it is the last piece in the book to be dated – January 1832.

21. 'The Campbells are Comin''.

The words and music pertain to the Jacobite Rebellion of 1715. The key is A major and the time signature 6–8.

APPENDIX ONE

Footnotes

Abbreviations used in the Footnotes

Alexander and Sellars	*The Art of the Brontës*, Christine Alexander and Jane Sellars (1995)
Athenaeum	*Athenaeum* (Literary Journal) (1846)
Bärenreiter	*Beethoven's Symphonies, Urtext edition* (Nine Symphonies) (1999)
Barker	*The Brontës*, Juliet Barker (1994)
Barker Letters	*The Brontës: A Life in Letters,* Juliet Barker, Second edition (2010)
Berlioz	*A Critical Study of the Symphonies of Beethoven* (1843), (Downloaded translation)
Berlioz Memoirs	*The Memoirs of Hector Berlioz,* translated by David Cairns (1970)
Bewick, Thomas	*A History of British Birds* (1816)
Blackwood	*Blackwood's Edinburgh Magazine* (1830–1847)
Blom	*Beethoven's Pianoforte Sonatas Discussed,* Eric Blom (1938)
BPM	Brontë Parsonage Museum
BS	*Brontë Studies*
BST	*Brontë Society Transactions*

Calderdale	*Malcolm Bull's Calderdale Companion* (Downloaded)
Cecil	*Early Victorian Novelists: Essay in Revaluation* (1934)
Centenary	*A Centenary History of the Brontë Society 1893–1993* (1993)
Charlotte BN	'Biographical Notice', in preface to *Wuthering Heights* and *Agnes Grey* (1850) Charlotte Brontë Haworth Edition
Charlotte EP	'Editor's Preface' to *Wuthering Heights* (1850), Charlotte Brontë Haworth Edition
Chitham	*The Birth of* Wuthering Heights: *Emily Brontë at Work*, Edward Chitham (2001)
Companion	*The Beethoven Companion*, ed. Dennis Arnold and Nigel Fortune (1971)
Compendium	*Beethoven Compendium*, ed. Barry Cooper (1996)
Conservatoire	Conservatoire Royale de Bruxelles
Davies, Heretic	*Emily Brontë: Heretic*, Stevie Davies (1994)
Davies	*Emily Brontë*, Stevie Davies (1998)
Dingle	*The Mind of Emily Brontë* (1974)

Early Visitors	*Early Visitors to Haworth,* ed. Charles Lemon (1996)
Essays	*Essays in Biography and Criticism,* First Series, Peter Bayne (1857)
Everyman's Companion	*Everyman's Companion to the Brontës,* Barbara and Gareth Lloyd Evans (1982)
Fraser	*Fraser's Magazine for Town and Country,* Hugh Fraser and William Maginn
Gazette	*The Brontë Society Gazette*
Gérin	*Emily Brontë,* Winifred Gérin (1971)
Gérin AB	*Anne Brontë,* Winifred Gérin (1959)
Gezari	*The Poems of Emily Brontë,* ed. Janet Gezari (1992)
Grove	*Grove's Dictionary of Music and Musicians* Fifth Edition (1954)
Grove Beethoven	*Beethoven and His Nine Symphonies*, George Grove (1896)
Halifax CS	*Halifax Choral Society Souvenir Brochure* (1967)
Harmonicon	*Harmonicon* (1823–1833)
Hatfield	*The Complete Poems of Emily Jane Brontë,* C.W. Hatfield (1941)
Haworth WH	*Wuthering Heights,* Introduction, Haworth Edition (1900)

Higuchi	*The Brontës' World of Music,* Akiko Higuchi (2005)
Hymns A&M	*Hymns Ancient and Modern,* Standard Edition (1916)
Jerrold	*Douglas Jerrold's Weekly Newspaper*
Lane	*The Brontë Story*, Margaret Lane (1953)
Letters	*The Letters of Charlotte Brontë,* Volume One, Margaret Smith (1995)
Leyland, Francis A.	*The Brontë Family*, Two Volumes (1886)
Life	*The Life of Charlotte Brontë,* Elizabeth Gaskell, Haworth Edition (1900)
Liverpool Guide	*Liverpool Guide,* First Edition (1796)
Lock Dixon	*A Man of Sorrow*, John Lock and Canon W.T. Dixon (1965)
Lonoff	*The Belgian Essays*, Sue Lonoff (1996)
Monthly Magazine	*The Monthly Magazine*
Musical Library	*The Musical Library* (1834–1837)
Oxford Companion	*Oxford Companion to the Brontës* Christine Alexander and Margaret Smith (2005)
Peros	Nick Peros, quoted by Linda Lister, *The Brontës in the World of the Arts* (2008)

Ponden Sale	*Ponden Hall Sale Catalogue* (1899)
Roper	*The Poetry of Emily Brontë*, Derek Roper (1995)
Princeton	The 'Parrish Collection', Princeton University, New Jersey
QR	*Quarterly Review*
Robinson	*Emily Brontë*, Mary Robinson (1883)
Rolland	*Beethoven the Creator*, Romain Rolland (1929)
Rushton	*Incorporated Society of Musicians Journal*, article, Virginia Rushton (August 2011)
Rosen	*Beethoven's Piano Sonatas*, Charles Rosen (2002)
Schonberg	*The Lives of the Great Composers,* Harold C. Schonberg (1970)
Schindler	*The Life of Beethoven. Including his Correspondence with his Friends, Numerous Characteristic Traits, and Remarks on his Musical Works,* Translated by Ignaz Moscheles (1841)
Shirley	*Shirley*, Haworth Edition (1900)
Sutcliffe-Smith	*A Musical Pilgrimage in Yorkshire*, J. Sutcliffe-Smith (1928)

Symington	*Catalogue of the Museum and Library of the Brontë Society* (1927)
Thayer	*Thayer's Life of Beethoven*, A.W. Thayer, ed. Eliot Forbes (1967)
TLS	*Times Literary Supplement* – Robert Bridges' Review of *The Complete Poems of Emily Brontë*, ed. Clement K. Shorter
Tovey's Essays I and V	*Tovey's Essays in Musical Analysis*, Volumes One and Five, Donald Francis Tovey (1935 and 1937)
Wallace	*Emily Brontë and Beethoven; Romantic Equilibrium in Fiction and Music*, Robert K. Wallace (1986)
WH	*Wuthering Heights*, Haworth Edition (1900)
Wood	Steven Wood, email correspondence (2015).

Footnotes

Chapter One

A Social Context

(1) Shirley, Chapter 19, page 340 *et seq.*
(2) Barker, pages 471 and 655

Music in England

(1) Liverpool Guide, page 88
(2) Barker, page 247
(3) Barker, page 432
(4) Halifax CS, page 6
(5) Halifax CS, page 7
(6) Halifax CS, page 7
(7) 414, below
(8) 401, below
(9) BST, Part 95, Volume 18, No. 5
(10) BST, Part 3, page 20
(11) WH, Chapter 7, page 60
(12) Shirley, Chapter 16, page 308
(13) BST, Part 69, Volume 13, No. 4
(14) Early Visitors, page 106

Chapter Two

Haworth

(1) Life, page 32
(2) Calderdale, downloaded
(3) Letters, page 599
(4) Rushton, ISM article, August 2011
(5) BST, Part 75, Volume 14, No. 5
(6) BST, Part XXVII, page 185
(7) Symington, page 21
(8) Centenary, page 30

(9) Wallace, page 159
(10) BPM, Letter to the author dated 2 July 2012 and email from Juliet Barker, former Curator, BPM, 29 July 2013
(11) Page 414, below
(12) Page 133, below
(13) Lock Dixon, page 325
(14) Wood, email to the author, 3 September 2015
(15) Barker, page 342, quoting *Halifax Guardian*, 20 October 1838
(16) BST, Part LVII, Volume XI, No. 2
(17) Letters, page 130
(18) Life, page 139
(19) Page 45, below
(20) Ponden Sale
(21) BS, Volume 40, No. 2
(22) BS, Volume 32, Part 3, page 193, *et seq.*
(23) Barker, page 172

Brussels

(1) Letters, page 285
(2) Lonoff, pages 140–141
(3) BST, Part LX, Volume XI, No. 5
(4) Bewick , Volume 2, page xviii
(5) Gérin, page 127
(6) Gérin, page 130; Life, page 240
(7) BST, Part XXIII
(8) Centenary, page 17
(9) Robinson, Chapter 7, page 90
(10) Letters, page 311
(11) Letters, page 289
(12) Villette, Chapter Twenty, page 250

(13) Gérin, page 133, quoting C.K. Shorter, *The Brontës: Lives and Letters,* Volume 1, page 249 (1908)
(14) BST, 1982, Part 92, No. 2 of Vol. 18
(15) Conservatoire, Letter to the author from the librarian dated 10 November 2012
(16) Higuchi, pages 179–180 and 274; *Villette*, Chapter Thirty-eight
(17) Letters, page 299
(18) Barker Letters, page 110
(19) Letters, page 299
(20) Oxford Companion, page 93
(21) *Villette*, Chapter 19, page 230, *et seq.*
(22) Conservatoire, letter to the author dated 10 November 2012
(23) Grove: *Beethoven and his Nine Symphonies* (1896)
(24) Robinson, Chapter 14, page 166
(25) BST, Part 81, Volume 16, No. 1, page 57
(26) *Villette*, Chapter 20, page 244, *et seq.*

Beethoven

(1) Hatfield, number 5
(2) Dingle, page 103
(3) Charlotte EP, page lv
(4) Thayer, page 356
(5) Charlotte BN, page li
(6) Schonberg, pages 91 and 93
(7) Rolland, pages 33 and 118
(8) Berlioz Memoirs, page 528
(9) Gérin, page 94
(10) Rosen, page 149
(11) Berlioz, page 3
(12) Compendium, page 214

(13) Grove Beethoven, page 44, quoting *Allgemeine Musikalische Zeitung* (Universal Musical Times), 23 July 1828
(14) QR, December 1848
(15) Jerrold, 15 January, 1848
(16) Chitham, page 227
(17) Essays
(18) Bärenreiter, Symphony Number 3, page III
(19) Pages 139 and 176, below
(20) Thayer, page 349
(21) Thayer, page 920
(22) Page 281, below
(23) Bärenreiter, Symphony Number 3, page IV
(24) Chitham, page 190
(25) Pages 208 and 209, below
(26) Pages 342 and 343, below
(27) Berlioz, page 10
(28) Page 207, below
(29) Berlioz, page 13
(30) Hatfield, number 168
(31) Life, page 142
(32) Gérin, page 60
(33) Page 44, above
(34) Hatfield, number 191
(35) Thayer, page 482
(36) Tovey Essays V, pages 165 and 166
(37) Hatfield, number 174
(38) Wallace, Chapter One
(39) Rosen, page 249
(40) Wallace, Chapter Three
(41) Schindler, pages 18–19; Thayer, page 58
(42) WH, Chapter 4, page 36

(43) Hatfield, page 239
(44) Blackwood, Volume 27, March 1830, pages 472 and 479
(45) Blackwood, Volume 50, November 1841, page 564
(46) Blackwood, Volume 58, July 1845, page 43
(47) Blackwood, Volume 59, February 1846, page 175
(48) Blackwood, Volume 62, October 1847, pages 420–421

Romanticism

(1) Anderson, 1136
(2) Schonberg, page 91
(3) Oxford Companion, page 55
(4) BST, Part XXXVI, Volume VII, No. 1, page 22
(5) Hatfield, number 184
(6) Hatfield, number 190
(7) Thayer, pages 408–409
(8) Thayer, page 480
(9) WH, pages xxv and xxviii
(10) Hatfield, number 135 and Chitham, page 143
(11) Everyman's Companion, page 239
(12) Letters, page 130
(13) Gérin, page 45
(14) Gérin, page 45
(15) WH, Chapter Nine, page 82, *et seq.*
(16) Thayer, pages 851–852

Chapter Three

Musical and Literary Rhythm

(1) Gazette, Issue 55, September 2011
(2) Roper, page 21
(3) Charlotte BN, page xliv

(4) Athenaeum, 4 July 1846, 'Poetry of the Million', Sydney Dobell
(5) Blackwood, Volume 82, July 1857, page 89
(6) TLS, 12 January 1911
(7) Davies, page 44
(8) Peros, page 225
(9) Cecil, Chapter 5
(10) Hatfield, number 62
(11) Hatfield, numbers 59 and 76
(12) Hatfield, numbers 173, 177 and 12
(13) Hatfield, numbers 65–74
(14) Hymns A&M, 520
(15) Hatfield, number 66
(16) Hatfield, numbers 36–38
(17) BST, Part 67, Volume 13, No. 2, page 91
(18) Page 69, above
(19) Page 17, above
(20) WH, Chapter 31, page 312
(21) WH, Chapter 32, page 321
(22) WH, Chapter 9, page 78

Emily the Pianist

(1) Gérin AB, page 74
(2) Wallace, page 174; Companion, page 175; Gérin AB, page 74
(3) Conservatoire, email to the author dated 26 June, 2017
(4) Page 60, above
(5) Robinson, Chapter 7, page 84
(6) Page 31, above
(7) WH, Chapter 24, page 257

Chapter Four

The 'Parrish Collection'

(1) Page 76, above
(2) Page 52, above
(3) Page 414, below
(4) Oxford Companion, page 226

Three Bound Volumes of Sheet Music from the 1830s

(1) Sutcliffe-Smith, pages 233–234
(2) BST, Part XLV, No. 4 of Vol. VIII
(3) Monthly Magazine, Volume 37, page 65
(4) Letters, pages 309-310

The Musical Library – Instrumental'

(1) Page 136, above
(2) Page 27, above
(3) Page 137, above
(4) Page 65, above
(5) Page 186, below
(6) Page 139, above
(7) Pages 52 and 126, above
(8) Page 69, above
(9) Grove Beethoven, page 251
(10) Page 67, above
(11) Page 116, above
(12) Page 68, above
(13) Tovey's Essays I, page 46
(14) Hymns A&M, number 545
(15) Harmonicon, Volume 5, page 164
(16) Page 62, above
(17) Page 66, above

The Musical Library – Vocal

(1) Page 67, above

(2) Page 84, above

Anne Brontë's Songbook

(1) Life, page 162

(2) Page 414, above

(3) Page 112, above

(4) Page 408, below

(5) Gérin, page 40

(6) Page 266, above

Branwell Brontë's Flute Book

(1) Leyland, Volume One, page 119

(2) Leyland, Volume One, page 238

(3) Leyland, Volume Two, page 37

(4) Leyland, Volume One, page 173

(5) Page 142, above

(6) Leyland, Volume Two, page 100

(7) Shirley, Chapter 24, page 438

APPENDIX TWO

Select Bibliography

Select Bibliography – Brontë

Alexander, Christine and Sellars, Jane	*The Art of the Brontës* (CUP)
Alexander, Christine and Smith, Margaret (eds.)	*The Oxford Companion to the Brontës* (OUP)
Barker, Juliet	*Sixty Treasures* (Brontë Society)
Barker, Juliet	*The Brontës* (Abacus)
Barker, Juliet	*The Brontës: A Life in Letters* (Viking)
Barnard, Robert	*Emily Brontë* (The British Library)
Barnard, Robert and Louise	*A Brontë Encyclopaedia* (Wiley-Blackwell)
Bell, Currer, Ellis and Acton *'Poems '*	(Smith, Elder and Co., London)
Bellamy, Joan	*Mary Taylor* (Kirklees Cultural Service)
Bentley, Phyllis	*The Brontës* (Pan Books)
Bentley, Phyllis	*The Brontës and Their World* (Book Club Associates)
Brontë, Anne	*Anne Brontë's Songbook* (Boethius Press)
Brontë, Anne	*Agnes Grey* (The Haworth Edition. Smith, Elder and Co., London, 1900)
Brontë, Anne	*The Tenant of Wildfell Hall* (The Haworth Edition. Smith, Elder and Co., London, 1900)

Brontë, Anne	*Poems* by Anne Brontë (The Haworth Edition. Smith, Elder and Co., London, 1900)
Brontë, Branwell	*Branwell Brontë's Flute Book* (Boethius Press)
Brontë, Charlotte	*Emma: A Fragment* (The Haworth Edition. Smith, Elder and Co., London, 1900)
Brontë, Charlotte	*Jane Eyre* (The Haworth Edition. Smith, Elder and Co., London, 1900)
Brontë, Charlotte	*Poems* by Charlotte Brontë (The Haworth Edition. Smith, Elder and Co., London, 1900)
Brontë, Charlotte	*Shirley* (The Haworth Edition. Smith, Elder and Co., London, 1900)
Brontë, Charlotte	*The Professor* (The Haworth Edition. Smith, Elder and Co., London, 1900)
Brontë, Charlotte	*Villette* (The Haworth Edition. Smith, Elder and Co., London, 1900)
Brontë, Emily	*Wuthering Heights* (The Haworth Edition. Smith, Elder and Co., London, 1900)

Brontë, Patrick, Revd.	*Cottage Poems* (The Haworth Edition. Smith, Elder and Co., London, 1900)
Brontë, Patrick, Revd.	*Collected Works'* (T.Harrison and Sons)
Brontë Society	*Brontë Society Transactions*, 1895–2001
Brontë Society	*Brontë Studies*, 2002 to date
Brontë Society	*Gazette*, 1990 to date
Chadwick, Ellis H.	*In the Footsteps of the Brontës* (Downloaded)
Chitham, Edward	*A Life of Emily Brontë* (Amberley)
Chitham, Edward	*The Birth of Wuthering Heights: Emily Brontë at Work* (Palgrave)
Chitham, Edward	*The Poems of Anne Brontë* (Macmillan)
Davies, Stevie	*Emily Brontë* (Northcote House Publishers)
Davies, Stevie	*Emily Brontë: Heretic* (The Women's Press)
Dingle, Herbert	*The Mind of Emily Brontë* (Martin Brian and O'Keefe)
Davis, Mark and Dinsdale, Ann	*In the Footsteps of the Brontës* (Amberley)
Dinsdale, Ann	*At Home with the Brontës* (Amberley)
Dinsdale, Ann	*The Brontës at Haworth* (Frances Lincoln)

Dinsdale, Ann and White, Kathryn	*The Brontë Parsonage Museum* (Brontë Society)
Dinsdale, Ann Laycock, Sarah, and Akhurst, Julie	*Brontë Relics: A Collection History*(Brontë Society)
Duckett, Bob (ed.)	*The Brontë Novels: 150 Years of Literary Dominance* (The Brontë Society)
Du Maurier, Daphne	*The Infernal World of Branwell Brontë* (Penguin)
Duthie, Enid L.	*The Foreign Vision of Charlotte Brontë* (MacMillan)
Forshaw, Chas. H.	'The Poets of Keighley, Bingley, Haworth and District' (W.W.Morgan)
Gardiner, Juliet	*The World Within – The Brontës at Haworth*
Gaskell, Elizabeth	*Life of Charlotte Brontë* (The Haworth Edition. Smith, Elder and Co., London, 1900)
Gaskell, Elizabeth	*Life of Charlotte Brontë* (D. Appleton, NY, 1857)
Gérin, Winifred	*Anne Brontë* (Allen Lane)
Gérin, Winifred	*Branwell Brontë* (Radius/ Hutchinson)
Gérin, Winifred	*Charlotte Brontë* (OUP)
Gérin, Winifred	*Emily Brontë* (Clarendon Press)
Gezari, Janet (ed.)	*Complete Poems of Emily Brontë* (Penguin)

Gezari, Janet	*Last Things* (OUP)
Glen, Heather (ed.)	*The Cambridge Companion to the Brontës* (CUP)
Green, Dudley	*Patrick Brontë: Father of Genius* (History Press)
Hagan, Sandra and Wells, Juliette	*The Brontës in the World of the Arts* (Ashgate)
Hatfield, C.W. (ed.)	*The Complete Poems of Emily Jane Brontë* (Columbia University Press)
Heaton, Robert	*Sale Catalogue of the Heaton Library* (Ogden and Shuttleworth)
Hewish, John	*Emily Brontë: A Critical and Biographical Study* (Macmillan)
Higuchi, Akiko	*Anne Brontë's Songbook and Branwell Brontë's Flute Book* (Yushodo)
Higuchi, Akiko	*The Brontë's World of Music* (Yushodo)
Ingham, Patricia	*The Brontës* (Oxford World's Classics)
Jay, Betty	*Anne Brontë* (Northcote House)
Kellett, Jocelyn	*Haworth Parsonage* (The Brontë Society)
Knight, Charmian and Spencer, Luke	*Reading the Brontës* (The Brontë Society)
Lane, Margaret	*The Brontë Story* (Heinemann)

Lemon, Charles	*A Centenary History of the Brontë Society 1893–1993* (The Brontë Society)
Lemon, Charles	*Early Visitors to Haworth* (The Brontë Society)
Lewis, Naomi	*A Peculiar Music* (Bodley Head)
Leyland, Francis A.	*The Brontë Family with special reference to Patrick Branwell Brontë* (Hurst and Blackett)
Lister, Philip	*Ghosts and Gravestones of Haworth* (History Press)
Lloyd Evans, Barbara	*Everyman's Companion to the Brontës*and Gareth (Dent)
Lock, J and Dixon, W.T	*A Man of Sorrow* (Nelson)
Lonoff, Sue	*The Belgian Essays* (Yale University Press)
Macdonald, Frederika	*The Secret of Charlotte Brontë* (Gutenberg ebook)
Miller, Lucasta	*The Brontë Myth* (Vintage)
Moore, Virginia	*The Life and Eager Death of Emily Brontë* (Rich and Cowan)
Pepetone, Gregory G.	*Kaleidoscopic Images: A Comparison of Robert Schumann and Charlotte Brontë* (University of Georgia)
Raymond, Ernest	*In the Steps of the Brontës* (Rich and Cowan)

Petit, Jean-Pierre (ed.)	*Emily Brontë* (Penguin Critical Anthologies)
Ratchford, Fannie E.	*The Brontës Web of Childhood* (Columbia)
Robinson, Mary	*Emily Brontë* (W.H. Allen and Co)
Roper, Derek	*The Poetry of Emily Brontë* (OUP)
Ruijssenaars, Eric	*Charlotte Brontë's Promised Land* (The Brontë Society)
Scruton, William	*The Brontës* (Arthur Dobson Publishing Co.)
Shorter, Clement	*The Brontës and their Circle* (Dent)
Sinclair, May	*The Three Brontës* (Hutchinson)
Smith, Anne (ed.)	*The Art of Emily Brontë* (Barnes and Noble)
Smith, Margaret	*The Letters of Charlotte Brontë, Volume One 1829–1847* (Clarendon Press)
Smith, Margaret	*The Letters of Charlotte Brontë, Volume Two 1848–1851* (Clarendon Press)
Smith, Margaret	*The Letters of Charlotte Brontë, Volume Three 1853–1855* (Clarendon Press)
Spark, Muriel and Stanford, Derek	*Emily Brontë – her Life and Work* (Owen)
Steed, Michael	*A Brontë Diary* (Dalesman)

Symington, J.A.	*Catalogue of the Museum and Library of the Brontë Society* (The Brontë Society)
Symington, J.A.	*The Shakespeare Head Brontë Bibliography* (Oak Knoll)
Trapenard, Augustin	*Emily Brontë – Devoirs de Bruxelles* (Mille et une Nuits)
Walker, Arthur D. and Duckett, Robert J.	*The Brontë Society Transactions 1895–2001: An Index and History* (Brontë Society)
Whitworth, Alan	*The Old Bell Chapel* (Culva House)
Wilks, Brian	*Illustrated Brontës of Haworth* (Tiger Books International)
Wilks, Brian	*The Brontës* (Hamlyn)
Wroot, Herbert E.	*The Persons and Places of the Brontë Novels* (The Brontë Society)

Select Bibliography – Music

Anderson, Emily	*The Letters of Beethoven* (Macmillan)
Barford, Phillip	*Beethoven Companion – The Piano Music II* (Faber and Faber)
Barlow, Harold and Morgenstern, Sam	*A Dictionary of Musical Themes* (Faber and Faber)

Berlioz, Hector	*A Critical Study of the Symphonies of Beethoven* (Downloaded)
Berlioz, Hector	*Memoirs*, translated by David Cairns (Readers Union)
Blom, Eric	*Beethoven's Piano Sonatas Discussed* (Da Capo Press)
Bory, Robert	*Beethoven* (Thames Hudson)
Cooper, Barry	*Beethoven and the Creative Process* (OUP)
Cooper, Barry (ed.)	*Beethoven: The Thirty-five Piano Sonatas* (Associated Board)
Cooper, Barry (ed.)	*The Beethoven Compendium* (Thames and Hudson)
Cudworth, W.	*Musical Reminiscences of Bradford* (W. Byles and Sons)
Drake, Kenneth	*Beethoven's Sonatas and The Creative Experience* (Indiana University Press)
Drake, Kenneth	*Beethoven's Piano Sonatas as He Played and Taught Them* (Indiana Press)
Ellsworth, Therese and Wollenberg, Susan	*The Piano in Nineteenth-Century British Culture* (Ashgate Publishing Ltd.)
Finane, Ben	*Handel's* Messiah *and his English Oratorios* (Magnum Opus series)

Frost, Maurice (ed.)	*Historical Companion to Hymns Ancient and Modern* (William Clowes and Sons)
Grove, George	*Beethoven and His Nine Symphonies* (Novello)
Grove, George	*Dictionary of Music and Musicians, 5th Edition* (10 Volumes), (Macmillan)
Halifax Choral Society	*Halifax Choral Society 150th Anniversary Souvenir Brochure*
Hennessy, John	*Beethoven – An Analysis of the Piano Sonatas* (Hennessy)
Hennessy, John	*Emily Jane Brontë and Ludwig van Beethoven* (Hennessy)
Kennedy, Michael (ed.)	*The Oxford Dictionary of Music* (OUP)
Knight, Charles	*The Musical Library* (8 Volumes) (W. Clowes and Son)
Knight, Charles	*The Musical Library Supplement* (W. Clowes and Son)
Latham, Alison (ed.)	*The Oxford Companion to Music* (OUP)
Levarie, Siegmund	Le Nozze di Figaro: *A Critical Analysis* (Da Capo Press)

Marston, Nicholas	*Beethoven Compendium – Symphonies* (Thames and Hudson)
Milford, Humphrey (ed.)	*The English Hymnal* (OUP)
Nicholson, S.H. (ed.)	*Hymns Ancient and Modern* Standard Edition (W. Clowes and Son)
Princeton University	*The Parrish Collection Catalogue* (Princeton University Press)
Ringer, Alexander L.	'Beethoven and the London Pianoforte School' from *The Musical Quarterly* (Oxford Journals)
Robbins Landon, H.C.	*Beethoven* (Arts Book Society)
Rolland, Romain	*Beethoven the Creator* (Victor Gollancz)
Rosen, Charles	*Beethoven's Piano Sonatas – A Short Companion* (Yale University Press)
Schindler, Anton, ed. Ignaz Moscheles,	Life of Beethoven. Including his *Correspondence with his Friends, Numerous Characteristic Traits, and Remarks on his Musical Works* (Henry Colburn)
Scholes, Percy M.	*The Oxford Companion to Music* (OUP)
Schonberg, Harold C.	*The Lives of the Great Composers* (Davis-Poynter)

Scott, Marion	*Beethoven* (Dent)
Swafford, Jan	*Beethoven Anguish and Triumph* (Faber and Faber)
Temperley, Nicholas	*The Music of the English Parish Church* (2 Vols.) (Cambridge University Press)
Thayer, Alexander W.	*Thayer's Life of Beethoven*, Revised and Edited by Elliot Forbes (2 Volumes) (Princeton University Press)
Tovey, Donald Francis	*A Companion to Beethoven's Pianoforte Sonatas* (Associated Board)
Tovey, Donald Francis	*Beethoven* (OUP)
Tovey, Donald Francis	*Essays in Musical Analysis, Volume 1 – Symphonies* (OUP)
Tovey, Donald Francis	*Essays in Musical Analysis Volume 4 – Illustrative Music* (OUP)
Tovey, Donald Francis	*Essays in Musical Analysis, Volume 5 – Vocal Music* (OUP)
Tyson, Alan	*The Authentic English Editions of Beethoven* (Faber and Faber)
Wallace, Robert K.	*Emily Brontë and Beethoven: Romantic Equilibrium in Fiction and Music* (University of Georgia Press)

Wesley, John	*The Methodist Hymn Book* (Methodist Conference Office)
Wesley, John	*The United Methodist Hymnal* (United Methodist Publishing House)

Select Bibliography – Beethoven Scores

Adelaide, opus 46
Ah! Perfido, opus 65
Bagatelle in A, opus 33, no. 4
Canon, *Kühl, nicht lau,* WoO 191
Coriolan Overture, opus 62
Das Glück der Freundschaft, opus 88
Das glücklische Land, opus 75, no. 1
Diabelli Variations, opus 120
Fidelio, opus 72
Five Variations on *Rule Britannia*, WoO 79
Große Fuge, opus 133
In questa tomba, WoO 133
Kleine Blumen, opus 83
La Marmotte, opus 52, no. 7
Leonore Overtures, 1, 2 and 3, opus 72a
Mass in D, *Missa Solemnis,* opus 123
Nine Variations on Paisiello's *Quanto* è *bello – La Molinara,* WoO 69
Piano Sonata in A, opus 2, no. 2
Piano Sonata in D, opus 10, no. 3
Piano Sonata in C minor, opus 13, *Pathetique*
Piano Sonata in A flat, opus 26

Piano Sonata in F minor, opus 57, *Appassionata*
Piano Sonata in C minor, opus 111
Romance in G for Violin and Piano, opus 40
Rondo in C, opus 51, no. 1
Septet, opus 20
Serenade for Flute and Piano, opus 41
Serenade for Violin, Viola and Cello, opus 8
Seven Variations on *God Save the King*, WoO 80
Six Easy Variations on an Original Theme, WoO 77
Six Variations on *Nel cor più non mi sento – La Molinara*, WoO 70
Sonata for Horn and Piano, opus 17
String Quartet in A, opus 18, no. 5
String Quartet in B flat, opus 130
String Quartet in C# minor, opus 131
String Quartet in A minor, opus 132
Symphony Number 1 in C, opus 21
Symphony Number 2 in D, opus 36
Symphony Number 3 in E flat, opus 55, *Eroica*
Symphony Number 4 in B flat, opus 60
Symphony Number 6 in F, opus 68, *Pastoral*
Symphony Number 7 in A, opus 92
Symphony Number 9 in D minor, opus 125, *Choral*
Twenty-four Variations of Righini's *Venni amore*, WoO 65
The *Creatures of Prometheus*, opus 43
Waltz in E flat, WoO 14 Anh.
Waltz in F minor, WoO 14 Anh.
Wellington's Victory (or the *Battle of Vitoria*), opus 91
Wie herrlich leuchtet mir die Natur, opus 52, no. 4
Zärtliche Liebe, WoO 123

Select Bibliography – Literary and Miscellaneous

Allom, Thomas — *Views in the Northern Counties* (Fisher, Son and Co.)

Bayne, Peter — *Two Great Englishwomen* (James Clarke and Co.)

Bewick, Thomas — *A History of British Birds*, Volumes 1 and 2 (Walker)

Blackwood, William — *Blackwood's Edinburgh Magazine*, Volumes 27–62 (Blackwood)

Bunyan, John — *'Pilgrim's Progress'* (George Virtue)

Burns, Robert — *The Poetical Works of Robert Burns* (Henry Frowde)

Byron, Lord George Gordon — *The Complete Poetical Works* (George Routledge and Sons)

Britannica — *Encyclopaedia Britannica*

Cecil, Lord David — *Early Victorian Novelists: Essays Revaluation* (Fontana)

Collins — *German Dictionary*

Collins-Robert — *French Dictionary*

Drabble, Margaret (ed.) — *The Oxford Companion to English Literature* (Guild Publishing)

Ford, Boris (ed.) — *From Byron to Blake* (Penguin)

Fraser, Hugh and Maginn, William	*Fraser's Magazine for Town and Country* 1830–1848 (Fraser)
Goethe, Johann Wolfgang von	*Selected Poetry* (Libris)
Gregg, Pauline	*A Social and Economic History of Britain 1760–1972* (Harrap)
Hannon, Paul	*Brontë Way* (Hillside)
Haworth Parochial	*Haworth Parish Church Guide* (Church Council)
Hayward, John (ed.)	*The Penguin Book of English Verse* (Penguin)
Horne, Oliver	*A History of Savings Banks* (Oxford)
Magnusson, Magnus (ed.)	*Chambers Biographical Dictionary* (TSP)
Milford, H.S. (ed.)	*The Oxford Book of English Verse of the Romantic period 1798–1837* (Clarendon)
Milton, John	*The Poetical Works of John Milton* (Henry Frowde)
Moore, Thomas	*The Poetical Works of Thomas Moore* (The Grand Colosseum Warehouse)
Moss, W.	*The Liverpool Guide*, First Edition, 1796
Osbourne, Harold (ed.)	*The Oxford Companion to Art* (Clarendon Press)

Oxford University Press	*Book of Common Prayer* (Presented in accordance with the will of Philip, Lord Wharton, 1696) (OUP)
Oxford University Press	*Holy Bible* (Presented in accordance with the will of Philip, Lord Wharton, 1696) (OUP)
Oxford University Press	*Oxford Dictionary of Quotations* (OUP)
Oxford University Press	*Oxford English Dictionary* (OUP)
Scott, Walter	*The Poetical Works of Sir Walter Scott* (Henry Frowde)
Shelley, Percy Bysshe	*Poetical Works of Shelley* (OUP)
Sutcliffe-Smith, J.	*A Musical Pilgrimage in Yorkshire* (Richard Jackson)
Thornton Antiquarian History Society	*Footpaths and Byways Map and Potted Trail*
Wordsworth, William	*The Poetical Works of William Wordsworth* (Henry Frowde)

APPENDIX THREE

Brief Chronology

Brief Chronology

1818 30 July	Emily Jane Brontë born at Thornton to Patrick and Maria Brontë, the fifth of six children
1818 20 August	Christened at St. James' Church, Thornton, by William Morgan; her godparents are Revd. John and Jane Fennell and their daughter Jane
1820 17 January	Birth of Anne (christened 25 March)
1820 April	Family moves to Haworth upon Patrick's taking up the incumbency there
1821 15 September	Maria Brontë dies of cancer
1824 25 November	Emily follows her sisters Maria, Elizabeth and Charlotte to Cowan Bridge Clergy Daughters' School
1824 2 September	Crow Hill bog-burst
1825 January/February	Tabitha Aykroyd engaged as a servant
1825 February – June	Maria (14 February) and Elizabeth (31 May) leave Cowan Bridge to come home to die of consumption (respectively 6 May and 15 June). Charlotte and Emily hastily removed from school by Patrick on 1 June
1826 29 May	The cherry tree incident, when Emily climbs out of an

	upstairs window and breaks off a branch; she and Tabby try to cover up the damage with soot
1826 5 June	Patrick Brontë brings home the toy soldiers from Leeds
1827 1 December	Bed plays started by Charlotte and Emily
1831 17 January	Charlotte goes to Roe Head, Miss Wooler's School, Mirfield (leaves May 1832)
1832	Patrick has the Sunday School built – Charlotte is the first Superintendent
1833 10 July	Ellen Nussey's first visit to the Parsonage
1834	Organ installed in Haworth Church
1834 24 November	First of Emily's and Anne's diary papers
1835 29 July	Emily goes to Roe Head School as a student; Charlotte goes with her as a teacher. Emily stays only three months, Anne replacing her in October
1836 12 July	First extant poem – 'Will the day be bright or cloudy?'
1837 26 June	Diary paper signed with Anne
1838 February	Keeper, Emily's mastiff, arrives at the Parsonage
1838 9 June	Mary and Martha Taylor visit the Parsonage for the first time
1838 September	Emily takes up position as

	teacher at Miss Patchett's School, Law Hill, Halifax
1839 March/April	Emily returns home from Law Hill
1839 August	William Weightman comes to Haworth as curate
1840 February/March	Emily nicknamed 'The Major' by Ellen Nussey
1841 30 July	Diary paper mentions the sisters' plan to open their own school; nothing comes of it
1841 27 October	Emily paints her pet merlin 'Nero'
1842 8 February	Emily and Charlotte begin their journey to Brussels in order to study at the Pensionnat Heger , arriving there on 15 February
1842 31 March	Branwell is dismissed from his post in the railway company
1842 6 September	Death from cholera of William Weightman
1842 12 October	Martha Taylor dies of cholera in Brussels
1842 29 October	Death of Aunt Elizabeth Branwell
1842 5 November	Emily and Charlotte leave Brussels hastily upon receiving news of the death of their Aunt Elizabeth Branwell, arriving at Haworth on 8 November
1843 27 January	Charlotte returns to Brussels; Emily remains at home

1843	Anne and Branwell return to Thorp Green as governess and tutor, respectively
1844	Emily begins the task of copying her poems into two notebooks – Gondal and non-Gondal
1845	Probably the year in which Emily started writing *Wuthering Heights*
1845 25 May	Revd. Arthur Bell Nicholls comes to Haworth as curate
1845 30 June	Emily and Anne travel to York for two nights
1845 July	Branwell dismissed from his position at Thorp Green
1845 30 July	Diary paper signed by Emily (albeit probably written a day later)
1845 September/October	Discovery by Charlotte of one of Emily's poetry notebooks
1846 May	Publication, by Aylott and Jones, of *Poems*, by Currer, Ellis and Acton Bell
1847 16 October	*Jane Eyre* by Currer Bell published by Smith, Elder and Company
1847 December	*Wuthering Heights* and *Agnes Grey,* by Ellis and Acton Bell, eventually published by T. C. Newby, after much disreputable dealing on his part; authors'

	copies containing many errors received 14 December
1848 24 September	Death of Branwell Brontë. Emily catches a cold at his funeral on 28 September
1848 19 December	Emily Jane Brontë dies of pulmonary tuberculosis (consumption)
1848 22 December	Emily's funeral conducted by Revd. Arthur Bell Nicholls.

APPENDIX FOUR

Notes on Playing the John Green Upright Cabinet Piano

by

Ken Forrest

No apologies need be made for this instrument. It is not a modern piano, and cannot produce the effects which the latter can. However, it is a musical instrument of high quality in first-class playing condition, and can play with great sensitivity any music written for the piano before and during its year of manufacture – c1825. I would suggest that at least half an hour's playing-in is essential for any pianist coming to the John Green for the first time, to get the feel for the dynamic range available and to immerse themselves into its contemporary sound-world and touch.

Fragility: However, one must also remember that the John Green is relatively fragile compared with a modern instrument. It is what might be termed a 'Mozart' piano, in other words it was built for music of the Classical era of Mozart and Haydn. The Romantic approach to music, with plenty of emotional expression, gave pianists the licence to play *fff* at will, and pianos were developed to provide the strength to resist the unrestrained outpourings of emotion. Beethoven, as we know, broke his pianos; Liszt demanded that piano-makers build instruments to resist his phenomenal virtuosity, and gradually he broke fewer and fewer hammers and strings as the years passed and the hammers grew stronger. If the pianist imagines that John Green's hammer shanks (thin dowels, at the top of which are glued the hammers) are made of glass, then this perhaps would give an insight. The Parsonage piano was a domestic instrument built to cater for the earlier repertoire. Upright pianos soon caught up with the greater demands on the action, but not in the John Green era! Its falling into dereliction could well be through the attempt to play Romantic era music on it, the Liszt-style virtuosity, which would quickly have broken the hammer shanks and sprung the leather and vellum hinge joints. Those who do get to play on it should be aware of the gentle dynamic range it has, almost as great as the modern instrument, but from *ppp* to *mf,* and the delicate touch required to control it. The pianist must learn to rein in the dynamic and develop the touch to take advantage of the softer tones. A pianist who has attained concert level should be tactfully reminded that this is a disadvantage in some ways as regards the John Green piano. To play with 'the emotions in the forearms', as pianists using the modern piano do, is a recipe for broken components. The emotions must 'stay in the hands' on this delicate instrument. So long as the pianist does not bring iron fingers to the piano, even Prokofiev can safely be played thereon.

Light touch: The delicacy of the piano and its fragility go with a very light touch. The piano, at first, seems uncontrollable, but during the familiarisation playing-in, the touch graduation needed to achieve the extremes of dynamic available on the John Green becomes ever more natural within its sound-world.

Repetition: The piano does not have the advantage of the modern upright action, which will repeat a note from 'half-touch'. On this piano, the note will not repeat unless the key has risen completely to rest. Half-finger articulation is essential. The action will repeat very rapidly, if this principle is remembered, and the finger virtually leaves the key between successive repetitions.

Shift pedal: The sustaining pedal lifts all the dampers as usual. The 'soft' pedal is a shift mechanism giving a true *una corda* from the bichord-strung instrument (throughout – lowest bass to top treble). The John Green action cannot be adjusted to the same degree of accuracy as the modern grand piano, and leather hammer coverings do not react in the same way as modern felt. Thus the shift pedal does not like being used in graduated positions as, while some hammers miss the second string altogether on half depression, some will brush the second string and create a faint zinging sound. It is best to think of it as 'on' or 'off' only, providing a terrace dynamic (and to a degree timbre) change similar to a harpsichord.

Tuning: Old pianos go out of tune with each breath of change in the weather. The iron strings are stretched between wooden anchoring, and as the temperature rises, and the humidity reduces, so the strings expand and the wooden structure contracts. The two forces are acting together to skew the tuning. The iron frame across which modern strings are stretched takes away this double problem almost completely, a good thing when there are about 225 strings to tune each time! Normally, in domestic use, the small daily movement would not be enough to bother with, but for a concert, when the piano is expected to sound at its very best, a touch-over is advisable on the day of performance, following the full tuning the day before.

APPENDIX FIVE

Illustrated Talk at Haworth

Emily Jane Brontë and
Ludwig van Beethoven
5 June 2015

Emily Brontë's Poetry and '*Wuthering Heights*
Beethoven's Music
Alexandra Lesley (Speaker)
Isabelle Oehmichen (Piano)

'High Waving Heather'
Sonata in D minor, opus 31, no. 2, 1st movement

'It is too Late to Call Thee Now'
String Quartet in A minor, opus 132
Heiliger Dankgesang eines Genesenen an die Gottheit in der Lydischen Tonart

'To Imagination'
Sonata in E, opus 109, Final movement theme

'Silent is the House'
Allegretto from Symphony Number 7 in A, opus 92

Extract from *Wuthering Heights*, Chapter 15
Sonata in F minor, opus 57, *Appassionata* – 1st movement

Extract from *Wuthering Heights*, Chapter 34
Das Liedchen von der Ruhe, opus 52, no. 3

'No Coward Soul is Mine'
String Quartet in B flat, opus 130, Cavatina

A Talk
John Hennessy

The potential influence of Beethoven's music and personality upon Emily Brontë's literary creativity

APPENDIX SIX

Playing the Parsonage Piano
By Isabelle Oehmichen

The piano which Patrick Brontë acquired for his children is unique. Pianos which stand upright have long since been popular but, as we now know them, they are not of the height of the Parsonage piano which stands 1.99 metres tall, and is thus called a cabinet (not upright or cottage) piano. The hammers are extremely long with small heads which give them the fragility of glass, and the keyboard is of far less range than that of modern pianos. It is very tricky to play this instrument as it is always necessary to ensure that the keys are not struck too hard, which could very quickly break hammers which have been so remarkably rebuilt by Ken Forrest.

Right from the start, I was surprised at the instrument's sonority which appeared to be somewhere between that of a harpsichord and early piano. The notes seemed somewhat uneven, and the touch was especially light. The distinct feeling was one of an instrument which, from a technical point of view, was very different from that which a modern-day pianist is used to playing. There was also the impression that this was not a piano which was easily controllable, of there being a feeling of its 'dragging' during playing.

I found the left pedal particularly interesting, it being an *una corda,* which permits the playing on only one of the two strings, which each note of this piano has. This one string seems to be regulated differently from its neighbour – it produces a very different sound from that produced on a modern instrument. Thus, one cannot absolutely reproduce the effect of a modern *una corda* pedal on this piano, which creates a different sonority or atmosphere. Once this fact is understood, however, one can consider various interpretations of the music which was being written at the time when the instrument was built – circa two hundred years ago.

At first, until I became used to playing the Parsonage piano, I was concerned about adapting my technique to an instrument where *ff* on a Steinway meant little more than *mf* on this one. This could, potentially, have been a problem in the playing of the first movements of the *Tempest* (opus 31, no. 2) and *Appassionata* (opus 57) sonatas of Beethoven. Yet suddenly, I do not know why, the magic seemed to operate; I began to feel how this piano should be played in such a challenging repertoire. Of course, this is not an instrument designed for the concert hall nor, perhaps, even for salon recitals. But I think that it offers many possibilities for the interpretation of Beethoven, his contemporary composers, and those who preceded them – perhaps with scope for carefully selected recordings. I wonder how such a fragile instrument was, all those years ago, conveyed from the manufacturers to its successive owners before ending up at the Parsonage? (I believe also that it subsequently passed through other hands before eventually being returned to the Brontë Society). And I can't help wondering how Emily, with her very singular personality, handled it.

Certainly I was affected by the experience of playing on the Brontë piano. It was a privilege, and I think one that suggests a re-think of one's approach to the music of Haydn, Mozart and Beethoven and that of their contemporaries – Clementi, Dussek, Field and Czerny. For my part, there is necessarily a 'before and after' which leads me to consider modern methods by which to interpret those works which were, of course, written for instruments of the period. Just one example – the sonority obtained by use of the *una corda* pedal on the Parsonage piano could easily evoke that of a glass harmonica of Mozart's time, for which instrument he wrote a number of pieces; an area for further research, I am sure.

There were particular problems with the playing of the first movement of *Appassionata.* The 'toning down' of the dynamics from *ff* to *mf,* while retaining the tension and extraordinary drama of the movement (which, in the recital was coupled with a reading from one of the most dramatic chapters of *Wuthering Heights*) is an obvious example. But, equally challenging was the fact that the numerous repeated *allegro assai* notes, middle C in particular, were close to being impossible to play. This was of particular concern given that C is the dominant of F minor, the key of the sonata, and Beethoven makes considerable use of the rapid repetition of this note. My technique was challenged!

Ultimately, it was a wonderful experience to be afforded the opportunity to play on this unique and historic instrument and, in the context of the whole occasion, an emotional one, especially knowing that I was placing my hands on the keyboard which Emily had once played. Could I perhaps feel her presence?

APPENDIX SEVEN

Music Settings by John Hennessy

'It is too Late to Call Thee Now'
'No Coward Soul is Mine'

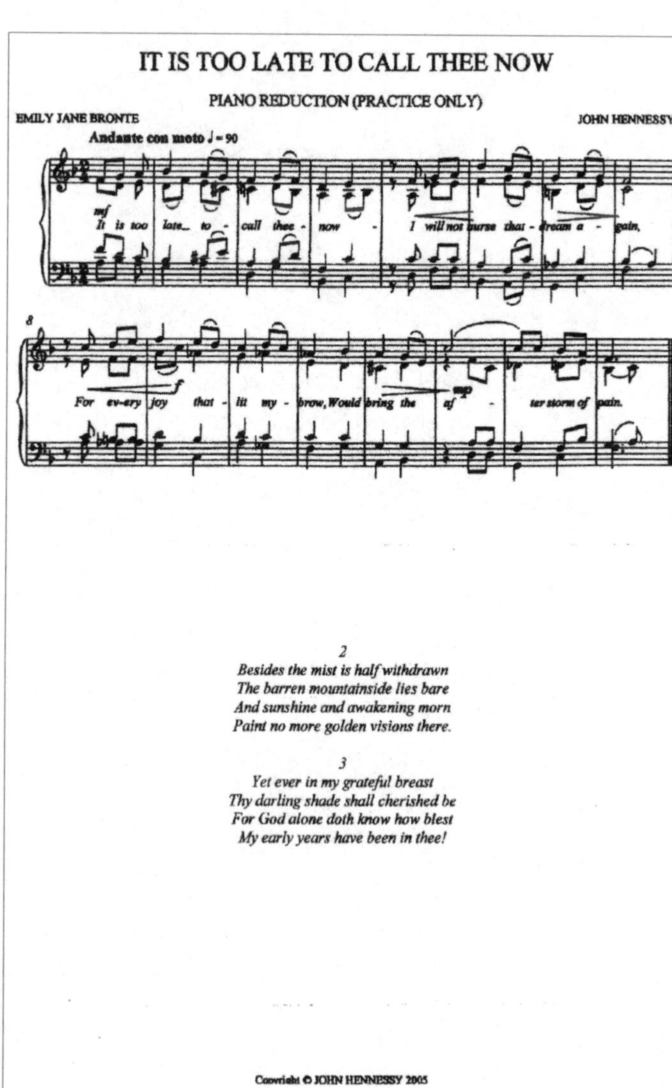
IT IS TOO LATE TO CALL THEE NOW
PIANO REDUCTION (PRACTICE ONLY)
EMILY JANE BRONTE
JOHN HENNESSY
Andante con moto ♩ = 90
mf
It is too late_ to - call thee - now - I will not nurse that - dream a - gain,
8
For ev-ery joy that - lit my - brow, Would bring the af - ter storm of pain.
f
mp
2
Besides the mist is half withdrawn
The barren mountainside lies bare
And sunshine and awakening morn
Paint no more golden visions there.
3
Yet ever in my grateful breast
Thy darling shade shall cherished be
For God alone doth know how blest
My early years have been in thee!
Copyright © JOHN HENNESSY 2005

NO COWARD SOUL IS MINE
PIANO REDUCTION (PRACTICE ONLY)
EMILY JANE BRONTE
JOHN HENNESSY
Andante con moto
♩=100
No cow-ard soul is mine No trem-bler in the world's storm troub-led sphere I see heav-en's glo-ry - shine And
decresc.
Faith shines bright-ly arm - ing me from fear. O God with-in my breast, Al-might-y ev-er pre-sent De-it
y Life that in me hath- rest, As I un dy-ing Life - have power in Thee. Vain - are the
decresc.
thou-sand creeds that move men's hearts un utter-ab-ly vain, Worth-less as wither-ed weeds, Or idlest - froth a
mid the bound - less main, To wa-ken doubts in one, Hold-ing so fast to thine in -

fin-it-y, So sure-ly an-chor-ed on The stead-fast rock of Imm-or-tal-it-y.
With wide em-bra-cing love Thy spi- rit an-i-mates e-ter-nal years - Per-vades and broods a-bove,
Chan-ges, sus tains-, dis solves-, cre-ates-, and-rears, Though Earth - and moon were gone And
sun and un-i-ver-ses cease to be, And thou wert left a-lone Every ex-ist-ence would-ex-ist in
Thee. There is not room for Death, Nor a-tom that his might could ren-der void. Since

64
thou art Be-ing and - Breath, And what thou art may ne - ver be des - troyed.
ff

Indexes

Index – Excluding Composers in Chapter Four

Index of Composers in Chapter Four

Each of the scores of piano music that Emily Brontë owned at Haworth has been discussed in the previous pages, along with brief biographical details of each of the composers. However, many composers featured more than once, and in such cases their details will be found in their first appearance in the text, on the page listed in this index.